Teaching Secondary Students Through Their Individual Learning Styles

Practical Approaches for Grades 7–12

RITA DUNN
St. John's University

KENNETH DUNN
Queens College

ALLYN AND BACON
Boston London Toronto Sydney Tokyo Singapore

Library of Congress Cataloging-in-Publication Data

Dunn, Rita Stafford, 1930–
    Teaching secondary students through their individual learning
    styles : practical approaches for grades 7–12 / Rita Dunn, Kenneth
    Dunn.
          p.   cm.
    Includes bibliographical references (p.   ) and index.
    ISBN 0-205-13308-8
    1. Individualized instruction—United States   2. Cognitive
    styles—United States.   3. Teaching—Aids and devices.   I. Dunn,
    Kenneth J.   II. Title.
    LB1031.D819   1992
    373.13′94—dc20   91–45749
                                                                CIP

Printed in the United States of America

10 9 8 7 6   99 98 97

—— DEDICATION ——

To those scholars and researchers at more than seventy institutions of higher education throughout the world, and to those administrators and teachers in hundreds of secondary schools across the United States who have reported results and provided feedback:

We thank you, with the deepest appreciation, for your consistent energy and willingness to experiment, accept difficult challenges, persist, test this model of learning style, improve it, and share what you learned for the benefit of secondary students everywhere. We recognize your valuable contribution and dedicate this book to you.

Among those outstanding professionals are the following who have made particularly unique contributions:

Researchers

Dr. Marianne M. Cholakis, St. Johns University graduate
Dr. Corine Cody, Temple University graduate
Dr. Thomas C. DeBello, St. John's University graduate
Dr. Christina DeGregoris, Hofstra University graduate
Dr. Joan DellaValle, St. John's University graduate*
Dr. Mary Ellen Freeley, St. John's University graduate
Professor Gene Geisert, St. John's University faculty, Administration and Supervision
Dr. Mary Cecelia Giannitti, St. John's University graduate
Professor Josephine Gemake, St. John's University faculty, Reading
Professor Shirley A. Griggs, St. John's University faculty, Counseling
Dr. Helene Hodges, St. John's University graduate*
Dr. Dennis Kroon, St. John's University graduate
Dr. Peter Lynch, St. John's University graduate*
Dr. Maureen Martini, St. John's University graduate*
Dr. Barbara Miles, St. John's University graduate*

*Research award recipients.

Professor Roberta M. Milgram, Tel Aviv University, Israel
Professor John B. Murray, St. John's University faculty, Psychology
Professor Louis Primavera, St. John's University faculty, Psychology
Professor Gary E. Price, University of Kansas, Lawrence
Professor Peter Quinn, St. John's University faculty, Instructional
   Leadership
Dr. Thomas C. Shea, St. John's University graduate*
Professor Richard Sinatra, St. John's University faculty, Reading
Professor John N. Spiridakis, St. John's University faculty, Bilingual
   Education
Dr. Virginia Flemming Tappenden, Kent State University
Professor Donald Treffinger, State University College at Buffalo
Professor Jennie Venezzia, St. John's University faculty, Research and
   Statistics
Professor Solange Wechsler, Departmento de Psicologica, Universidade
   de Brasilia, Brazil
Dr. Regina White, St. John's University graduate*
Professor Robert Zenhausern, St. John's University faculty, Psychology

Practitioners

Mrs. Gayla Beauchamp, Florida
Mrs. Terri Brantz, Wyoming
Mr. Rudy Bruehler, New York
Mrs. Carolyn Brunner, New York
Dr. David Cavanaugh, Ohio
Dr. Linda Cohen, Minnesota
Mr. Bryce Cool, Wyoming
Mrs. Sherrye Dotson, Texas
Ms. Karol Gadwa, Washington
Dr. Mary Cecelia Giannitti, New York
Dr. T. Y. Harp, Texas
Dr. Jeff Jacobson, Wyoming
Mr. Bruce Jones, Minnesota
Mr. Philip Kelley, Pennsylvania
Mrs. Jane Kitley, Indiana
Dr. Mary A. Lafey, Missouri
Ms. Jewel Lewis, Illinois
Mr. Lee Marcus, New York
Dr. Michael Martin, Canada
Mrs. Lana Orsak, Texas
Mrs. Sherri Patterson, Indiana

*Research award recipients.

Dr. Janet Perrin, New York
Mrs. Luanne Reabe, Indiana
Ms. Mary Ellen Kasak-Saxler, Minnesota
Dr. Jacqueline Simmons, Illinois
Ms. Margaratha Smit, Illinois
Mrs. Mollye Sparks, Texas
Ms. Barbara Vine, Illinois

CONTENTS

PREFACE

Research on the Dunn and Dunn model of learning styles is more extensive and more thorough than the research on most previous educational movements. As of 1992, that research had been conducted at more than 70 institutions of higher education, at grade levels from kindergarten through college, and with students at most levels of academic proficiency, including gifted, average, underachieving, at-risk, dropout, special education, vocational, and industrial arts populations. Furthermore, the experimental research in learning styles conducted at the Center for the Study of Learning and Teaching Styles, St. John's University, New York, received two regional, twelve national, and two international awards/citations for their quality between 1980 and 1990.

That wealth of well-conducted research verifies the existence of individual differences among students—differences so extreme that the identical methods, resources, or grouping procedures can promote achievement for some and inhibit it for others.

This book is designed to assist teachers, administrators, college professors, and parents to discover the learning style of each youngster and then to suggest practical approaches for teaching students through their individual learning style strengths. Each chapter presents practical, tried and tested ideas and techniques that can be used as quickly as the personnel in a given school can absorb them and put them into practice. The ideas and strategies include the following:

- A thorough analysis of each of the 21 elements of learning style and an instrument and observational methods for recognizing them
- Detailed blueprints for redesigning secondary school classrooms to accommodate a wide variety of learning style differences
- Step-by-step guidelines for creating instructional spaces for secondary students, such as Interest Centers (for global students), Game Tables (for tactual/kinesthetics), Media Corners (for youngsters with specific perceptual strengths), and a Reading Corner (for people who cannot concentrate on printed text in an environment with classmates' movements, sounds, or other distractions)
- Descriptions and examples of small-group instructional strategies for peer-oriented students, such as Team Learning, Circle of Knowledge, Brainstorming, and Case Study

- Detailed explanations for designing Programmed Learning Sequences, Contract Activity Packages, Multisensory Instructional Packages, and tactual and kinesthetic instructional resources—different methods for teaching the identical information to secondary students with different learning styles
- Sample individual printouts that permit readers to test their developing ability to diagnose and prescribe for individuals with diversified learning styles
- An instrument for identifying the teacher's learning style and another for identifying the teacher's teaching style to determine the degree to which each teacher teaches the way he or she learns—or the way he or she was taught
- An instrument for identifying the teacher's learning style and each of his or her students' learning styles to determine the degree of match between the two

In a practical sense, these tried and tested techniques, all based on valid and reliable research findings, may be used by all people concerned with the instructional process at the secondary level.

- Teachers can use the text as a how-to guide to respond to the learning style requirements of individual students.
- Administrators can use the descriptions of methods and approaches as supervisory tools when assessing and aiding teachers to respond to the learning style characteristics of their students.
- Central office personnel can use the separate chapters as a basis for staff development to build instructional skills among faculty.
- Colleges and university professors can use the text as a basis for a course in theory and its practical translation into responsive methods for the preparation and retraining of teachers—who increasingly are being required to diagnose and prescribe on the basis of individual learning style differences.
- Parent groups can use this book to understand, monitor, and support improved instructional programs and to assist their own offspring at home.
- School districts can protect themselves against the increasing number of educational malpractice suits by accurate identification of student learning differences and provision of instructional prescriptions based on accurate data.
- Motivated secondary students can use the strategies included herein to teach themselves how to: (a) do their homework through their learning style strengths; (b) translate their textbooks and other printed materials into instructional resources through which they can teach themselves new and difficult information; and (c) cope with their teacher's style if it happens to be dissonant from how they learn.

This book, then, was written to translate accepted research theory into practical techniques that any teacher, administrator, professor, or parent can use and try immediately. It also includes the first guidelines for teaching secondary students how to teach themselves based on their unique learning style traits. The acquisition of new skills, the redesign of conventional classroom areas, and the provision of varied and style-responsive resources and approaches will, in a relatively short period of time, build an instructional process that will respond directly to the individual learning styles of each of your students.

Previous Books by Rita and Kenneth Dunn

- *Practical Approaches to Individualizing Instruction: Contracts and Other Effective Teaching Strategies* (1972)
- *Educator's Self-Teaching Guide to Individualizing Instructional Programs* (1975)
- *Administrator's Guide to New Programs for Faculty Management and Evaluation* (1977)
- *How to Raise Independent and Professionally Successful Daughters* (1977)
- *Teaching Students through Their Individual Learning Styles: A Practical Approach* (1978)
- *Situational Leadership for Principals: The School Administrator in Action* (1983)
- *Teaching Students to READ through Their Individual Learning Styles* (1986) (with Marie Carbo)
- *Bringing Out the Giftedness in Every Child: A Guide for Parents* (1992) (with Donald Treffinger)

Previous Prentice-Hall Books by Rita and Kenneth Dunn Translated into Foreign Languages

- *Procedimentos Practicos para Individualizar la Enseñanza* (1975)
- *Programmazione Individualizzata: Nuove Strategie Practiche per Tutti* (1977)
- *La Enseñanza y el Estilo Individual del Aprendizaje* (1978)

Previous Book by Rita Dunn

- *Learning Styles: Quiet Revolution in American Secondary Schools* (with Shirley A. Griggs) (1988)

Previous Book by Kenneth Dunn

- *Using Instructional Media Effectively* (with Jack Tanzman) (1971)

ACKNOWLEDGMENTS

Rita and Ken Dunn wish to express loving appreciation for the valuable word-processing expertise, attention to detail, willingness to revise the manuscript, and ever-present sunshine emanated by Madeline Larsen, Executive Secretary, Center for the Study of Learning and Teaching Styles, St. John's University, New York.

We also are indebted to Dr. Lewis Grell, Executive Director, Association for the Advancement of International Education (AAIE), who graciously permitted us to incorporate articles written by Rita Dunn, and previously published in that association's newsletter, into several chapters. We also wish to thank Patricia Broderick, editor and associate publisher of *Teaching K–8,* for permitting us to include the essence of "Presenting Forwards Backwards" (October 1988) in Chapter 4 of this text. In addition, Miss Broderick has been a continuing advocate of our learning style concept for more than a decade. She has provided a forum in which elementary teachers throughout the nation have been exposed to the theory and related practices of individualization through learning style and could, if they were so inclined, learn how to implement them through many series of articles on this topic. It is our belief that she and *Teaching K–8* have contributed ongoing excellence to education by providing practical instructional know-how unavailable in many teacher education courses.

1

Understanding Learning Style and the Need for Individual Diagnosis and Prescription

The research on learning styles explains why, in the same family, certain children perform well in school whereas their siblings do not. It demonstrates the differences in style among members of the same class, culture, community, profession, or socioeconomic group, but it also reveals the differences and similarities between groups. It shows how boys' styles differ from girls' and the differences between youngsters who read well and those who read poorly.

More important than the documentation of how conventional schooling responds to certain students and inhibits the achievement of others, the research on learning styles provides clear directions for either teaching individuals through their style patterns or teaching them to teach themselves by capitalizing on their personal strengths.

Everybody has strengths, although parents' strengths tend to differ from each other's, from their offsprings', and from their own parents'. Thus, mothers and fathers often learn differently from each other and from their children. Nevertheless, a common parental practice is to insist that children study and do their homework as those adults did when they were young. That is not likely to be effective for at least some of the siblings because, in the same family, members usually learn in diametrically opposite ways.

What Is Learning Style?

When a child is ill, a competent physician examines more than just the part of the anatomy that hurts—the throat, the eyes, or the chest. Professionalism requires that the child be examined thoroughly to determine what might be contributing to the health problem; thus, doctors get at the *cause,* not just the symptoms. So it is with learning style. Although some pioneers identified style as only one or two variables on a bipolar continuum (Dunn, DeBello, Brennan, Krimsky, & Murrain, 1981; DeBello, 1990), style is a combination of many biologically and experientially imposed characteristics that contribute to learning, each in its own way and all together as a unit.

Thus, learning style is more than merely whether a child remembers new and difficult information most easily by hearing, seeing, reading, writing, illustrating, verbalizing, or actively experiencing; perceptual or modality strength is only one part of learning style. It also is more than whether a person processes information sequentially, analytically, or in a "left-brain" mode rather than in a holistic, simultaneous, global, "right-brain" fashion; that, too, is only one important component of learning style. It is more than how someone responds to the environment in which learning must occur or whether information is absorbed concretely or abstractly; those variables contribute to style but, again, are only part of the total construct. We must not look only at the apparent symptoms; we need to examine the whole of each person's inclinations toward learning.

Learning style, then, is the way in which *each* learner begins to concentrate on, process, and retain new and difficult information. That interaction occurs differently for everyone. To identify a person's learning style pattern, it is necessary to examine each individual's multidimensional characteristics to determine what is most likely to trigger each student's concentration, maintain it, respond to his or her natural processing style, and cause long-term memory. To reveal that, it is necessary to use a comprehensive model of learning style because individuals are affected by different elements of style and so many of the elements are capable of increasing academic achievement for those to whom they are important within a short period of time—often within six weeks. Only three comprehensive models exist, and each has a related instrument designed to reveal individuals' styles based on the elements included in that model (DeBello, 1990). It is *impossible* to obtain reliable and valid data from an unreliable or invalid assessment tool. The instrument with the highest reliability and validity, and the one used in most research on learning styles, is the Dunn, Dunn, and Price *Learning Style Inventory* (LSI).

Teachers cannot identify correctly all the elements of learning style (Dunn, Dunn, & Price, 1977; Marcus, 1977; Beaty, 1986); some aspects of style are not observable, even to the experienced eye. In addition, teachers often misinterpret behaviors and misunderstand symptoms. Chapter 2 explains which instruments are appropriate at different age levels and how to prepare students to answer their questions. Chapter 2 also describes how to administer a learning style instrument to obtain accurate information.

The Dunn and Dunn Learning Styles Model

Evolution of the Model

In 1967 Professor Rita Dunn was invited by the New York State Department of Education to design and direct a program that would help "educationally disadvantaged" children to increase their achievement. Freed from teaching responsibilities, and thus able to focus on how individuals were responding to alternative instructional approaches, she observed the widely diverse effects of exposure to identical methods and teaching styles on same-age and same-grade youngsters. She and Dr. Kenneth Dunn then scrutinized the educational and industrial literature concerned with *how* people learn. They found an abundance of research, accumulated over an eighty-year period, that repeatedly verified the individual differences among students in the way each begins to concentrate on, process, absorb, and retain new and difficult information or skills.

Initially, the Dunns identified 12 variables that significantly differentiated among students (Dunn & Dunn, 1972); three years later they reported the existence of eighteen (Dunn & Dunn, 1975); by 1979 they had incorporated hemispheric preference and global/analytic inclinations into their framework. Over the past two decades, research conducted by the Dunns, their colleagues, doctoral students, graduate professors, and researchers throughout the United States have documented that when students are taught through their identified learning style preferences, they evidence statistically increased academic achievement, improved attitudes toward instruction, and better discipline than when they are taught through their nonpreferred styles (*Annotated Bibliography,* 1991; *Learning Styles Network Newsletter,* 1980–1991).

Currently, research is being focused on additional variables, such as the amount and kind of space that people need when concentrating on new and difficult information or the effects of color. By 1990, however, the Dunn and Dunn model included 21 elements that, when classified, revealed that learners are affected by their (1) *immediate environment* (sound, light, temperature, and furniture/seating designs); (2) *own emotionality* (motivation, persistence, responsibility [conformity versus nonconformity], and need for either externally imposed structure or the opportunity to do things in their own way); (3) *sociological preferences* (learning best alone, in a pair, in a small group, as part of a team, or with either an authoritative or a collegial adult; and wanting variety as opposed to patterns and routines); (4) *physiological characteristics* (perceptual strengths, time-of-day energy levels, and need for intake and/or

FIGURE 1-1 Learning Styles Model
Designed by Dr. Rita Dunn and Dr. Kenneth Dunn

4

mobility *while* learning); and (5) their *processing inclinations* (global/analytic, right/left, and impulsive/reflective) (see Figure 1–1).

Theoretical Cornerstone of the Dunn and Dunn Model

Learning style is a biological and developmental set of personal characteristics that make the identical instruction effective for some students and ineffective for others. Though initially conceived of as an outgrowth of practitioners' observations combined with university researchers' studies, this learning style model traces its roots to two distinct learning theories—cognitive style theory and brain lateralization theory.

   Cognitive style theory suggests that individuals process information differently on the basis of either learned or inherent traits. Many previous researchers investigated the variables of field dependence/independence, global/analytic, simultaneous/successive, and/or left- or right-preferred processing. As we conducted studies to determine whether relationships existed among these cognitive dimensions and students' characteristics that appeared to be more or less responsive to environmental, emotional, sociological, and physiological stimuli, we found that selected variables often clustered together. Indeed, relationships appeared to exist between learning persistently (with few or no intermissions), in quiet and bright light, in a formal seating arrangement, and with little or no intake, and being an analytic Left processor (Dunn, Bruno, Sklar, & Beaudry, 1990; Dunn, Cavanaugh, Eberle, & Zenhausern, 1982). Similarly, young people who often requested breaks while learning and who learned more, more easily, in soft lighting, with sound in the environment, seated informally, and with snacks, often revealed high scores as Right processors. Field dependence versus field independence correlated in many ways with a global versus analytic cognitive style and, again, seemed to elicit the same clustering as left- and right-preferred students did.

   In some cases, more attributes allied themselves with global/right tendencies than with their counterparts'. Thus, although global/rights often enjoyed working with peers and using their tactual strengths, analytic/lefts did not reveal the reverse, nor did their sociological or perceptual characteristics evidence consistent similarities.

   As the relationships among various cognitive style theories were evidenced, brain lateralization theory emerged, based to a large extent on the writings of the French neurologist Paul Braco, whose research had led him to propose that the two hemispheres of the human brain have different functions. Subsequent research by the Russian scientist Luria and the American scientist Sperry demonstrated that the left hemisphere appeared to be associated with verbal and sequential abilities, whereas the right hemisphere appeared to be associated with emotions and with spatial, holistic processing. Those conclusions, however, continue to be challenged. Nevertheless, it is clear that people begin to concentrate, process, and remember new and difficult information under very different conditions.

Thus, the Dunn and Dunn model is based on the following theoretical assumptions:

1. Most individuals can learn.
2. Instructional environments, resources, and approaches respond to diversified learning style strengths.
3. Everyone has strengths, but different people have very different strengths.
4. Individual instructional preferences exist and can be measured reliably (see Appendixes A and B).
5. Given responsive environments, resources, and approaches, students attain statistically higher achievement and attitude test scores in matched, rather than mismatched treatments (see Appendix A).
6. Most teachers can learn to use learning styles as a cornerstone of their instruction.
7. Many students can learn to capitalize on their learning style strengths when concentrating on new or difficult academic material.

Assessing the Elements of Learning Style

What Do We Know about Processing New and Difficult Information?

The terms *analytic/global, left/right, sequential/simultaneous,* and *inductive/ deductive* have been used interchangeably in the literature; the descriptions of these variables tend to parallel each other (Dunn, Beaudry, & Klavas, 1989). Analytics learn more easily when information is presented step by step in a cumulative sequential pattern that builds toward a conceptual understanding. Globals learn more easily when they either understand the concept first and then can concentrate on the details, or are introduced to the information with, preferably, a humorous story replete with examples and graphics. What is crucial to understanding brain functioning, however, is that both types reason, but by different strategies (Levy, 1979; Zenhausern, 1980); each strategy "is a reflection of a trend toward optimalization of efficient use of neural space" (Levy, 1982, p. 224).

Thus, whether youngsters are analytic or global, left or right, sequential or simultaneous, or inductive or deductive processors, they are capable of mastering identical information or skills if they are taught through instructional methods or resources that complement their styles. That conclusion was documented in mathematics at the elementary (Jarsonbeck, 1984), high school (Brennan, 1984), and community college (Dunn, Bruno, Sklar, & Beaudry, 1990) levels; in high school science (Douglas, 1979) and nutrition (Tanenbaum,

1982); and in junior high school social studies (Trautman, 1979). Processing style appears to change; the majority of elementary school children are global, but the older children are and the longer they remain in school, the more analytic some of them become.

What is fascinating is that analytic and global youngsters appear to have different environmental and physiological needs (Cody, 1983; Dunn, Bruno, Sklar, & Beaudry, 1990; Dunn, Cavanaugh, Eberle, & Zenhausern, 1982). Many analytics tend to prefer learning in quiet, well-illuminated, formal settings; they often have a strong emotional need to complete the tasks they are working on; and they rarely eat, drink, smoke, chew, or bite on objects *while* learning. Conversely, globals appear to work with what teachers describe as distractors; they concentrate better with sound (music or background talking), soft lighting, an informal seating arrangement, and some form of intake. In addition, globals take frequent breaks while studying and often prefer to work on several tasks simultaneously. They begin a task, stay with it for a short amount of time, stop, do something else, and eventually return to the original assignment.

Neither set of procedures is better or worse than the other; they are merely different. Globals often prefer learning with their peers rather than either alone or with their teacher, and also often prefer to structure tasks in their own way; they tend to dislike imposed directives. What is interesting is that most gifted children with an IQ of 145 or higher are global (Cody, 1983). On the other hand, most underachievers also are global. The difference between the high-IQ and underachieving global students tends to be motivation and perceptual preferences.

It is understandable that the motivation levels of underachievers would be lower than those of achievers, but what may separate the two groups is the biological development of their auditory, visual, tactual, and kinesthetic senses. Although we currently do not know how to intervene in their biological development, we have been successful in teaching them through their existing perceptual preferences (Bauer, 1991; Carbo, 1980; Gardiner, 1986; Ingham, 1989; Jarsonbeck, 1984; Kroon, 1985; Martini, 1986; Urbschat, 1977; Weinberg, 1983; Wheeler, 1983).

Beginning Steps for Practitioners

Teachers need to know how to teach both analytically and globally. Chapter 4 describes that process and will help develop beginning skills in teaching both ways. However, global students often require an environment very different from the conventional classroom. They also appear to need more encouragement and short, varied tasks because of their lower levels of motivation and persistence. Most children learn more easily when lessons are interesting to them, but globals *require* that new and difficult information be interesting, be related to their lives, and permit active involvement. Hart (1983) insists that these are requirements for all youngsters; without doubt, they are necessary if globals are to master academic requirements.

What Do We Know about Students' Environmental Needs?

Although many students require quiet while concentrating on difficult information, others literally learn better with sound than without (Pizzo, 1981, 1982). For the latter group, music without lyrics provide an atmosphere more

Some students need to wear sweaters or jackets in exactly the same environment in which others feel comfortable with short-sleeved blouses or shirts. The need for different levels of warmth or coolness is biologically determined and seems to remain fairly consistent over a long period of time. (Photograph courtesy of Blake Middle School, Hopkins, Minnesota.)

conducive to concentrating than do melodies with words, and baroque music appears to cause better responsiveness than rock (DeGregoris, 1986). Similarly, although many people concentrate better in brightly illuminated rooms, others think better in soft light than in bright light. Indeed, fluorescent lighting overstimulates certain learners and causes hyperactivity and restlessness (Dunn, Krimsky, Murray, & Quinn, 1985).

Temperature variations affect individual students differently. Some achieve better in warmth and others in cool environments (Murrain, 1983). Similar differences are evidenced with varied seating arrangements. Some prefer studying in a wooden, plastic, or steel chair, but many others become so uncomfortable in conventional classroom seats that they are prevented from learning.

Few educators are aware that, when a person is seated in a hard chair, fully 75 percent of the total body weight is supported by four square inches of bone (Branton, 1966). The resulting stress on the tissues of the buttocks causes fatigue, discomfort, and frequent postural change, for which many youngsters are scolded on a daily basis. Only people who, by nature, happen to be sufficiently well padded exactly where they need to be can tolerate conventional seating for long periods of time.

Everywhere that teachers teach, they testify to the fact that boys tend to be more hyperactive and restless than girls, and seating arrangements contribute to this phenomenon. But when students were permitted to learn and/or take tests in seating that responded to their learning style preferences for either a formal or an informal design, they achieved significantly higher test scores when matched with their design preferences than when mismatched. That occurred in high school English (Nganwa-Baguma, 1986; Shea, 1983) and mathematics (Orsak, 1990), in junior high school mathematics (Hodges, 1985), and in elementary school reading and mathematics (Lemmon, 1985) (see Table 1–1.)

Beginning Steps for Practitioners

Redesign conventional classrooms with cardboard boxes and other usable items placed perpendicular to the walls to create quiet, well-lit areas and, simultaneously, sections for controlled interaction and soft lighting. Permit students who want to do so to work in chairs; on carpeting, bean bags, or cushions; and/or seated against the walls, as long as they pay attention and perform as well as or better than they had previously. Turn the lights off and read in natural daylight with underachievers, or whenever the class becomes restless. Establish rules for classroom decorum as you feel comfortable—for example, no feet on desks, no shoes on chairs, do not distract anyone else from learning. You also may require better test performance and behavior than ever before. You will be surprised at the positive results that will occur (Dunn, 1987).

For easy-to-follow suggestions for redesigning classrooms without any cost and in a minimum of time, see Chapter 3.

In every school at every grade level, some students concentrate best in informal seating whereas others only can work well on difficult academic tasks while at conventional desks and chairs. (Photographs courtesy of the Blake Middle School, Hopkins, Minnesota, Midwest High School, Midwest, Wyoming, and Worthington High School, Worthington, Ohio, respectively.)

What Do We Know about the People with Whom Students Learn Most Easily?

For years, many teachers taught their students whatever had to be learned rather directly. When youngsters had difficulty in acquiring knowledge, teachers believed that their charges had not paid attention. Few realized that despite the quality of the teaching, some children were incapable of learning directly from an adult. These young people were uncomfortable when under pressure to concentrate in either teacher-dominated or authoritative classes. They were fearful of failing, embarrassed to show inability, and often too tense to concentrate. For such students, learning either alone or with peers is a better alternative than working directly with their teachers in either an individual or a group situation. Indeed, research demonstrates that when students' sociological preferences were identified and the youngsters then were exposed to multiple treatments—both congruent and incongruent with their identified learning

TABLE 1-1 Experimental Research Concerned with Learning Styles and Instructional Environments

Researcher/ Date	Sample	Subject Examined	Element Examined	Significant Effects	
				Achievement	Attitudes
DeGregoris, 1986	6th-, 7th-, 8th-graders	Reading comprehension	Kinds of sound needed by sound preferents	+[a]With moderate talking	Not tested
DellaValle, 1984	7th-graders	Word recognition memory	Mobility/passivity needs	+	Not tested
Hodges, 1985	7th-, 8th-graders	Mathematics	Formal/informal design preferences	+	+
Krimsky, 1982	4th-graders	Reading speed and accuracy	Bright/low lighting preferences	+	Not tested
Lemmon, 1985	3rd–6th-graders	Reading and mathematics	Design and time	+	Not tested
MacMurren, 1985	6th-graders	Reading speed and accuracy	Need for intake while learning	+	+
Miller, 1985	2nd-graders	Reading	Mobility/passivity needs	+	Not tested
Murrain, 1983	7th-graders	Word recognition/ memory	Temperature preference	0	Not tested
Nganwa-Baguma, 1986	High schoolers	English	Formal/informal design preferences		Not tested
Pizzo, 1981, 1982	6th-graders	Reading	Acoustical preference	+	+
Shea, 1983	9th-graders	Reading	Formal/informal design preferences	+	Not tested
Stiles, 1985	5th-graders	Mathematics testing	Formal/informal design preferences	0	Not tested

Source: Adapted by permission from "Survey of Research on Learning Styles" by R. Dunn, J. Beaudry, and A. Klavas, March 1989, *Educational Leadership, 46*(6), p. 51, copyright © 1989 by the Association for Supervision and Curriculum Development.
Note: Price (1980) reported that the older students became, the less they appeared able to adapt to a conventional setting. Thus, design may be far more crucial to secondary students' ability to concentrate than to that of fifth-graders, who may be better able to adjust to this element (Stiles, 1985). Dunn and Griggs (1988) described the importance of design to high schoolers throughout the United States.
[a] + represents significant positive findings at $p < .01$ or greater; 0 = no differences or slight trend.

styles—each achieved significantly higher test scores when taught in congruent patterns (Dunn, Beaudry, & Klavas, 1989). Four studies also examined the effects of sociological preferences on attitude toward learning and found statistically higher attitude scores when students were taught in matched situations (DeBello, 1985; Dunn, Giannitti, Murray, Geisert, Rossi, & Quinn, 1990; Miles, 1987; Perrin, 1984) (see Table 1–2). Indeed, gifted students strongly prefer to learn by themselves rather than with others (Cross, 1982; Griggs &

TABLE 1–2 Experimental Research Concerned with Sociological Preferences

Researcher/Date	Sample	Subject Examined
Bauer, 1991	44 junior high school Resource Room students	Mathematics was taught through perceptually different strategies—auditory/visual, tactual/visual; and kinesthetic/visual.

Findings: Math underachievers attained statistically higher achievement *and* attitude test scores when taught with a combined tactual/visual approach, followed by a kinesthetic/visual reinforcement approach.

Cholakis, 1986	106 underachieving, inner-city, parochial school seventh- and eighth-graders	Vocabulary development was provided through three strategies—by the teacher, alone by themselves, and in a peer group treatment.

Findings: Those who preferred learning alone, scored significantly higher (.01) than those who preferred learning either with peers or the teacher. However, all students attained significantly higher achievement (.001) and attitude (.01) scores when learning with an authority figure.

DeBello, 1985	236 suburban eighth-graders	Students wrote social studies compositions and then experienced revision strategies that were congruent *and* incongruent with their sociological preferences.

Findings: Peer learners scored significantly higher when matched wtih the peer-conferencing technqiue (.01). Authority-oriented learners, when revising through the teacher-conference, achieved statistically higher (.01) than when revising either through peer conferencing or self-review. And those who preferred to learn alone scored significantly higher (.01) when matched, rather than mismatched, with self-review. No learning style group achieved better than any other, but a significant interaction occurred between individual sociological style and the matched method of revision (.001). In addition, the attitudes of students who preferred to learn alone or with an adult were significantly more positive (.01) when they were assigned to approaches that matched their styles.

Giannitti, 1988	104 suburban, parochial and public school sixth-, seventh-, and eighth-graders	Social studies was taught through both a mini–Contract Activity Package (CAP) and a small-group strategy, Team Learning.

Findings: Peer-oriented students achieved significantly higher test and attitude scores when learning through Team Learning than through the mini-Cap (.01). Learning-alone preferents attained significantly higher test and attitude scores (.01) through the mini-CAP than with their peers. Non-preferred students achieved better through the mini-CAP than through the Team Learning and liked working alone better than in groups. A significant interaction occurred between learning alone and peer-preferred learning and the method of learning (mini-CAP and Team Learning).

Miles, 1987	40 inner-city fifth- and sixth-graders	Twenty-two who preferred to learn alone and 18 who preferred to learn with peers were assigned randomly to two instructional groups that taught career awareness and career decision-making concepts in conditions both congruent and incongruent with their preferences.

(Continued)

TABLE 1–2 *Continued*

Researcher/Date	*Sample*	*Subject Examined*

Findings: The matching of sociological preference with complementary grouping patterns increased achievement significantly on career awareness (.01) and career decision making (.01). In addition, students' attitude scores were statistically higher when they were taught career awareness (.01) and career decision-making concepts (.05) in patterns accommodating their sociological preferences. With the exception of career awareness achievement, neither sociologically preferred group achieved better than the other but learning-alone preferents scored higher (.05) than peer-preferred individuals.

Perrin, 1984	104 gifted and nongifted suburban first- and second-graders	Problem solving and word recognition were taught through both individual and peer-group strategies. Learning with the teacher was eliminated as a strategy when not a single gifted child preferred to learn that way.

Findings: Analysis of the mean gain scores revealed that achievement was significantly higher (.05) whenever students were taught through approaches that matched their diagnosed sociological preferences. Although the gifted tended to prefer to learn alone in their heterogeneously grouped classes, a small group of seven gifted, who previously had known each other from participation in a special, part-time program for the gifted, actually performed best when learning in isolation with other gifted children.

Source: Adapted by permission from ''Survey of Research on Learning Styles'' by R. Dunn, J. Beaudry, and A. Klavas, March 1989, *Educational Leadership, 44*(6), p. 54, copyright © 1989 by the Association for Supervision and Curriculum Development.

In CLIP, a Washington high school alternative program, students are encouraged to complete assignments as they feel comfortable sociologically—alone, in a pair, in a small group, or directly with the teacher. (Photographs courtesy of the CLIP Program, Edmonds School District, Washington, DC.)

Price, 1980; Kreitner, 1981; Price, Dunn, Dunn, & Griggs, 1981). These research data were supported in schools throughout the United States when site visitations, observations, and evaluation collection documented that adolescents achieved more, behaved better, and liked learning better when they were permitted to learn through their sociological preferences as revealed through the *Learning Style Inventory* (Andrews, 1990; Dunn & Griggs, 1988; Lemmon, 1985; Harp & Orsak, 1990; Sinatra, 1990). Since 1984, schools have been experimenting with teaching students to teach themselves by capitalizing on their sociological and other learning style preferences (Dunn, 1984); the results to date are very promising (Clark-Thayer, 1987, 1988; Dunn, Deckinger, Withers, & Katzenstein, 1990; Griggs, 1990; Knapp, 1991; Miller & Zippert, 1987).

Beginning Steps for Practitioners

It is easy for teachers to post an assignment with specific objectives and/or tasks and say to the entire class, ''You may work on this alone, in a pair, in a team of three, or with me. If you wish to work alone, sit wherever you will be comfortable in the room. If you wish to work in a pair, take a moment to decide where you want to work, but allow privacy to classmates who need to be by themselves.'' After a momentary pause, those students who want to work cooperatively may move together quietly; after that, those who wish to work directly with the teacher or an aide may move to a specifically designated area of the room.

We strongly recommend, however, that Team Learning and Circle of Knowledge—specific small-group strategies to *introduce* and to *reinforce* difficult information—become an integral part of the class's repertoire *prior* to permitting many sociological choices. Those strategies enable students to work efficiently with a tape recorder and printed illustrated materials, either alone or in a small group, for a lengthy period. Thus, once youngsters are familiar with these strategies and can function independently or with a peer or two, teachers find themselves with sufficient time to teach the smaller group while others are engaged in Team Learning or independent study. These small-group instructional strategies, as well as others, can be found in Chapter 5.

What Do We Know about Triggering Concentration and Increasing Retention through Perceptual Strengths?

When students were *introduced* to new material through their perceptual preferences, they remembered significantly more than when they were introduced through their least preferred modality. That was true for primary (Carbo, 1980; Urbschat, 1977; Wheeler, 1980, 1983) elementary (Hill, 1987; Weinberg, 1983), *and* secondary (Bauer, 1991; Kroon, 1985; Martini, 1986) students, as well as for adults (Ingham, 1989). Furthermore, when new material was reinforced through students' secondary or tertiary preferences, they achieved significantly more than when it merely was introduced correctly—an additional .05 (Kroon, 1985) (see Table 1–3).

Considering that most secondary children are not auditory (they rarely remember at least three-quarters of what they hear in a normal forty- or fifty-minute period), lectures, discussions, and talking are the *least* effective way of teaching. Few teachers, however, know how to *introduce* difficult new material tactually or kinesthetically—the sensory preferences of most young or un-

TABLE 1–3 Experimental Research Concerned with Perceptual Learning Styles

Researcher and Date	Sample	Subject Examined	Perceptual Preference Examined	Significant Achievement
Bauer, 1991	Junior high school underachievers	Mathematics	Auditory, visual, tactual, kinesthetic	+
Buell & Buell, 1987	Adults	Continuing education	Auditory, visual, tactual	+[a]
Carbo, 1980	Kindergartners	Vocabulary	Auditory, visual, "other" (tactual)	+
Ingham, 1989	Adults	Driver safety	Auditory/visual, tactual/visual	+
Jarsonbeck, 1984	Fourth-grade under-achievers	Mathematics	Auditory, visual, tactual	+
Kroon, 1985	Ninth-, tenth-graders	Industrial arts	Auditory, visual, tactual, sequenced	+
Martini, 1986	Seventh-graders	Science	Auditory, visual, tactual	+
Urbschat, 1977	First-graders	CVC Trigram Recall	Auditory, visual	+
Weinberg, 1983	Third-grade under-achievers	Mathematics	Auditory, visual, tactual	+
Wheeler, 1980	Learning-disabled second-graders	Reading	Auditory, visual, tactual, sequenced	+
Wheeler, 1983	Learning-disabled second-graders	Reading	Auditory, visual, tactual	+

Source: Adapted by permission from "Survey of Research on Learning Styles" by R. Dunn, J. Beaudry, and A. Klavas, March 1989, *Educational Leadership, 46*(6), p. 53, copyright © 1989 by the Association for Supervision and Curriculum Development.
Note: It is important to note that the Carbo (1980), Ingham (1989), and Martini (1986) studies won national awards for the "best research" during the year each was published. Each demonstrated the statistically higher test scores that occurred when students *initially* were introduced to new and difficult academic information through their perceptual preferences—rather than through their less preferred modalities (see Appendix B).
[a] + represents significant positive findings.

derachieving students. Easy-to-make tactual resources are described in Chapter 6 and should be used *before* discussing new content.

1. Using all four modalities without a matched sequence does not insure that each youngster is *introduced* to difficult material correctly (through his or her perceptual strength/preference); neither does it insure that each will be *reinforced* correctly—and that is what caused achievement gains and/or retention in the studies cited earlier.

2. Young children or underachievers are almost exclusively tactual/kinesthetic learners (Crino, 1984; LeClair, 1986; Keefe, 1982; Price, 1980). Teaching them new and difficult information auditorially at the onset almost guarantees confusion and/or difficulty for many. If their auditory skills are to be developed, we must *reinforce* that way and patiently wait for the day when, as usually happens, their modalities mature and they are "ready" to learn our way. In the meantime, only a small percentage of what we say is absorbed and understood. As a general guideline, it is better to teach underachievers tactually and experientially first and then speak to emphasize and reinforce.

3. Underachieving, at-risk, and dropout students almost exclusively are tactual/kinesthetic learners; when they have auditory preferences, they usually are only tactual/kinesthetic/auditory—missing the visual, which often is a typical "learning-disabled" or "LD" profile. So-called learning-disabled students often are tactual/kinesthetic or tactual/auditory, but it is easier for them to learn tactually than in other ways. Introducing them to new material with Flip Chutes, Pic-a-Holes, Multipart Task Cards, and/or Electroboards (see

The young lady seated on the couch needs to read *her textbook aloud onto a tape recorder. She then plays the tape back to* hear *the difficult information read to her. The two on the floor are taking turns* reading *the textbook to each other so that they can cooperatively decipher the difficult words and, simultaneously,* see *and* hear *the material. The front group in the third photo are each taking* notes *(writing) to retain what they are* reading. *(Photographs courtesy of the CLIP Program, Edmonds School District, Washington, and Cedar Crest High School. Lebanon, Pennsylvania.)*

Chapter 6) and then reinforcing with auditory and visual supplements is likely to help them achieve almost at grade level and in approximately the same amount of time that most average achievers require.

4. A system for introducing each student to new material through his or her perceptual strengths and reinforcing through his or her secondary or tertiary modality is available (see Chapters 6 and 11), is easy to use, costs little or nothing, and does not require repetition through various forms of whole-class instruction provided at different times in four different ways.

Beginning Steps for Practitioners

Identify students' primary perceptual preferences with the *Learning Style Inventory* (Dunn, Dunn, & Price) and use the sequence for introducing new material through individuals' strengths and reinforcing through their secondary and tertiary modalities whenever you teach by talking or discussing (see Chapter 11). *Before* you lecture, introduce tactual students to the new content tactually—with Electroboards, Flip Chutes, Pic-A-Holes, Multipart Task Cards, and so on as described in Chapter 6. If you need help remembering which youngster needs what, obtain or design your own "Homework Charts," available from the Center for the Study of Learning and Teaching Styles at St. John's University (see Chapter 12). Use programmed Learning Sequences to *reinforce* for essentially tactual learners. Tape record the printed material for poor/slow readers (see Chapter 7).

What Do We Know about Time-of-Day Preferences?

Task efficiency is related to each person's temperature cycle (Biggers, 1980); thus, it is related to *when* each student is likely to learn best. For example, junior high school math underachievers became more motivated and better disciplined, and produce a trend toward statistically increased achievement, when they were assigned to afternoon math classes that matched their chronobiological time preferences—*after* they had failed during their energy lows (Carruthers & Young, 1980). One year later, Lynch (1981) reported that time preference was a crucial factor in the reversal of chronic initial truancy patterns among secondary students.

Later, the matching of elementary students' time preferences and instructional schedules resulted in significant achievement gains (.001) in both reading and math (Dunn, Dunn, Primavera, Sinatra, & Virostko, 1987). The following year, teachers' time preferences were identified and inservice sessions were conducted in both matched and mismatched sessions (Freely, 1984). Interestingly, teachers implemented innovative instructional techniques significantly more often (.01) when they were instructed at their preferred times. Then Lemmon (1985) administered the *Iowa Basic Skills Achievement Tests* in reading and math to elementary school students whose time preferences matched their test schedule—either morning or afternoon. She reported significantly higher test gains in both subjects compared with each youngster's previous three years' growth as measured by the same test.

Most students are *not* alert early in the morning. Primary school children experience their strongest energy highs between 10:00 A.M. and 2:00 P.M.: Only approximately 28 percent are "morning" people (Price, 1980). Approximately one-third of junior high schoolers are alert in the early morning when academics are accented but, again, the majority first "come alive" after 10:00 A.M. In high school, almost 40 percent are "early birds"; a majority, however, continue to be late morning/afternoon preferents and, for the first time since infancy, 13 percent are "night owls" (Price, 1980). There are exceptions to these data, but test *your* pupils to determine their individual style patterns.

Beginning Steps for Practitioners

Advise students to do all their studying during their energy highs at their best time of day. Offer demanding subject material at varied times of the school day and assign underachieving, at-risk, and dropout students to their most important subjects when they are most alert. Time is one of the most crucial elements of learning style and demands attention—particularly for potential underachievers (Gardiner, 1986; Gadwa & Griggs, 1985; Griggs & Dunn, 1988; Johnson, 1984; Thrasher, 1984), for whom learning at their energy high increases achievement.

What Do We Know about Restlessness and Hyperactivity?

Most students referred to psychologists for "hyperactivity" are not clinically hyperactive; instead, they often are normal youngsters in need of mobility (Fadley & Hosler, 1979). The less interested the learners are in what is being taught, the more mobility they need. A disquieting point is that such youngsters are "almost always boys" (p. 219).

Restak (1979) substantiated that "over 95 percent of hyperactives are males" (p. 230) and that the very same characteristic, when observed in girls, is correlated with academic *achievement*. He deplored the fact that boys are required to be passive in school and are rejected for aggressive behaviors there, but are encouraged to engage in typical male aggressions in the world at large—a situation that Restak suggested might lead to role conflict. He added that conventional classroom environments do not provide male students with sufficient outlet for their normal movement needs and warned that schools actually cause conflict with societal expectations that boys not be timid, passive, or conforming.

Tingley-Michaelis (1983) corroborated Restak's warnings and affirmed that boys labeled "hyperactive" in school often were fidgety because their teachers provided experiences for them "to think about something"; instead,

Teachers who capitalize on students' need for mobility by incorporating kinesthetic instructional activities report increased achievement and better behavior than when those same youngsters are restricted to their seats. For example, one science teacher required that each student hold the name of an element in one hand. When she called out a compound, the two who held its component parts were required to come forward and place their signs together to signify that a combination of the chemicals formed that compound—for example, hydrogen (H) + chlorine (CL) = hydrogen chloride (HCl). (Photograph courtesy of the P. K. Yonge Laboratory High School, Gainesville, Florida.)

those young people needed "to do something" (p. 26). Tingley-Michaelis also chastised educators for believing that activities prevented—rather than enhanced—learning!

When researchers began redefining hyperactivity as students' normal need for mobility, they experimented with providing many opportunities for learning while engaged in movement. Reports then began to document that,

Boys from all cultural groups appear less able than girls to sit still in wooden, plastic, or steel chairs for more than 10 or 15 minutes. At Franklin Central High School, many teachers permit students mobility while they are engaged in completing activities other than listening to a lecture. (Photograph courtesy of Franklin Central High School, Franklin Township, Indiana.)

when previously restless youngsters were reassigned to classes that did not require passivity, their behaviors were rarely noticed (Fadley & Hosler, 1979; Koester & Farley, 1977). Eventually, teachers began indicating that, although certain students thrived in an activity-oriented environment that permitted mobility, others remained almost exclusively in the same area—despite frequent attempts to coax them to move (Hodges, 1985; Miller, 1985). That led to Fitt's

(1975) conclusions that no amount of persuasion increased selected students' interest in movement, whereas others found it impossible to remain seated passively for extended periods. "These are cases of a child's style . . . governing his interactions with and within the environment" (p. 94).

Add to all that the knowledge that almost 40 percent of youngsters require informal seating while concentrating, and it is not difficult to understand why so many—particularly boys—squirm, sit on their ankles and calves, extend their feet into aisles, squirrel down into their seats, and occasionally fall off their chairs.

DellaValle (1984)* documented that almost 50 percent of a large, urban junior high school's students could not sit still for any appreciable amount of time. Twenty-five percent could remain immobile if interested in the lesson, and the remaining 25 percent preferred passivity. DellaValle clearly demonstrated the importance of the mobility/passivity dimension of learning style. When students' preferences and their environment were matched, they achieved significantly higher test scores (.001) than when they were mismatched. Students who required mobility moved from one part of the room to another in order to master all the information in the lesson and performed better than when they sat for the entire period. On the other hand, students who disliked moving performed worse when required to learn while walking and significantly better when permitted to sit quietly and read. Table 1–4 reports the post hoc analysis used to determine exactly where the interaction occurred. This analysis was conducted after the initial repeated measures design indicated a significant interaction at the .001 level.

Beginning Steps for Practitioners

Establish varied areas in the classroom so that mobility-preferred youngsters who complete one task may move to another section to work on the next. See Chapter 3 for easy-to-follow guidelines for redesigning a conventional classroom so that it responds to multiple learning style characteristics.

TABLE 1–4   Analysis of Preference × Environment Interaction

	Means	
	Passive b_1	Active b_2
Passive a_2	8.70	5.45
Active a_2	7.15	9.10

Source: Adapted by permission from "Survey of Research on Learning Styles" by R. Dunn, J. Beaudry, and A. Klavas, March 1989, *Educational Leadership,* 46(6), p. 51, copyright © 1989 by the Association for Supervision and Curriculum Development.
Note: a = preference; b = environment, N = 20.

*DellaValle's research won three national awards (see Appendix B).

Whenever possible, incorporate kinesthetic activities into each lesson so that, while demonstrating points, acting, role playing, brainstorming, interviewing (whether simulated or real), or observing phenomena, students may move. Permit those who can be trusted to behave *and* who require mobility (as revealed through their behavior and/or the LSI) to move to the varied areas you have established in the classroom. Some may need only the space available in their own "office" or "den"; others may require movement to one classroom area (such as a Library Corner, an Interest Center, a Media Section, or a sectioned-off space near the door in a hall). One or two responsible students might be permitted to work in the corridor immediately outside the classroom under the supervision of a volunteer parent, older student, or aide. Youngsters become increasingly trustworthy when they see that you recognize their needs and are aware that they will lose a privilege if they abuse it. Many of the most difficult-to-contain youngsters are precisely those who cannot sit and, thus, require opportunities to stretch (Dunn, DellaValle, Dunn, Geisert, Sinatra, & Zenhausern, 1986; Miller, 1985).

In addition, do not forget to experiment with a form of independent study such as Programmed Learning Sequences (see Chapter 7) or Contract Activity Packages (see Chapter 8), where students may move as they concentrate without disturbing others. Finally, be certain to experiment with the small-group techniques such as Team Learning for *introducing* new and difficult material and Circle of Knowledge for *reinforcing* it (see Chapter 5). Peer-oriented learners who need mobility will function well with these instructional strategies because of their responsiveness to both the sociological and physiological characteristics.

What Are Some Important Ramifications of Style?

Both Restak (1979) and Thies (1979) ascertained that three-fifths of learning style is genetic; the remainder, apart from persistence, develops through experience. Individual responses to sound, light, temperature, seating arrangements, perceptual strengths, intake, time of day, and mobility are biological, whereas sociological preferences, motivation, responsibility (which correlates with conformity), and structure versus need-for-providing-self-direction are thought to be developmental. The significant differences among the learning styles of students in diverse cultures tend to support this theory (Dunn, 1990b; Gemake, Jalali, Zenhausern, Quinn, & Spiridakis, 1990; Dunn & Griggs, 1990; Guzzo, 1987; Jacobs, 1987; Jalali, 1989; Lam-Phoon, 1986; Mariash, 1983; Roberts, 1984; Sims, 1988; Vazquez, 1985).

The one variable that may provoke disagreement concerning whether its origin is biological or developmental is persistence. Analytics tend to be more persistent than globals; globals tend to concentrate on difficult academic studies for relatively short periods of time, need frequent breaks, and work on several different tasks simultaneously. Once strongly analytic students *begin* a task, they appear to have an emotional need to complete it.

Within each culture, socioeconomic stratum, and classroom there are as many within-group differences as between groups. Indeed, within each family, some members are analytic and others are global—each with many of the learning style traits that tend to correlate with one processing style or the other.

Every person has a learning style pattern and every person has learning style strengths. People tend to learn more when taught with their *own* strengths than when taught with the teacher's strengths (Buell & Buell, 1987; Cafferty, 1980).

No learning style pattern is better or worse than another. Each style encompasses similar intelligence ranges. Students tend to learn and remember better, and to enjoy learning more, when they are taught through their learning style preferences. More than fifty studies documenting that statement exist (see *Annotated Bibliography,* 1991; *Learning Styles Network Newsletter,* (1980–1991).

Beginning Steps for Practitioners

Ask the teachers and administrators in your building or district to take the *Productivity Environmental Preference Survey* by Dunn, Dunn, and Price) (1979, 1985, 1991; see Chapter 2) to identify their learning styles. Compare your style and the learning style of the teacher you like best—and least—or wish most or least to emulate. Notice where the two individual printouts differ.

Decide to learn a little more about learning style. Administer the appropriate test to those students with whom you are most concerned. Examine their styles. Discuss their individual printouts with them. Ask questions about how they believe their styles have affected their attitudes toward school and why. If possible, visit a learning styles school (Andrews, 1990; DellaValle, 1990; Dunn & Griggs, 1988, 1989a, 1989b, 1989c, 1989d, 1989e; Orsak, 1990; Sinatra, 1990).

Next, decide which students are of most concern to you. If you are *visual* read the chapters in this book that help you work with the styles of those youngsters. For example, if you want to attend first to bright, achieving youngsters and enhance their ability to teach themselves more rapidly than could occur in a heterogeneous class, read Chapters 1, 2, 8, 11, and 3, in that order—and you will be able to help those students. However, if you are more concerned with an at-risk and potential dropout population, read Chapters 1, 12, 11, 2, 3, 4, 6, 7, 9, and 10, in that order. If you are global or nonconforming, pay no attention to *our* sequence; we know you will design your own! If you prefer a structure for learning and can identify a specific type of student you wish to help, you probably will adhere to our suggested pattern (see Table 1-5). It really does not matter where you start and how you proceed; what is important is that you *do* start and experiment with the suggestions so that you can determine for yourself whether, in fact, students achieve higher tests scores when taught through their styles than when not.

TABLE 1–5 A Guide to Reading This Book for Visual Learners

Students with Whom You Are Concerned	Chapters to Read in Indicated Sequence											
	1	2	3	4	5	6	7	8	9	10	11	12
Slow Learners	1	2	3	7	6	4	8		5		9	
Gifted but under-achieving learners	1	2		4		5		3		7	6	
Fidgety children who do not concentrate	1	2	3		5	4	7	6	8	10	9	
Dropouts and the turned-off	1	4	5	6			7	8		9	10	3	2
Behavior problems	1	2	4		3	5	6	8	7	11	10	9
Bright, achieving learners	1	2	5					3			4	
All	1	2	3	4	5	6	7	8	9	10	11	12

If you are *not* a visual learner, examine Chapter 11's resources and purchase one of the Teacher Inservice Packages (TIPs) available for learning tactually or auditorially. You will learn kinesthetically as you begin to implement the methods you choose. Study in an environment that complements *your* style for sound, light, temperature, and design. Examine your sociological preference and decide to work either by yourself, with a friend or colleague (or two), or with an authority—another teacher, an administrator, or a college professor.

If you have no strong primary perceptual preference, you can use this book *if you are motivated;* if not, you are likely to learn better with one of the videotapes described in Chapter 11 or through an on-site visitation.

Table 1–5 may be a good guide for involving you in learning styles–based instruction. Once you decide with which children you are most concerned, find that group in the table and then follow its itemized chapter sequence.

In the meantime, if you want to begin *tomorrow* and have little time to read and absorb today, experiment with those of the following suggestions *that most appeal to you.* Almost any effort to complement students' learning styles produces positive effects. Try—and encourage your colleagues to experiment with—one or more of the following suggestions. Look for improvements in students' behaviors, attitudes, and test scores.

- Tell them what is "important." As you mention the items you want remembered, give them clues: "Make note of this!" "Write this down!" "This is important!" "This could be on your test!" This provides *structure* for those who need it.

- When you mention important items, walk to the chalkboard and, in big print, write a word or two that synthesizes that content so that *visual* learners can see it and others can copy it onto their papers.
- When you write on the chalkboard, illustrate important information; stick figures will do. If you can't draw, ask students to do it for you. Encourage *global* students to illustrate their notes. *Visual left* processors seem to respond to words and numbers; *visual rights* pay attention to drawings, symbols, and spatial designs. *Global rights* often are strongly *tactual;* they are the doodlers who pay attention better if they use their hands while they are listening. Use colored chalk on blackboards or colored pens on overhead transparencies for global learners.
- Give strongly *visual* children a short assignment to read to introduce new and difficult material. Then they should listen to you speak or participate in a discussion of the topic. Strongly *auditory* students should hear your explanation first and then read materials that will reinforce it. Visual children should copy notes while they listen; auditory learners should copy notes while they read.
- When working with youngsters who read poorly, read in natural daylight. If necessary, turn off the classroom lights or darken a section of the room. Low light relaxes and permits better concentration for 8 out of 10 children who do not read well.
- Write a three- or four-word illustrated outline of the lesson on the chalk board at the beginning of each period. That overview helps the *visual* learner who cannot focus well to keep track of the lesson's emphasis. From time to time, draw attention to the outline and say, "Now we're moving into this part of the topic."
- Laminate 30 or 40 numbered, colored footprints and 6 or 8 handprints. With masking tape folded against itself to provide two sticky surfaces, place the prints into a Twister Game pattern in a less busy part of the classroom so that walking on it in sequence requires body contortions. When youngsters with short attention spans lose interest in a task they should be doing, give them a chance, one at a time, to "walk the footprints." *Kinesthetic* youngsters, or those in need of *mobility,* will benefit greatly. After just one minute, they will be able to return to their seats and concentrate—for another ten minutes or more. These kinesthetic prints can be designed to incorporate educational games as well.
- Encourage highly *kinesthetic* children to walk back and forth while they are reading their assignments. Somehow, this helps them understand better.
- Encourage youngsters to study at their best time of day, whether it is early in the morning *before* they leave for school, during lunch or free periods, immediately after school, or in the evening before they go to bed.
- Permit children who need *intake* while they are concentrating to bring raw vegetables to school. Establish firm rules: They cannot make noise

while eating (you need quiet!); the custodian must never know what you are permitting; no leftovers should remain in the classroom; whatever they don't want must be placed into wastebaskets; and they must get better test grades than they ever have before—otherwise it's not helping!

- Begin reading this book tomorrow, if you can't possibly begin today! Experiment with the suggestions made in each of the chapters you read.

__2__

Identifying Students' Individual Learning Style Characteristics

Why Use an Identification Instrument?

Learning style encompasses at least 21 different variables, including each person's environmental, emotional, sociological, physiological, and cognitive-processing preferences. Thus, a comprehensive instrument that measures all, or at least *most,* of those elements has a distinct advantage over more limited instruments such as those used for bipolar models (see DeBello, 1990). The very variable *not* examined by a limited instrument may fail to identify an element or style pattern crucial to the successful learning of an individual.

Teachers cannot correctly identify all the elements of a student's learning style pattern through observation. Some elements of style are not observable even to the experienced eye, and the behaviors associated with other elements often are misinterpreted (Dunn, Dunn, & Price, 1977; Marcus, 1977; Beaty, 1986). For example, children who do not sit quietly in their seats often are seen as hyperactive, immature, troubled, or troublesome; few adults ever consider that these youngsters may have an unusually high energy level throughout the day (a sign of good health!) or may require an informal seating design, a great deal of mobility, or opportunities to move from one area of the room to another *while* learning. Those characteristics can be dealt with easily once a knowledge of learning style exists by permitting the student to sit on a pillow or carpet and/or to move from one section of the instructional environment to another as tasks are completed (see Chapter 3).

It is important to identify learning style with a comprehensive instrument, and it is *crucial* to use one that is both reliable and valid. An unreliable or invalid instrument will provide incorrect information. The extensive experimental research on learning styles verifies that students *can* tell you their learning style preferences accurately, but the concept of style *should be explained to them clearly before* they are tested.

Preparing Students for Taking a Learning Styles Test

We know that many youngsters cannot remember three-quarters of what they either hear or see, and many of those students do not read well. Such learners cannot possibly feel good about themselves in our auditory/visual-dominated schools. Thus, it is extremely important to identify their learning styles to determine whether—if they *are* low-auditory/low-visual—they have tactual or kinesthetic strengths through which they can be taught. Tactual students taught with tactual instructional resources (see Chapter 6) achieve almost as well and as rapidly as auditory students taught auditorially and visual students taught visually (Carbo, 1980; Kroon, 1985; Martini, 1986; Wheeler, 1983).

Begin by explaining the differences in learning styles that exist among all classes, families, and cultures. Tell the students that their mothers' styles are likely to be different from their fathers' and that their own styles are probably different from one another's and from their sisters' and brothers' styles.

After some discussion, read either *Two-of-a-Kind Learning Styles* (Pena, 1989) (grades 5–8) about Global Myrna and Analytic Victor, two middle schoolers who do most of their leisure-time activities together but who must study separately because their learning styles are so different, or use *A Guide to Explaining Learning Styles to High School Students* as a basis for developing understanding of the concept. Both are obtainable from the Center for the Study of Learning and Teaching Styles at St. John's University (see Chapter 11).

As you read the story to the middle school or junior high school class, tape record it and explain to the students why you are doing so. Then break the small tab at the top of the tape to prevent accidental erasure of the contents, and glue the plastic box in which the tape came to the back of the story book. Tell the students that any time individuals wish to hear that story read again, they can use the tape attached to the back of the book and hear it as often as they wish. Some young people will choose to hear the tape repeatedly. If the tape was made so that each time a page in the book was turned, the reader indicated that whoever is using the tape should also turn the page, the books will be read and reread repeatedly.

Encourage students to guess the styles of members of their own family and then write why they believe those are their relatives' styles. Eventually, they can graph their family's styles and compare them with those of their classmates' families. They can illustrate their own learning styles and write poems about how they *feel* now that they know about their style.

Explain that it is important for each person to understand his or her style *strengths*. Accentuate that everyone *has* strengths but that each person's are different from his or her friends' and relatives'. Introduce the idea of learning about one's strengths through a series of questions—which each person must answer truthfully, or there is no way to learn how each should be taught, or do homework, or study efficiently. Tell students in advance that one day in the near future you are going to ask all of them many questions about how they prefer to learn new and difficult information. When you get the results back from the computer, you will be able to tell each boy and girl exactly how he or she should study in order to remember anything that ordinarily would be difficult.

Using the Learning Style Inventory

The *Learning Style Inventory* (LSI) (Dunn, Dunn, & Price, 1975, 1978, 1984, 1986, 1987, 1989) is the first comprehensive approach to the assessment of an individual's learning style in grades 5 through 12. This instrument is an important first step toward identifying the conditions under which each person is

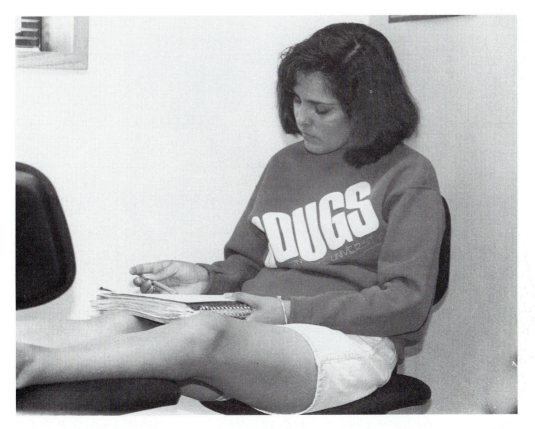

This young lady concentrates best in an informal *seating arrangement; her* Learning Style Inventory *Individual Printout registered 32. She is a responsible, serious Manson Secondary School student but can absorb new and difficult academic information better in an easy chair than at a conventional desk. (Photograph courtesy of Richard R. Uhlhorn, Manson, Washington.)*

most likely to concentrate on, learn, and remember new and difficult academic information.

Careful analysis of each student's LSI Individual Printout identifies those elements that are crucial to the individual's learning style. Further, the instrument aids in prescribing the type of environment (see Chapter 3), instructional resources (see Chapters 4, 6, 7, 8, and 9), social groupings (see Chapter 5), and motivating factors that maximize personal achievement. Many of the questions in the instrument are highly subjective and relative—and that, of course, is precisely why they contribute to an understanding of how each student learns in ways that are different from those of his or her peers.

Each student's learning style is based on a complex set of reactions to varied stimuli, feelings, and previously established patterns. Those patterns

This young man's Learning Style Inventory *registered 24 on Learning Alone—a Strong Opposite Preference for Learning with Peers—and 72 on Tactual—a Strong Preference for learning new and difficult information through a hands-on approach. Because his teacher permits him to learn independently with tactual resources and games, his attitude is positive and his behavior has become exemplary. (Photograph courtesy of Robeson High School, Chicago, Illinois.)*

*Working as a pair is ideal for these two young la-
dies. They always work on assignments together
and then succeed individually on tests. Each registered 62 on Peer-Oriented and, when questioned,
promised that they would complete the entire task
if permitted to do so together. (Photograph courtesy of Franklin Township Middle School, Franklin
Township, Indiana.)*

tend to be repeated when the person concentrates on new or difficult material.
Thus, the words *think, learn, read, write,* and *concentrate* are used interchangeably throughout the inventory, and it is not necessary for the respondent to differentiate among their meanings. Comparisons of answers to questions that include these words, and to others that seem to ask the same thing
in different ways, contribute to the accuracy of the student's overall profile.

The inventory does not measure underlying psychological factors, value
systems, or the quality of attitudes. Rather, it yields information about the
patterns through which learning occurs. It summarizes the environmental,
emotional, sociological, physiological, and global/analytic processing preferences a student has for learning—not *why* they exist.

Some students learn best in groups of three or four. These youngsters opted to tackle a difficult assignment in a team by beginning with a media explanation. Their printouts revealed scores of between 60 and 80 on the Peer-Oriented continuum. (Photograph courtesy Cedar Crest High School, Lebanon, Pennsylvania.)

Finally, the inventory does not assess the finer aspects of an individual's skills, such as the ability to outline procedures, organize, classify, or analyze new material. Again, it gives evidence of *how* students prefer to learn, not the skills they use (Dunn, Dunn, & Price, 1989, pp. 5–6).

The LSI uses dichotomous items and can be completed in approximately 30 or 40 minutes. It reports a Consistency Key to reveal the accuracy with which each respondent has answered the questions. The National Center for Research in Vocational Education at The Ohio State University published the results of its two-year study of instruments that diagnose learning styles and reported that the LSI had established impressive reliability and face and construct validity (Kirby, 1979). Since examination by that center more than a decade ago, the LSI has evidenced remarkable predictive validity (Dunn, Bruno, Sklar, & Beaudry, 1990; Dunn, DellaValle, Dunn, Geisert, Sinatra, & Zenhausern, 1986; Dunn, Dunn, & Freeley, 1984; Dunn, Dunn, Primavera, Sinatra, & Virostko, 1987; Dunn, Gemake, Jalali, Zenhausern, Quinn, & Spiridakis, 1990; Dunn, Giannitti, Murray, Geisert, Rossi, & Quinn, 1990; Dunn, Krimsky, Murray, & Quinn, 1985; Dunn, White, & Zenhausern, 1982; Miller & Zippert, 1987).

These students scored 60 or above on the Learning Style Inventory *on both Peer-Oriented and Tactile Learning. They chose to complete their assignment together by making and studying with multipart Task Cards. (Photograph courtesy Troutdale High School, Troutdale, Oregon.)*

In a comparative analysis of the style conceptualization and psychometric standards of nine different instruments that measure learning style instructional preference, the Dunn, Dunn, and Price *Learning Style Inventory* (LSI) was the *only* one rated as having good or very good reliability and validity (Curry, 1987). Of the 18 instruments reviewed in the document, including an additional 9 concerned with information processing, the LSI was one of only 3 with good or very good reliability and validity. The LSI is an assessment that is easy both to administer and to interpret. Perhaps because of that, Keefe (1982) revealed that it "is the most widely used in elementary and secondary schools" (p. 52).

Information Provided by the LSI

The LSI assesses individual preferences in the following areas: (1) immediate environment (sound, light, temperature, and seating design); (2) emotionality

Some learners prefer competing against themselves, reflected in a score below 40 on the Learning Style Inventory. *That is often true of gifted youngsters. This independent Manson Secondary School student capitalizes on her visual and tactile strengths with computer-assisted instruction. (Photograph courtesy Richard R. Uhlman, Manson, Washington.)*

(motivation, persistence, responsibility/conformity, and need for internal or external structure); (3) sociological factors (learning alone, in a pair, as part of a small group or team, with peers, with an authoritative or collegial adult, and/or learning in a variety of ways or in a consistent pattern); (4) physiological factors (auditory, visual, tactual, and/or kinesthetic perceptual preferences; food or liquid intake, early morning, late morning, afternoon, or evening time-of-day energy levels, and mobility needs; and, through correlation with sound, light, design, persistence, peer-oriented, and intake scores (Dunn, Cavanaugh, Eberle, & Zenhausern, 1982), indications of global (right) or analytic (left) cognitive/psychological processing inclinations (see Figure 2–1).

Junior high school youngsters in an alternative education program tested above 70 on Tactual and Kinesthetic preferences. They succeeded in learning all major subjects through an integrated aerospace curriculum. Model planes, rockets, wind vectors, Task Cards, and Learning Circles were the resources through which they mastered the theory and history of flight. Their classrooms reflected their essentially hands-on approach to learning. (Photograph courtesy of Madison Prep, New York City.)

The LSI Inventory

The inventory does the following:

- Permits students to identify how they prefer to learn and also indicates the degree to which their responses are consistent.

Secondary students with tactual and/or visual scores of 60 or above designed creative tiles for a liteature unit in Shirley Jackson's English class. (Photograph courtesy Cedar Crest High School, Lebanon, Pennsylvania.)

- Provides a computerized summary of each student's preferred learning style; that summary is called an *Individual Profile* (see Figure 2–2).
- Suggests a basis for redesigning the classroom environment to complement many students' needs for sound, quiet, bright or soft light, warmth or coolness, or formal or informal seating (see Chapter 3).
- Describes with whom each student is likely to achieve most efficiently—for example, alone, in a pair, with two or more classmates, with others with similar interests or talents (peers), with either an authoritative or a collegial teacher, and/or with all, none, or only one or two of these possibilities.
- Explains for whom to provide options and alternatives and for whom direction or structure is appropriate.
- Sequences the perceptual strengths through which individuals should *begin* studying and then *reinforce* new and difficult information and how each student should do his or her homework (see Chapter 12).
- Indicates the methods through which students are likely to achieve well—for example, through Contract Activity Packages (CAPs), Programmed

FIGURE 2-1 Learning Styles Model
Designed by Dr. Rita Dunn and Dr. Kenneth Dunn

Learning Sequences (PLSs), Multisensory Instructional Packages (MIPs), tactual/kinesthetic manipulatives, or a combination thereof.

- Extrapolates information concerning which children are nonconforming, and how to work with those who are.
- Pinpoints the best time during the day for each child to be involved in required difficult subjects, and thus permits grouping students for instruction based on their learning style energy-high strengths.
- Itemizes the types of students for whom snacks, *while learning,* are an integral part of the process.
- Notes the types of students for whom movement *while* learning, may accelerate the learning process.
- Suggests for which students analytic or global approaches to learning new and difficult material are likely to be important (see Chapter 4).

These questions are sample items from the LSI:

- I study best when it is quiet.
- I study best at a table or a desk.
- I can ignore most sound when I study.
- I like to study by myself.

Name: Elizabeth Patrice   **Sex:** F   **Year In School:** 11   **Date of Birth:** 6/74   **I.D. No.:** 1406

Group Identification: Malverne Public Schools   **Special Code:** G/T   **Date:** 1-24-1991   **Group No.:** 9021

PREFERENCE SUMMARY

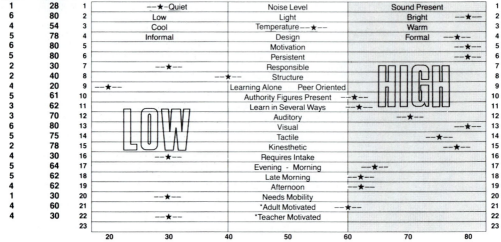

Raw Score	Standard Score	No.	Scale
1	28	1	—★— Quiet / Noise Level / Sound Present
6	80	2	Low / Light / Bright —★—
4	54	3	Cool / Temperature —★— / Warm
5	78	4	Informal / Design / Formal —★—
6	80	5	Motivation —★—
5	80	6	Persistent —★—
2	30	7	—★— Responsible
2	40	8	—★— Structure
4	20	9	—★— Learning Alone / Peer Oriented
5	61	10	Authority Figures Present —★—
3	62	11	Learn in Several Ways —★—
3	70	12	Auditory —★—
6	80	13	Visual —★—
5	75	14	Tactile —★—
2	78	15	Kinesthetic —★—
4	30	16	—★— Requires Intake
5	64	17	Evening - Morning —★—
5	62	18	Late Morning —★—
4	62	19	Afternoon —★—
1	30	20	—★— Needs Mobility
4	60	21	*Adult Motivated —★—
4	30	22	—★— *Teacher Motivated

CONSISTENCY: 100   *These scales are on LSI profile only.   **PROFILE NO.:**

FIGURE 2-2 Individual Profile
Learning Style Inventory

- When I can, I do my homework in the afternoon.
- The things I remember best are the things I hear.
- I concentrate best on difficult subjects seated on a couch or easy chair.
- I think best when I work on hard tasks with a friend.
- It's hard for me to sit in one place for a long time.
- Music helps me concentrate when I have to learn difficult things.

Individual Profile

The Individual Profile (see Figure 2-2 for an example) for the LSI includes the student's name or number, gender, date the inventory was administered, school, teacher, grade, and class number. A Consistency Score, which indicates how accurate the responses are for this particular student, is provided in the lower left-hand corner of each Individual Profile (see Figure 2-2). To interpret an individual's profile, follow these guidelines:

1. Note that the rectangle that constitutes the Preference Summary for each student has numbers beginning with 20 at the upper left-hand side through to 80 at the upper right-hand side.

a. Bracket the upper section to include everything between 70 and 80. Label that section "Strong Preference." Any learning style element that falls within the range from 70 to 80 on an Individual Profile is *extremely important* to that person. That person will *always* learn new and difficult information more easily and retain it better when that particular element is responded to. Thus, in Figure 2–2, Elizabeth Patrice will always learn better in *bright* than in low lighting, at a conventional desk and seat than on an easy chair, and when given a variety of resources or methods (Learning in Several Ways) than when following patterns or routines.

b. Bracket the upper section to include everything between 60 and 69. Label that section "Preference." A preference is almost as important as a strong preference, but the person with a preference has some limited options. That learner will *usually* or *often* learn new and difficult information more easily and retain it better when that particular element is addressed. That learner, however, *occasionally* can learn well despite the failure to address that element. It is important to remember that more than three-fifths of learning style appears to be biologically imposed (Restak, 1979; Thies, 1979). Thus, it is not easy for students to overcome their preferences, and it is very difficult indeed to overcome a strong preference.

c. Bracket the upper section to include everything between 20 and 29. Label that section "Opposite Strong Preference." An opposite strong preference is just as important as a strong preference, but it responds to the *opposite* of the element printed in the *center* of the Preference Summary. Thus, Elizabeth Patrice (Figure 2–2), who scored 28 on needing quiet, will *always* work better in a quiet rather than in a sound-filled environment. This is not a young person who can work well with music or any kind of sound while she is concentrating on new or difficult academic material.

d. Bracket the upper section to include everything between 30 and 39. Label that section "Opposite Preference." An opposite preference is just as important as a preference, and almost as important as an opposite strong preference. The individual *occasionally* can overcome an opposite preference—but not too often.

e. Bracket the entire middle upper section of the Preference Summary and label it "Not Important" or "It Depends." Elements that fall within this middle section suggest that the individual has the *ability* to learn in that way but will use it only when *interested in the topic* or motivated.

Thus, the *Learning Style Inventory* (LSI) Individual Profile for each student represents how he or she responded to the series of questions for each subscale. That information describes how the student should be taught, with whom, in which section of the environment, at what time of day, and with which methods or approaches (Contract Activity Packages, Programmed Learning Sequences, Multisensory Instructional Packages, or tactual/kinesthetic resources). As an example, consider Figure 2–2, the Individual Profile of Elizabeth Patrice.

Interpreting Elizabeth Patrice's Individual Profile: What Is Her Learning Style and How Should She Be Taught?

When "reading" a profile, first scan the student's demographic information to learn age, gender, and how accurate this information is for that individual—the consistency score. Elizabeth Patrice is a seventeen-year-old girl in the eleventh grade. Her Consistency Score (lower left corner) is 100 percent. You may use any data with a Consistency Score of 70 or above; do *not* use information on an Individual Profile with consistency below 70 percent. If that occurs, and you have read *Two-of-a-Kind Learning Styles* or *A Guide to Explaining Learning Styles to High School Students,* retest and send the new Answer Sheet to Price Systems, where it will be reprocessed at no cost.

Environmental Information.   Scan the first four elements of the environmental stimulus and determine each student's preferences for either a quiet (40 or below) or sound-filled (60 or above), well-illuminated (60 or above) or softly illuminated (40 or below), cool (40 or below) or warm (60 or above), and formal (60 or above) or informal (40 or below) classroom. Elizabeth prefers quiet; because her LSI score is below 30, that is a strong preference of hers. She also strongly prefers bright light and seating at a conventional desk. Temperature, because her score is in the 41–59 range, is not important to her. When she is interested in what she is learning or doing, she is unaware of temperature except when it is at an extreme; when she is bored, however, she will become aware of temperature discomfort.

Emotional Information.   Elizabeth is highly motivated and persistent (scores in the "Strong Preference" range of 70 or above), does not require external structure, and sometimes prefers to provide her own structure. Her low Responsibility score suggests that she is a nonconformist and likes to do things *her* way. When working with nonconforming students, experiment with doing the following three things.

1. Explain why whatever you want the student to do is important to *you.*
2. Speak collegially. Do *not* address the nonconforming student in an authoritative or directive tone. Instead, make believe you are talking with the teacher next door (assuming you respect the teacher next door!).

3. Give the student choices of how he or she can show you that what you requested has been completed.

For example, you might say, "Liz, it is important to me that you translate this chapter into a Contract Activity Package you can use, because I have not had the time to create one on this topic and I do not want to keep you at the class's pace. I know you can progress faster than most students, and I do not want you to become bored. However, if you do not find the material interesting, speak with the librarian, Mrs. Roberts; perhaps she can help you find multimedia related to this topic. Or you might see whether our local museum can add information that we do not have in our school library. Also, if you prefer, you can translate the material into a videotape or another media form that might make the topic more interesting. Which of these alternatives make sense to you?" Once a nonconformist commits to a choice, he or she often will follow through.

Teachers often believe that having motivated, persistent students in their classes makes teaching easy. Liz, however, as you will see when we examine other elements of learning style, is a bright student who remembers easily by listening, seeing or reading, taking notes or using manipulatives, and experiencing. Because she *is* motivated, she enjoys learning; because she is persistent, once she begins an assignment or project, she continues until it has been completed. Thus, she works attentively and finishes tasks before most of her classmates do. Because she is a nonconformist and is motivated, she will not hesitate to tell her teacher that she has done the assignment and requires that it be corrected (high on Authority Figures Present, thus wants feedback from her teacher). If told to wait for the others to complete their work, she will respond that *she* is ready to continue. She is not "fresh," but she does not need social approval for things she believes in. Thus, an Elizabeth Patrice who has completed her assignment, is motivated to learn, and is highly persistent *and* a nonconformist will ask for individual attention. If her teacher either is whole-class-oriented or does not understand that this adolescent's learning style dictates her need for constant involvement, tension is likely to develop both within the two individuals *and* betweeen them. Many gifted students experience such frustration, and many teachers are unaware of why those young people do not perform well in school or become angry with the process of schooling.

Sociological Information.   Elizabeth is a strong Learning Alone student (only 20 on the LSI Individual Profile); she is not peer-oriented. Elizabeth may be offered the choice of working with peers when she wishes, but she should be permitted to do difficult assignments on her own if she chooses. Elizabeth is *not* a good candidate for cooperative learning or small-group techniques unless *she* opts for those strategies when permitted to choose.

Despite her high nonconformity score (Responsibility score below 31), Elizabeth wants feedback from from the authority or authorities in her life (LSI score of 61). She also likes variety (LSI score of 62 on Learning in Several

Ways) and thus becomes bored quickly when required to engage in patterns and routines. Given this information about Liz, her teacher would be wise to permit her to work either alone, with peers, or with media *or adults* when she prefers to do so. The variety of sociological choices is, in and of itself, enticing to her.

Perceptual Strengths.   Most people have just a single perceptual strength, as indicated by LSI scores of 60 or higher. Scores between 41 and 59 indicate that a person *can* remember what is learned through that modality, but only if interested in what is being studied. Liz's scores are all above 70, indicating that she remembers easily what she hears, what she sees or reads, what she writes or manipulates, and what she experiences. Thus, Liz has *multisensory* perceptual strengths. Unlike most students, Liz does not need to sequence her perceptual exposures when she is introduced to new and difficult material. She can learn through all senses. That gift contributes substantially to high achievement in school, and thus it is easy to conjecture that Liz performs very well academically, particularly because those high perceptual strengths are combined with high motivation and high persistence.

Other Physiological Information.   Liz's low intake score (below 31) indicates no need for snacking while learning. Her chronobiological scores (60 or above on every segment of time of day) suggest a consistently high energy level—which "keeps her going"! Most people have only a single energy high each day, but Liz has *three*. Such students often are labeled hyperactive by teachers who do not understand why they never sit still. The reason is simply that they have so much energy, they *cannot* contain it.

Hypothesize a student with high energy levels, who is motivated and persistent, who completes work quickly because of strong perceptual strengths and a need for variety. It is easy to understand why that student is always "on the go." Because few people experience such energy drive, in contrast with an average level, that youngster *appears* to be hyperactive. Consider, too, Tingley-Michaelis' (1983) admonition that youngsters labeled hyperactive in school often were fidgety because their teachers provided them with experiences "to think about something"; instead, those children needed "to do something" (p. 26). Tingley-Michaelis also chastised teachers for believing that activity prevented—rather than enhanced—learning. Indeed, when previously restless youngsters were reassigned to classes that did not require passivity, their behaviors were rarely noticed (Fadley & Hosler, 1979; Koester & Farley, 1977).

Observe Liz's low mobility score (30 on the LSI); she does not need to be in constant motion. Instead, she needs to learn experientially—through *doing*. Such a youngster should be permitted to choose from among alternative projects of which the teacher approves and should be enabled to complete them through *any* perceptual strength. Thus, she might build, paint, draw, act out or role play, demonstrate, graph or chart, and so forth. The choice of projects should respond to her need for variety, multiple strengths, preference for learning alone, and need to complete many tasks at her own fast pace.

Adult Motivation Scores.   Although Liz wants to please *some* adult in her life, it probably is her parent or an other-than-teacher figure. Her low teacher motivation score (30 on the LSI) suggests she is not in need of pleasing her teacher—although she *does* want feedback (high on Authority Figure Present).

Analysis of LSI Data from Individual Profile.   Let's consider what a teacher looking at Elizabeth Patrice's LSI Individual Profile might do to improve instruction for her. In terms of classroom environment, Liz might be seated near a window or under a direct light. Because of her need for quiet, her desk should be away from the center of activity—perhaps even in a corner of the room. If the floor is uncarpeted, a small rug placed beneath Liz's desk and seat would help to absorb sound.

Contract Activity Packages (CAPs) (see Chapter 8) would be an excellent instructional method for Liz. They provide the choices that nonconformists respond to and suggest multisensory materials that a good student like Liz could use easily and well. The teacher should set aside some time to review Liz's work periodically, add comments to her grade to provide the feedback she needs, and permit her a range of choices of ways to demonstrate mastery of objectives. Because Liz is capable of becoming an independent learner, she should be able to design her own Activity, Reporting, and Resource Alternatives after just a few experiences using the CAP system. Eventually she would develop the ability to read textbook information and convert it into a CAP through which she could teach herself anything required by her teachers—or anything else of interest to her.

Determining Global or Analytic Processing Inclinations.   Previous studies revealed correlations between individual learning style characteristics and global and analytic processing styles (Cody, 1983; Dunn, Bruno, Sklar, & Beaudry, 1990; Dunn, Cavanaugh, Eberle, & Zenhausern, 1982). Global learners tend to prefer learning with what conventional teachers think of as distractions—sound (music, tapping, or conversation), soft illumination (covering their eyes or wearing sunglasses indoors), an informal design (lounging comfortably), peer orientation (wanting to work with a friend), and a need for intake (snacks) *while* studying. Furthermore, globals tend not to be persistent; they begin working with a burst of energy which lasts for a relatively short period, and then they want a "break." Globals return to their task and work again for another short interval; then they want another break. Globals also dislike working on one thing at a time; they often become engaged in multiple tasks simultaneously and concentrate on several in varying sequences. Thus, globals may begin an assignment in the middle or at the end.

Analytics, on the other hand, tend to prefer learning in silence, with bright lighting, and a formal design—a conventional classroom. They rarely eat, chew, drink, or smoke *while* learning; instead, they eat afterward. Analytics tend to be persistent; they may not always start an assignment immediately, but once they *do* begin, they have a strong emotional urge to continue until the task is done or until they come to a place where they feel they can stop.

These five elements—sound, light, design, persistence, and intake—correlate significantly (.01) with processing style. Many global learners also prefer to learn with peers and have strong tactual perceptual preferences. That is true of many fewer analytics at the high school level.

It is not necessary to have all five elements to be either a global or an analytic processor; the presence of three of the same group indicates tendencies in that direction. Thus, Liz prefers quiet, bright light, a traditional desk and chair, and no intake; she also is persistent. Liz has five analytic qualities, and thus the teacher would be safe to assume that Liz learns best via step-by-step sequential lessons that begin with the data or details and gradually build up to an understanding (see Chapter 4).

Interpreting a Second LSI Individual Printout

Now examine Figure 2–3, Keith David's Individual Profile. Keith is a twelve-year-old seventh-grader attending Carey Middle School. His Consistency Score is 88, which is fine.

Environmental Information.   Scan the first four elements of the environmental stimulus and determine which learning style elements are important to Keith. In contrast to Elizabeth Patrice, who requires quiet, Keith prefers sound—music or conversation in the background—while learning. He also prefers soft lighting and an informal design. Conventional seating makes Keith physically uncomfortable and unable to concentrate on new and difficult information for any length of time. But when he is permitted to study on a floor, rug, beanbag, or pillows, Keith's attention span increases and his power of concentration is enhanced. Temperature is not important to him.

Emotional Information.   Keith is unmotivated (LSI score of 33) and has a low responsibility score (33), suggesting that he is a nonconformist (Dunn, White, & Zenhausern, 1982). When he is interested in what he is learning, he can be persistent and function with an average amount of structure. But when he is either uninterested or unable to master the material, he reveals a short attention span and does not follow directions.

Sociological Information.   Keith is strongly peer-oriented (LSI score of 64), wants feedback from an authority (LSI score of 80), and prefers a great deal of instructional variety rather than patterns or routines (LSI score of 66). Unlike Elizabeth Patrice, he does not enjoy learning alone but, rather, will perform better when permitted to learn with peers.

Name: Keith David   Sex: M   Year In School: 10   Date of Birth: 4/69   I.D. No.: 40000000

Group Identification: Carey H.S.   Special Code: Date: 02-05-1984   Group No.: 110

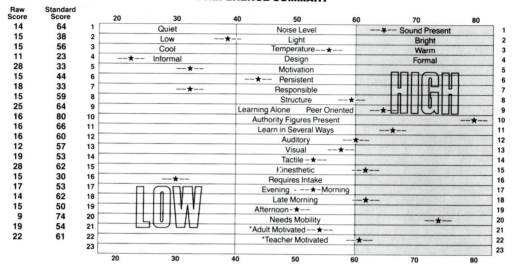

PREFERENCE SUMMARY

Raw Score	Standard Score						
14	64	1	Quiet	Noise Level	--★-- Sound Present		1
15	38	2	Low --★--	Light	Bright		2
15	56	3	Cool	Temperature--★--	Warm		3
11	23	4	--★-- Informal	Design	Formal		4
28	33	5	--★--	Motivation			5
15	44	6	--★--	Persistent			6
18	33	7	--★--	Responsible			7
15	59	8		Structure --★--			8
25	64	9	Learning Alone Peer Oriented	--★--			9
16	80	10		Authority Figures Present	--★--		10
16	66	11		Learn in Several Ways	--★--		11
16	60	12		Auditory --★--			12
12	57	13		Visual --★--			13
19	53	14		Tactile -★--			14
28	62	15		Kinesthetic --★--			15
15	30	16	--★--	Requires Intake			16
17	53	17		Evening - --★-Morning			17
14	62	18		Late Morning --★--			18
15	50	19		Afternoon-★--			19
9	74	20		Needs Mobility	--★--		20
19	54	21		*Adult Motivated --★--			21
22	61	22		*Teacher Motivated --★--			22
		23					23

CONSISTENCY: 88   *These scales are on LSI profile only.   PROFILE NO.:

FIGURE 2–3 Individual Profile
Learning Style Inventory

Perceptual Strengths. Keith has good perceptual strengths. He remembers nicely the things he hears (LSI score of 60) and experiences (LSI score of 62 on Kinesthetic), and his visual and tactual scores (57 and 53 respectively) are good, provided he is interested in what he is being exposed to.

Other Physiological Information. Keith's best time of day for difficult learning is in the late morning (LSI score of 62), but, if interested, he is capable of learning at any time of day. He needs frequent mobility (LSI score of 74).

Adult Motivation Scores. Although he wants to please another adult in his life when he is interested in what he is learning and can do so, Keith is strongly teacher-motivated. When a student's score on Teacher Motivated is 60 or above, also note the LSI score on Authority Figure Present. If both are 60 or above, that youngster may need an authoritative teacher—someone warm but firm. However, if the LSI Teacher Motivated score is 60 or above and the Authority Figure Present score is 40 or below, a collegial rather than an authoritative teacher would appear to be a better match of teaching and learning style.

Analysis of LSI Data from Individual Printout. Keith's low motivation may be reversed if his teacher responds to his learning style characteristics. The conventional classroom itself is unmotivating to students like Keith, who thrive in the midst of activities, variety, peer interaction, and choice. The first step is to redesign a section of the room to permit casual seating arrangements. Obviously, regulations need to be established—for example, students may do their work anywhere they wish as long as they are: (1) responsive to the teacher's directions; (2) considerate of others and not distracting to anyone; (3) able to complete their assignments; and (4) evidencing better grades than they achieved before they were permitted to choose their work places.

Keith needs soft lighting. Undoubtedly, he will choose a section of the classroom away from the lights and windows, perhaps even underneath or in back of a piece of furniture. Noise not only does not disturb Keith, he probably uses it to block out extraneous sounds (such as classmates breathing or moving in their seats) of which many of us are unaware. The teacher might be willing to experiment with either earplugs, earmuffs, clean cotton, or earphones to help him concentrate. Again, the same rules should apply: Keith may use the sound blocks provided he is responsive to his teacher's directions, does not distract or interfere with classmates' learning, completes his work, and achieves better than previously.

Another way to motivate Keith may be to permit him to study, learn, and complete assignments with classmates, rather than alone. Many young people function poorly cognitively when required to concentrate on difficult tasks by themselves; they simply are not loners. Conversely, they are stimulated by interaction with others. His teacher should experiment with permitting Keith to work with others *providing* all students in the group complete their tasks; function in an orderly, quiet manner; *and* perform as well as or better than they have previously. Normally, we suggest that students must perform *better* than previously; in Keith's case, however, to increase his desire to achieve, working with classmates is just an initial step forward.

In addition to permitting Keith to complete tasks with classmates, his teacher must give him the feedback he needs. He should understand that she is trying to help him perform better than before and is there to assist, question, monitor, and guide him on a frequent basis (because of his need for an authoritative presence).

Keith's perceptual strengths are fine; he is auditory (LSI score of 60) and kinesthetic (LSI score of 62), and his visual and tactual scores are all in the middle of the Individual Profile, indicating that, when interested, he is capable of remembering what he sees or reads and what he writes, draws, or expresses manipulatively. Keith's problems are his low Motivation score, his inability to adjust to traditional classroom settings, and his preference for working with others rather than alone. He also wants a variety of instructional experiences; he becomes bored with patterns and routines.

Keith does not require intake and, if interested, can concentrate at any time of day, but his *best,* most alert period is in the late morning. Thus, he should be scheduled for his most important subject between 10:00 A.M. and 12:00 noon, with some variation to respond to his need for variety.

Keith's strong need for mobility undoubtedly causes problems in school. Teachers often do not understand that, when a person is seated in a wooden, steel, or plastic chair, fully 75 percent of the total body weight is resting on just four square inches of *bone* (Branton, 1966). Only people who are sufficiently well endowed exactly where they need to be can sit for more than 10 or 12 minutes in such seating. Keith's teacher would be wise to experiment with permitting him to sit on a cushion on his chair or on a beanbag, pillow, carpet, or couch (if one is available).

Keith's willingness to please his teacher (LSI score of 61 on Teacher Motivated) will help increase this young man's motivation *and* achievement.

When choosing an instructional method appropriate for Keith, the knowledge that he has good perceptual memory, wishes to learn with peers, likes variety, and is a nonconformist is helpful. Ordinarily we would not recommend Contract Activity Packages (CAPs) for unmotivated learners because successful use of a CAP demands a strong measure of independence. However, Keith is *capable* of learning through this method because he can learn easily when interested (no perceptual strengths below 40), and his problems appear to stem from the mismatch between his learning style and the traditional school environment. A CAP would permit Keith to work anywhere in the classroom where he felt comfortable, with a peer or two, and would provide the variety (choices of Resource, Activity, and Reporting Alternatives, and even of Objectives) (see Chapter 8). However, Keith also could work well with a Programmed Learning Sequence (PLS), which provides more structure than he necessarily needs but would permit another alternative while learning (see Chapter 7). A Multisensory Instructional Package is unnecessary for someone so capable of learning. Keith could use tactual/kinesthetic materials if he were attracted to them, but could *create* those himself as part of the Activity Alternatives of a CAP.

Determining Global or Analytic Processing Inclinations. Here is Keith's *real* problem. You may recall that global people prefer to have sound while learning, soft illumination, an informal design, and intake; they also are not persistent learners; they rarely stay on task for any extended period when engaged in difficult academic studies. No wonder Keith is unmotivated. He has five of five possible global characteristics and, in addition, prefers working with peers, is tactual, and requires a great deal of movement rather than passivity. Traditional classrooms respond better to analytics than to globals, and Keith's additional needs for mobility and peer interaction are more than enough to reduce his motivation to learn. Awareness of this will encourage the teacher to begin new units with an anecdote (a short story related to the topic and demonstrating why this subject matter is relevant and interesting), humor, illustrations, and/or symbols—to gain the concentration and attention of global learners.

Graphic Overview of Interpreting LSI Individual Profiles

Global readers will find Table 2–1 an easy-to-follow representation of how to interpret LSI Individual Profiles. Extrapolation to which methods are appropriate for which learners will be addressed directly in each of the chapters concerned with instructional resources—Chapters 5, 6, 7, 8, and 9. You might care to test a few of your students with the LSI at this point and see whether you can identify their learning styles by following the guidelines in this chapter.

TABLE 2-1 Graphic Overview of Interpreting LSI Individual Profiles

Elements	20–29	30–39	41–59	60–69	70–80
Sound while learning	Always needs quiet when learning. A	Usually needs quiet when learning. A	It depends on what is being learned; sometimes needs quiet and sometimes does not.	Often works with some kind of sound. Is it radio? Records? TV? Conversation? G	Always/usually works with sound. What is listened to? Radio? TV? Conversation? G
Light while learning	Always works in very low light G	Sometimes works in low light. G	It depends on what is being done.	Likes light. It does not have to be extremely bright, but likes more light than less. A	Always has lights high when learning. Prefers them bright. A
Temperature while learning	Likes it very cool; is "warm" when others are cool! G	Likes it more cool than warm, but can adjust if needs to.	It depends on what is being done, the season, how student feels.	Likes it warm—not very warm, but nowhere near cool.	Feels better in the warmth and loves sunshine.
Design while learning	Always does best thinking work on a bed, lounge chair, floor, or carpet. G	Often does best thinking in an informal environment. G	It depends on what is being done.	Student thinks best on a wooden chair and desk, as in a library, classroom, or kitchen. A	Always works in a formal setting; doesn't do best work unless in "hard" chair. A
Motivation for academic learning	Is not really tuned in to school academic learning in a conventional classroom.	Occasionally enjoys academic learning—but not too often and not conventionally.	It depends on what is supposed to be learned. Sometimes student "turns on," but if he or she is not interested, no one can make him or her do it.	Likes to learn most of the time, especially when interested.	Enjoys learning. Gets a sense of accomplishment from achieving.

Continued

TABLE 2-1 Continued

Elements	20–29	30–39	41–59	60–69	70–80
Persistence during learning	Starts many things that are not finished; enjoys working on several tasks simultaneously.	There are things student has started that are still not done—but it does not happen too often, only occasionally. **G**	Whether or not student completes what he starts depends on his interest in it.	Usually completes the things he begins. **A**	Always completes the things begun; in fact, it bothers him not to. **A**
Responsibility for academic learning	Likes to do things that most other people usually don't do; does not respond well to authority but *does* to collegiality.	Sometimes enjoys doing things that he knows he would be better off *not* doing; is fairly nonconforming.	Whether or not student does unconventional things depends on what the task is, how he feels, what the circumstances are, etc.	Usually does the things that he believes he *ought* to do.	Feels best when he does the things he knows he should do, and that is what he does most of the time; is conforming.
Structure versus options while learning	Student can't stand other people telling him what to do or how to do it.	Really likes to do things in own way.	What is being done, with whom, why are what determine whether it gets done the student's way, someone else's way, or cooperatively.	Doesn't mind at all being told what to do or how to do it—as long as student likes the person who's telling him!	Student feels best when told exactly what is required, all the guidelines (including the date it is due), and when he knows exactly how to proceed before starting.
Learning alone	Student works best alone and gets more done that way.	Student prefers doing most things alone.	It depends on what needs to be done—and with whom.	Student really prefers doing things with someone else. **G**	Should be the chairperson of the committee. **G**
Learning with an authority	There aren't many things that a teacher suggests that this student will actually do, unless made to. Try a collegial approach; give options.	Often does the *opposite* of what a teacher suggests. Try a collegial approach; give options.	It depends on whether or not student respects the teacher.	Student *likes* to do what teacher asks; feels better when he does than when he doesn't. Provide frequent feedback.	Usually does what teacher requests—unless he disagrees on the issue, at which point motivation determines action. Provide frequent feedback.

54

Needing variety	Likes routines and patterns. Does not feel comfortable doing new/different things too often.	Prefers doing essentially the same thing in the same way, but can tolerate some change.	It depends on what is being done, why, how, when, and with whom.	Likes change. Gets bored with the same old routine.	Rarely does the same thing in the same way twice in a row. Needs variety.
Learning by listening (auditory)	Often sits at a lecture and doesn't really know much of what is being said. Finds it difficult to listen for long periods of time.	Sometimes sits at a lecture and "tunes out." Has to concentrate to "stay with" a speaker.	If interested, can learn by listening; if bored, doesn't know what is going on.	Finds it easy to learn by listening.	Remembers things heard, can concentrate and "pull back" people's voices and reconstruct a lot of what they have said.
Learning by reading or viewing (visual)	Often reads a page, comes to the end, and thinks, "I don't know what I've read!" Then rereads the page.	Sometimes needs to reread a page because although it has been read, virtually no meaning has been absorbed.	If interested, can retain a great deal of what has been read; if not, can go through the text without absorbing what the words actually mean.	Remembers a great deal of what has been read.	Can concentrate on things read long afterward; closes eyes, "sees" the open book, the section of the page and the paragraph, focuses on the print—and remembers what was read.
Learning by touching (tactual)	Never/rarely takes notes. Is also not too great at doing things with the hands.	Only takes notes for numerical data or things that can't be remembered easily.	Whether or not student takes notes during a lecture depends on how difficult/interesting the topic is.	Often takes notes either during a lecture or when reading something new or difficult that student wants to learn. Global tactuals often draw or doodle to remember; they enjoy hands-on learning.	If student forgets shopping list, he/she remembers most of the things on it. If hands were *not* used during a lecture (by note-taking, doodling, knitting or a similar activity) student would find it difficult to listen.

Continued

TABLE 2-2 Continued

Elements	20–29	30–39	41–59	60–69	70–80
Learning by doing (kinesthetic)	Would rather drive than walk.	Does not often engage in energetic, action-oriented learning.	Student's degree of involvement in doing things is determined by what is being done—and by whom.	Likes being active and involved.	Becomes involved in many energetic activities, and people comment on high energy level.
Needing intake while learning	Never eats, drinks, smokes, chews, or gets involved with intake while studying.	Rarely eats, drinks, smokes, chews, or gets involved with intake while studying.	Whether or not student uses intake when learning depends on what is in the refrigerator.	Often uses intake when studying. G	Always uses some kind of intake when studying. G
Evening–morning energy levels	Remembers best the things studied at night.	Remembers best the things studied in the evening.	Time of night or day is not important; what is important is what is being done and with whom.	Remembers best the things studied in the morning.	Remembers best the things studied early in the morning.
Late morning energy levels	Not really "alive" just before lunchtime.	Can function, but learning does not come easily late in the morning.	The time is not important; what is important is what is being done and with/for whom.	Can learn very nicely in the late morning.	Learns extremely well in the late morning.
Afternoon energy levels	The afternoon is a *terrible* time for studying. Avoid making important decisions of any kind at that time!	Can get through an afternoon—but not easily.	The time is not important; what *is* important is what is being done and with/for whom.	Learns nicely in the afternoon.	Afternoon is an excellent time for learning.
Mobility while learning	Can sit still for long periods of time when interested in what is being learned.	Sitting still is not much of a problem.	If interested, can sit still; if bored, can't.	Finds it difficult to sit still for long periods of time.	Finds it impossible to sit still for long periods of time.

Note: A = Analytic; G = Global.

*Some analytics prefer a softly lit room with a bright, intense light focused directly on the page they are reading.

__3__

Redesigning the Educational Environment

Designing an Effective Instructional Environment

The secret of designing an effective instructional environment at no cost (or very little) involves using what you already have in new patterns. The desks, chairs, tables, bookcases, file cabinets, and other furniture are moved to take maximum advantage of the space available and the individual learning styles of students.

Begin slowly, be flexible and receptive to new ideas and approaches, plan carefully, and continually evaluate how well the new design meets your objectives for each of the students in the class.

Room Redesign Based on Individual Learning Styles

Many teachers alter the seating assignments in their classrooms in response to discipline problems. Changing an individual to another seat without changing his or her total learning environment is a little like playing Russian roulette—one never knows what will happen.

For example, a student who likes to work with one or two peers might be moved away from friends because their voices disturb others. That youngster may become very unhappy and, as a result, may not be able to concentrate on his or her studies. How much better it would be to establish ground rules for when, how, and under what circumstances students may teach each other and discuss what they are learning, so that peer-oriented students may have time to learn together.

To begin redesigning your classroom to provide for varied learning styles, you first must identify each of your student's learning styles—either

57

with the *Learning Style Inventory* (LSI) (see Chapter 2). Then, using the following checklist, begin to identify the parts of the room that might lend themselves to each of the following:

- Places where several students may meet to discuss what they are learning
- Well-lit reading areas
- Warmer areas
- Desks or tables and chairs
- Sections that permit responsible students to work without direct supervision
- Sections that permit students to work alone, with a friend or two, in a small group, with an adult, or in any combination thereof, provided they show academic progress
- Essentially quiet and screened study areas for individuals or pairs
- Darker sections for media viewing, photography, or dramatizations
- Cooler areas
- Carpeted informal lounge sections with couch and easy chairs
- Sections that permit close supervision of less responsible students
- An area where snacking may be available (preferably raw vegetables and fruits, nuts, and other nutritious foods)

Changing the Classroom Box into a Multifaceted Learning Environment

Some teachers can visualize an entire room redesign by closing their eyes. Others must move one seat or section at a time. Still others must try several alternatives before deciding on a relatively permanent arrangement.

Planning Step 1: Locating Dividers

The first planning step is to identify and locate as many things as possible that can be placed perpendicular to walls, unused chalkboards, and spaces between windows. Such items include file cabinets, desks, bookcases, tables, shelves, material displays, screens, charts that can stand unsupported, and cardboard cartons or boxes that may be attractively painted or decorated. Even your desk can be used effectively this way. Do not overlook bookcases that may be partially fixed to a wall or those, such as library stacks, that may seem too unstable to stand out into the room.

The custodians will enjoy the experience and novelty of assisting you in this venture. They are your "design engineer assistants" and will be proud of having helped you. To enlist their support, tell them why you are changing your room and that your room will be easier to move around in and to clean—because it will be. The custodians will also respond positively to the need to build supports and add backings to rickety bookcases. They may have good suggestions and, once involved, might be able to obtain that extra table, too.

Step 1 is the key to providing different types of areas and more space than you realized was possible.

Examples of Waist High Dividers Used by Teachers

Cardboard boxes	Cardboard carpentry
Bookshelves	Homosote
Filing cabinets	Closets
Wooden crafts	Colored yarn
Bulletin boards	Fish nets
Coat racks	Fish tanks
Boards on wheels	Long tables
Plastic six-pack holders	Voting booths
Shower liners	Shower curtains
Wire and posters	Bed sheets
Burlap	Plastic wall covering
Styrofoam	Piping
Planters and plants	Drop cloths
Display cases	Cutting boards
Art easels	Awnings

Planning Step 2: Clearing the Floor Area

Look at your room. Walk around. There are likely to be boxes, books, papers, and assorted teaching materials. Temporarily place these materials outside the room or into a closet or corner. Later you will place these resources on top of the perpendicular units to provide additional screening and separation of the instructional areas such as the Learning Station, Interest Center, office area, Game Table, Library Corner, Quiet Reading Area, Role-Playing Stage, Media Corner, and so forth.

When moving the furniture and developing the physical environment, it is usually wise to do it with the students. They should be aware of what is going to be created and why, and that it will take a while to become acclimated to the change. Their involvement in the development of the design invariably creates a positive attitude of acceptance for the revision, and, of greater importance, the youngsters' suggestions and reactions help to correctly place students with specific learning styles.

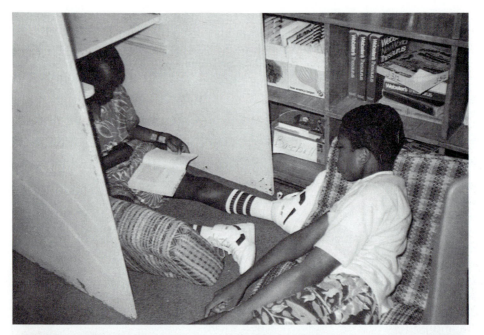

Bookshelves, individual carrels, and homosote or plywood dividers placed perpendicular to classroom walls provide spaces for formal and informal study areas, reading alcoves, and small-group instruction. (Photographs courtesy: Madison Prep Junior High School, New York City; Sacred Heart Seminary, Hempstead, New York; and Franklin Township Middle School, Franklin Township, Indiana.)

Planning Step 3: Involving the Students

Should you elect to involve all your students, you might begin your conversation by explaining that, as in their apartments or homes, the way the furniture is arranged in an area should make sense for the people who live there; that some of the boys and girls who "live" in their classroom (and it is living for four or five hours each school day!) may enjoy the arrangement just as it is, but that others might feel uncomfortable because people are different from each other and some need certain things that others do not.

For example (and here begin to personalize with them), everyone in the present arrangement is seated, in a sense, out in the open, even if there are separations between groups. With many students at close range it must be difficult for some of them to concentrate as they see and hear the door opening, chairs and people moving, and materials being used and replaced. Some need a quiet place to concentrate on their studies; for those people you would like to create small offices, dens, or alcove areas where they can be by themselves, or with a friend or two, to complete their work.

At this point you are certain to have their undivided attention; they will be curious, stimulated, intrigued, and individually motivated to redesign their classroom. You might ask how many students would like to serve as assistant interior decorators to aid you in rearranging the room to create spaces in which they will enjoy doing their schoolwork.

One of the first things you will suggest is the establishment of some areas where small groups of students may literally turn their backs on what is happening in the room and become absorbed in their work. This can be done by facing their chairs toward any available wall space.

You can increase bulletin board space by using the backs of file cabinets, bookcases, closet doors (that can be left closed) and rarely used chalkboard sections. Plywood, cardboard, wallboard, and other building materials can be added to one side of bookcases that are open in both directions or to the side of a file cabinet.

Describe how you plan to clear one section of the room at a time; explain the kind of den or office it will be (number of students it can hold, light or shady, warm or cool, open or partitioned); and tell the students that if individuals would like to try locating in that area (either alone or with a friend or two, or occasionally three), they should so indicate by any method you suggest (raised hands, quietly spoken words). Preface any decisions by clearly explaining that students who shout for recognition, call out "Oooooh!," or in any way behave disruptively will slow down the process and will have to wait longer for their turn. (Do not confuse excitement with disruptiveness; be prepared to be flexible.)

It is also necessary to explain that they really have to understand themselves, that some of them work best alone. These students should not volunteer to sit with their friends, for if they do not complete their work, their seats will have to be changed; it's better to diagnose themselves correctly in the beginning. Conversely, if youngsters promise they will work well with a friend (even if they previously played more than they worked and therefore made little academic progress), give them an opportunity to try to do so. Warn them, however, that if they do not show increased achievement, their seating arrangements will be altered. Students frequently become highly motivated when allowed to share a secluded section of the room with a friend or two, and they often will gradually conform to higher standards of behavior and effort than previously shown.

Mention to your students in this pre-redesign discussion that, just as they are used to the placement of the furniture in their homes, they are currently at home with the placement of the various items in their classroom. Explain that it takes time for people to adjust to new things, but that the more flexible they are, the faster they adjust. (This will encourage many of the students to experience positive reactions to the emerging redesign. In turn, they will then assist others to become acclimated to the new arrangements.)

Finally, assure the students that if they do not like the redesigned room, you will help them return to the present arrangement. Ask them, however, to agree to live with the new placement for at least one week before deciding whether to keep it or to revert to the way the room was arranged before the proposed change.

Once the students indicate a willingness to experiment with the classroom furniture and to remain with the change for at least a one-week trial period, you are ready to actually redesign. At this time, distribute the students' individual printouts, teach them how to interpret them, and discuss their decisions concerning their choices of location on the basis of differences revealed by the LSI.

Redesign: Preliminary Considerations

The major objective of changing the placement of furniture in the classroom is to provide different types of areas to permit students to function through patterns that appear to be natural for them and for their learning styles. Some students, however, may not know how they work best or where they prefer to sit; they can only try new placements and determine whether the arrangement is good or appropriate for them on the basis of how they react after the change. Therefore, rather than asking students where they would like to sit, begin by establishing the areas. Then, one by one, explain the advantages and disadvantages of each, describing the responsibilities of those who elect to sit in that den, alcove, office, corner, or section.

Next, describe the learning styles that the area will complement and request volunteers. Students need only try the area for a one-week period; if they either are dissatisfied or are unable to work there, changes can be made on a flexible basis with your approval.

Step-by-Step to Partial or Total Redesign: Some Problems and How to Begin

This section will present a sample redesign plan. It is, of course, only one of an infinite variety of arrangements to meet the learning style needs of students and instructional objectives of the teacher. Further, if you have some trepidation or doubt based on the commonly expressed concerns that follow, try some of the suggestions in this description. It is crucial that you feel confident and able to live with the approach you select. Then measure the results with your students after six weeks!

Expressed Concerns

- I have too much material to cover. I will never finish if students are all over the room doing different things.
- I could lose control. These students are difficult enough when I can see all of them in rows.
- The principal would never let me do this.
- The parents will be upset if I don't lecture to the students every day.
- How could I possibly address the whole group in this setup?
- I have wall-to-wall students now. Some of them almost have to hang their feet out the windows as it is.
- We have no money, no resources, no bookshelves. . . . I'm fortunate to have a tablet arm-desk for each student.
- I am a traveling teacher. I have five classes in five different rooms.
- I might be able to do this, but the teacher who follows me will complain.

As a teacher who once taught three basic subjects on two different grade levels in two different buildings, Ken has deep empathy for all instructors who face these and other problems and obstacles not cited herein. Nevertheless, room redesign will generate more space, not less; improve learning, self-image, and discipline; permit additional time to help individuals and facilitate learning for all; involve students positively in the instructional process; creatively and inexpensively improve the educational environment; develop student responsibility for replacing seating arrangements for the next teacher; and reveal new approaches to large-group instruction. These results will become evident over time. If, however, you wish to retain a whole-class lecture option as a possibility each day, begin with the next section in this chapter. If you would like to try a more complete design sooner, consider the following type of plan.

One last word of encouragement before you begin: This is an accurate story, and variations of it have been told to us repeatedly.

I'm a veteran math teacher who is known as the toughest disciplinarian in the high school. Last semester I ran into one of those average-ability classes that just couldn't master geometry no matter how I explained it, or reviewed it, or drilled it. I had read an article by the Dunns and, in desperation, I told the students to listen to the day's lecture and then to study any where in the room that they chose. They could work wherever they wished if they exercised self-control and learned what was taught. The students became very quiet. Finally one youngster said, Do you mean it? When I assured him that I did, students excitedly moved into all types of positions and areas. Two girls sat on the windowsill; one came to my desk; several sat on the floor, threee pushed their desks together; and so forth. I never had a better class!

Establishing Instructional Areas

A simple way to begin is to clear a section of the room other than a window wall. Then identify all the movable objects in the room that can be used as perpendicular extensions to break up the linear effect and to provide small areas. If there are few movable items such as bookcases, file cabinets, tables, or chests available, low-cost dividers can easily be constructed with cardboard boxes in which house appliances are delivered.

The movable objects may be used in a variety of ways in different sections of the room. For example, bookcases of varying lengths and widths may separate pairs of desks to provide privacy and to permit quiet areas (see Figure 3–1). Small groups of desks (three or five) may be isolated in a charming little

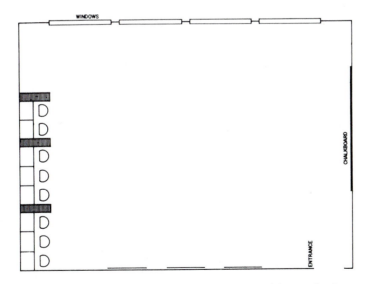

FIGURE 3–1 Bookcases, file cabinets, extra tables, and other movable items may separate desks that have been arranged to face the wall so that students have their backs to the center of the room and thus can turn away from the hub of activity to concentrate on their work. The wall space directly in front of the desk is used for a personal bulletin board. The divider provides privacy for occupants on both sides of it.

den or alcove that encourages small-group teamwork (see Figure 3–2). The movable objects may also set apart resource instructional areas such as Learning Stations or Media Corners so that students may conduct their work out of the mainstream of activity (see Figure 3–3). In addition, dividers may be used to separate the motivated, persistent students from those who do not follow through on their prescriptions and who require constant supervision (see Figure 3–4).

When you have cleared the first section of the room, you may begin by saying, "Here is an area that is far from the windows. The lighting will probably be soft and the temperature may be a little cooler in the summer and warmer in the winter" (if that is true). "If you think you'd like to work where the lighting is less bright and it's a little less warm than in other areas of the room, you may sit here with one or two friends—if you are certain that you'll work quietly with those friends and learn, too. This area, because it is next to the wall, will have a bulletin board space. Remember, if you accept the responsibility of the bulletin board, you'll have to keep it looking attractive, neat, and interesting. Is there anyone who would like to sit here with a friend or two?"

If one student volunteers, ask him with whom he would like to sit. If he

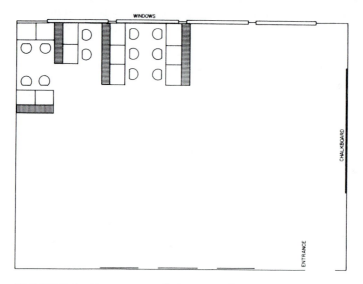

FIGURE 3–2 To create small den areas for two or more pairs of students (selected by student preferences), separate the desks from adjacent groups by placing the movable objects perpendicular to the walls. Face each pair or small group of desks toward the divider so that the paired students have their backs to other pairs. This arrangement is conducive to the development of close peer relationships between the members of each paired group, but not necessarily among the members of the two groups.

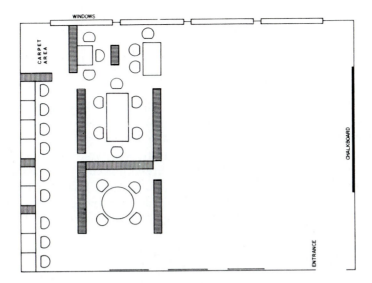

FIGURE 3-3 Cleverly used dividers can separate the active area of the classroom (which frequently centers around Interest Centers and Learning Stations) from the Library Corners and other study-reading areas. Such an arrangement provides students with the options of either working in the center with others or studying alone or with a friend at one's desk or den area.

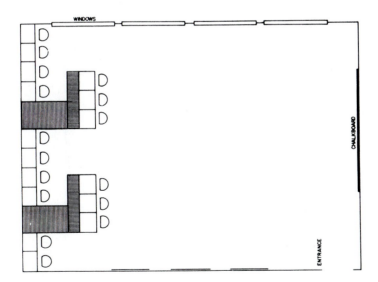

FIGURE 3-4 Dividers also may be used to separate those students who are capable of working independently from those who need constant supervision. The former are provided with den or alcove areas on the periphery, while the latter are seated toward the center of the room where the teacher is closer and may work with them more directly.

names one or two friends, ask them if they would like to sit together with the person who nominated them. If so, ask them each to bring their seats and desks to the area (see Figure 3–2).

Show the students the wall section that will hold their bulletin boards and ask them again if they are willing to assume the responsibility for keeping their bulletin boards attractive, up-to-date, and interesting. If they respond affirmatively, give them an opportunity to try with your approval. They may immediately obtain the construction paper and masking tape (it does not pull off paint when removed) and begin mounting their boards. Move the first object that will be used as a divider and place it perpendicular to the wall at the end of the grouped desks to form the first private section in the room (see Figure 3–5).

If the divider that you have used to mark off the first den area is long enough to place two side-by-side desks on the other side, you can begin the second den area by describing that arrangement to the class. This would be an area that would tend to be a little lighter than the first and a little warmer, and would, again, offer a relatively secluded space to its occupants. This section also would contain space for individual bulletin boards. Again, request volunteers and, depending on your and their preferences, place their desks either directly against the wall as in Figure 3–5 or in back-to-back pairs (see Figure 3–6). Combinations of the two designs provide increased interior interest, but some people prefer either one or the other pattern. Exact placement

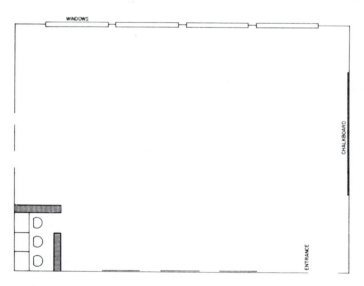

FIGURE 3–5 The first step in classroom redesign is to divide available wall space into small dens or alcoves to provide privacy and relative quiet for those students who need these elements to function effectively.

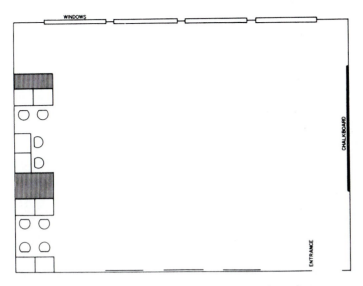

FIGURE 3-6   This is an alternative beginning plan where two pairs of students share the same den area.

is not of prime importance; what is necessary is that small groups of young-sters each have a place of their own in which to escape the activity and accom-panying classroom distraction so that they may work effectively alone or with a friend or two.

Some dividers, such as a single file cabinet, aid in isolating an individual youngster who prefers to work alone. Explain that this is an area that permits a person to work quietly and independently, and encourage the students to know themselves and to select a placement that will enhance their learning style.

Reading Corner

After the second or third den area has been situated, identify two long dividers that can delineate a Reading Corner (a quiet, casual reading-meditating corner of the room where absolutely no discussion is permitted). This area should be close to the windows if the students who use it need bright light, or away from illumination if they tend to be global and prefer soft lighting. It is a place where students may go to relax, to read in silence, or to rest if they need to do so.

The Reading Corner permits students to withdraw temporarily from the noise and activities of the class, thus transforming this section into the quietest area in the environment. It usually is carpeted and/or pillowed and holds no chairs, desks, or hardware, although many schools provide a couch or easy chair to accommodate those who prefer this type of informal seating to the floor. The Reading Corner includes many appropriate books of varied levels and types; textbooks are included but are not the only books available. There are other places in the room (shelves, bookcases, display counters) that also house interesting books on many subjects, but those are easily accessible to all students who are in the area as long as they choose to remain. The teacher may be flexible, of course, and permit students to take books out of the Corner to be read elsewhere (perhaps by a pair), but the object of maintaining a current display there is to prevent other students who may want to browse through or take a book away from this intimate section to avoid intruding on the privacy of the youngsters who are actually in that Corner because they think best in solitude. The authors therefore suggest that a special group of nonmovable books (which may have duplicates in other sections of the room) be kept in this special location, if possible.

To establish the Reading Corner, use two bookcases (or cardboard open-shelf dividers) at right angles to each other in the corner of the room at the other end of the wall on which you began to establish the den areas. This should be a corner near or at a windowed section (to provide light for the readers). Place the two dividers so that each is perpendicular to one of the corner walls (as in Figure 3–7), but not touching each other. Leave room for a small entranceway.

Merchants who sell carpeting often will donate last year's samples and remnants to local schools when they receive a letter on official stationery requesting leftover sections. Those pieces—or the squares or rectangle samples from floor covering display books, may be placed end to end inside the Reading Corner to provide a clean, relatively soft, inviting place to concentrate in

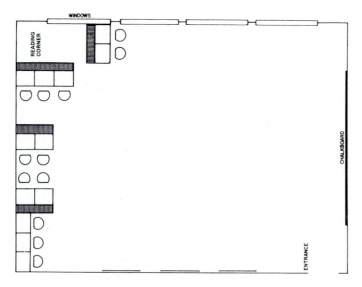

FIGURE 3–7 Note the formation of a Reading Corner, a casual, carpeted area where students may read or meditate in silence.

comparative quiet. You may wish to use strips of double-stick masking tape beneath the carpet sections to keep them in place.

It is wise to establish rules limiting the number of students who may use the Reading Corner at one time. The number will vary in accordance with the size of the area, but allow for at least two or three more than the actual number whose LSI printouts indicate the need for an informal design. The number may vary, but a Reading Corner should be designed to be used by no more than five or six students at a time.

Should your printouts reveal a large group of global students, many of those should be directed to global, interdisciplinary, and thematic areas in relatively low light that also contain Reading Corners. These reading areas provide privacy and quiet zones to permit focus and concentration. Students assigned there or permitted to use them should not be disturbed.

Expanding the Den Area Concept

Once the Reading Corner has been established, you will be able to determine how many desks may be placed against each of the two dividers that were used to mark off its boundaries. Show the students that you plan to place desks snugly up against each of the dividers to begin the formation of additional dens.

If the back of the divider is solid, place this solid part so that it faces the front (or the inside) of the room. When a desk is pushed up against that surface, the back of the divider (if high enough) becomes a bulletin board for each youngster who faces it. If the divider has only one open side (such as a one-sided bookcase), use the bookshelf part on the inside of the magic carpet area and the closed shelf part on the outside to form a bulletin board surface. If both sides of the divider are open, place the books in the divider so that the bindings are accessible to the students inside the Reading Corner.

Explain the attributes of each of the two newly created den areas to the students—for example: "This section is near the windows. It is likely that the light will be brighter than elsewhere in the room. It is also near the heater. If you volunteer for this space, be certain that you like warmth. You'll also be near the Reading Corner, so you'll have to be able to avoid socializing with students as they enter and leave that section. Can you work quietly with only the friend you elect, and can you ignore the traffic going in and out of the area? If so, this may be a good location for you. If you would like to sit here with a friend or two, raise you hand."

After each of the two sections behind the two dividers that border the Reading Corner have been occupied by their new tenants, survey the entire wall area with which you have been working. Do you have room for an additional pair, a single youngster who wants to work alone, another divider to provide even more privacy? Add whatever appeals to you aesthetically and makes sense educationally. Your first wall should be near completion and may look something like the model in Figure 3–8 or 3–9. If not, do not be concerned. As long as the students are positive about their seating arrangements

Many individuals, pairs, and small groups of students are most productive in mini-den areas. These may include either formal or informal seating arrangements. (Photographs courtesy: Troutdale High School, Trautdale, Oregon; Robeson High School, Chicago, Illinois; Midwest High School, Midwest, Wyoming; Corsicana High School, Corsicana, Texas; and Franklin Township Middle School, Franklin Township, Indiana respectively.)

and you are willing to try the design, further adjustments may be made as the need for them becomes evident.

Once the far wall has been designed to your initial satisfaction, the front wall directly opposite the one you have just completed should be redesigned. Begin with the section of the front wall that is directly opposite the Reading Corner. Establish a den by using two dividers to enclose the corner. Determine if you wish to place two pairs of youngsters, two groups of three students, or some other number. The width and depth of the den will depend on the number of desks and chairs you place there.

Once each of the dividers has been located perpendicular to one of the two right-angled corner walls, the students' desks may be placed so that they either face the interior wall (as in Figure 3–10) or face the back side of either one or both of the dividers (as in Figure 3–11). The latter placement is directly opposite from the way we used the dividers in the Reading Corner where stu-

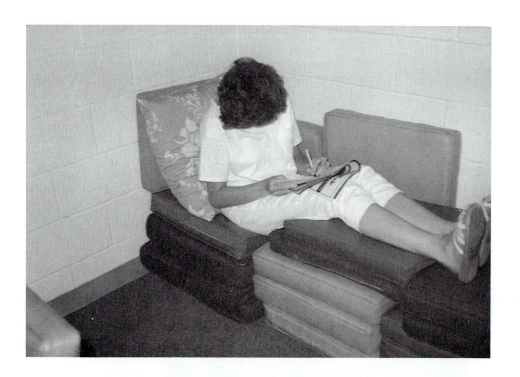

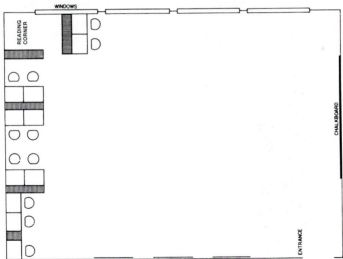

FIGURE 3–8   This is one plan for the development of small den or alcove areas where two to four students may share their efforts toward completing their individual or group prescriptions. On the upper left, near the window corner, is the Reading Corner.

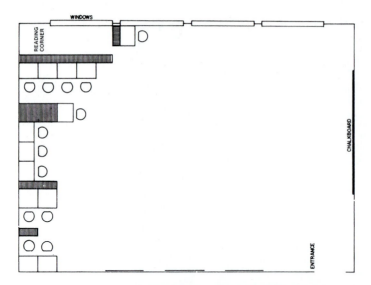

FIGURE 3–9 This is an alternative plan for redesigning a far wall in a traditional classroom. This arrangement also features the Reading Corner near the windows (to provide light) and on the far, rear wall (to provide quiet).

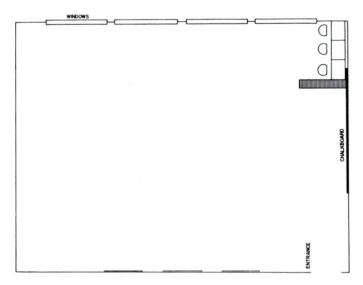

FIGURE 3–10 Students in this corner den have placed their desks so that they face against the interior wall, which provides bulletin board space for its occupants.

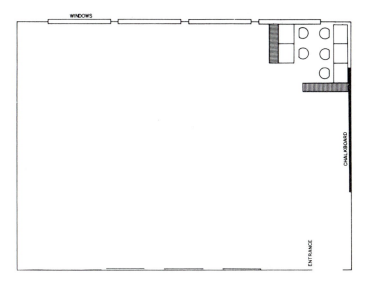

FIGURE 3–11   In this corner den some of the students' desks face against the back of one of the dividers and others face the interior wall.

dents inside needed to be able to reach whatever occupied the shelves or drawers of the dividers used to form the area; here it will be the students who do not share this area who will need to be able to get to the materials housed in the dividers without intruding on the youngsters inside.

If a bookcase or cabinet is used as a divider on the outside of the corner den, two or three additional students may be placed at right angles to it on the outside of the corner area. These new desks could face the front wall and begin to form the next area. If the divider on the front wall of the corner area has neither side shelf nor side drawer space (such as a file cabinet where the drawers face the center of the room), desks may be placed up against the divider itself. A table may be used as a material resource center and may be flanked on both sides by dividers. This arrangement would permit an additional area where students who do not share a den area may meet to work together during a small-group instructional activity such as a circle of knowledge, simulation, or case study (see Figure 3–12).

Any of the techniques for grouping two to five students may be used to continue the pattern of establishing small den or alcove areas. The section nearest the door lends itself well to being a material resource section. Dividers may be placed at right angles to the walls near the entrance to provide an open passageway where books and manipulatives (games, subject area materials, and so forth) may be selected easily without intruding on others (see Figure 3–13).

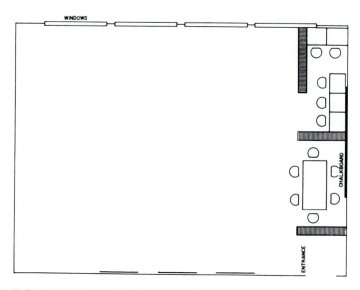

FIGURE 3–12   A table has been designated as a material resource center (for example, a place where subject area materials may be available) and placed between two dividers to facilitate easy access to the materials and privacy when using
them. This area also can be used as a small-group center where
students who do not share a den may meet to work together.

Behind the bookcases on the side wall near the door, two or three students' desks may be placed to form another den. When a wall includes a clothing closet, it may be feasible to establish only one den area behind the entranceway bookcase. The remaining section must be free for access to the
closet. In older, traditional buildings, closets frequently have some stationary
doors. These may be used for individual youngsters who prefer to work alone.
Their desks may be placed against the nonmovable doors that may then be
used as bulletin boards (see Figure 3–14).

Where large, old-fashioned heating units are exposed to view it is possible to cover the surface with a protective, fireproof material and to use the
units themselves as areas against which one or two desks may be placed, using
the portion of the unit above the desk heights as a bulletin board.

When sections of the room appear to be unusable for desk placement
(such as long sections of wardrobe walls, built-in bookcase walls, or sink and
other wet areas), it is appropriate to leave an aisle between these sections and
a series of horizontally placed dividers. This arrangement creates an attractive
resource aisle on the periphery of the room and permits small dens to be established toward the inner part. Access to the materials placed in the dividers
does not interfere with students engrossed in their studies outside the area (see
Figure 3–13).

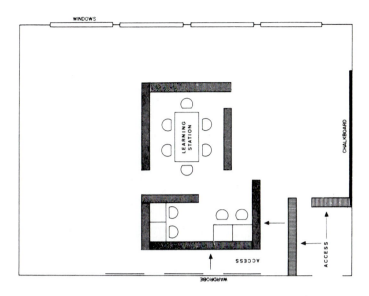

FIGURE 3–13 The entrance to a room serves effectively as a resource center, providing easy access to learning materials without intrusion on working students. Built-in wardrobes or bookcase walls may be made more functional by placing dividers three to four feet in front of them with access to the materials they house from the side away from the middle of the room. Students' desks then may be placed against the dividers on the inside of the room to create new den areas.

The various patterns of separating the rear and front walls of the classroom into small den areas to accommodate between two and five students should be extended all around the outer area of the room with the exception of closets or sinks. If sufficient space is available, it may be possible to establish one or more material resource centers or small-group meeting areas within the total design. The outer sections of the room should be maintained as quiet work areas for independent, paired, or small-group work. The teacher should move from youngster to youngster and from small group to small group to check each student's progress, respond to questions, guide youngsters in need of assistance, and evaluate the quality of what has been completed.

Initially, redesign efforts should be restricted to the outer perimeter of the room. The center should be reserved for areas where students may work together in more gregarious or mobile activities. The den areas that foster privacy and small-group work will aid in keeping the noise level down and student concentration high. Youngsters may work alone, in pairs, or in small teams in their dens or in the small-group instructional areas that have been established on the outer edge of the room. For more interactive activities, they may work in the center of the room. With this method, youngsters involved

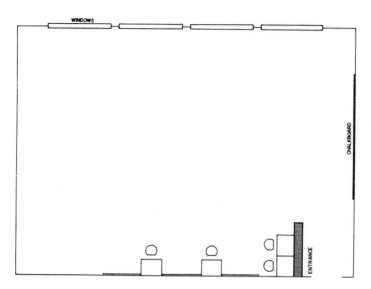

FIGURE 3-14   Behind the entranceway bookcase is the first side wall den area. If this is a clothing closet wall and the closets include some nonmovable doors, individual youngsters may occupy the spaces directly in front of the stationary doors and may use the doors as bulletin boards. An alternative would be to establish a resource aisle directly in front of the wardrobe area by placing dividers approximately four feet away from the closets and permitting access to materials from the closet side (see Figure 3-13).

in their independent prescriptions can literally turn their backs on the activity in the center and remain with their tasks. Should it be appropriate to join those involved in the center of the room, at a thematic interest center for example, they merely need to move to the larger area. Basic rules and procedures for moving from one area to another should be established to promote positive learning activities for all.

The center area might include a Learning Station or two, an Interest Center, or a Game Table. If the teacher and class prefer, one of the corner den areas may be used as a Resource Center or a Media Corner. The room arrangement may be as creative as the teacher, but much of the practicality of this kind of redesign will not become apparent until experienced by the group for a week or more. The room should be revised, especially in the early stages, to meet needs as they emerge.

As you reconstruct your classroom, it is important to teach the students to use it effectively. This necessitates the ability to cooperate with peers; to choose from among appropriate alternatives; to complete assignments or tasks; to locate, use, share, repair, and return resources; and to function independently in an environment that requires increased decision making and student responsibility.

Figure 3–15 depicts a completely redesigned model classroom that provides for different learning styles.

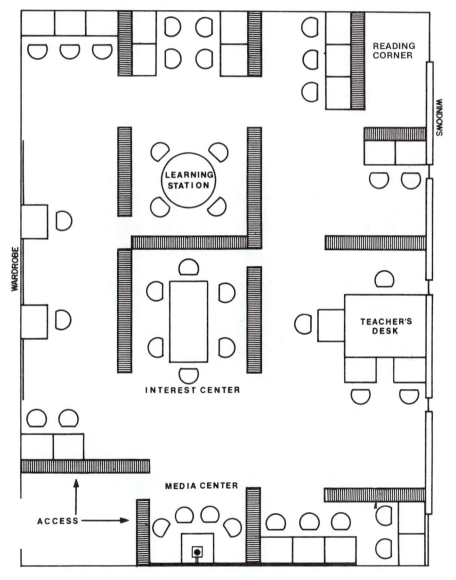

FIGURE 3–15   This depicts a completely redesigned model classroom that provides for different learning styles. It is but one of an infinite number of redesign options.

Adding Designer Touches

Aluminum Foil, Construction Paper, and Paint Leftover holiday wrappings, colored construction paper, unused paint, clear food wrappings, or aluminum foil can be used effectively to decorate walls, bulletin boards, cardboard dividers, and the backs and sides of file cabinets. Remnant wallpaper, shelf liner, and sections of carpeting, burlap or cut-up old jeans can be used to create montages and attractive backs for dividers, walls, shelves, and mounted objectives. In addition to creating an attractive learning environment, you will promote interest and enthusiasm if you let the students and, occasionally, their parents help in the interior decorating process.

Living Room Areas
A large number of junior and senior high students concentrate best while reading either on carpeting or in a lounge chair. They often seek an overhead cover

Designer touches and mini-living room arrangements provide positive room redesign alternatives for informal-preferenced and nonconforming learners. Improved behaviors, attitudes, and test scores result (Griggs & Dunn, 1986). (Photographs courtesy: Brockport Middle School, Brockport, New York; P. K. Yonge Laboratory School, Gainesville, Florida; and Midwest High School, Midwest, Wyoming respectively.)

and settle themselves below a shelf or a table. Some like open spaces while studying or conversing. Still others achieve quickly and well while listening to music. Successful alternative schools around the nation recreate living rooms or homelike dens for those who learn best in an informal environment. Students often enjoy the creativity and results when given the opportunity to design informal areas that differ substantially from the institutionalized structures of traditional high school classrooms.

Understanding and Using Varied Instructional Areas

Once the room has been totally redesigned, rules should be established for the use of varied instructional areas. Those students who demonstrate that they can learn effectively together by using any three or four small-group techniques without supervision should begin to use instructional areas such as Learning Stations, Interest Centers, Game Tables, Reading Areas, Media Corners, and Resource Centers. In this way, youngsters may continue to work independently or with partners at defined learning spaces while the teacher focuses attention on the ones who cannot achieve without adult direction. Each instructional area serves specific purposes and thus attracts students with different learning styles, interests, and goals at varying times.

Separating the learning environment into multi-instructional areas encourages students to consider where they will find it most appropriate to do their work; where they will find the resources through which they may achieve

their objectives; and whether they prefer working alone, with a friend or two, in a small group of peers, or directly with the teacher.

The instructional areas that may be established have characteristics in common. These include the following:

1. Clearly stated objectives, usually with some choice permitted, such as ''Complete three (3) of the following five (5) objectives''
2. Small-group techniques with which the students are familiar, such as Circle of Knowledge, Team Learning, Brainstorming, Case Study, Group Analysis, Role Playing, or Simulations
3. Introductory, reinforcement, and evaluative activities related to the important objectives
4. Alternative activities on different levels of difficulty: written assignments, creative tasks, problem-solving requirements, and so forth

5. Self-correcting activities: student-made Electroboards, Pic-A-Holes, and multipart Task Cards
6. Multiple options so that the student is required to make some choices as he progresses
7. Multisensory resources whenever available
8. Opportunities for creative and imaginative projects
9. Attractive signs and decorations
10. A self-contained space to provide privacy and a feeling of personal involvement

Each area should be designed so that a given number of students may use it at one time. Depending on the size of the area, the number may vary from four to six. See Figure 3–15 for the placement and design of various instructional alternatives.

Decide whether you will use a table, desk, carpeting, or selected furniture inside the area. If shelves are available, materials may be placed on them for use. If shelves are not available, a table or other such item may be necessary for the display and use of related Task Cards, books, activity sheets, packages, and other similar materials. Use attractive and lively colors to decorate the dividers, the inner walls, and the materials. Clear contact paper is a useful covering, for it lasts a long time and prevents deterioration of much-used resources.

Identify the major theme or topic to which a first center will be devoted for the present. Develop clearly stated behavioral objectives that indicate to the students what they will need to learn about the current topic. Print some of the objectives on colored signs or banners and mount them on the inner walls. Have others duplicated for distribution to the youngsters working in this area. List the resources that are available for students for mastering the objectives you designed. Organize the resources for easy use through either shape or color codes, either to indicate various levels of difficulty or as suggestions for student selection based on ability.

As you move more deeply into instructional area teaching, develop additional resources and have students develop others. There should be a number of multisensory materials available to provide appropriate learning aids that match the perceptual learning style strengths of each youngster. Secondary students will redesign the classroom for you if you provide these suggestions.

Learning Stations

A Learning Station is an analytic instructional area that houses multilevel resources related to a specific curriculum topic. Step-by-step worksheets, varied tests, printed directions, diagrams, Programmed Learning Sequences and other analytic teaching materials are available for students to work on alone or with others. Learning Stations are most effective with sequential, analytic students—those who proceed step by step and prefer specific directions (see Chapter 4).

Interest Centers

A second instructional area where students may congregate to learn is called an Interest Center. This section of the learning environment should house interdisciplinary resources concerned with a selected theme (topic, unit, study) such as energy, pollution, cultural diversity, the short story, contemporary music lyrics, genetics versus environment, changes in eastern Europe, technology in the twenty-first century, mathematics and the stock market, the greenhouse effect, geometry in everyday life, and so forth. This center is usually best for global students—those who like large, sweeping themes and holistic approaches (see Chapter 4).

Interest Centers serve many purposes. They are available as another option for students—an alternative way of obtaining information and concepts about a given theme. Also, they provide students with a means of gathering facts and concepts independently or with one or more other students. Although self-pacing is an important instructional goal, many youngsters prefer working with others. For them, isolated studying and learning may not be desirable. Indeed, even those students who seem to think best while working on independent units occasionally need to interact with others in order to test ideas and to grow.

Games Tables

Educational games are used extensively in schools today. Their major contributions to the learning process include: (1) introduction of a topic or concept; (2) application of information or concepts; (3) increased motivation and stimulation; (4) provision of an alternative teaching method or device; (5) opportunities for either individual or small-group focus on information through alternative media-learning resources; (6) opportunities for independent concentration; (7) activities for small-group and interage shared experiences; (8) review or reinforcement of previously discussed or studied information; (9) remediation purposes; and (10) opportunities for learning difficult material in a relaxed and motivating setting for many.

Media Corners

Many schools have limited equipment and must distribute their resources equitably among all classes in a given building. It is desirable, however, to provide each large group of youngsters (twenty-five to thirty-five) with enough hard-

Many tactual/visual students enjoy designing games which emphasize subject matter to be learned. Whether literature or mathematics, such youngsters master information by creating and then sharing their original educational resources. (Photographs courtesy Corsicana High School, Corsicana, Texas.)

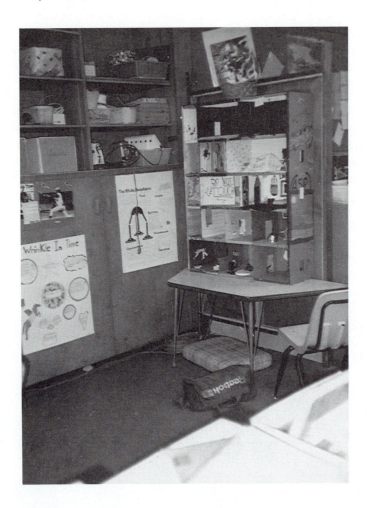

ware so that students may use the media equipment to obtain information, study concepts, and develop skills.

Students should be free to take computer software, filmstrips, cassettes, slides, and so forth from either the Interest Center or the Learning Station to the Media Corner and use them there as learning resources. The materials should be replaced carefully when the student no longer needs them. Cadres of students should form team task forces to assume the responsibility for demonstrating how to use, care for, repair, replace, and organize the equipment and resources that complement the media center.

When one student begins to view materials, others are drawn into the procedure by interest, curiosity, or social awareness. Students should be permitted to join each other in viewing, discussing, studying, or analyzing the materials, provided each of the participants is receptive to the cooperative effort.

Informal Reading Section

Many students prefer and can concentrate much better in an informal carpeted area that contains couches, easy chairs, pillows, lamps, and a living room atmosphere. This area should be quiet, although two students could work together if learning something difficult requires joint effort. Rules for appropriate use of the Reading Corner could be posted, and students using this or any other special area must demonstrate improved performance.

Perpendicular bookcases are ideal to establish boundaries and to provide books and reading material for use in this informal area. Texts and other printed matter may be brought to the Reading Corner by students assigned there or during times of student choice.

Resource Center

An alternative or addition to the Learning Station and the Interest Center is a Resource Center that includes a variety of global and analytic learning materials at different levels. This area literally becomes an interesting repository or library, with texts, pictures, tapes, cassettes, computers, films, filmstrips,

This young man in a school with an essentially gifted student population does his "best reading" extended on the floor. Other adolescents in different sections of the nation reported exactly the same thing! (Photograph courtesy Blake Middle School, Hopkins, Minnesota.)

A number of students in this urban high school of 2,300 young adults returned to classes and began to achieve when permitted to concentrate on their academic requirements in informal study areas with carpeting, rocking chairs, couches, and/or cushions. Most teachers are unaware that, when seated in conventional wooden, steel, or plastic chairs, fully 75 pecent of one's total body weight is resting on four square inches of bone. That pressure on the buttocks is likely to cause restlessness, fatigue, discomfort, and/or physical distress for youngsters who are not sufficiently well padded exactly where they need to be. (Photograph courtesy Robeson High School, Chicago, Illinois.)

sound filmstrips, games, worksheets, manuals, directories, and tactual/kinesthetic materials, all of which relate to the current objectives to be learned. The Resource Center should include desks, tables, an alcove or two, and informal seating such as a couch or easy chairs and footstools.

Individual and Small Group Seating
Private study areas, alcoves for two, and team tables should be available for scheduled assignment. These should be located to take advantage of learning strengths—for example, well lit or subdued, with lamps, facing the wall or out in the open, near the teacher, and so forth, as described earlier in the chapter. Students will contribute the items they wish to use.

Changing Rooms

Although groups of students change classrooms, as do the teachers, it is possible to establish a few learning areas that vary the usual rows or circles in secondary classrooms. If several teachers who use a room can agree on leaving one, two, or even three instructional areas in place day after day, they will discover that the Media Corners, Resource Centers, or Learning Stations are useful in meeting the instructional and learning style needs of their students to the point where the inconvenience of making administrative arrangements is far outweighed by increased student interest and involvement. In this regard, the Resource Center is one that teachers may prefer as a beginning step because several functions may be incorporated there—for example, Media Corner, Interest Center, Learning Station, and some informal seating.

Youngsters at various high schools prefer reading difficult academic material on bean bags, soft plastic seats, and/or easy chairs with foot rests. Some sit upright while others prefer horizontal positions. Skeptical teachers always find that relaxing the seat code produces fewer discipline problems and, simultaneously, statistically higher achievement among informal preferents. (Photographs courtesy: Brockport Middle School, Brockport, New York; Midwest High School, Midwest, Wyoming; and Corsicana High School, Corsicana, Texas.)

Alternative Room

Teachers should be comfortable and confident when attempting to stretch their natural teaching styles to meet the learning styles of their students (see Chapter 10). Thus, a number of instructors approach room design cautiously and with careful step-by-step planning and continuous evaluation of the results. Some have elected to begin by simply dividing the room into formal and informal areas so that they may continue large-group instruction (Figure 3–16). Others elect to begin with one area (Figure 3–17) and then build toward a combination of large-group instruction with several areas available for small-group instruction and varied individual and cooperative learning arrangements (Figure 3–18). For small-group or large-group lessons, an overhead projector can be used to assist in teaching. The screen should be placed near the ceiling on braces at a 45 degree angle so that everyone can see what-

Classrooms should include opportunities for students to work alone, in pairs, in teams, and with the teacher as determined by their individual learning styles provided *youngsters abide by established rules and earn at least as high and higher test scores than previously. (Photographs courtesy: Sacred Heart Seminary, Hempstead, New York; Midwest High School, Midwest, Wyoming; and Contracted Learning for Independent Progress program, Edmonds School District, Lynnewood, Washington.)*

This youngster consistently bends one knee under the other and the second over the first—a typical adolescent practice. It is difficult for growing young adults of varying physical stature to sit comfortably in same-sized chairs and concentrate on often-uninteresting academics for long periods of time in conventional seats and desks. (Photograph courtesy Cedar Crest High School, Lebanon, Pennsylvania.)

ever you write or illustrate. Using an overhead projector with class lights off will increase attention and improve behavior during a lecture or discussion.

Gaining Parental Support

Now that you have redesigned your room to base your instructional program on individual learning styles, it is important to gain the support of your students' parents. Parents are interested in and often concerned about the concepts and strategies to which their children are being exposed, especially if they are new. Once the class has become adjusted to the redesigned room, invite parents in to visit and to discuss the rationale of the room or area redesign. Explain the advantages of capitalizing on each youngster's learning style and describe how the students participated in the developing arrangement. Once parents understand why the instructional environment has been altered, they usually are willing to support the effort until sufficient time has elapsed

The fatigue, discomfort, and frequent postural change caused by conventional classroom seating causes many adolescents to be scolded daily by teachers who forget how uncomfortable they become when required to sit for more than an hour during inservice sessions. Corsicana High School accommodates certain students' need for an informal design by permitting them to sit on carpeting or bean bags as long as each behaves politely, completes assignments, and achieves better than previously. (Photograph courtesy Corsicana High School, Corsicana, Texas.)

to yield both objective and subjective results, such as student responsiveness, teacher reactions, academic progress, and increased provision for individual differences and learning styles. Actually, the students themselves will presell the change with the enthusiasm they express at home about their new interior decoration.

In some cases, single-parent or dysfunctional families may not be involved in their charges' education as one might wish. But even here, room design and advice on how to do homework in home environments that match individual learning styles can stimulate renewed interest and involvement.

As you read through subsequent chapters and experiment with having students make the Tactual Resources, Contract Activity Packages, Programmed Learning Sequences, and Multisensory Instructional Packages they

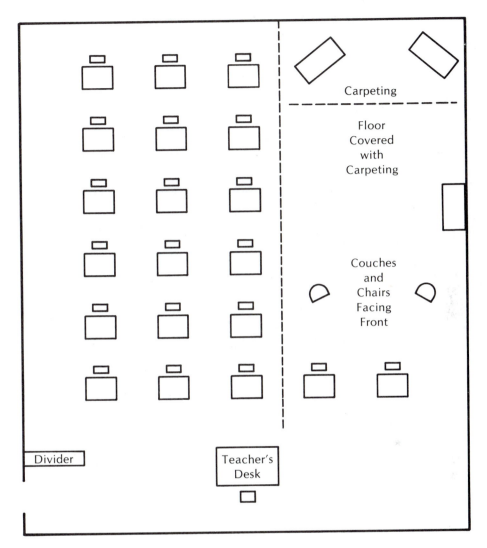

FIGURE 3–16   Formal and Informal Areas—A Beginning.

can use for learning, remember that any or all of these may be placed into classroom instructional areas when appropriate. Also, having students *create* their own learning materials is one of the best ways we know of helping them master information and knowledge.

Redesigning the instructional environment to respond to students' learning style characteristics is a new consideration for secondary teachers. Dependent on your teaching style (see Chapter 10) and your ability to accept/experiment with change (take the *Productivity Environmental Preference Survey* (see

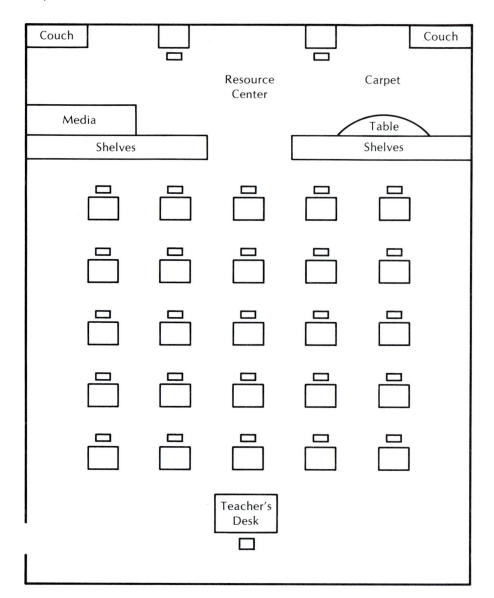

FIGURE 3–17

Appendix C) and examine your score on Learning in Several Ways versus patterns and routines to determine your inclination toward change) you may be willing to try one thing only, or several suggestions, or none at all. Whatever you *can* do to accommodate your students' styles will help them feel comfortable, be better able to concentrate in their way, and gradually improve their

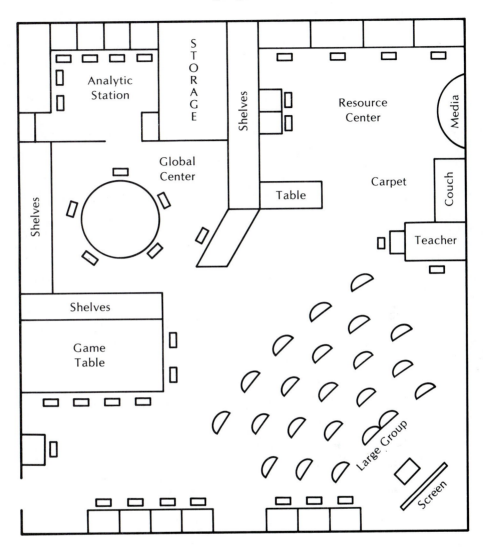

FIGURE 3–18   Large Group plus Several Areas.

grades and attitudes toward school. If you decide to experiment, do so using whatever *you* feel comfortable with. If room design is more than you can do, move on into the next chapters and find something you *can* try.

Regardless of any hesitation you may have personally, given the opportunity to redesign their classroom to respond to their important learning style traits, secondary students usually do a wonderful job of it and reciprocate for the opportunity with better behavior, attitudes, and grades. How willing are you to chance it?

4

Global and Analytic Approaches to Teaching

Forward Can Be Backward for Many Students

Have you ever analyzed your own teaching style? Not through an observation form, your supervisor's evaluation, or even a peer conference but, rather, by focusing on how you *begin* a lesson? Most of us initially consider the content objectives, what was taught during the previous period, which items need reinforcement, what might constitute a motivating opening. Sometimes the introduction is humorous, or interestingly related to a recent event, or it may seize students' attention because it reflects something that happened at the school or in their lives.

Even when we have planned well, however, some students do not respond to what we believe should be motivating, and others soon drift off into their own thoughts as the lesson sinks into a relatively dull, fact-by-fact development of a concept. Often the problem is that some of us are teaching in a way that is the reverse of the way in which many students learn.

Do you introduce new concepts with one fact after another until, gradually, your students begin to understand the idea? If you do, you are engaged in *analytic* teaching. This requires analytic processing, which means that a youngster's mind must be able to absorb many small pieces of information and then synthesize them into an overall understanding. That's the way many people learn, but it is not the way *most* people learn. In fact, the younger the children, the more likely they are to be *global* processors. At the secondary level, between 50 and 60 percent of all students tend to be global. An even higher percentage of those students who achieve slowly or of those having

This chapter is based on ''Presenting Forwards Backwards,'' *Teaching K–8,* by R. Dunn and K. Dunn (October 1988). Norwalk, CT: Early Years, Inc. 19(2), 71–73.

difficulty in school—as many as 85 percent—cannot learn successfully in an analytic mode.

As you are probably aware, analytic students are concerned with details, rules, procedures, and directions; they like specific, step-by-step instructions. Global students, on the other hand, are concerned with end results; they need overviews and the "big picture"; they like general guidelines, variety, alternatives, and different approaches.

Does the inability to remember facts mean that globals are less intelligent than analytics? Not at all. Several studies have verified that globals and analytics are equally able academically, but that, each group achieves best when taught with instructional approaches that match its individual members' learning styles. Unfortunately, of the thousands of teachers we have tested, fully 65 percent are analytic. Thus, a serious mismatch between analytic teaching styles and global learning preferences occurs far too often, resulting in disaffected students with low scores, poor self-discipline, and damaged self-image.

But what about you? How do you begin a lesson? If you don't know, just listen to yourself as you introduce each new topic. Do you begin with one detail followed by another? If you do, you are teaching analytically. Or, instead, do you tell a story that gives your students the major focus of the lesson and then fill in the gaps with the pertinent details? That is a global approach. Neither approach is better than the other, but matching the instructional strategy to the appropriate student is crucial.

Many teachers, either intuitively or by design, use both global and analytic approaches when introducing lessons. If you do not, you would do well to examine the results in your classroom. Here is how you go about it: First, test your students to determine which are global and which are analytic. The *Learning Style Inventory* offers an easy way to tell which is which; see Chapter 2. Next, analyze your teaching style to see which approach you tend to use most often. Then examine the grades of the students who match your style and the grades of those who do not. You will find that the children who learn the same way you teach will achieve higher test scores than those who do not.

Guidelines for Teaching Global Students

If you are analytic and wish to teach your global students in ways that make it easier for them to understand and remember, try the following:

1. *Introducing material:* Begin the lesson with either a story, an anecdote, a humorous incident, or a joke that is directly related to the content you are teaching. If possible, relate the introduction to the students' experiences. If that is not feasible, relate the introduction to something that is realistic to them.

2. *Discovery through group learning:* Avoid telling the students too many facts directly; instead, get them to unravel the information by them-

Global students learn by examining an overall result or outcome first. *They then analyze the end product so that they see the relationship between it and all its component parts. Thus, these middle school art students designed huge blocks that included important information about Picasso's paintings and life. After studying the entire block puzzle, they were able to explain why Picasso won recognition as an artist. (Photograph courtesy East Islip Middle School, East Islip, New York.)*

selves. To do this, suggest that they divide into small groups—rather than work as individuals—unless specific students prefer to work toward solutions by themselves. Usually, global students find it less threatening and more fun to solve problems with others. For four easy-to-use small-group techniques that enable students to learn together in an organized, controlled way, see Chapter 5.

    3. *Written and tactual involvement:* In addition to encouraging global students to think through by themselves or in a small group those details related to what they must learn (rather than telling them the answers), have them graph or map their new information and, if they can, illustrate it. Globals tend to draw meaning from pictures, photographs, symbols, and other visual representations; they respond less well to words and numbers. Thus, have them demonstrate their mastery of specific objectives by developing di-

Because global students often learn through simulations and role playing, these high school students are demonstrating a trial and what occurs when defense and prosecuting attorneys present alternative sides of the same information. (Photograph courtesy Robeson High School, Chicago, Illinois.)

oramas, graphs, charts, games, and so on. Since it helps for globals to dramatize what they are learning, you might also suggest creating pantomimes or plays and making puppets to demonstrate what they have learned. In addition, encourage students to develop their own teaching devices to share with classmates, so that others can learn through alternative strategies.

Guidelines for Teaching Analytic Students

If you are global and wish to reach your analytic students, try the following:

1. *Explanations and visual reinforcement:* Explain the procedures and approaches to be used in reaching specific objectives. Write key words on the chalkboard as you speak. (Analytics respond to words and numbers.) Answer questions about details directly, and use printed visuals on either an overhead projector, slides, or the chalkboard.

French teacher, Mary Ellen Kasak-Saxler, encourages global students to role-play daily activities in which they engage in their homes. As they describe their experiences, they gradually become familiar with the translation into French of the necessary nomenclature. (Photograph courtesy Blake Middle School, Hopkins, Minnesota.)

2. *Directions:* List all assignments, directions, test dates, and specific objectives on ditto sheets, and provide one for each student. If paper is in short supply, list the directions on a chart and have the students copy them.

3. *Learning through direct teaching or related resources:* Proceed step-by-step through the details that need to be assimilated to reach understandings or to acquire skills. Put key words on the chalkboard; distribute duplicated materials and fact sheets; underline important sections; check homework and notebooks daily. Teach students how to use the library independently and how to find and use reinforcing material directly related to the specific objectives of the sequence.

4. *Testing and feedback:* Test frequently; provide instant feedback on details in the sequence; respond to questions as soon as possible; itemize your expectations and requirements; if you give an assignment, check it; when you say you will test, do so.

Analytic students often prefer learning through words and numbers rather than through anecdotes, jokes, illustrations, or symbols. This student has just explained the process he used on a sequential software computer program. (Photograph courtesy Contracted Learning for Individual Pacing (CLIP) program, Edmonds School District, Lynwood, Washington.)

Clues to Recognizing Analytic and Global Students; What They Are Likely to Say

Analytics	*Global*
Does spelling count?	Why are we doing this?
Should I use a pen or a pencil?	Not now! I'll do it later!
Should I skip lines?	I need a break!
Will this be on the test?	Don't touch the piles on my desk.
When is this due?	Why does it really matter?
Can't I have some more time?	Let's start this project—and that one too!
What comes first? second?	Why can't I skip around in the book?
Why can't we do one thing at a time?	I'll come back to this later!
Please check my work before I submit it.	
What are you really looking for?	

Analytic and Global Lesson Starters:
Quickie Quiz—Global or Analytic?

In each of the following lesson-starters, Teacher 1 and Teacher 2 are introducing the same lesson. One teacher is using an analytic approach; the other, a global approach. Can you tell who is using which? Even more important, do you recognize your own teaching style? The answers are at the bottom of the quiz. Remember, one approach is not better than the other. Matching the technique to the strength of the student is critical to total success by the learner.

Sample Lesson 1: The Science Experiment (Grades 6–8)

Teacher 1

Today we're going to boil equal amounts of water and seal the two quantities in Ehrlenmeyer flasks with corks. Then we'll cool one down to 40 degrees Fahrenheit and keep the other at 110 degrees. Now we'll place both in the refrigerator and see which one freezes first. Note that we've left room for expansion so that the flasks won't break.

From time to time you'll hear people say that hot water freezes first. Well, that happens for a number of reasons in an uncontrolled laboratory situation. First of all, we drive the air out of water when we heat it. Air acts as an insulator and helps to prevent cold water from freezing first. Second, there is a rapid loss of heat from the boiling or hot water once the source of heat is removed. This heat gradient, when plotted on a chart, is a sharp downward curve compared to the cold water. Third, you must have equal volumes of water to be frozen, and last, you must prevent evaporation before the experiment begins.

Teacher 2

Last night we had a flood in our basement. One of the pipes burst. The plumber said it was our hot water pipe. We know that water expands when it freezes, but shouldn't cold water freeze first? After all, the temperature of cold water is closer to freezing than hot water is.

I want you to design an experiment to demonstrate which freezes first—hot or cold water. Under which circumstances will the hot water freeze first? Consider the exact laboratory conditions that must exist for the cold water to freeze first.

You can find clues to this mystery through books in the library that describe: air as an insulator; heat gradient; volumes of cold and hot water in equal containers; and the evaporation of hot liquids. You also could visit or call a manufacturing plant that makes ice cubes commercially. Ask the people in charge why their ice cubes are clear, whereas yours in the refrigerator are cloudy.

Sample Lesson 2: The Better Paragraph (Grades 11–12)

<table>
<tr><td>

Teacher 1

I have distributed two paragraphs that describe the same incident. The first is by Ernest Hemingway and the second is a flowery, romaticized version. Please read both descriptions quietly and prepare arguments to support this statement: "Ernest Hemingway was a master of understatement and point of view." Be specific. Note the length of sentence, the dearth of adjectives, the short powerful descriptor verbs, the linkage of sentences, and the intensity pictured for us by the author.

</td>
<td>

Teacher 2

Inhuman things often happen during a war. Brothers kill brothers and life seems to become valueless. Some writers have the ability to capture the power and the meaning of history in a short intense paragraph. Others waste words in an orgy of flowery description. I am going to read two paragraphs to you. Then I would like you to answer the following questions by yourself, in pairs, or in groups of three or four, as you choose.

1. Which is the better paragraph?
2. Why? Support your arguments by referring to the words and sentences in the two paragraphs.
3. Who might the author be? Use the classroom or school libraries. *Hint:* These were written between 1910 and 1940.
4. Describe your emotions (if any) as you listened to or read each paragraph. Which description evoked stronger emotional reactions? Why?

</td>
</tr>
</table>

A. They shot the six cabinet ministers at half-past six in the morning against the wall of a hospital. There were pools of water in the courtyard. There were dead leaves on the paving of the courtyard. It rained hard. All the shutters of the hospital were nailed shut. One of the ministers was sick with typhoid. Two soldiers carried him downstairs and out into the rain. They tried to hold him up against the wall, but he sat down in a puddle of water. The other five stood very quietly against the wall. Finally the officer told the soldiers it was

Note: Paragraph A is from *In Our Times* by Ernest Hemingway (New York: Charles Scribner & Sons, 1925; renewal copyright 1953, Ernest Hemingway, p. 63 Reveal this reference only after the assignment has been completed. Paragraph B is from *A Quest for Questions*, The Education Council, Mineola, New York, 1966.

no good trying to make him stand up. When they fired the first volley, he was sitting down in the water with his head on his knees.

B. The six cabinet ministers were shot at half-past six in the morning. They were stood up against a hospital wall, their faces as white as their unbuttoned shirts. There was a courtyard there with pools of water in it, dirty-colored and desolate. Dried leaves scudded across the bricks, driven by the soft wind. It was simple enough to kill five of the ministers; a crash of arms, a sharp command from the nattily uniformed officer, a thudding volley of shots. That was all. But the sixth man was sick with typhoid, and it was necessary to carry him downstairs. They tried to prop him against the wall, but he slid pitifully to the ground, his wasted body falling into the water. At last, the officer, thin, arrogant, and impatient, cried petulantly that it was impossible to make him stand, and so they let him lie where he had fallen. Then they fired into him. A moment later, it was quiet, with only dying echo of the rifle fire in the air.

Sample Lesson 3: Growing Up in Athens (Grades 9–10)

Teacher 1	Teacher 2
Let us step into our time machine and travel back more then 2,000 years to ancient Greece. At your age you've been sent off to learn a trade, like making tools or weapons, building, or construction—that is, if you are a male. Boys remain in school to learn geography, mathematics, and how to debate. If you are female and fortunate enough to have literate slaves in your home, you might have learned to read, but you do not go to school as the boys do.	Our studies of ancient Greece continue today with some written material entitled "Growing up in Ancient Athens." Please read the selection and answer the questions that follow. You may do this either alone or in groups.

Team Learning*
Team Members:

1. _____   4. _____

2. _____   5. _____

3. _____   6. _____

        Recorder: _____

*This Team Learning was designed by Dr. Maureen Martini.

Growing Up in Ancient Athens

At seven years of age young boys from Athens were sent to schools. Girls stayed home and, at times, were taught some academics by literate slaves.

Classrooms in Ancient Athens were small and bare. Manuscript rolls were the books of the time. They were hung on walls for all the students to use and stored in baskets when not needed. Pupils sat on low benches.

At school in Athens, boys were taught manners, how to write with a writing stick on a wax tablet, and how to count using their fingers, pebbles, or on the abacus. In the late morning, boys went to music school to be taught singing and how to play a lyre, which is a small harplike instrument.

In the afternoon, the boys were marched off to the gymnasium, which was a complex of playgrounds. At gym, they went through a program to build the muscles of their bodies. Ancient Greeks tried to model themselves after their physically perfect gods and so this part of the day was very important to them. The gym program included wrestling, boxing, jumping, running, and discus and javelin throwing.

At twelve years old, most boys left to learn a trade. The rest went on to secondary school to be taught debate, geography, and mathematics.

Read the Team Learning that I have distributed, discuss life in ancient Athens, and compare it with your own. Then, design a role-play of boys and girls, ages 12–14, debating whether girls, as well as boys, should attend high school in ancient Greece.

Other options

- Write a poem describing ancient Greece. Include comparisons with your school and community life.
- Illustrate what an Athenian classroom looked like.

Assignment

1. At what age did Athenian boys begin school? _____

2. How and where did the girls of Ancient Athens learn? _____

3. Describe the classrooms of the Ancient Athenians _____

4. Name at least two (2) things the Athenian boys were taught in school during the morning.

   1. _____

   2. _____

5. What is a lyre? _____

   _____

6. Why was the gym program so important to the Ancient Greeks?

   _____

7. Name at least four (4) sports that the Athenian boys were involved in during their gym time.

1. _____

2. _____

3. _____

4. _____

You are terrific if you can name two (2) more.

5. _____

6. _____

Try teaching globally at least part of the time. More than half your students will be motivated and interested in what happens next. Do not be surprised when analytics indicate displeasure with your global lessons. After all, for them global teaching is just as backward as analytic teaching is for globals. Note the youngster who becomes impatient with your storytelling and asks, "Is this important? Is it going to be on a test?" Chances are, you have an extreme analytic on your hands, and you probably are going to have to teach that lesson both ways.

Well, why not? It certainly is not fair to teach to one style and not to the other. In addition, you will be successful with more students because you will be teaching forwards for *both* groups. And you are certain to find that when you teach globally to globals and analytically to analytics, the lesson moves more quickly than when one group is, in effect, being mis-taught.

Teaching to Both Groups Simultaneously

If you are willing to experiment once or twice to see the effects of teaching to each group correctly, try giving global students a Team Learning with creative assignments, inference questions, and factual material in that order at the beginning of a period while, simultaneously, you teach exactly the same information to analytics in reverse order. Succinctly instruct the analytics and then direct them to do the same Team Learning. Then bring the globals together and *elicit* the answers from them. Next, ask students to describe their reactions

Answers: "The Science Experiment," Teacher 1 (analytic), Teacher 2 (global); "The Better Paragraph," Teacher 1 (analytic), Teacher 2 (global); "Growing Up in Athens," Teacher 1 (global), Teacher 2 (analytic).

to this dual, matched instruction. Pay particular attention to the test results on the unit involved. Chances are good that most students will perform better after being *introduced* to the information through the correct processing style. They also should enjoy learning better than in nonmatched learning.

Effective Use of Computers: Assignments Based on Individual Learning Style

Once upon a time, a couple of decades ago, scientists were predicting the widespread use of computers to provide individualized instruction in schools across the nation. Indeed, within the past few years, zealous technology proponents have advocated a computer for each student in every classroom. That has not happened—partly because of the costs involved and partly—perhaps more so—because not everyone "takes" to computers. Why not? The mechanisms certainly provide explicit, to-the-point, step-by-step information in ways that any sequential mind should be able to absorb. However, the lack of computer literacy may be attributable to *exactly* that problem. Everyone does *not* process information sequentially—the style in which most software is presented. Whether or not specific software responds to how an individual learns depends essentially on the differences in learning style that exist among students at every age and grade level (K–12).

The Problem with Most Computer Software: Global versus Analytic Introductions to the Content

With few exceptions, most computer programs are designed for analytic (left) processors who think in a step-by-step sequential pattern—which is *the reverse of the way global processors think*. Globals learn in an overall holistic manner; instead of examining a plethora of facts, absorbing them, and extrapolating into either an understanding or conceptual framework, globals try to understand the idea or concept *first;* only then do they attend to the facts or details. Globals also learn from anecdotes, humor, and illustrations.

Analytics have few problems focusing on details. Conversely, globals need to understand *why* it is important that they memorize specific information *before* they subsequently are able to do so. Once they understand or are convinced that mastery is important, globals can do it, but the belief system must be in operation prior to the exertion of effort. Analytics, on the other hand, will memorize if they *need* to do so but are less concerned about why it is being required. Merely the fact that they must do so is sufficient to have many of them try to engage in the learning process.

What does all this have to do with computers? It determines whether or not a particular student is likely to fare well with one software program rather than another. If teachers were aware of which students need global and which students need analytic packages, it would be intelligent to prescribe accordingly—or to demand that producers supply both kinds, which then could be prescribed on the basis of matches and avoided when perceived as mismatches. Is the match between students and globally or analytically formatted packages likely to affect achievement significantly? Let's examine some of the research.

Research Concerned with Global/Analytic Matching versus Mismatching

Nearly 1,100 developmental mathematics students in an urban technical college were required to master two analytic and two global lessons of equal difficulty—one matched to, and the other dissonant from, their learning style. Significantly higher mean test scores ($p < .0001$) were revealed in the matched treatments (Dunn, Bruno, Sklar, & Beaudry, 1990). Similar results were obtained in high school mathematics (Brennan, 1982), biology (Douglas, 1979), and nutrition (Tanenbaum, 1982); in junior high school social studies (Trautman, 1979); and in elementary school mathematics (Jarsonbeck, 1984).

Another Problem with Computer Use: Research on Perceptual Strengths

In well-designed, well-controlled research conducted during the past decade, individual perceptual strengths were identified, and each student experienced multiple treatments in both matched and mismatched conditions. (Carbo, 1980; Ingham, 1989; Jarsonbeck, 1984; Kroon, 1985; Martini, 1986; Urbschat, 1977; Weinberg, 1983; Wheeler, 1980, 1983). Please note that the *quality* of those studies earned national recognition three times. The findings across all those investigations evidenced that when students were *introduced* to new and difficult material through their primary perceptual strength (auditory, visual, or tactual), they achieved statistically higher test scores than when they were introduced through their secondary or tertiary channel. When they were *introduced* through their primary strength and then *reinforced* through their secondary or tertiary modality, they achieved even higher scores than when only initially taught through a primary strength—an additional $p < .05$! (Kroon, 1985; Wheeler, 1980).

Computer-literate advocates, however, assume that the computer is responsive to *everyone*, and Martini's data tend to support that belief. However, because of the findings concerned with the effects of sequencing instruction to respond to primary and supplementary modality strengths, would computer packages be *more* responsive—and thus more effective—if: (1) students' primary perceptual strengths were identified with the *Learning Style Inventory*, the instrument administered to diagnose the learning styles of the populations in most of the aforementioned studies, and then (2) the computer were used to introduce new and difficult material in the correct sequence to each youngster? If that were to be tested, auditory students would hear a lecture first and then use the computer packages for reinforcement; visual students might begin by either reading a visual printed selection or working directly on the computer program, and then could be reinforced through either a tape or lecture—or by hands-on manipulatives if their second modality were the sense of touch. Strongly tactual students would begin with manipulatives such as Task Cards, Electroboards, Flip-Chutes, or Pic-A-Holes (see Chapter 6), and then use the computer. *Would* that sequencing incorporated into the use of computer instruction make a significant difference in student achievement?

To Increase Computer Effectiveness

This section is intended to increase the effectiveness of computer use in schools. It highlights two main problems:

1. Most computer programs are written analytically. However, the research is clear: Global students do not achieve well when instructed analytically. Thus, computer packages need to be rewritten to present the identical material both globally and analytically, so that students with both learning styles find the instruction responsive.

2. Computer programs currently are visual and slightly tactual; when accompanied by verbal instructions, they are auditory as well. The research is clear on this point, too. Multisensory instruction is not sufficient for many students. What works is *introducing* difficult material through each student's strongest perceptual modality and then *reinforcing* through supplementary modalities. Thus, if we were to identify students' strengths and use computer packages in a responsive sequence, we would be likely to increase their effectiveness.

__5__

Designing Small-Group Instructional Techniques

Importance of Small-Group Techniques

Many students respond best to a learning situation that involves from two to five of their peers. Some of these youngsters may not be authority- or teacher-oriented for a variety of reasons. They may feel intimidated, anxious, or overly directed by adults or those in charge. Some may need the interaction of friends to stimulate them to learn; others are motivated by a team effort. Many relax when a group, rather than each of them individually, is responsible for a task, contract, or project. There also are students who gain persistence through group goals or who can deal more effectively with a short, specific portion of an assignment rather than with an entire task. Such youngsters often feel more responsibility to their peers than to either themselves or adults. For these reasons, or simple gregariousness, many youngsters' learning styles are best served if they are often permitted to work in groups.

First Concrete Step toward Individualization of Learning

Group work is a first step toward independence within the instructional setting, and working with others in school is early training toward that eventuality for most people in adult life.

Diagnose or observe the sociological elements of learning style for each of your students. Once you are convinced that a given youngster will learn best from and with peers, assign that student to a variety of small-group experiences.

Students who have been parent- or teacher-directed for most of their lives should first learn to make simple decisions and to assume the responsibility for completing simple tasks free of constant adult supervision. Use of selected techniques such as Circle of Knowledge, Team Learning, Brainstorming, Case Study, and Simulation provides a structure wherein learning occurs through cooperative small-group effort without the teacher serving as a constant guide or fountain of knowledge.

Small-group interactions also permit youngsters to solve problems in cooperation with other students so that they need not fear failure or embarrassment. Even if errors are made, sharing the responsibility with a group of peers sharply reduces the tension or trauma. Further, the small-group techniques help students to understand how other people reach decisions and work toward solutions. Finally, interaction with peers creates sounding boards on which to reflect ideas, build solutions, and suggest conclusions to the group and to the teacher.

The Impact of Peer Interaction on Student Achievement

Over the years, a number of researchers examined teams and groups as they strove toward achievement. Homans (1950) postulated that groups are separate entities and cannot be viewed simply as the total of its members. Argyris (1957), Lorge, Fox, Davitz. and Brenner (1958); Hankins (1979), and others in and out of education demonstrated repeatedly that small teams often obtained better results than their individuals accomplished when working alone or with an adult. Poirier (1970) studied students as partners and reported increased learning, as did Bass (1965), who pointed toward group recognition, respect, and affection, as well as fun, as motivating factors toward higher achievement.

The emphasis on peer and team grouping was revived during the 1980s with cooperative learning (Slavin, 1983; Johnson, 1987). However, neither the newer proponents of peer group instruction nor any of their predecessors addressed the major variable of individual differences.

One deficiency of the research on peer learning is that none of the previous studies exposed the same students to a variety of interactive experiences to determine whether, indeed, all students perform best in small groups. The designs of previous studies did not permit analysis of how well *individuals* achieved when permitted a variety of treatments, and whether those same students *consistently* performed best in one condition or another.

Once researchers began to recognize that individuals learn differently from each other, they designed experimental studies that provided a series of varied instructional treatments for the same students. Thus, although the various investigations differed from each other, the subjects of each experienced multiple opportunities for learning alone, with peers, and or with adults. In some studies, students experienced different kinds of groupings (cooperative versus competitive) and adults (authoritative versus collegial); sometimes, media or methods were substituted for human interactions.

What was found was that, for many students, *with whom* they learned was almost as important as either how or when they learned. Some students had *no* sociological preferences; they could learn with almost anyone—but that group was small indeed. However, wanting to learn with others can vary from year to year; it tends to be developmental and is dependent upon each youngster's experiences, emotionality, age, grade, processing style, and achievement level. However, when their sociological preferences were diagnosed and students then were exposed to multiple treatments both congruent and incongruent with their identified learning styles, each achieved statistically higher test (*and* often attitude) scores when matched, rather than mismatched (DeBello, 1985; Dunn, Giannitti, Geisert, Murray, & Quinn, 1986; Miles, 1986) with their learning style preferences.

Research has shown (Cholakis, 1986; DeBello, 1985; Dunn, Giannitti, Murray, Geisert, Rossi, & Quinn, 1990; Giannitti, 1988; Miles, 1987; Perrin, 1984) that when students' sociological preferences were identified and the youngsters then were exposed to multiple treatments both congruent and incongruent with their identified learning styles, each achieved significantly higher test scores in matched conditions and significantly lower test scores when mismatched. In the three studies where attitudes were included as a dependent variable, those also were significantly higher as an outcome of matched conditions. In the one investigation where an interaction effect did not occur (Cholakis, 1986), the population had been made up of students who had attended a parochial school for their entire education. The researcher suggested that the history of strong authority orientation of those youngsters may have skewed the results. However, those students learned equally well in both conditions.

Studies revealed that students learned more and liked learning better when they were taught through their identified learning styles. Those data were supported in secondary schools throughout the United States when site visitations, observations, interviews, and evaluation collection documented that students achieved more, behaved better, and liked learning best when they were permitted to learn through their sociological preferences (Dunn & Griggs, 1988).

Since 1984 (Dunn, 1984), we have been experimenting with teaching students to teach themselves by capitalizing on their learning style strengths—of which sociological preference is only one variable. However, the first results are promising (Dunn, Deckinger, Withers, & Katzenstein, 1990; Knapp, 1991; Mickler & Zippert, 1987) and several additional studies currently are in progress.

Learning Style Characteristics Responsive to Small-Group Techniques

Many small-group techniques can be designed to accommodate multiple variations among students. Small-group strategies are especially appropriate for students who are peer-oriented, motivated, persistent, and responsible. They provide structure as well as auditory and visual experiences. Students who act as the recorder will gain additionally by writing (tactual) experiences.

Small-group techniques will accommodate the elements of light, temperature, design, time, intake, and mobility. Furthermore, motivation, persistence, and responsibility may be enhanced by the group process; members can exert positive peer pressure on those who are not strong in these areas.

Obviously, those who prefer to work alone or with adults and those who are creative and do not require structure are less likely to benefit from small-group techniques.

Descriptions and Samples of Small-Group Techniques

Circle of Knowledge

The Circle of Knowledge technique is highly motivating and is an ideal technique for reinforcing skills in any subject area. It provides a framework for review in which everyone learns more or solidifies what he or she has already mastered.

This instructional approach permits students to:

- Review previously learned information in an interesting way.
- Focus thinking on one major concept at a time.
- Contribute to a group effort as part of a team.
- Serve as catalysts for additional responses.
- Develop ingenuity in helping team members to contribute.
- Be exposed to and learn information without becoming bored.

Procedures

Several small circles of four to five chairs (no desks) are positioned evenly about the room. One student in each group should either volunteer, be drafted, appointed, or elected as the recorder—or the teacher can arbitrarily determine a means of selection—for example, "the person wearing the most of the color *blue*"; members also may take turns. Only the recorder writes, although everyone participates and concentrates on thinking of many possible answers.

A single question or problem is posed and, whether printed on a chalkboard or reproduced on paper, it must have many possible answers. Examples include naming all the presidents of the United States, all the requirements for becoming a citizen, as many Shakespearean characters as can be remembered, all the ways of saying "thank you" in a foreign language, as many examples of metaphors as can be recalled, all the causes of World War I, and so forth.

Each Circle of Knowledge team will respond to the same question simultaneously (but quietly). A member in each group is designated as the first to begin, and the answers are then provided by one member at a time, clockwise or counterclockwise. No member may skip a turn, and no one may provide

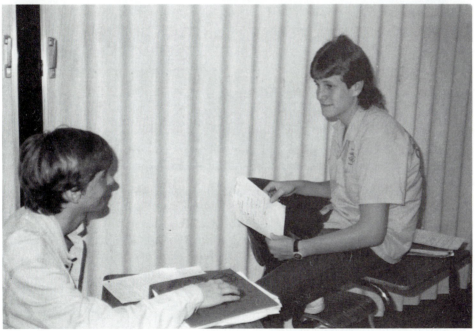

Although small-group instructional techniques were designed—and are most appropriate—for teams of students, some learners prefer to study in a pair. When placed into a larger group of three or four—or more, they sometimes destroy the group. Such youngsters work best only in pairs. (Photographs courtesy Franklin Township High School, Franklin Township, Indiana.)

Despite our personal beliefs concerning the importance of students learning how to live and work cooperatively with others, we must remember that approximately 13 percent of the school-age population prefers learning new and difficult material alone—a condition that those students do not equate with being lonesome. (Photograph courtesy Corsican High School, Corsicana, Texas.)

an answer until the person directly before him has delivered his; therefore, the answers stop while a member is thinking or groping for a possible response. No teammate may give an answer to another, but anyone in the group may act out or pantomime hints to help the person remember an item, an answer, or a possible response. Only the recorder may write, and he jots down (in a phrase or two only) the suggestions (answers, responses, thoughts) of each participant as the Circle of Knowledge continues.

Peer-oriented students profit greatly from involvement with classmates, particularly when learning new and difficult information. These youngsters are engaged in a Circle of Knowledge, and their involvement is evident. One boy is leaning forward with one knee on his chair, the recorder is busily writing the group's answers, another is scrutinizing the developing list to be certain there are no duplicates, and two are trying to reach consensus concerning a disputed response. (Photograph courtesy Robeson High School, Chicago, Illinois.)

At the end of a predetermined amount of time, the teacher calls a halt to the knowledge sharing, and all recorders must stop writing their groups' answers. The number of responses produced by each group is noted, but credit is not given for quantity.

The teacher divides the chalkboard or overhead transparency into columns and numbers them so that each represents one of the groups. In turn, a representative from each circle offers one of the answers suggested by that group. When an answer is provided, the teacher writes it in that group's column, and all the recorders in the room look at the list of answers developed by their group. If that answer is on the circle's list, the recorder crosses it off, thus gradually decreasing the length of the list until only the answers that have not yet been reported to the group and written on the board remain. This procedure continues until no circle has any remaining answers on its list. Recorders should add missing answers to the list and then cross them off immediately.

The answers given by each Circle of Knowledge can be awarded points that are then recorded on the board to produce competition among the teams.

The teacher might decide that each correct response will earn one point (or 5 to 10 points) and that the circle achieving the most points will be the winner. Any time an answer is challenged by a rival circle, the teacher must decide whether it is right or wrong. If the answer is right and the challenger incorrect, the challenger's circle loses the number of points given for one correct answer. If the answer is incorrect and the challenger was right, the circle that sponsored the answer loses the points and the challenger's circle gains them.

The important thing to remember about Circles of Knowledge is that they may be used only to review something that already has been introduced and taught. Because the information required has been made available to the students previously, the time span permitted is usually a short one (two to five minutes).

Middle or Junior High School

- Name as many chemical elements as you can in three minutes.
- Give as many synonyms as you can for the adjective *small*.
- List as many units of measurement and their metric equivalents as you can in five minutes.
- List the possible causes of war.
- Name as many American poets as you can.
- Name as many American plays as you can.
- Name as many books as you can that were written by Louisa May Alcott.
- List all the reasons that you can for people putting down other people.
- What are the things that you value most in life?
- Make up as many examples as you can where, when you use addition, subtraction, multiplication, and division (all four in one example), your answer equals 25.
- List as many rules as you can for writing a correct business letter.

High School

- What were the political implications of the caste system?
- Develop as many analogies as you can in four minutes.
- Name as many reasons as you can for changing the electoral college system.
- List as many ways as you can that pop art benefits our culture.
- Name as many eighteenth-century French painters as you can.
- List as many algebraic equations as you can using two unknowns and resulting in an answer of four.
- List as many causes of the Civil War as you can in three minutes.
- List all the natural forces that have changed the surface of our planet.

The format for presenting a Circle of Knowledge to students at any level is illustrated in Figure 5–1.

FIGURE 5-1 Sample format for Circle of Knowledge.

HIGH SCHOOL ENGLISH

Circle of Knowledge
Circle members:

1. _____   4. _____

2. _____   5. _____

3. _____

Recorder: _____

The Question: 2½ minutes

List the titles of as many of Shakespeare's plays as you can:

1. _____   19. _____

2. _____   20. _____

3. _____   21. _____

4. _____   22. _____

5. _____   23. _____

6. _____   24. _____

7. _____   25. _____

8. _____   26. _____

9. _____   27. _____

10. _____   28. _____

11. _____   29. _____

12. _____   30. _____

13. _____   31. _____

14. _____   32. _____

15. _____   33. _____

16. _____   34. _____

17. _____   35. _____

18. _____   36. _____

37. _____

Continued

FIGURE 5–1 *Continued*

Shakespeare's Plays

All's Well That Ends Well	Macbeth
Antony and Cleopatra	Measure for Measure
As You Like It	The Merchant of Venice
The Comedy of Errors	The Merry Wives of Windsor
Coriolanus	A Midsummer Night's Dream
Cymbeline	Much Ado about Nothing
The Famous History of the Life of	Othello, the Moor of Venice
King Henry VIII	Pericles, Prince of Tyre
Hamlet	Romeo and Juliet
Julius Caesar	The Taming of the Shrew
King Henry IV, Part 1	The Tempest
King Henry IV, Part 2	Timon of Athens
King Henry VI, Part 1	Titus Andronicus
King Henry VI, Part 2	The Tragedy of King Richard II
King Henry VI, Part 3	The Tragedy of King Richard III
King Lear	Troilus and Cressida
The Life and Death of King John	Twelfth Night
The Life of King Henry V	Two Gentlemen of Verona
Love's Labor Lost	The Winter's Tale

Could you have done as well with his sonnets?

Teacher's Score Card
For any Circle of Knowledge (on chalkboard or overhead projector)

	Circle 1	Circle 2	Circle 3	Circle 4	Circle 5
Round 1	1	1	1	1	
Round 2	2	2	2	2	
Round 3	3	3	3	3	
Round 4	4	4	4	4	
Round 5	5	5	5	5	
Round 6	6	6	6	6	
Round 7	7	7	7	7	
Round 8	8	8	8	8	
Round 9	9	9	9	9	
Challenges	Challenges	Challenges	Challenges	Challenges	
Won _____	Won _____	Won _____	Won _____	Won _____	
Lost _____	Lost _____	Lost _____	Lost _____		
Lost _____					
Total _____ _____ _____ _____ _____					

Team Learning

Team Learning is an excellent technique for introducing new material. All the advantages of peer interaction and support described earlier are apparent in this approach. Enthusiasm, motivation, good spirits, positive results, division of labor, responsibility, persistence, self-image, and group recognition of individual efforts usually result.

Procedures

Begin by writing original material or by copying sections of commercial publications to form short paragraphs containing new information to be learned. Secondary students should be able to understand and discuss entire articles, poems, or sets of diagrams with explanations. By developing Team Learning exercises of varied difficulty, you will not only be able to respond to different

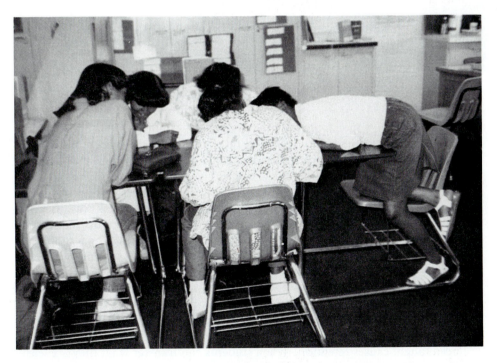

These high school students almost dive into their Team Learning. They are peer-oriented and enjoy reading together, answering factual and higher level cognitive questions coopertively, and creating an original instructional resource to demonstrate their mastery of the new and difficult material. Other youngsters at the same school prefer to work on computer-assisted instruction as a team. (Photographs courtesy Robeson High School, Chicago, Illinois.)

learning styles, you will also be able to establish groups to work on new material according to the ability level and rate of learning in each small team.

At the end of the printed reading (or diagramatic) material, list a series of questions that should be answered by the group. Some of the questions should be related directly to the printed reading passages; others should be answered through inference and analysis by the group. In this way, students will develop two skills, and will more likely retain the new information. By finding answers in the assigned material through rereading, underlining, or discussion, the individuals in the group will learn how to seek and to obtain specific information. The more difficult inference questions will promote reasoning and group decision making. In addition, add questions or assignments that require creativity—for example, translating the essence of a lesson into poetry or a rap, describing the concept through music with lyrics, drawing the main idea, pantomiming it, and so forth. Creative *application* of what has been taught causes retention. When students can transfer what they are learning into another medium, they remember it.

When the printed materials are ready, you may assign students to groups of four or five. (Five should be the maximum for most small-group techniques.) As students demonstrate responsibility, you might permit some degree of self-selection of groups. Groups should be allowed to sit on the floor or at clustered tables according to their preferences. Other variations include a round circle of chairs, hassocks, or a couch and chairs in a conversational grouping. The learning style elements of design, mobility, time, intake, and so on should be considered as part of the Team Learning assignment.

When comfortable, the group should elect, assign, or accept a volunteer to serve as recorder. It is the recorder (and only the recorder) who needs to write the group's responses to the questions. Short, succinct answers are important to keep the discussion and learning process moving. Some of the other students may elect to write the answers, too, but only because they believe they'll remember the material through note-taking.

Any member may help other participants on the same team, but all the effort must be concentrated within the group. One way to promote quiet and order if teams are in competition in a specific Team Learning exercise is to tell the class that teams are free to use answers that are overheard from other groups working on the same exercise.

After one or two Team Learning experiences, groups of students will develop team relationships and begin to question and analyze the material with enthusiasm and animated but productive conversation. You will need to walk

In schools where students are taught to teach themselves new and difficult academic material through Team Learning, they gradually become independent learners capable of progressing through the curriculum at their own rate and in their own learning style. Inevitably, such students become higher achievers than they have ever been previously. (Photographs courtesy Sacred Heart Seminary, West Hempstead, New York.)

around and assist with the process the first time or two, but you will discover newfound freedom to work with individuals or other groups very soon after the students gain initial experience with this teaching strategy.

Time limits may be imposed or left open, depending on the learning style and need for structure of the members of each group. An alternative to strict time limits would be to assign some Team Learning prescriptions to a group as homework or as free-time activity.

For the purposes of comparison, participation, and reinforcement, the recorders of teams working on the same assignment should be asked to share with the entire group those responses to the material that were developed and approved by their membership. This is done by numbering each group and then asking Team 1 for a response to a question, asking Team 2 for a second one, and so on, in rotation.

Write each recorder's responses on the chalkboard and instruct students to cross an answer off their lists if it duplicates theirs; they thus will be left with only answers that have not yet been called out. Other team members should respond on the second or third round. The recorders should pass their lists to the students who will be answering next. Eventually, you and the class will proceed through all the questions, permitting most of the team members to participate. In this way, errors and misinformation are not likely to be retained. Moreover, all questions will be answered, and everyone will have had a chance to participate actively.

As with the Circles of Knowledge, you and your class may elect to use a team competition approach with points based on the correct number of answers given by each team. Competition among teams is usually friendly and stimulating; often different teams win. Furthermore, the competition does not pit one individual against another, where loss of self-image is a serious risk.

Team Learning presents new material in a fashion that responds to such important learning style elements as structure, design, time, mobility, intake, learning with peers, motivation, persistence, responsibility, and visual and auditory perceptual strengths. (Kinesthetic and tactual resources could be added to Team Learning exercises for those who require them.) Sample Team Learnings are shown in Figure 5–2, and 5–3.

FIGURE 5–2   Sample format for team learning

Middle or Junior High School

Team Learning
Team Members:

1. ————————————————————————————————
2. ————————————————————————————————
3. ————————————————————————————————
4. ————————————————————————————————
5. ————————————————————————————————

Recorder: —————————————

Learning about the Eye*

Read the following:

Light is reflected from an object. It passes through the cornea, a clear covering that protects your eye. Then it passes through some liquid called "aqueous hu-

---

Continued

*This Team Learning, "Learning about the Eye," was designed by Irene K. Flatley, Rosedale, New York, for her Contract Activity Package, "Learning about Our Eyes: Here's Looking at You."

FIGURE 5–2   *Continued*

mor" and then through the pupil—the "window of your eye." (The pupil looks like a black dot in the middle of your eye.) A muscle opens the pupil when there is not much light and makes the opening smaller if there is a lot of light. The muscle is called the "iris." The iris is the colored part of your eye. Behind the pupil is the lens, which is something like the lens in a camera. The lens turns the picture upside down and projects it onto the retina, which is like a screen on the rear wall of your eyeball. Millions of nerve endings in the retina send messages through your optic nerves to your brain. Your brain turns the picture right side up again.

Your eye has three protectors outside the eyeball. Shading your eyes are the eyelids, which protect them from lights that are too bright and from strong gases such as ammonia. You close you eyelids when you sleep, and you close them automatically when you blink. Blinking spreads tear fluid over the corneas and cleans them as windshield wipers clean the glass in an automobile. The eyelids and the eyelashes also protect your eyes from flying insects and bits of dirt. The eyelids close automatically when an object, such as a ball, comes toward your eyes. The eyebrows above the eyes are protectors, too. They act as cushions against blows from above and keep perspiration from dropping into your eyes.

Assignment:

  1. What are some parts of the eye mentioned in this writing?

       a. _____

       b. _____

       c. _____

       d. _____

       e. _____

       f. _____

    Can you name at least four (4) more?

    _____

    _____

    _____

    _____

  2. What are the functions of at least seven (7) parts of the eye?

       a. _____

       b. _____

       c. _____

       d. _____

FIGURE 5–2 *Continued*

e. ————————————————————

f. ————————————————————

g. ————————————————————

3. Name the three protectors of the eye.

a. ————————————————————

b. ————————————————————

c. ————————————————————

4. How do each of the protectors do their work?

a. ————————————————————

b. ————————————————————

c. ————————————————————

5. Explain in your own words how the eye sees.

————————————————————————

————————————————————————

————————————————————————

————————————————————————

————————————————————————

————————————————————————

————————————————————————

6. Think of what a camera looks like and think about its parts. Are there any similarities or differences between a camera and the eye? If so, list them.

————————————————————————

————————————————————————

————————————————————————

————————————————————————

————————————————————————

Continued

FIGURE 5–2 *Continued*

7. If you were unable to see, how would you find out what some things looked like?

_____

_____

_____

_____

8. Write a short poem explaining how the eye works.

_____

_____

_____

_____

_____

High School

Team Learning
Team Members:

1. _____

2. _____

3. _____

4. _____

5. _____

Recorder: _____

FIGURE 5–3   Team Learning on Haiku Poetry*

Directions: Read the following objectives. If you are analytic, then read the passage that describes this special type of poetry and complete the assignment that follows. Follow up by reading at least four (4) different selections of haiku poetry and noting, in writing, how they exemplify traditional haiku.

If you are global, read the four (4) examples of haiku immediately *before* reading the objectives. *Then* complete the following assignment. Next, note how the examples you read reflected what the passage on the next page describes.

If you process either or both ways, choose the pattern you wish and follow it. Be certain to: (a) read the passage and the four haiku selections; (b) write how the four selections represented what the passage below describes; and (c) complete the following assignment.

1. Identify the primary purpose of haiku.

    _____

    _____

2. List at least four (4) characteristics of classical Japanese haiku. If you can list a fifth, you are extremely able.

    _____

    _____

3. Name one way in which haiku poets use the concept of *association*.

    _____

    _____

    _____

4. Explain why the reader of haiku is as important as the writer.

    _____

    _____

    _____

Continued

*This Team Learning was designed by Dr. John M. Jenkins for a Contract Activity Package (CAP) for high school students at the P. K. Yonge Laboratory School, University of Florida, Gainesville. The entire CAP is available through the Center for the Study of Learning and Teaching Styles, St. John's University, New York.

FIGURE 5-3 *Continued*

5. Use your imagination. Why would Japanese poets have developed such a short form of poetry?

_____

_____

_____

6. Again, using your imagination, why would Japanese poets have decided to use a reference to the seasons in most haiku?

_____

_____

7. Write an original haiku poem. Include as many of the characteristics of this type of poetry as you can.

_____

_____

Characteristics of Haiku Poetry

A haiku is a very *short* poem with special characteristics. It is intended to *express and evoke an emotion,* and all haiku truly worthy of the name are *records of special* high *moments.*

Haiku has a traditional, classic form. As a rule, a classical Japanese haiku consists of *17 syllables* (5 on the first line, 7 on the second, and 5 on the third). It usually *contains some references to nature; refers to a special, particular event;* and then *presents that event as if it were happening now,* rather than in the past.

Haiku may be either happy or sad, deep or shallow, religious, satirical, humorous, or charming. But because it is shorter than other forms of poetry, in order to produce an effect, it must *depend on the power of suggestion.* As you read several examples of haiku poetry, you will see that they gain their effects by suggesting a mood and also by providing a clear-cut picture that serves as a starting point for trains of thought and emotion. However, because of their shortness, haiku seldom provide the picture in detail. Instead, only the outline or *important parts* are drawn; the reader must fill in the remaining parts.

To protect their effect, haiku writers make excellent use of *association of ideas.* The older haiku writers concluded that one experience common to all persons was the seasonal changing of weather. Thus, they introduced the *season* (or *ki*) into all their poetry. Therefore, in all of the older haiku poets' creations, there is some word or expression that indicates the *time of year.* That reference to the season provides a background for the mental picture that the poet is trying to create in each reader's mind.

Brainstorming

Brainstorming is an exciting group participation designed to develop multiple answers to a single question, alternative solutions to problems, and creative responses. It is an associative process that encourages students to call out— one of the few times this is permitted in our schools. Thus it responds to personal motivation and does not suppress natural spontaneity.

In addition to increasing motivation, the technique of Brainstorming offers many practical advantages. Brainstorming is:

- *Stimulating:* It offers a unique, freewheeling, exciting, and rapid-fire method that builds enthusiasm in nearly all participants.
- *Positive:* Quiet and shy students usually become active participants because they are not put down; their contributions are masked by the group process. Conversely, those who usually dominate endless discussions are structured into offering succinct suggestions.
- *Focused:* Diversions and distractions are eliminated. Stories and speeches irrelevant to the question or otherwise not pertinent are eliminated.
- *Spontaneous and creative:* Students serve as a sounding board that generates new ideas. Creativity is released during the momentum of the process.
- *Efficient and productive:* Dozens of suggestions, facts, ideas, or creative solutions are generated in a matter of minutes. Additional steps or plans of an activity can be Brainstormed, as well as more specific answers for general responses (subset Brainstorming).
- *Involving and image-building:* Self-image is enhanced for students who see their ideas listed. Group pride and cohesiveness increase, too, as the members begin to feel a part of the unit that created the lists.
- *Ongoing and problem solving:* The results are recorded and may be modified and used in new situations.

Procedures
The Brainstorming leader also acts as recorder. His or her functions include recording all responses, asking for clarification or repetition, synthesizing large phrases into short key ideas, and keeping the group focused on each single topic. The leader should not comment, editorialize, or contribute; his or her effort should be concentrated on producing an effective and productive session.

Setting
From five to ten students should form a fairly tight semicircle of chairs facing the leader. (Larger groups can be effective at times.) Behind the leader is a wall containing three to five large sheets of lecture pad paper or newsprint double-folded to prevent strike-through marks on the wall (see Figure 5–4).

FIGURE 5-4 For optimum results, a brainstorming session consists of a tight semi-circle of five to ten participants.
Designed by Dr. Edward Manetta, Chairman, Department of Fine Arts, St. John's University, New York.

These sheets, approximately twenty to twenty-four inches wide and thirty to thirty-six inches high, should be attached to the wall with masking tape and placed a few inches apart at a comfortable height for recording. The leader should use a broad-tipped felt marker for instant visability by the entire group. A timekeeper should be appointed for the two- or three-minute Brainstorming segments, but he or she may participate. It is useful to have additional sheets available and an overhead projector to permit groups to analyze, plan, or do subset Brainstorming for specific aspects of general answers.

Rules for Participants

1. Concentrate on the topic—"storm your brain."
2. Fill the silence—call out what pops into your head.
3. Wait for an opening—don't step on someone's lines.
4. Record the thoughts in short form.
5. Record *everything*—no matter how far out.
6. Repeat you contribution until it is recorded.
7. Be positive—no put-downs, body language, or editorial comment.
8. Stay in focus—no digressions.
9. Use short time spans—one to three minutes.
10. Analyze later—add, subtract, plan, implement.
11. Brainstorm from general to specific subsets.

Examples
Middle or Junior High School
   List the desirable characteristics of good leaders.

Middle or Junior High School
   Provide synonyms for an entire sentence, one word at a time:

	(adjective)	(noun)	(verb)			(noun)
The	large	boy	ran	to	the	hill.

   Take one minute (60 seconds) for each word. Then consider the enormous number of combinations for finding the: (a) funniest sentence, (b) most precise description of an item or person, (c) most creative arrangement of words, (d) most alliterative series, and so forth. Ask students what they believe is the number of different sentences that can be generated. For example, 20 words in each column yields 20 to the fourth power, or 160,000 sentences!

High School
   List all the solutions you can think of to car pollution.

High School
   Call out as many ways as are possible to prevent poverty.

High School
   Or consider the following way to do three-part problem solving through Brainstorming.

[Take Three Minutes] What would constitute an ideal energy program?	*[Take Three Minutes]* What might the obstacles to this ideal program be?	*[Take Three Minutes]* What can we citizens do to overcome the obstacles and guarantee adequate energy?

High School
List all the clichés that you can think of in three (3) minutes. Then Brainstorm each cliché in an "action" sentence. For example, instead of "as quiet as a mouse," try:

   As quiet as a _____ _____ing.

   As students become familiar with brainstorming, they will demonstrate increasing creativity and gradually become skilled in this enjoyable form of critical thinking. Once the first person calls out something charming or clever—like "As quiet as an eyelid closing," or ". . . a heart breaking," or

". . . a thought forming," or ". . . blood pressure rising," others will follow suit, taxing their brains for nuances and witty alternatives. Thereafter, your charges will delight you with their spontaneous giftedness.

Case Study

A case study stimulates and helps to develop analytical skills. Four to five students can spend considerable time discussing and interpreting short, relevant stories that teach them something you believe they ought to learn.
Case studies provide:

- A strategy for developing material within the student's frame of reference. The characters, situations, and events can, if constructed properly, strike responsive and understanding chords.
- An approach that can be stimulating and meaningful if student identification is fostered and debate is structured to understand different points of view on recognized problems and situations.
- Safe, nonthreatening situations for students who can enter the analysis without direct personal effects.
- Training and development in problem solving, analytical skills, arriving at conclusions, and planning for new directions in learning situations and in real life.

Guidelines for the Development of Case Studies

Format   Case studies may be written as very short stories, audio- or video-taped dramatizations, films, psychodramas, news events, or historical happenings—real or fictional. The use of chronological sequence aids students in following the flow of events and in analyzing key issues. Flashbacks and other complex approaches should be avoided except for the most advanced students.

Focus   The case should focus on a single event, incident, or situation. Ability to analyze is aided by a high degree of concentration on the factors that precipitated the event, the attitudes prevailing during a given incident, or the sharply defined points of view of those dealing with a problem.

Relevance   Reality or "potential credibility" related to the frame of reference of the students is critical to the success of this small-group technique. The participants involved in analyzing the case must be able to recognize, understand, or even identify with the people in the situation because what they do or say seems authentic or possible. The style of writing should attempt to capture the flavor of familiar places, people, and their actions at a level that is at, or slightly above, the levels of understanding of the participants.

Increasing Motivation   After initial training in the analysis of case studies, involve students in the actual writing and acting out of roles in subsequent cases. Both relevance and motivation will increase as students become involved and begin to feel a sense of ownership of their new creation or variation of an older case.

Procedures

Elect, seek volunteers, or appoint a leader and a recorder from among the four to five participants. Have the group read the case at the beginning of the session. As the students become more familiar with this approach, you may wish to assign the materials as prior reading exercises to increase the amount of time devoted to group discussion.

The leader should not dominate the session but should keep the group on target for the allotted time. The recorder should participate and also concentrate on capturing the essence of the group's responses to various analytical questions. He or she must periodically verify all notes with the group to obtain consensus.

Key questions for the case study or short story must be developed in advance, although others may be suggested by the group as they delve deeply into the problem or situation. Questions may begin with factual checkpoints but then should move quickly into possible reasons, alternative motives, and analysis of the subtleties and complexities of human experiences and interactions as well as values, standards, and other abstractions. Finally, students should be asked to reach conclusions and to apply developing insights to new situations.

Analyzing case studies should build student powers of interpretation, synthesis, description, observation, perception, abstraction, comparison, judgement, conclusion, determination, and prediction.

Sample Case Study: Middle or Junior High School— Living History

Purpose: Understanding emotions and attitudes, coping with a difficult situation, developing alternative solutions.

The Unwanted Visitor

At the time of the Boston Massacre, British soldiers were feared, despised, and unwanted by many colonists who still considered themselves loyal British subjects under the rule of King George III. Nevertheless, the crude, red-uniformed soldiers were housed in homes in Boston where they ate the food, used the bedrooms, and sometimes engaged in mistreatment of the local citizens. Their red uniforms earned for them the derogatory term "lobster back."

For their part the British soldiers were not pleased to be far from home among hostile "barbarians." Some youngsters, perhaps of your age, undoubtedly found those red-coated lobster backs inviting targets for snowballs in the winter. This type of harassment, added to the irritable confrontations on the streets and commons of Boston, may very well have led to an accidental, or at least unnecessary, firing by the troops on the unarmed citizens of Boston.

Analysis Questions:

- If you had lived in Boston during the American Revolution, how would you have felt about British soldiers living in your home? Why?
- Why was "lobster back" a derogatory term? Why was this term used instead of another one, such as "red flannel-head"?
- How would you feel if you were one of the British soldiers?
- What would you have done to ease the tension in town to prevent the massacre and needless loss of life?
- Have there been similar situations in history since the Revolutionary War?

Sample Case Study: Senior High School—English
A series of incidents or consecutive events may be interesting in and of themselves. For example:

What Happens Next?
Mark stretched. The muscles rippled across his back. His mind came awake slowly, and he smiled as the memory of yesterday spread across his consciousness like warm waves at a tropical beach. He pulled himself out of the bed. The sunshine bathed his lean body; the future belonged to him!

Analysis Questions
- How do you know Mark was feeling good?
- What might have happened yesterday?
- How does the passage support your position?
- Have you ever felt the way Mark did? Explain why.
- Describe what happened next in Mark's life.
- Use the selection to indicate why you believe the next series of events you created is plausible.

Alternative Case Study Assignments Select a favorite novel, short story, or narrative poem.

1. Write the next chapter.
2. Send a letter to one of the main charactes describing what happens next.
3. Have the main character write a story or journal of succeeding events.
4. Report the next series of events to the newspapers.
5. Write a soap opera scenario for television about the main characters just after the end of the novel or story.

A Final Word on Small-Group Techniques

These four small-group techniques and others you use or devise are essential to building independence and for responding to those youngsters whose learning style clearly indicates a need to work with peers.

- *Circle of Knowledge* reviews and reinforces previously learned material.
- *Team Learning* introduces new material and uses both factual and inference questions.
- *Brainstorming* releases creative energy and aids in planning and solving problems.
- *Case Study* develops analytical skills and builds empathy and understanding of people as they work together to solve problems or cope with crises.

There are variations and other small-group techniques such as simulations, role playing, group analysis, task forces, and research committees.

Each technique should focus on a specific objective—learning new material, developing higher order thinking skills, and so forth. Select or develop those that will respond to varied learning styles, and your instructional role eventually will take less effort and will be far more rewarding for you and for your individual students.

6

Designing Tactual and Kinesthetic Resources to Respond to Individual Learning Styles

Students who do well in school tend to be the ones who learn either by listening in class or by reading. Because of this, most of us believe that the brighter students are auditory and/or visual learners. In reality, however, we usually teach by telling (auditory) and by assigning readings (visual) or by explaining and writing on a chalkboard (auditory and visual). Therefore, youngsters who are able to absorb through these two senses are, of course, the ones who retain what they have been taught and, thus, respond well on our tests, which also are usually auditory (teacher dictates) or visual (written or printed).

Our own research during the past two decades verifies that many students who do not do well in school are tactual or kinesthetic learners; their strongest perceptual strengths are neither auditory nor visual. These boys and girls tend to acquire and retain information or skills when they either are involved in handling manipulative materials or are participating in concrete "real-life" activities. Because so little of what happens instructionally in most classes responds to the tactual and kinesthetic senses, these students are, in a very real sense, handicapped. What's more, once they begin to fall behind scholastically, they lose confidence in themselves and either feel defeated and withdraw (physically or emotionally) or begin to resent school because of repeated failure.

Many young children appear to be essentially tactual or kinesthetic learners. As they grow older, some youngsters begin to combine their tactual inclinations with a visual leaning; for these, the resources suggested in this chapter will be helpful. Eventually, some youngsters develop auditory strengths and are able to function easily in a traditional class where much of the instruction is through discussion or lecture; this group, however, does not represent the majority.

Although we have found some parallels between age and perceptual strengths among students, many high schoolers continue to be unable to learn well by either listening in class or by reading. Sensory strengths appear to be so individualized that it is vital to test each student and then to recommend resources that complement their strengths rather than their weaknesses. When you recognize that selected students are not learning either through their readings or from class discussions or lectures, experiment with several of the following resources to provide tactual or kinesthetic instruction that should prove to be helpful.

Learning Style Characteristics Responsive to Tactual and Kinesthetic Resources

Because tactual and kinesthetic materials tend to be gamelike, they usually are naturally motivating, particularly for underachievers. When they are perceived as being babyish, however, they can cause embarrassment and turn off many

These three photos illustrate Robeson High School's widespread use of tactual resources for young people who do not remember well the information they hear during lectures or class discussions. The first photo shows one student using computer-assisted instruction while her classmate learns the same information through a manipulative Flip Chute.

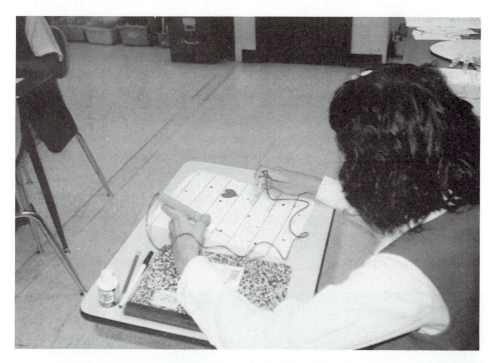

The second photo reveals a tenth-grader's involvement with an Electroboard, and the third shows a teacher initially introducing these tactual resources to adolescents whose learning style strengths they complement. All the students are learning exactly the same information, but each is using the medium most responsive to his or her strengths. (Photographs courtesy of Robeson High School, Chicago, Illinois.)

youngsters. It is important that the students to whom these resources are assigned are positive about them and therefore are willing to follow directions for their use, care, and replacement. If they enjoy learning in this way, they will become persistent and will continue using the materials until they have achieved the goals or objectives that have been outlined for them. All the materials are self-corrective, so that should youngsters experience difficulty while using them, they are able to manipulate them to find the correct answers. Nevertheless, the motivation for using these materials is necessary if the students are to be responsible for them—for the parts or sections of each set need to be kept intact, returned to holders or boxes, and generally maintained in good condition. However, as we have observed previously, apathetic students may become highly motivated because of their interest in and enjoyment with Learning Circles, Task Cards, Electroboards, Pic-A-Holes, Flip Chutes, and floor games (for kinesthetic learners).

One of Luanne Reabe's Resource Room students is independently using a self-designed puzzle to teach himself social study requirements. Placing the correct answers side by side the specified questions enables this youngster to manipulate the information in small doses in whichever sequence appeals to him. Thus, he can handle the material in the number and kind of steps responsive to his interest and ability to internalize. (Photograph courtesy of Franklin Township High School, Franklin Township, Indiana.)

Other than the directions for using the resources, little structure is provided through these materials; students using them may, therefore, need some structure—but not too much. Beyond the need for motivation, persistence, responsibility, and structure, these resources respond to students who have visual-tactual, tactual-kinesthetic, or visual-kinesthetic inclinations and who do not learn easily by listening or by reading. Be certain, however, to emphasize to the entire class that all students will be responsible for learning and mastering the identical objectives, but each will learn the information through his or her learning style strengths.

Learning Style Characteristics to Which Tactual and Kinesthetic Resources Can Be Accommodated

Because these resources may be used in a classroom, in a library, in a corridor, or in an instructional resource center as well as at home, they can accommo-

These highly creative students spend a great deal of time developing subject matter games to demonstrate mastery of their specific objectives. They then use one or more of their classmates' original creations to determine whether the included information is correct. (Photographs, courtesy of Robeson High School, Chicago, Illinois.)

date each student's environmental and physical preferences. Because they may be used independently, in pairs, with a small group, or with an adult, they also respond to each student's sociological needs.

Step-by-Step Guide to Designing Tactual Resources

Developing tactual resources is easy. Once you have designed one or two samples, middle, junior, and high school students can duplicate and create additional samples for you. Although many of these materials are available in primary and elementary schools, they often are used indiscriminately rather than with those youngsters whose perceptual inclinations would complement them, and they usually are commercially produced and do not respond directly to either the topics that are taught or the objectives on which the teacher focuses. After you have made a few samples for experimentation and observed the progress that certain students make through their use, you will become committed to their availability as an instructional resource for your classroom. Another advantage is that they save labor by being adaptable to different levels, questions, and even subject areas—for example, a Learning Circle with interchangeable parts. However, at the secondary level, students can create their own tactual resources. Once they have learned to do so, they find that

These adolescents are competing to see who knows the most about Vectors in their Algebra 2 class. Their instructional resource is a modified commercial game one created. (Photograph courtesy of Corsicana High School, Corsicana, Texas.)

they remember difficult academic information more easily than they ever could before.

In effect, the ability to take difficult information in a text and translate it into resources that facilitate memory retention is a first important step toward becoming an independent learner—a stage toward which most underachievers rarely aspire. However, the research documents very clearly that tactual/kinesthetic learners *become* poor learners because their teachers lecture or require readings *as the basic source of introductory learning.* When such students experience initial concentration tactually, they find how much easier it is for them to succeed.

Chapter 10 describes how, once teachers and students become aware of individuals' perceptual strengths, they can learn to *sequence* exposure to the teacher's lectures by capitalizing on strengths in the beginning and hearing the lecture afterward. Chapter 10 also describes how students can be shown to design their own tactual instructional resources.

A small group of ninth-graders is checking the accuracy of a game designed for a literature class. At the same time, they are reinforcing the information they learned through their textbooks. (Photograph courtesy of Corsicana High School, Corsicana, Texas.)

Tactual students who enjoy learning alone complete many objectives successfully when permitted either to design their own manipulative resources or to use those developed by classmates. (Photograph courtesy of Worthington High School, Worthington, Ohio.)

Understanding Task Cards

Task Cards are easy-to-make, multisensory resources that respond to a youngster's need to see and to touch simultaneously. Often designed in sets or groups, each series teaches related concepts or facts. This resource tends to be effective with students who cannot remember easily by listening or by reading. They are used both to introduce new material and to reinforce something the student has been exposed to but did not learn.

The most effective task cards are those that are self-corrective. These (1) permit students to recognize whether they understand and can remember the material, (2) allow no one other than the youngster using the cards to see errors made—thus preserving the student's dignity and self-image, (3) enable students who do make mistakes in their responses to find the correct answers, and (4) free the teacher to work with other students.

Youngsters at any age or grade level who have trouble understanding specific math concepts or practices often learn easily when permitted to manipulate concrete materials. (Photograph courtesy of Midwest High School, Midwest, Wyoming.)

Task Cards can be made self-corrective through any one of several methods: color coding, picture coding, shape coding, or the provision of answers. Task Cards for high school students can be either simple or multipart, complex, exacting, and challenging at many different levels. They may be used by individuals, pairs, or a small group. They permit self-pacing. Students may continue to use them until they feel secure in their knowledge of the topic; they can be reused as a means of reinforcement if specific data have been forgotten. They are gamelike in character and often win and sustain youngsters' attention. They appeal to young people who cannot learn through other available resources, and, therefore, they are important for those they do teach.

Students who select or are assigned Task Cards may work with them at their desks, in an instructional area such as a Learning Station or Interest Center, in the library, on carpeting, or anywhere they prefer in either the school or home environment.

*This sixth-grader is learning about figures of speech through a Learing Circle—
a round instructional resource on which he places the correct answer (printed on
a clothespin) against its matching question. The back of each question on the
Circle and the back of each answer is color-coded to make this instructional resource self-corrective. (Photograph courtesy of P. K. Yonge Laboratory School,
Gainesville, Florida.)*

Designing Task Cards

Task Cards are easy-to-make and extremely effective resources for tactual students at all levels. Begin by listing exactly what you want your students to
learn about a specific topic, concept, or skill. Then translate your list into
either questions and answers concerning what they should learn or samples of
the answers—some true and others false. For example, if you were concerned
about teaching the derivation of commonly used American words, you would
list the words and the people who coined them.

Example

Words	Derivation
Prairie	French
Oasis	Greek
Shanty	French
Pretzel	German
Piano	Italian
Sputnik	Russian
Canoe	American Indian
Algebra	Arabic
Vanilla	Spanish
Cereal	Latin

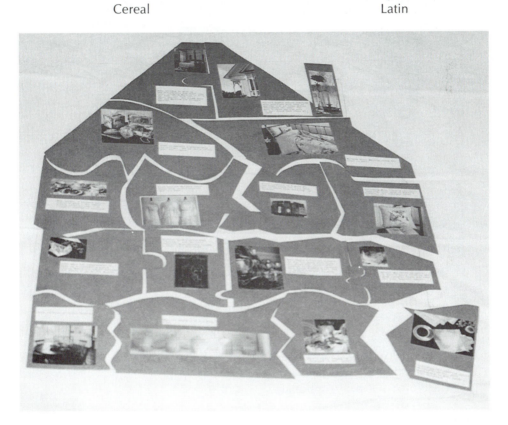

Task Cards may be made in any shape related to the content they are designed to teach and should be attractive and neat. The sequence of events that occurs in Anne of Green Gables *can be deduced from this example created by Vivian Lynch. Another set, part of a Multisensory Instructional Package on Ancient Greece, is housed in a replica of the Greek flag. (Photographs courtesy of Center for the Study of Learning and Teaching Styles, St. John's University, Jamaica, New York.)*

Materials

- Colored oaktag or cardboard
- Black thin-line felt pens
- Colored felt pens (optional)

Directions

1. Cut the colored oaktag or cardboard into three- by twelve-inch rectangles.

2. On the left side of each of the rectangles, in large, easy-to-read letters, print one of the words on your list. On the right side of the rectangle print the corresponding derivation of the word. Be certain to leave space between the word and its derivation.

This Learning Circle complements the Ancient Greece Task Cards. Both are tactual resources in a Multisensory Instructional Package on Greece." (Photograph courtesy of Center for the Study of Learning and Teaching Styles, St. John's University, Jamaica, New York.)

3. Either laminate or cover each rectangle with clear Contact paper.

4. Cut each rectangle into two parts by using a different linear separation for each (to code them according to shape). For examples, see Figure 6–1.

5. Package the set in an attractive box and place a title on top that describes the task cards inside. For the set we just discussed, appropriate titles might include:

How Did You Learn the Foreign Words You Use?

or

The Background of Words We Use Every Day

or

Foreign Words in Our Everyday Vocabulary

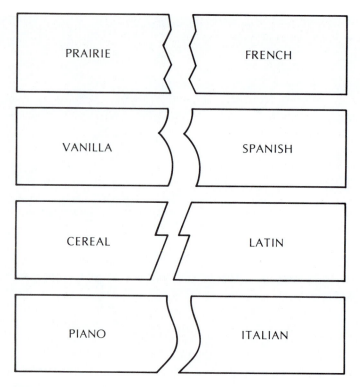

FIGURE 6–1 Sample Task Cards on word derivations.

6. Either laminate or cover the box in clear Contact paper so that it remains sturdy and can be wiped clean whenever necessary.

7. If the box top is not very tight, use a couple of strong rubber bands to hold the lid down and the cards inside.

One teacher, interested in getting her students to understand the concept of the Depression and its impact on people, worked backward. She folded a large yellow envelope, and on the back flap she printed:

What Do You Know about the Depression?

Below the title she also printed:

The Depression was a period in our history during which times were very hard for most people in the United States.

Then she thought of several facts concerning the Depression of 1929 and printed a question related to the fact on the left side of each card and its answer on the right side. When she had developed at least a dozen question and answer cards, she divided each card into two sections and shape-coded them by cutting the two halves in irregular patterns so that only the matching left side would "fit" with its original right half. The end product, a set of Task Cards, became an interesting strategy for either teaching or reinforcing basic factual information concerning that dismal economic period in American history (see Figure 6–2).

Then the teacher combined a series of related facts into three- and four-part Task Cards (see Figures 6–3 and 6–4). She also added pictures to appeal to visual/global students. The sections of the multipart Task Cards were scrambled and then placed into an envelope labeled appropriately, for example, "Three-Part Task Cards on the Great Depression" or "Four-Part Task Cards on the Great Depression."

For homework the next day, the teacher assigned a reading on the Depression and the activity to "Design a set of two-, three, or four-part Task Cards to teach the information I did *not* include in my sets of Task Cards." The day the assignment was due, students were directed to share the Task Cards they had created for homework with at least one classmate, and to have the student with whom they had shared, initial his or her name on the back of one Task Card half *if* willing to document that all the information in the set was correct. The class was warned that, if initials were found on the rear of a card and any information in the set was wrong, both students—the one who designed the set *and* the one who had verified the accuracy of the information, would lose points on their final grade for that unit. However, if a student's card was initialed and the information was later verified as correct by the teacher, both students would gain extra points toward their final grade on that unit.

Students began learning an enormous amount of information concerned with the Depression—some of it trivia that they had uncovered through earnest research efforts. Many became fascinated with the topic and with mastery of what they previously had termed "irrelevant facts." Some appeared to be gaining a sense of pride over the number and kind of facts they could unearth and recall. In fact, so much information was retrieved from a multitude of sources that the teacher added a test question to the final exam on that unit: "For extra points toward your grade, list at least 10 Depression trivia items that you learned during this unit—but never thought you'd *want* to!" The conversations concerning the many minuscule bits of information that had been absorbed ceased only after the group had gotten well into the *next* unit!

In science, Task Cards were designed to supplement a Contract Activity Package on "Ants." The task is to match the description on one set of cards to the type of ants on the other set.

When designing task cards for middle or high school students, you might consider:

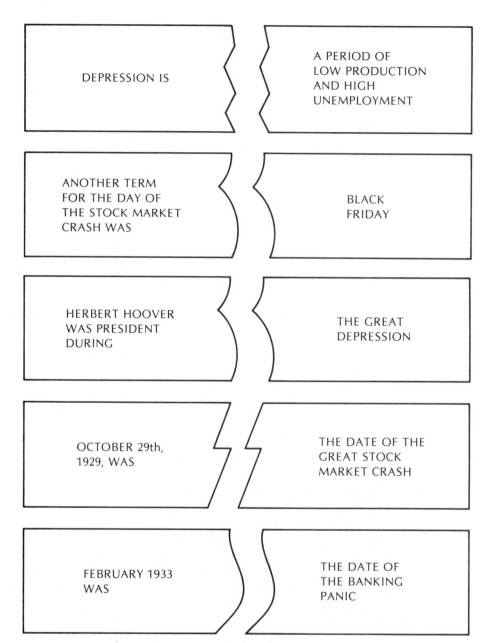

FIGURE 6–2   Sample Task Cards on the Depression.

Source: The Task Cards on ''The Great Depression: Don't Let It Get You Down'' (Figures 6–2, 6–3, and 6–4) were designed by Camille Sinatra, Reading Specialist, Manhasset Junior-Senior High School, Manhasset, New York, to complement the Programmed Learning Sequence (PLS) in Chapter 7 and the Contract Activity Package (CAP) in Chapter 8; they are part of the Multisensory Instructional Package in Chapter 9, as is the Electroboard (Figure 6–11) and the Pic-A-Hole (Figure 6–21).

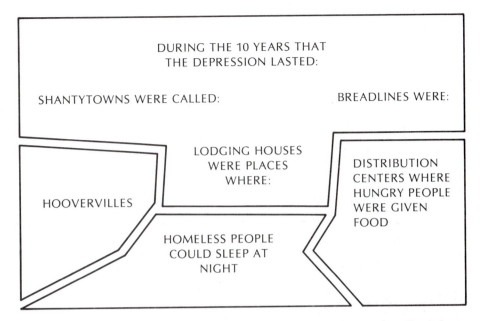

FIGURE 6–3   Sample of four-part Task Card on "The Great Depression: Don't Let It Get You Down!"

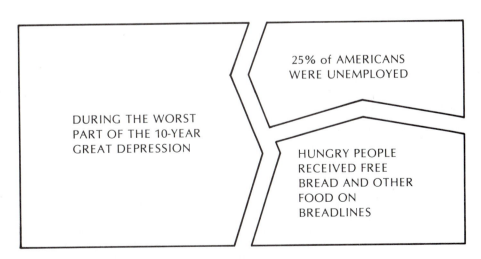

FIGURE 6–4   Sample of three-part Task Card.

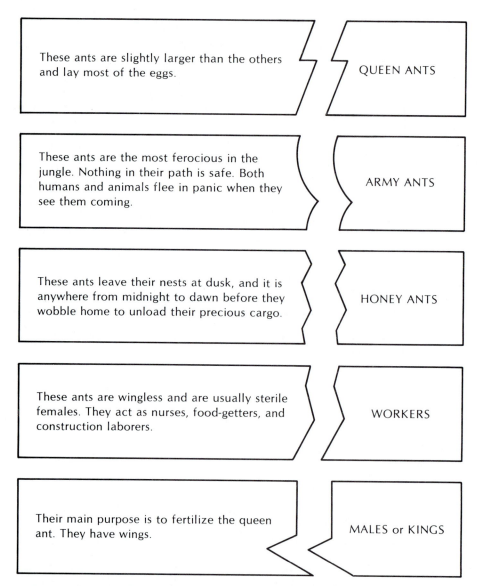

These ants are slightly larger than the others and lay most of the eggs.

QUEEN ANTS

These ants are the most ferocious in the jungle. Nothing in their path is safe. Both humans and animals flee in panic when they see them coming.

ARMY ANTS

These ants leave their nests at dusk, and it is anywhere from midnight to dawn before they wobble home to unload their precious cargo.

HONEY ANTS

These ants are wingless and are usually sterile females. They act as nurses, food-getters, and construction laborers.

WORKERS

Their main purpose is to fertilize the queen ant. They have wings.

MALES or KINGS

FIGURE 6–5 Sample set of Task Cards on ants.

Source: The Task Cards to supplement a Contract Activity Package on ''Ants'' were designed by Fran Ryan, Freeport, New York.

1. Outlining the shape of each of the original states; adding their official state nicknames, their capital cities, and the rank order in which they became a state: then having the youngsters piece the facts together (see Figure 6–6).

2. Identifying famous buildings through illustrations (see Figure 6–7).

3. Placing the name of a state, the person who founded it, and the year in which it was founded all on one Task Card that is divided into three sections; then having students piece together an entire set—perhaps entitled "Who Founded What and When?"

4. Completing a puzzle that combines all the parts of the eye into a single Task Card (see Figure 6–8).

There is no limit to the intricacy and complexity that task cards may reach when subdivided into many parts. They are an effective introductory and reinforcement device for tactually and visually inclined students and often are successful in motivating students toward achievement after many previous methods have failed.

To arouse interest in the novel, *Anne of Green Gables,* a set of Task Card pieces was designed introducing the characters and the sequence of events. When placed together correctly, the resulting picture resembles the house in the story (Figure 6–9).

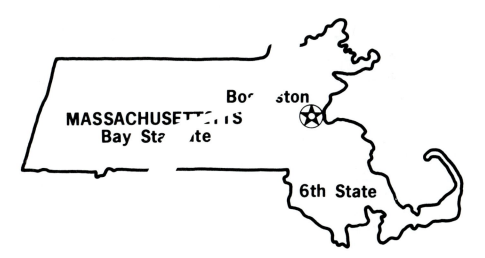

FIGURE 6–6 These Task Cards in the shape of states were designed to help students recognize each state on a map and recall its capital, its nickname, and the order in which it entered into the Union.

Source: Designed by Dr. Jeanne Pizzo, Director of Federal Funding, Community School District #24, Middle Village, New York.

The Supreme Court Building

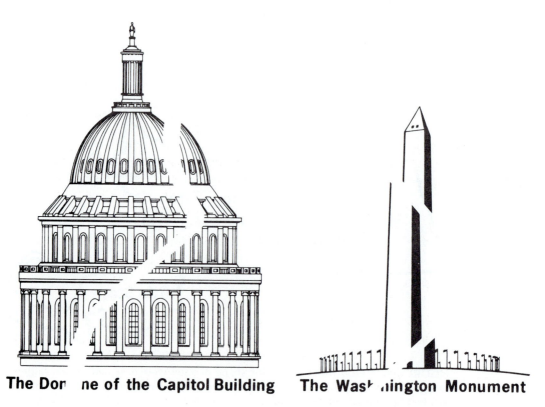

The Don ne of the Capitol Building   **The Wash ington Monument**

FIGURE 6–7   Sample Task Cards on famous buildings and monuments in Washington, D.C.
Source: Designed by Dr. Jeanne Pizzo, Community School District #24, Middle Village, New York.

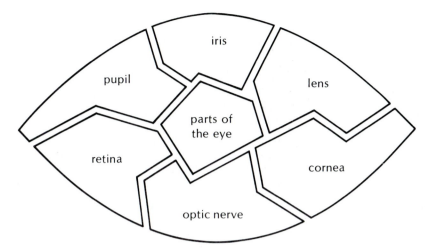

FIGURE 6–8 This sample, multipart Task Card includes the names of the parts of the eye and, if pieced together correctly, forms the shape of an eye.
Source: This multipart Task Card on ''Parts of the Eye'' was designed by Irene K. Flatley, Rosedale, New York.

Basic Task Cards

Figure 6-10 provides a sample pattern for basic Task Cards. Although this pattern facilitates the creation of Task Cards for students (and teachers) who are not very tactual, we encourage you to design the sample set you will use to introduce learners to this resource in the *shape* of the subject, concept, or ideas you are trying to teach. Once secondary students *see* and *use* shape-related Task Cards, and are given the directions for making them (see Chapter 10), many will become innovative and will design their sets in interesting, subject-related shapes too. Varied shapes are responsive to the learning styles of visual and/or tactual learners.

Designing an Electroboard

Perhaps the most effective instructional resource for tactually and visually oriented students is the Electroboard. It is difficult to find secondary students who can resist learning with this device, unless they are highly auditory—and, even then, many will be intrigued by it for at least a short time.

Creatively vary the outer dimension of each Electroboard to represent either the unit or topic the students will be studying. Should the topic not lend itself to a pattern, use any shape that is different from a standard 8 × 10 textbook—to attract the attention, and thus the concentration, of the tactual

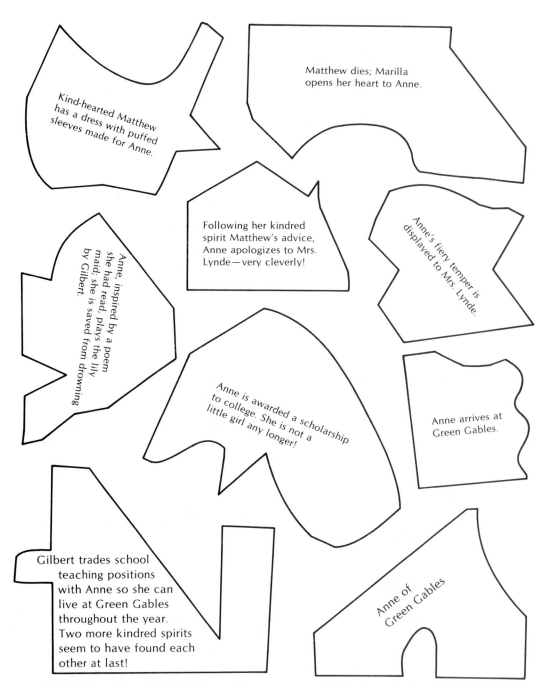

Kind-hearted Matthew has a dress with puffed sleeves made for Anne.

Matthew dies; Marilla opens her heart to Anne.

Following her kindred spirit Matthew's advice, Anne apologizes to Mrs. Lynde—very cleverly!

Anne's fiery temper is displayed to Mrs. Lynde.

Anne, inspired by a poem she had read, plays the lily maid; she is saved from drowning by Gilbert.

Anne is awarded a scholarship to college. She is not a little girl any longer!

Anne arrives at Green Gables.

Gilbert trades school teaching positions with Anne so she can live at Green Gables throughout the year. Two more kindred spirits seem to have found each other at last!

Anne of Green Gables

FIGURE 6–9   Task Card puzzle on *Anne Of Green Gables* novel. When reproduced, pasted onto a piece of cardboard, and placed together correctly, these pieces form the shape of the house and the sequence of major events in the story.

Anne makes an honest mistake at the tea party with Diana—she gives her currant wine instead of raspberry cordial. Mrs. Barry forbids Anne, who is broken-hearted, to play with Diana.

Minnie May Barry is saved by Anne's quick thinking and good nursing; Diana and Anne can play together again.

Gilbert Blythe calls Anne "Carrots," and the hot-tempered Miss Shirley breaks a slate over his head!

Anne uses her imagination to make up a confession about losing Marilla's brooch because she wants to go to the picnic.

Marilla decides to let Anne stay.

Mrs. Allan, a kindred spirit, comforts Anne—who baked a very original cake with liniment instead of vanilla!

Following Miss Stacy's excellent teaching, Anne goes to Queen's Academy. Her academic rival is Gilbert!

Source: Task Card puzzle on *Anne of Green Gables* was designed by Vivian Lynch, Associate Dean, St. John's College, Utopia Parkway, Jamaica, New York, to complement the Programmed Learning Sequence in Chapter 7 and the Contract Activity Package in Chapter 8; it is part of the Multisensory Instructional Package in Chapter 9.

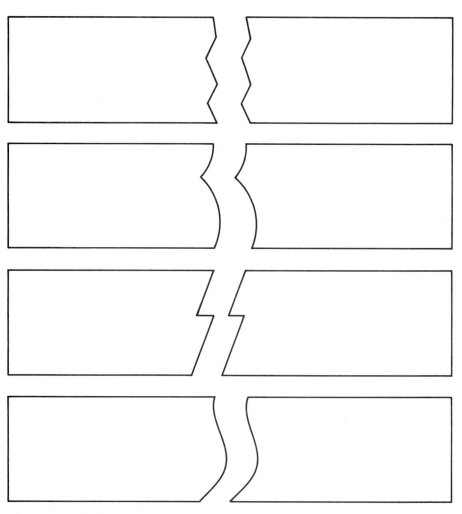

FIGURE 6–10 These basic Task Card shapes may be used as a pattern for helping students design sets of their own. However, if the subject matter lends itself to a shape, encourage that the students' sets reflect a shape related to the topic or theme they are studying.

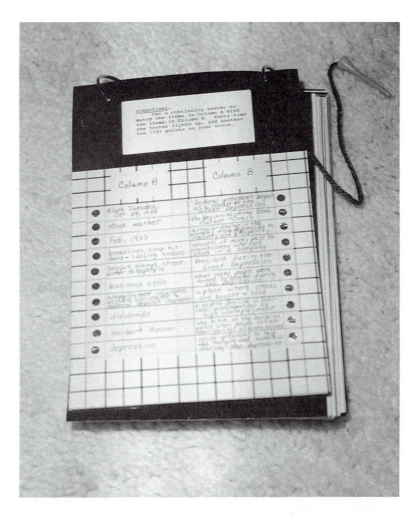

Electroboards come in a variety of sizes, colors, shapes, and levels of difficulty. The one in the first photo complements a Multisensory Instructional Package on The Great Depression. The map Electroboard teaches objectives related to Ancient Greece. The Chicago, Illinois, Robeson High School student in the third photo is engaged in memorizing multiplication facts by noting which answer makes the continuity tester bulb light up. In the fourth photo, two East Islip Junior High School students in New York are testing their knowledge of a required science unit. (Photographs courtesy of Center for the Study of Learning and Teaching Styles, St. John's University, Jamaica, New York.)

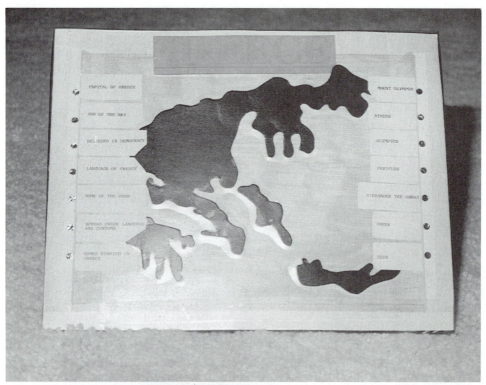

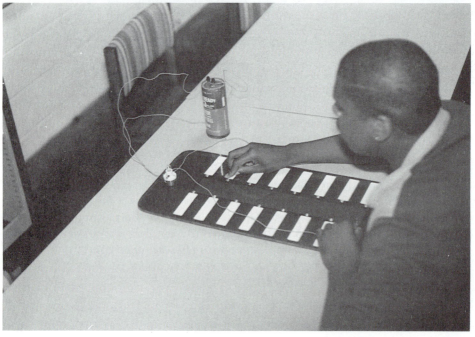

and visual youngster. Thus, for an Electroboard to use with a unit on war, you might use a helmet, a flag, or any other symbol of fighting or patriotism. For one on interplanetary transportation, consider a rocket or starship. For one on computing the perimeter of a triangle, a three-sided geometric representation would be appropriate. If studying about a specific country, use the shape of that political entity or a representative product. For a foreign language unit, the shape of the nation, an outline of a piece of its traditional clothing, or one of its famous products might complement the theme.

When assigning the development of an Electroboard for homework, indicate that its shape should reflect its contents, but permit wide latitude of the specific pattern designed by individuals. Sometimes young people add touches of creativity to an idea that professional adults rarely consider. Merely advise the youngsters that they should be able to cogently explain why they selected the specific shape they did for this Electroboard.

1. Begin with two pieces of either posterboard or oaktag cut into exactly the same size and shape.

2. List the exact questions you want the Electroboard to ask; then list their answers. Count the number of questions and divide the face of the left side of the Electroboard into evenly divided spaces so that the questions all fit on the left side.

3. Use a paper hole puncher to make one hole on the left side of the face of the Electroboard for each question you developed. Then punch corresponding holes *on the same horizontal level as the beginning of each question*—but on the *right* side; those holes are for the answers to the questions.

4. Print the questions and each answer separately in large, black, capital letters either directly on the oaktag or posterboard, or to secure very neat, attractive lines, onto *double*-line opaque white strips of correction tape. This tape can be obtained in most large stationery stores or directly from the Dennison Manufacturing Company, Framingham, Massachusetts 10701. When you are satisfied with the printing of the questions and their corresponding answers, peel the correction tape from its base and carefully place each question next to one of the prepunched holes on the left side of the developing Electroboard's face. Be certain that each is placed horizontal to the other and leaves even spaces between. Then peel off and place the answers onto the right side of the Electroboard near the other prepunched holes, but *be certain to randomize the answers so that none is on the same horizontal level as its matched question.*

5. Turn the oaktag or posterboard face over, and on its back create circuits made with aluminum foil strips and masking tape. Lay strips of aluminum foil "connecting" each question and its correct answer. Then use masking tape that is wider than the foil strips to cover each foil strip. Be certain to press both the foil and the masking tape cover so that they: (1) completely cover the punched holes and (2) remain permanently fixed.

6. Note the positions of each question and its answer so that you have a self-corrective guide in case one is necessary for substitute teachers or aides. Write the name and number (assuming you have several) of the Electroboard at the top of the code. Place into a secure place where access is available when necessary.

7. Using a continuity tester, which can be purchased in any hardware store, check every circuit to be certain that each is working. Do that by touching each question with one prong of the circuit tester and its related answer with the other prong. If the circuits were put together correctly, the tester's bulb should light. Experiment with touching several questions and *incorrect* answers (one at a time) to be certain that the bulb does *not* light.

8. Next tape the second, identically shaped and sized piece of oaktag or posterboard to the *back* of the first piece on which you have been doing all this tactile work; the second piece will serve as a cover to conceal the circuits so that your students do not know which questions are paired with which answers. Then tape the entire perimeter of both cards together, or as Bruno and Jessie suggest (1983, p. 3), "connect the cards using double-faced tape."

Thus, for the unit on "The Great Depression: Don't Let It Get You Down," the Electroboard was designed in the shape of a loaf of bread to suggest the bread lines that were evident during that era (see Figure 6–11). For the unit on "Basic Bookkeeping: The Dollars and Cents of It," the Electroboard was designed in the shape of a ledger (see Figure 6–12).

Designing Flip Chutes

Some secondary students (and many secondary teachers) resist Flip Chutes because of this resource's basic simplicity; they perceive it as being "elementary." We have observed few resources more effective when teaching highly routinized, factual materials—such as multiplication tables, spelling or vocabulary words, or dull facts—with the exceptions of calculators and computer games—which also are tactual!

Experiment with a Flip Chute for mastery of required facts students need to remember. Then teach the youngsters to make their own. Once they overcome their initial hesitation about using tactual devices, many students will cling to this resource because it *does* make it easy for them to learn.

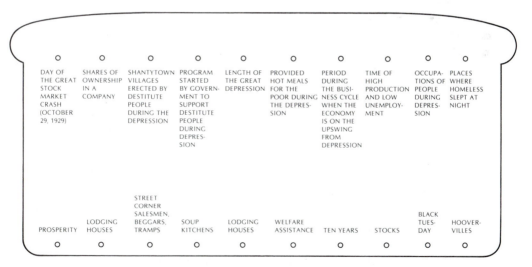

FIGURE 6–11   This Electroboard in the shape of a loaf of bread was designed to complement the unit on "The Great Depression" (Programmed Learning Sequence in Chapter 7, Contract Activity Package in Chapter 8, and Multisensory Instructional Package in Chapter 9).

O Land is an example of _____ asset.	What customers owe. O	
O Longterm Notes Payable	is the dollar value of the stock on hand. O	
O Debits	Borrowing to be repaid after one (1) year. O	
O Credits	are on the <u>left</u> side. O	
O Initial Capital	Any business deal that involves money. O	
O Journal	is the money & assets the owner contributes to start a business. O	
O Transaction	Capital O	
O Accounts Payable	is money owed to outsiders. O	
O Inventory	Basic tool for recording. O	
O Accounts Receivable	are on the <u>right</u> side. O	

FIGURE 6–12 This Electroboard was designed to complement the unit on "Basic Bookkeeping: The Dollars and Cents of It," and is in the shape of a bookkeepers's ledger.

Directions for Constructing Flip Chutes*

1. Pull open the top of a half-gallon milk or juice container.
2. Cut the side folds of the top portion down to the top of the container.

*Flip Chute directions were developed by Barbara Gardiner (1983).

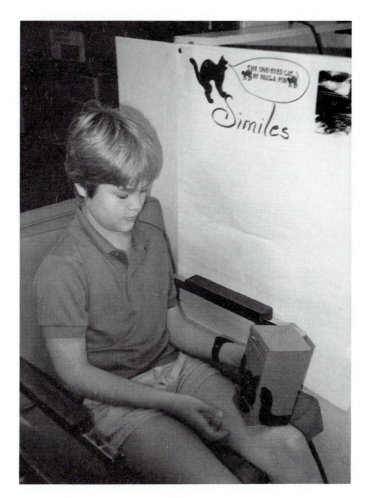

*Flip Chutes may be the best way to teach multiplication
tables to tactual students. However, in this photo, the
young man is using one to test his knowledge of similes.
(Photograph courtesy of P. K. Yonge Laboratory School,
Gainesville, Florida.)*

3. On the front edge, measure down both: (a) $1\frac{1}{2}$ inches, and (b) $2\frac{1}{2}$ inches.
   Draw lines across the container. Remove that space.
4. Mark up from the bottom: (a) $1\frac{1}{2}$ inches, and (b) $2\frac{1}{2}$ inches. Draw lines
   across the container. Remove that space.
5. Cut one 5×8 index card to measure $6\frac{1}{2}$ inches by $3\frac{1}{2}$ inches.
6. Cut a second index card to measure $7\frac{1}{2}$ inches by $3\frac{1}{2}$ inches.

This innovative Flip Chute was designed to complement a unit on Ancient Greece. (Photograph courtesy Center for the Study of Learning and Teaching Styles, St. John's University, Jamaica, New York.)

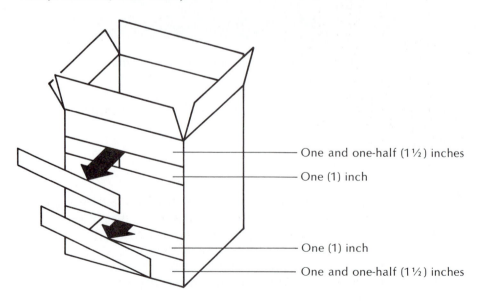

One and one-half (1½) inches

One (1) inch

One (1) inch

One and one-half (1½) inches

7. Fold down ½ inch at *both* ends of the smaller strip. Fold down ½ inch at *one* end of the longer strip.

7½ inches by
3½ inches

6½ inches by
3½ inches

8. Insert the small strip into the bottom opening with the folded edge resting on the upper portion of the bottom opening. Attach it with masking tape.

9. Bring the upper part of the smaller strip out through the upper opening with the folded part going down over the center section of the carton. Attach it with masking tape.

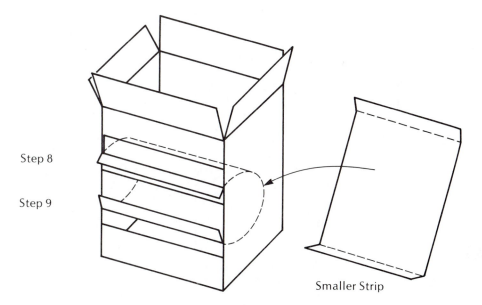

Step 8

Step 9

Smaller Strip

10. Working with the longer strip, one end is folded down, and the other end is unfolded. Insert the unfolded end of the longer strip into the bottom opening of the container. Be certain that the strip goes up along the

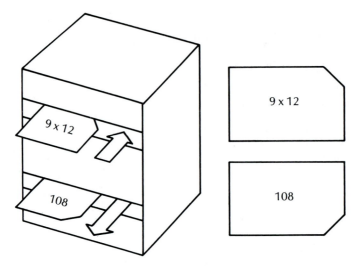

FIGURE 6–13 Sample Flip Chute developed by Barbara Gardiner, New York City teacher.

Side View of Container

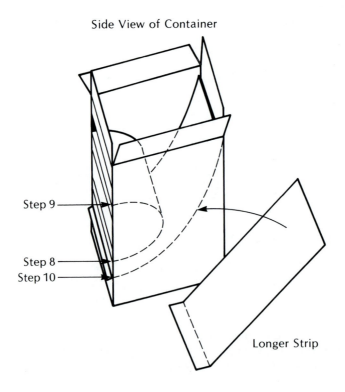

Step 9

Step 8
Step 10

Longer Strip

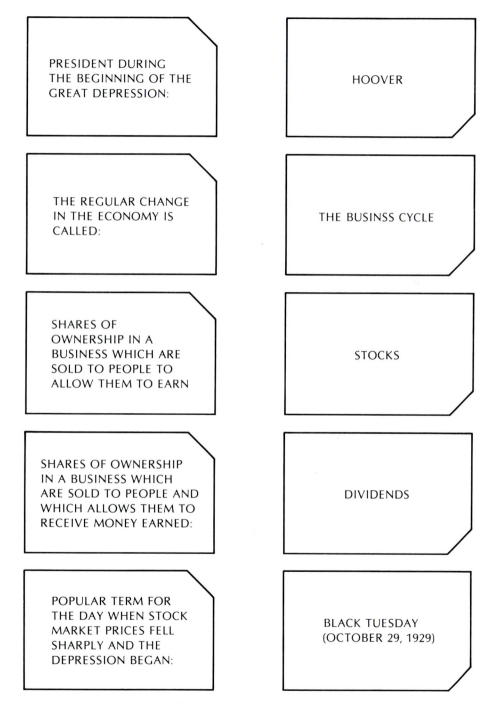

FIGURE 6–14   These sample Great Depression Task Cards show the types of questions and answers that lend themselves to this format.

back of the container. Push it into the container until the folded part rests on the bottom part of the container. Attach it with masking tape.

11. Attach the upper edge of the longer strip to the back of the container ⅝″ from the top, creating a slide. Secure it with masking tape. Follow the next illustration.

12. Fold down the top flaps of the container and tape them in place, forming a rectangular box.

13. Use small, 2″ × 2½″ cards to write the question on one side and the answer on the flip side.

If you want to make the Flip Chute reflect a particular theme or area of study, add a rounded section at the top to represent a head, arms or other "special effects." Paint, color, or cover with colored contact paper or vinyl wall covering and add lettering describing this particular Flip Chute's purpose. When completed, Flip Chutes that maintain secondary students' attention often are the ones they create themselves. Encourage them to "dress up" the Flip Chute to resemble the fact or concept basically being emphasized (see Figures 6–16 through 6–18 for samples related to PLSs, CAPs, and MIPs for the units in this book.

Designing a Touch-Compute Can

Although many teachers have been using a compute-can to facilitate addition and multiplication processes for youngsters who need assistance, the added touch of letting the studetns *feel* the answers may help younger or slower students to commit number facts to memory much faster than they could without the aid of this clever device.

Materials

- 2 sheets of different-colored construction paper
- 1 potato chip can or a similarly shaped product.
- Clear Contact paper
- Black, thin-line felt pens
- Scotch tape
- A glue stick
- Elmer's glue or similar nontoxic glue

Directions

1. Cut sheet #1, which is to be permanently attached to the can, as follows: 9¼ inches × 8¼ inches (see Figures 6–15 and 6–16).

2. Cover sheet #1 with contact paper on its top side and attach to the can. Cut the clear contact paper 10¾ inches long and 8¼ inches wide to fully cover sheet #1 (addition or multiplication), which is 9¼ inches high and 8¼

0 +		0	1	2	3	4	5	6	7	8	9
9 +		9	10	11	12	13	14	15	16	17	18
8 +		8	9	10	11	12	13	14	15	16	17
7 +		7	8	9	10	11	12	13	14	15	16
6 +		6	7	8	9	10	11	12	13	14	15
5 +		5	6	7	8	9	10	11	12	13	14
4 +		4	5	6	7	8	9	10	11	12	13
3 +		3	4	5	6	7	8	9	10	11	12
2 +		2	3	4	5	6	7	8	9	10	11
1 +		1	2	3	4	5	6	7	8	9	10

FIGURE 6–15   Sheet #1 to be used for addition.

inches wide. The additional ¾ inch at the top and ¾ inch at the bottom are used to attach sheet #1 to the can permanently. Use either glue or Scotch tape as you wrap sheet #1 around the can.

3. Outline the numerals with glue so that the children can feel the shape of the number as well as see them.

4. Cut sheet #2, which will rotate around the can, 9⅜ inches long and 7⅜ inches wide. Cut out and remove all the boxes marked with an "X" (see Figure 6-17). Cut contact paper the same size (9⅜ inches long and 7⅜ inches wide). Place the contact paper over the front of sheet #2 even with the top so

0 ×		0	0	0	0	0	0	0	0	0	0
9 ×		0	9	18	27	36	45	54	63	72	81
8 ×		0	8	16	24	32	40	48	56	64	72
7 ×		0	7	14	21	28	35	42	49	56	63
6 ×		0	6	12	18	24	30	36	42	48	54
5 ×		0	5	10	15	20	25	30	35	40	45
4 ×		0	4	8	12	16	20	24	28	32	36
3 ×		0	3	6	9	12	15	18	21	24	27
2 ×		0	2	4	6	8	10	12	14	16	18
1 ×		0	1	2	3	4	5	6	7	8	9

FIGURE 6–16   Sheet #1 to be used for multiplication.

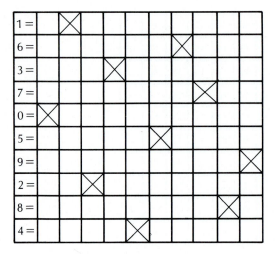

FIGURE 6–17   Sheet #2 to be used for either addition or multiplication.

that the additional 1 inch of length is at the bottom. When curling sheet #2 around the can, this additional inch will attach to the top forming a sleeve that can rotate around sheet #1, which is attached to the can. Sheet #2 may be used for addition and multiplication.

5. Place sheet #2 "sleeve" over sheet #1. The correct answers will appear in the cut-out boxes.

6. Label the Touch-Compute Can, adding the phrase (perhaps at the bottom), "Give me a turn!"

Demonstrate how to use this device for youngsters who need help with their number facts and then permit them to try it. Be certain to emphasize that, when they turn to the correct answer in the "boxed" cut-out, they also touch the numbers.

Designing Pic-A-Hole Resources

Tactual secondary students have used Pic-A-Holes successfully (Dunn & Griggs, 1988) in a variety of subject areas. The attached directions for constructing them initially require measuring and cutting accurately but, as you construct the first sample, *before you seal it, trace the pattern you made.* Students then will need only to copy that pattern and duplicating multiple replicas will become an easy task for them. On the other hand, the tactual/visual youngster for whom this resource will be effective, will be capable of measuring and cutting exactly according to directions.

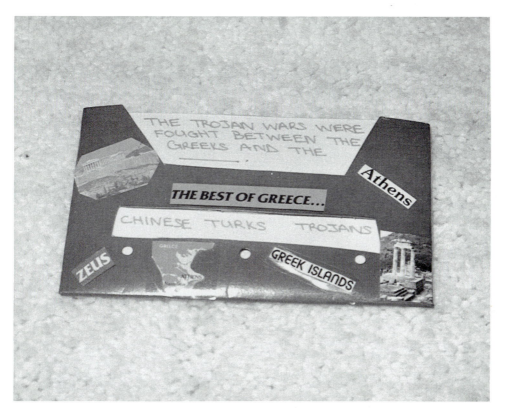

This Pic-A-Hole can either introduce or reinforce the same information included in the Learning Circle and the Flip Chute. All three are tactual components of a Multisensory Instructional Package on the topic, Ancient Greece. (Photograph courtesy Center for the Study of Learning and Teaching Styles, St. John's University, Jamaica, New York.)

Directions for Constructing a Pic-A-Hole*

1. Cut a colorful piece of cardboard or poster board 24⅜ inches by 6½ inches.
2. Following the guide below, measure and mark the cardboard (on the wrong side) to the dimensions given. Use a ball-point pen and score the lines heavily.

---

*Pic-A-Hole directions were developed by Barbara Gardiner (1983).

These tactual instructional resources—a set of Task Cards, a Flip Chute, a Pic-A-Hole, and an Electroboard—all complement the Contract Activity Package, the Programmed Learning Sequence and the Multisensory Instructional Package for the unit on the book, Anne of Green Gables. *(Photograph courtesy Center for the Study of Learning and Teaching Styles, St. John's University, Jamaica, New York.)*

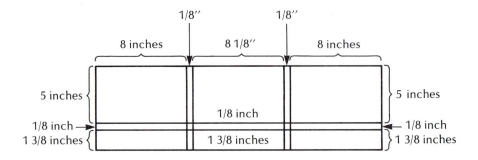

3. Remove the shaded areas. Use a ruler and a razor or exacto knife to get a straight edge. The piece of poster board then should look like the illustration below.

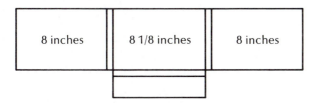

4. Working on the wrong side of the center section only, follow the measurement guide given below.

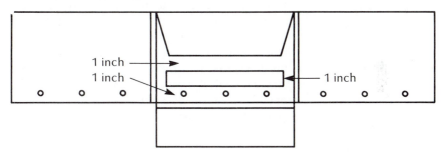

5. Remove the shaded areas with a ruler and razor or exacto knife.
6. Fold on all the drawn lines using a ruler as a guide to obtain sharp, straight fold lines.
7. Punch three holes as shown in the diagram.
8. Place an index card under the center section. Trace the openings onto the card. Remove the same areas from the index card. This will serve as a guide for placement of questions and answers, which can be written on 5 × 8 inch index cards in appropriate places. Punch out the holes.
9. Using 5 × 8 inch index cards, mark holes and punch them out. Use the guide for the placement of information.
10. Fold over the first side under the center section; then fold up the bottom flap; now fold over the last side. Paste or staple them together, being certain that the bottom flap is in between.

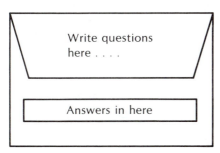

Figure 6–18 shows sample Pic-A-Hole cards on the Great Depression.

Figure 6–19 shows samples of Pic-A-Hole cards for a unit on *Anne of Green Gables,* and Figure 6–20 shows examples for another in bookkeeping. These resources are related to the Programmed Learning Sequences in Chapter 7 and to the Contract Activity Packages in Chapter 8, and are part of the Multisensory Instructional Packages in Chapter 9. If you are interested in experimenting with any of these samples, you may duplicate them and try them with one or more of your classes based on the students' identified learning style characteristics.

Pic-A-Holes are more of an *introductory* than a reinforcement type of resource, although, of course, they can be used in both ways. When employed as an opportunity for becoming familiar with the topic, they reduce student tension because of the choices permitted from among three possible alternatives; because they are self-corrective, they permit adolescents (and anyone else who uses them) the luxury of learning through trial and error without jeopardy of the embarrassment that can occur when teachers call on individuals and students must respond to whole-class inquiries. The self-corrective feature of all these tactual devices ensures eventual success in a private, non-threatening environment. Because the students for whom Pic-A-Holes and similar tactual resources are recommended for hands-on people, they learn more easily in this way than through other more conventional approaches.

When students consider options and then examine the three possible choices at the bottom, they may be conjecturing analytically about the correct answer. When they look, instead, for the answer and then read the question to determine how that answer is appropriate, they are attacking their assignment

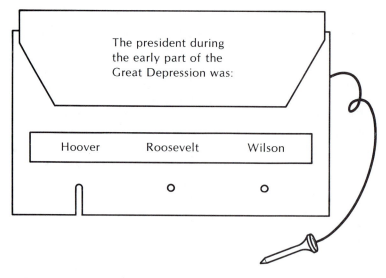

FIGURE 6–18   Sample Pic-A-Hole Cards.

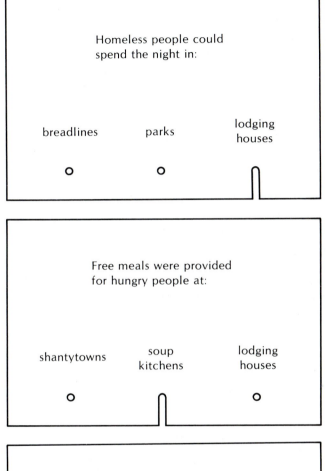

Homeless people could
spend the night in:

breadlines   parks   lodging
                                   houses

○   ○

Free meals were provided
for hungry people at:

shantytowns   soup   lodging
                kitchens   houses

○   ○

The Great Depression lasted:

8   3   10
years   years   years

○   ○

Continued

FIGURE 6–18 *Continued*

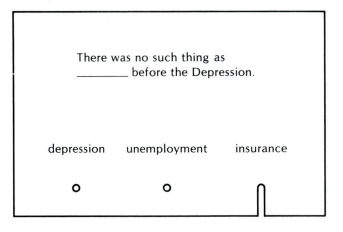

There was no such thing as
_____ before the Depression.

depression   unemployment   insurance

      O   O

Shares of ownership in a business
that are sold to people, and which
allow them to share some of the
money earned by the business or
company, are:

shareholders   stock   dividends

      O   O

_____ _____ was the day in
October 1929 when stock prices fell
sharply and the Great Depression
began.

Black   Black   Blue
Monday   Tuesday   Monday

      O   O

FIGURE 6–18 *Continued*

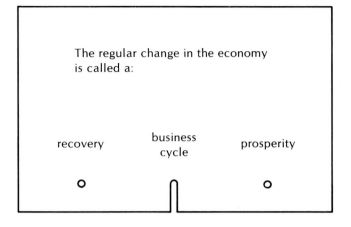

The regular change in the economy
is called a:

recovery   business   prosperity
                    cycle

     O   O

Street corner merchants selling
apples and pencils, beggars, and
former _____ were common
sights during the depression.

millionaires   tramps   politicians

                            O   O

Money paid to shareholders who
own stock in a company or business
is called:

shares   dividends   certificates

     O   O

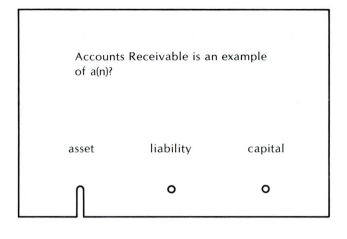

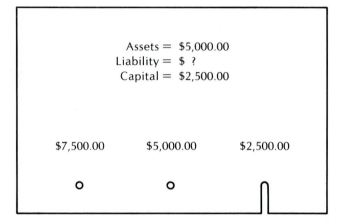

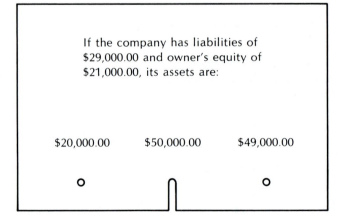

FIGURE 6–19   Sample Pic-A-Hole Cards for the Unit on Bookkeeping.

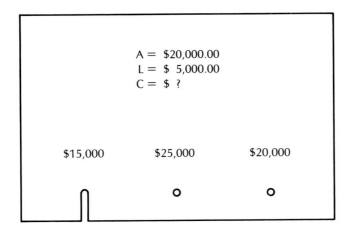

A = $20,000.00
L = $ 5,000.00
C = $?

$15,000 $25,000 $20,000

                    O   O

What is the account balance?
        Accounts   Payable
        $20,000.00 $40,000.00
                          $10,000.00

$70,000.00 $60,000.00 $30,000.00

        O   O

Money paid <u>in advance</u> for services
the business has <u>not</u> yet received is
called:

prepaid
items   inventory   supplies

                    O   O

globally. When analytics cope analytically and globals cope globally, they gradually learn; one is not necessarily a better sequence than the other.

With a tied-on golf tee, students place the point directly below the option they believe to be correct and then attempt to lift the question card. When the answer selected is correct, the card lifts easily and can be removed. The student then works with the card directly below the top one. Should the student's first (or second) choice be incorrect, the card will not budge (see Figure 6–18).

Step-by-Step Guide to Designing Kinesthetic Activities

Some youngsters can learn only by doing; for them, real-life experiences are the most effective way of absorbing and retaining knowledge. It is easy to teach students to convert pints to quarts and quarts to gallons through baking and cooking or to teach them inches and feet by helping them to build a scooter or antique doll house, but it is not simple to teach all the skills and information that must be achieved through reality-oriented activities. To begin with, such activities are time-consuming; second, many activities require supervision; finally, we are not used to teaching that way, and to do so requires an endless source of creative suggestions. There is, however, a new kind of kinesthetic (whole-body) game that you can design for classroom use, reuse, and ever-continuing learning by your tactual charges.

Designing Body-Action Floor or Wall Games

Many teachers save old things and then use them creatively to instruct their students. Now is the time to locate all the large plastic tablecloths, shower curtains, carpet and furniture coverings, and sails that may be hidden away in basements, attics, garages, and wherever else too-good-to-throw-away things are placed. Old sheets and bath towels may also be pressed into service, but they are not as durable as plastic, and when they are washed the printed matter on them often fades and occasionally disappears altogether. If you are not a collector of old valuables, you may need to either solicit cast-off materials from others or purchase a large sheet of plastic from your neighborhood bargain store.

Materials

- One large sheet of plastic, approximately 4 × 5, 5 × 5, or 5 × 6 feet, or another material within that size range
- Smaller pieces of multicolored plastic that can be cut into decorations and illustrations and then glued or sewn onto the larger sheet
- Black thin-line permanent ink pens
- Black and brightly colored permanent ink felt pens

This Floor Game complements the Contract Activity Package, the Programmed Learning Sequence, and the Multisensory Instructional Package for the Unit on The Great Depression. (Photograph courtesy of Center for the Study of Learning and Teaching Styles, St. John's University, Jamaica, New York.)

- Glue that will adhere plastic to plastic
- Assorted discarded items that, depending on your imagination and creativity, you use as part of the game you design
- Pad and pencil for sketching ideas

Directions

1. Identify the information or skills that you want your students to learn.

2. Consider ways in which you can either introduce that information or reinforce it through a body action game in which selected students can hop or jump or merely move from one part of the large sheet to another as they are exposed to the major (or finer) points of the topic, or where they can reach and extend their arms as if they are painting a huge wall mural.

Kinesthetic adolescents—who learn most easily through active participation—begin a unit with a Floor Game. They then either read or hear the information they need to remember, answer questions about it by writing or illustrating, and then use the knowledge by transferring it into an original instructional resource of their choice. (Photograph courtesy of East Islip Junior High School, East Islip, New York.)

    3. Sketch a design on a sheet of paper to work it out before you begin cutting, pasting, or sewing.

    4. When you are satisfied with your conceptualization of the game, plan a layout of the various sections on the plastic sheet that you will use; consider the placement of articles, and list the additional items that you can use, noting the ways in which you can use them.

    5. In pencil, lightly sketch on the large sheet where you will paste each item, the dimensions that you must plan for, and where you will place key directions.

6. Cut the smaller plastic pieces into appropriate shapes or figures and glue them onto the larger sheet.

7. With a felt pen that will not wash off, trace over those penciled lines that you wish to keep.

8. Develop a set of questions and answers or tasks that students may complete as they use the body-action game. Then either develop an answer card so that students may correct themselves or color-code or picture-code the questions and answers so that the game is self-corrective.

9. If you teach either non-English-speaking students or poor readers, develop a tape that will tell them how to play the game, what the game will teach them, and how they can recognize that they have learned whatever it is the game is designed to teach.

10. If your students are capable of reading and following printed sequences, print or type a set of directions for them and attach it to the sheet (perhaps in a pocket that you cut out and glue or sew onto its underside).

Examples. For an instructional package on "Perimeters," several activities were designed that taught students to find the perimeter of a series of different shapes (see Figure 6–21). As the culminating exercise, a body-action floor game was created with the following directions:

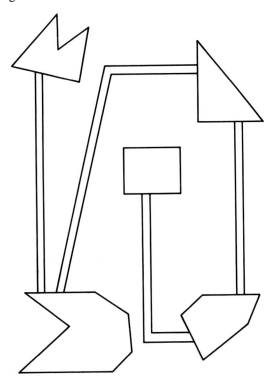

FIGURE 6–21

To play this game, you must find the perimeter of each shape as you come to it. Travel along the path according to the direction on the answer side of each card.

1. *Start at the center of the game.* What is the perimeter of the blue square if its sides measure 12 inches each?

2. Look at Answer Card 1 in the pocket on the underside of the game. If your answer is correct, hop on one foot to the next shape. If you are *not* correct, take "baby steps" to the next shape.

3. You now should be standing on the yellow shape. It has five sides. Three of its sides measure 12 inches each, and two of its sides are 10 inches each. What is the perimeter of the yellow shape?

The directions guided students through a series of varied geometric shapes, permitting them to check their answers and, if they had computed incorrectly, to learn why they were wrong. When the body game was completed, a duplicated sheet attached to the larger package tested them on their ability to determine the perimeter of a variety of shapes. When their teacher checked their Final Assessment responses to determine their grades, she was surprised to see how well students who had rarely achieved a passing grade on previous units had done!

For a social studies unit on "The Battle of Manila Bay: May 1, 1989," a floor game was designed to duplicate the geographical maps of the South China Sea, the Philippines, and Manila Bay. Students were asked to reenact the first and second battles in correct sequence by using miniature ships and other replicas.

For a unit on westward expansion, a map of the entire United States, including many geographical representations and divisions representing the acquisition of territories, was recreated on an eight by ten foot plastic sheet. Students were directed to play a game in which they identified which territories had been added and when, what their contribution to the country eventually had been, and the values of those contributions to present-day citizens.

Using Wall Games

For classrooms with a minimum of floor space, similar games can be designed for wall areas or outside-the-classroom hall walls. In fact, extremely large Pic-A-Holes or Flip Chutes can be made from the cardboard boxes in which appliances or television sets are delivered. Students delight in both creating and using such large instructional resources and they serve the same purpose as other resources; they teach students required information. In this case, however, they teach *kinesthetic* learners—the young people that only coaches and industrial arts and vocational education teachers appear to respond to positively in traditional education.

Using Tactual/Kinesthetic Resources in the Classroom

At least four valuable contributions are made by tactual/visual instructional resources. They:

1. Respond to the tactual/visual preferences of students (who rarely are introduced to difficult academic information through their strengths at the secondary level).
2. Permit such youngsters to work with responsive materials *first* and then be reinforced through approaches used with their classmates—so that they need not leave the class situation (for "extra help" or Resource Room instruction).
3. Teach students to convert required information into resources through which they can succeed—even beyond high school.
4. Gradually enable students to become independent learners—perhaps the best skill they can acquire during their education.
5. Demonstrate to adolescents, who often have poor self-image and a lack of confidence merely by virtue of being in transition between childhood and adulthood, that they *do* have strengths, *are* capable, *can* learn, and *are* worthy, but that everybody has different strengths and all strengths are valuable.

Allow either 10 to 15 minutes at the end of the period immediately before you plan to introduce a new unit *or* allow the same 10 to 15 minutes at the beginning of the period in which you plan to introduce a new unit. Tell the class:

> *Today we are going to develop beginning familiarity with a new, difficult unit. Please look at the chalkboard (wall chart, distributed ditto, or page ____ in the back of Chapter ____ in our ____ book). Those are the objectives for this new unit. The objectives tell you exactly what you need to remember for this unit.*
>
> *Every one in this class will be responsible for the same objectives; every one will take exactly the same test at the end of this unit. However, many of you will be using different resources to learn the exact same information.*
>
> *Students with tactual strengths, use either the Electroboard, Task Cards, Flip Chute, or Pic-A-Hole to work toward completing the unit's objectives. As long as you are using a tactual resource, the choice of the resource is yours.*
>
> *Students with visual strengths, read pages ____ through ____ in Chapter ____ of your ____ book to develop beginning familiarity with the information. You will have only 10–15 minutes to skim the material, so keep the objectives in mind as you seek answers to the questions in this unit.*
>
> *Students with kinesthetic strengths, try the Floor Game to initially seek the information required by the objectives. You may need to use the game with others if there are several with kinesthetic strengths, but if you prefer to work with it alone, come in during a free period or after school. It won't take more than 15 minutes to find most of the facts.*

> *Students with* auditory *strengths, please meet me in the far corner near the* ___ *for a quick overview of the basic facts required for this unit. If you care to bring your tape recorder, you may tape the information for review at a later time.*
>
> *I do not expect that any of you will remember all or most of the information you find in this short amount of time. Rather,* beginning *this unit with your strength will help you to begin concentrating on the information you will need to complete it successfully. Just concentrate on finding as much of the information as you can. You do not need to take notes or record the answers, unless you* want *to. You will begin to remember as you experience the different approaches we will use during this unit.*

Some secondary students may not wish to be labeled auditory, visual, tactual, or kinesthetic; until they recognize that each of these senses is a strength, many feel embarrassed. If that occurs, say:

> *Research suggests that people learn more easily and more rapidly through their preferences than through their nonpreferences, but if you do not wish to concentrate with the resource I indicated, use the material you do prefer. However, you must try to find as much of the required information as possible in the short amount of time I have allocated.*

Indicate that the youngsters may work alone, in a pair, or in a small group, but that they need to use their sociological preferences as revealed on the LSI. Thus, if their LSI score on Learning Alone was below 40, they should work alone. If their LSI score on that same element was 60 or above, they should work with one or two peers. If they are nonpreferenced (LSI score between 40 and 59), they may choose how they wish to learn—either alone, with a friend or two, or with you, the teacher.

Should students whose LSI scores indicate they need to work alone, wish to work with peers, you may allow them *one* opportunity to try learning that way, but advise them that, because they are not following their learning style prescription, if they do *not* learn everything they need to learn for this upcoming unit *or* if they do not perform well on the test (85 percent or better), they will thereafter be required to learn new material as directed, and not as they prefer.

Begin the new unit with this approach. If you are concerned that these resources tend to emphasize only the facts that need to be memorized and do not provide experiences with higher-level cognitive thinking, use Team Learning immediately after this short experience to reinforce some of the facts and to introduce cognitive strategies that enable youngsters to synthesize, extrapolate, compare, contrast, translate, analyze, and so forth.

For homework after the Team Learning, assign tasks that require translation of the information students are learning in class into original resources. Thus, for homework, students may be directed to *make* a set of Task Cards, a Flip Chute, an Electroboard, or a Pic-A-Hole that teaches the information required by this unit's objectives. However, recognize that those activities respond to tactual strengths. For the visual and auditory students, provide choices that include the writing of poetry, the development of a crossword puzzle, the designing of a game, or the making of a tape that teaches the information required for this unit. For kinesthetics, permit the pantomiming of the information or the creation of a ballet or dance that teaches it.

A Final Word about Tactual/Kinesthetic Instructional Resources

Most teachers have not been taught how to employ hands-on and body action resources in traditional academic teaching; somehow, we assume that by the time adolescents reach secondary school they should be sufficiently well equipped to be able to listen to what we tell them, read on their own, and direct their learning independently.

Despite that assumption, we all know that young people are different from each other. Some grow tall at a very early age; others shoot up overnight and, often, just before their parents give up on their ever reaching an appropriate height. Others remain diminutive throughout their lives.

Similarly, student's perceptual strengths develop independently of their wishes or control. Many *never* become auditory; they spend much of their adult lives insisting that they have *never* been told the things that others are certain have been said to them. Many *never* become visual; they *feel* their way through life doing what intuitively strikes them as being most appropriate.

We teachers are in command.

- We can choose to ignore student's differences.
- We can teach all youngsters in our classes in exactly the same way and verbalize that we believe they should all learn equally well through whichever approach *we* feel comfortable using.
- We can consign the low auditory and low visual students to failure, for they surely will fail unless we respond to their only strengths.
- We can continue to assign the responsibility for their instruction to special educators, Resource Room teachers, and psychologists. If we do that, however, we inadvertently will be harming them immeasurably. Children never recuperate from being labeled "Special Ed" or "Learning Disabled," and neither do their families. Such young people do not *belong* in special classes apart from other students merely because they find it difficult to remember 75 percent of what they hear in a normal 40 or 50 minute lecture; they are not necessarily deficient because they do not remember three-quarters of what they read in the same amount of time. They remember what they *do* and what they *experience*. Why shouldn't they be taught with tactual materials? Why shouldn't they be allowed to experience actively?

Being low auditory or low visual is not something that happens to *other* people's children. Ask any group of 100 or more educators how many have had youngsters of their own who neither liked nor did well in school, and you will be appalled at the number who raise their hands. And wait until it happens to your grandchildren.

We ask you as educators—among the most caring humans in the world, to *try* these tactual and/or kinesthetic resources with the young people who can't seem to "make it" in school. Try them with the unhappy students. Experiment by using them with the ostracized, the nonconformists, the potential dropouts. Obviously, if Flip Chutes, Electroboards, Pic-A-Holes, and Task Cards are not effective, you will stop. But if you observe that they pull some youngsters through to passing grades or better, perhaps you will teach those students to make their own resources and help them get started on the road to success. *That's* where these approaches lead—for more young people than most of us are willing to believe! (Andrews, 1990).

Designing Programmed Learning Sequences to Respond to Individual Learning Styles

Using Programmed Instruction for Selected Students

A second basic method for individualizing instruction is to program material so that it may be learned in small, simple steps without the direct supervision of an adult. Like any other method, programmed instruction is responsive to only selected learning style characteristics and, therefore, should not be prescribed for all students. The special type of programming described in this chapter is entitled Programmed Learning Sequences (PLS).

Commercial programs are designed around preselected concepts and skills, called *objectives,* that must be mastered by each student. Objectives range from the simple to the complex and are sequenced so that, after taking a pretest, students are assigned only those that they have not achieved before using this particular program. Each youngster then is introduced to the programmed materials at the point where the remaining objectives are either partially repetitive or introductory. All students proceed through the identical sequence but may pace themselves and use the program when and where they prefer to study. Programmed instruction is individualized only in terms of diagnosis, prescription, level, and, when used flexibly, selected aspects of learning style.

Programs that have been commercially produced have had only limited effectiveness because they are solely visual—similar to short workbooks—and therefore appeal most to students who either read fairly well and who can retain information by seeing. The firms that produce such programs maintain that cassettes and filmstrips occasionally supplement their resources. When multimedia materials are available, they should be used to facilitate the program's effectiveness for those youngsters who are auditory while serving as reinforcement for those who are visual.

In actual practice, students are each given a program for which they are responsible, and, as the various objectives and their related tests are completed, gradual progress is made toward completing the material. Unless learners need and seek assistance, they virtually may be isolated for long periods of instructional time. It also is possible for them to engage in hours of study without benefiting from either adult or peer interaction. There are youngsters who prefer to work alone, but the Poirier (1970) methods instituted at the University of California verify that for many students, retention is increased after peer discussions of what is being learned. A teacher who chooses to use programmed materials for students who are peer-oriented may overcome the isolation factor, however, by incorporating selected small-group techniques into the programs—such as Team Learning, Circle of Knowledge, Group Analysis, Case Study, Simulation, and Brainstorming.

Learning Style Characteristics Responsive to Programmed Learning Sequences

Because programmed materials are used independently (alone or with one classmate), it is important that those students to whom this resource is assigned enjoy working alone or in a pair and are motivated to learn the program's contents. They also should be persistent, suggesting that they normally would continue using the materials until the program has been completed. Should they experience difficulty, they either should review the previous frames and continue to try to progress, or they should seek assistance from appropriate persons.

By organizing everything that should be learned so that only one item at a time is presented, the sequenced materials in each program provide a great deal of structure. A student cannot proceed until what must be achieved at each stage has been fully understood, as demonstrated through a short quiz at the end of each frame or page. Youngsters who prefer to be directed and told exactly what to do will feel at ease with programmed learning, whereas creative students may find it boring and unchallenging.

Programmed Learning Sequences (PLS) are ideally suited to youngsters who prefer to work alone and to avoid the sounds, movement, and interaction of classmates. They also are a perfect match for students who learn best by seeing and for those who need to read and, perhaps, reread information before it is absorbed.

Teachers who believe that selected students are neither motivated nor persistent, but who recognize that they are average or slow achievers, visual learners, and in need of structure, should experiment with programmed instruction. Because this strategy presents concepts and skills simply, gradually, and repeatedly, and may be used alone—without causing either the embarrassment or the pressure that emerges when one has difficulty achieving among one's peers—many youngsters often become motivated, persistent, or responsible when using a PLS. When the "right" method is matched correctly with the "right" student, increased academic achievement and improved attitudes toward learning are likely to result.

Learning Style Characteristics to Which Programmed Learning Sequences Can Be Accommodated

Because a PLS may be used in a classroom, in a library, in a corridor, or in an instructional resource center as well as at home, it can accommodate each student's environmental and physical preferences. For example, the PLS can be taken to a silent area if quiet is desired, or it may be used in the midst of classroom activity by a learner who can block out sound. It can be moved to either a warm section of a room—near a heating unit—or to a cool area. It can be studied at a desk or on a carpet, in a well-lit space or away from the bright sunshine. A student may snack or not as he or she works, may use the package at any time of day that is convenient, and may take a break or two if mobility is necessary. Because the PLS is visual, it will utilize the perceptual strengths of students who learn best by reading or seeing. For auditory youngsters, a teacher should add a tape that repeats orally what the text teaches visually. When students are either tactual or kinesthetic learners, the teacher should add games that introduce the PLS's objectives through those senses. For students who learn slowly or with difficulty, it is wise to supplement a visual PLS with three other types of perceptual resources—auditory, tactual, and kinesthetic. When appropriate, a PLS may be completed by pairs or teams of students!

Case Studies Describing Students Whose Learning Styles Are Complemented by Programmed Learning Sequences

1. Only the sound of his own name was able to break through into his thoughts. As Mrs. Diamond's voice repeated the question, Kerry sat up in his seat. He had been so engrossed in contemplating the effects of the civil rights movement—an item on which the teacher had been focusing ten minutes earlier—that his imagination had carried him from the advent of slavery in the United States to the psychological implications of being a despised minority in a majority culture.

Mrs. Diamond's voice was sympathetic. "Do you know the answer?" Kerry sat up quickly in embarrassment.

"I'm sorry," he answered. "I was thinking about something else."

"What?" she asked. He merely shrugged. He was reluctant to reveal that he was mentally involved with an item that had been discussed a while before—one only tangentially related to what the class was studying.

"Please keep up with us," the teacher urged, and slowly shook her head in exasperation.

Students who are motivated to learn, but who need more time to consider items or to concentrate than is usually permitted by group instruction, may learn more effectively through Programmed Learning Sequences.

2. Mark could not work out the fifth example. He pulled his text out from the desk and fingered through its pages until he found the chapter that explained how to convert fractions. He read the section related to that process but was still not certain of how to apply the rule. He leaned over toward a classmate and asked for assistance. When the directions for solving the problem were clear to him, he turned back to the papers on his desk and continued working.

Students who are persistent—who continue working toward the completion of an assignment and find ways to do so—usually respond well to Programmed Learning Sequences.

3. Barbara's elbow was on her desk, her forehead rested on the fingers of her clenched hand, and her eyes had just closed tightly. She was trying to reconstruct the page she had read, which described the elements of a short story. Suddenly she recalled the page and was able to "see" the listing of elements. She relaxed, picked up her pen, and began to answer the text questions.

Students who are visual learners—who remember more by reading and seeing than they do by listening—usually respond well to Programmed Learning Sequences.

4. Tim was having a great time with the kids on his committee. As members tried to find the information for their assignment, he collected their pens, pencils, and notes and hid them inside his desk. When the boys reconvened to decide on how they would present their report, Tim alternated between wandering around the room and tipping his chair to see how far back it could go without falling. When the teacher chastised him to settle down and seated him apart from the group, he picked up a pencil and began to organize the presentation.

Students who do not work well in groups may work better alone knowing that they, personally, are responsible for completing an assignment. Such youngsters may respond well to Programmed Learning Sequences, Contract Activity Packages, or Multisensory Instructional Packages.

5. Claire was at her teacher's side again. "Mr. Dawes, am I doing this right?" she asked.

"You asked the same question five minutes ago!" the teacher responded.

"I know," Claire answered, "but I want to be sure!"

Students who require structure—who need to know exactly what to do and how to do it—usually respond well to Programmed Learning Sequences.

Basic Principles of Programmed Learning Sequences

Programmed Learning is designed on the basis of several important principles that tend to facilitate academic achievement for students with selected learning style elements. All programs tend to follow a pattern that includes each of the following characteristics:

1. *Only one item is presented at a time.* A single concept or skill that should be mastered is introduced through a simple written statement. After reading the material, the learner is required to answer a question or two to demonstrate that what has been introduced on that frame (page, section) has been understood. This procedure prevents the lesson from advancing faster than the student, and it does not permit the student to fall behind. The youngster may learn as quickly as he or she is capable of comprehending the material, or as slowly and with as much repetition as may be needed. Students should not continue into a subsequent frame or phase of the program until each previous one has been mastered.

Presenting one item at a time is effective for the analytic youngster who wants to learn (is motivated), who will continue trying (is persistent), and who wants to do what is required (is responsible/conforming). For students who are not persistent, being exposed to one item at a time breaks the content into small phases and the process into short steps that can be mastered gradually. Understandably, this process is not effective for the global student who needs to be exposed to a gestalt of the information—who, rather than piecing a totality together bit by bit, prefers to develop an overall view of the end product. It is also inappropriate for those who cannot continue to work with the same set of materials for any continuing period of time and who need diversity and variety. In addition, it appears to be a method that does not attract and hold creative students who want to add their own knowledge and special talents to what is being learned before they have accomplished the entire task.

2. *The student is required to be an active, rather than a passive, learner.* Unlike large-group instruction, where a student may merely sit and appear to be listening, PLSs require that students respond to questions related to each introduced item. Youngsters cannot progress through the program without responding, and only accurate answers permit continuation of this instructional process.

3. *The student is immediately informed of the correctness of each response.* As soon as a youngster has read the frame, he or she is required to answer a question based on the material that has just been read. The moment that the student's response has been recorded, the youngster may turn to the back of the frame, where the correct answer is stated. The student, therefore, is immediately made aware of the accuracy or inaccuracy of the response. This technique of immediate reinforcement is a highly effective teaching strategy with most learners.

4. *The student may not continue into the next phase of a program until each previous phase has been understood and mastered.* When the program reveals that a student's response to the questions related to each frame are correct, the student is directed to continue into the next section (frame, page, or phase). When students' responses are not correct, they can be directed either to restudy the previously read frames or to turn to another section of the program that will explain in a different way the material that has not been understood. Because each phase of the program must be mastered before students are permitted to continue into the next phase, learners do not move ahead aimlessly while grasping only parts of a concept or topic. Their base of knowledge is solid before they are exposed to either new ideas or related ones.

5. *The student is exposed to material that gradually progresses from the easy to the more difficult.* Frames are written so that the first few in a series introduce what should be learned in an uncomplicated, direct manner. Gradually, as the student's correct answers demonstrate his or her increasing understanding of what is being taught, more difficult aspects of the topic are introduced. Through this technique, students are made to feel both comfortable and successful with the beginning phases of each program, and their confidence in their own ability to achieve is bolstered. Youngsters who find themselves achieving are likely to continue in the learning process.

6. *As the student proceeds in the program, fewer hints and crutches are provided.* Programming uses a system of "fading," or gradually withdrawing easy questions or hints (repeated expressions, illustrations, color coding, and similar crutches) so that the student's developing knowledge is tested precisely. This technique also enables the teacher to accurately assess the youngster's progress and mastery of the material.

Step-by-Step Guide to Designing a Programmed Learning Sequence

Developing a program is not difficult, but it does require that you organize the topic that will be taught into a logical, easy-to-follow sequence. Begin with step 1 and gradually move through each of the remaining steps until you have completed your first program. Each subsequent program will become easier and easier to design. By their questions and responses, students will provide direct feedback on how to revise and improve your initial efforts. Subsequent programs will require fewer revisions.

Step 1 Begin by identifying a topic, concept, or skill that you want to teach. A good choice would be something that most youngsters in your classes need to learn. Since all students are not capable of learning at the same time, in the same way, and at the same speed, a program is one way of permitting individuals to self-pace themselves with materials whenever they are ready to achieve. Thus, some youngsters may use a specific program early in the semester, while others will use it later. Some will use it to learn before the remainder of the class is exposed to a new idea, and others will use it to reinforce an idea that you already have taught—but which they did not master.

Step 2 Write the name of the topic, concept, or skill that you have decided to teach as a heading at the top of a blank sheet of paper. Add a subtitle that is humorous or related to a real life experience. Plan to design the covers—or the entire PLS—in a shape that represents the topics to appeal to the tactual children. If you can include some humor, it will appeal to the more global students.

Examples

- Electricity: A Shocking Experience
- Math IV: Divide and Conquer
- Ancient Rome: No Toga Party
- Pronouns: Up Front and Personal

Step 3 Translate the heading that you have written at the top of the sheet into an introductory sentence that explains to the youngsters using the PLS exactly what they should be able to do after they have mastered what it is designed to teach.

Examples

- By the time you finish this Programmed Learning Sequence, you will be able to recognize adjectives and identify the nouns that each of the adjectives modifies.
- When you have completed this Programmed Learning Sequence, you should be able to explain at least five (5) ways in which your life is different from that of a youngster living in a terrorist family and at least five (5) ways in which your lives are similar.
- This Programmed Learning Sequence will teach you to complete at least five (5) basic geometric proofs.

The humorous subtitle on this Programmed Learning Sequence (PLS), "Ancient Greece: It Burns a Torch for You," appeals to cetain students who, otherwise, might find its contents uninviting. Its shape and color helps to attract visual and tactual learners. (Photograph courtesy Center for the Study of Learning and Teaching Styles, St. John's Univesity, New York.)

Step 4 List all the prerequisites for using the program effectively.

Examples

- Before you use this Programmed Learning Sequence, you should be familiar with the meanings of each of the following words: desert, nomad, oasis, arid, mirage.

Illustrations, cartoons, and symbolic representations all add to the appeal of this mathematics PLS on how to make change. (Photograph courtesy Center for the Study of Learning and Teaching Styles, St. John's University, New York.)

- Be certain that you begin using this Programmed Learning Sequence either on or near a large table so that you will have ample room to use the booklet, its materials, and the tape recorder at the same time.
- Because you may realize that certain knowledge or skills are prerequisites after you have moved beyond step 4, leave space on your paper so that you may insert additions as they come to mind.

Step 5 Create a global story, fantasy, cartoon, or humorous beginning that relates to the topic. Place this global opening just before the information and question frames begin. (See sample programs for global openings.)

Step 6 Decide which of the two basic types of programming you will use.

Type 1: Linear Programming
This type of programming presents material in a highly structured sequence. Each part of the sequence is called a *frame,* and each frame builds upon the

one immediately preceding it. Each frame ends with an item that requires an answer—in either a completion, a matching, or a multiple-choice format. Prior to the introduction of each subsequent frame, the answer to the previous frame is supplied. Program efficiency increases when the correct answer is accompanied by an explanation and a humorous comment or cartoon. Additional comprehension is developed when the incorrect answers also are accompanied by explanations Add other modes of response for variety as you develop additional frames—for example, circle the correct answer; match the correct answers to each question by connecting them with lines; and place the correct answer in the right space (see Figure 7–1).

Type 2: Intrinsic Programming

Intrinsic programming also presents material in a highly structured sequence, but the major difference between the linear and intrinsic types is that the intrinsic does not require that each student complete every frame. Intrinsic programming recognizes that some youngsters can move through learning experiences faster than others can, and it permits those who score correct answers to skip over some of the reinforcement frames.

When students may bypass frames that teach the same aspect of a subject, the system is called *branching*. Branching, in effect, permits a faster rate of self-pacing. When a student answers a question incorrectly, he must continue from one frame to the next, to the next, and so on until every frame in the entire program has been completed. When a student studies several introductory frames and then answers the questions correctly, he may branch over additional reinforcement frames if the program is an intrinsic one (see Figure 7–2).

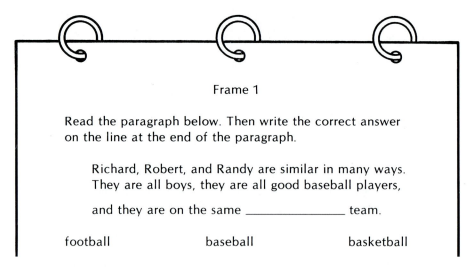

Frame 1

Read the paragraph below. Then write the correct answer on the line at the end of the paragraph.

Richard, Robert, and Randy are similar in many ways. They are all boys, they are all good baseball players,

and they are on the same _____ team.

football   baseball   basketball

FIGURE 7–1 This example of linear programming builds reading comprehension step by step through the provision of correct answers on the back of each frame accompanied by explanations.

FIGURE 7-1 *Continued*

Back of Frame 1

Answer: baseball

The paragraph tells us that the three boys are good *baseball* players. It does not tell us whether or not they play football or basketball.

Frame 2

Write the correct answer on the line at the end of the paragraph.

Richard, Robert, and Randy are all fourteen. They enjoy active sports. In addition to baseball, they each play

_____.

video games   monopoly   basketball

Back of Frame 2

Answer: basketball

The paragraph stated that they enjoy active sports, and basketball is an active sport. Video games and Monopoly are not. At least, not usually!

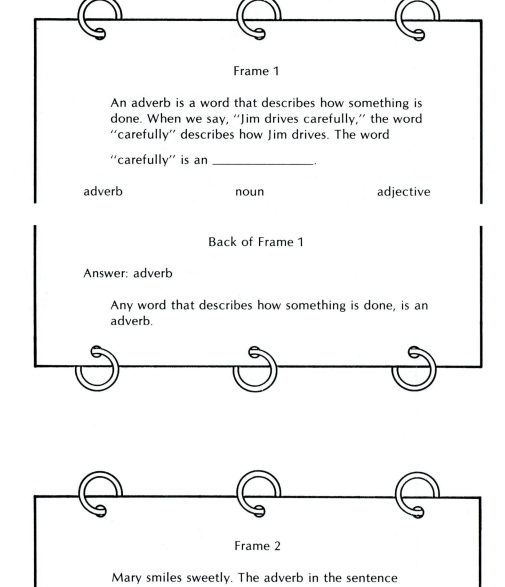

Frame 1

An adverb is a word that describes how something is done. When we say, "Jim drives carefully," the word "carefully" describes how Jim drives. The word

"carefully" is an _____.

adverb   noun   adjective

Back of Frame 1

Answer: adverb

Any word that describes how something is done, is an adverb.

Frame 2

Mary smiles sweetly. The adverb in the sentence

"Mary smiles sweetly," is _____.

Mary   smiles   sweetly

FIGURE 7–2 Intrinsic programming permits *branching,* a term that indicates a student may bypass one or more frames when a correct answer is given. This example outlines how branching is included within a structured sequence on adverbs.

FIGURE 7–2 *Continued*

Back of Frame 2

Answer: sweetly

"Sweetly" tells how Mary smiles. Mary is a girl's name. Mary is a noun. "Smile" is what Mary does. Smile is a verb. If you wrote that "sweetly" is an adverb, you understand how to recognize some words that are adverbs.

Turn to Frame 5. You may skip Frame 3 and 4. If you did not write that "sweetly" is an adverb, turn to Frame 3 for more practice in recognizing adverbs.

Frame 3

John walks quickly.

Circle the adverb in the sentence above.

Back of Frame 3

Answer: quickly

"Quickly" tells how John walks.
"John" is the boy's name. "John" is a noun.
"Walks" is what John does. "Walks" is a verb.

Step 7   Outline how you plan to teach the topic. Use short, simple sentences, if possible. Most people have two different vocabularies: One is used for speaking, the other for writing. When you begin to outline your program, pretend that you are speaking to the student who will have the most trouble learning this material. Use simple words and sentences. Then write exactly the words that you would use if you were actually talking to that youngster. In other words, use your speaking vocabulary rather than your professional writing vocabulary to develop the Programmed Learning Sequence.

Step 8   Divide the sentences in your outline into frames. Frames, which are equivalent to pages, are small sections of the topic that teach part of the idea, skill, or information. After listing the sentences that teach the information, ask a question that relates to the material. The student's answer will demonstrate his or her growing understanding of the subject. Think small! Most people who begin to write programs try to cover too much in a frame. Keep it a simple, small part of the total knowledge represented by your instructional objectives. In some cases, for global students, you may wish to start with a simple generalization and move to specific examples and applications.
  Pose fairly easy-to-answer questions in the first two or three frames to:

- Build a student's self-confidence.
- Demonstrate to the student that he or she can learn independently through the PLS.
- Provide the student with a couple of successful experiences by using the process of Programmed Learning Sequences.

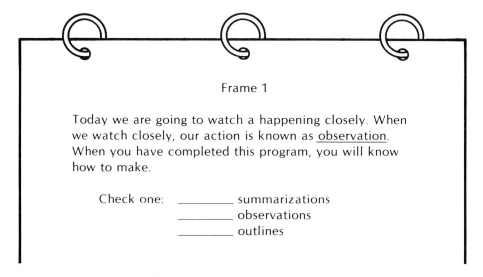

Frame 1

Today we are going to watch a happening closely. When we watch closely, our action is known as <u>observation</u>. When you have completed this program, you will know how to make.

Check one: _____ summarizations
              _____ observations
              _____ outlines

FIGURE 7–3   Initial frames in a sequence should be simple and concise. Think "small"! This example on vocabulary building is an easy-to-answer frame early in the program.

Step 9   Using a five-by-eight inch index card to represent each frame, develop a sequence that teaches a subject and, simultaneously, tests the student's growing knowledge of it.

Step 10   Refine each index card frame.

Step 11   Review the sequence to be certain that it is logical and does not teach too much on each frame.

Step 12   Check the spelling, grammar, and punctuation of each frame.

Step 13   Examine the vocabulary to be certain that it is understandable by the slowest youngsters who may use the PLS. Avoid colloquialisms that are acceptable in conversation but are less than professional in written form. Remember to use good oral language as opposed to good written language.

Step 14   Reread the entire series to be certain that each frame leads to the next one, and so on.

Step 15   When you are satisfied with the content, sequence, and questions on the frames, add colorful illustrations to clarify the main point on each index card. If you do not wish to draw, use magazine cutouts or gift wrapping paper to graphically supplement the most important sections of the text. The illustrations should relate directly to the PLS content.

Step 16   Read the written material on each frame onto a cassette so that poor readers may use the PLS by listening to the frames being read to them as they simultaneously read along. (See Chapter 6 for directions on making a tape.)

Step 17   Ask three or four of your students to try the PLS, one at a time. Observe each youngster using the material and try to identify whether any errors, omissions, or areas of difficulty exist. Correct anything that requires improvement.

Step 18   If necessary, revise the PLS based on your observations of your students' usage.

Step 19   Laminate each of the index cards that comprise the program or cover them with clear Contact paper. Student use will cause the index cards to deteriorate unless they are protected by a covering. Laminated programs have lasted for years and can be cleaned with warm water and soap. They can be written on with grease pencils, or water-soluble felt pens and then erased for use by another youngster.

Step 20   Add miniature tactual activities (Pic-A-Holes, Task Cards, or Electroboards) for reinforcement of the most important information in the PLS (see Chapter 6). The PLS, as designed through step 14, will respond only to youngsters who learn through either their visual or auditory strength. When you can add tactual reinforcements you provide youngsters who need to learn through their sense of touch with a method appropriate for them. Thus, you will add to the effectiveness of the PLS and increase the number of students who can learn successfully through it.

Step 21 Ask additional students to use the PLS.

Step 22 When you are satisfied that all the "bugs" have been eliminated, add a front and back cover (in a shape related to the topic). Place the title and global subtitle of the program onto the front cover, and, if possible, shape and illustrate the cover to represent the subject matter. Bind the covers to the index card frames. You may use notebook rings, colored yarn, or any other substance that will permit easy turning of the index cards. Be certain that the answers to each frame, which appear on the back of the previous frame, are easily readable and are not upside down. When the program has been completed, make it available to students whose learning styles are complemented by this resource.

Step 23 Design a record-keeping form so that you know which students are using and have used the program and how much of it they have completed successfully (see Figure 7–4).

Literature Programs Completed

Student	Vocab. Week 1	Test Score	Vocab Week 2	Test Score	Vocab Week 3	Test Score	Recommended Prescriptions
Adams, William	3/17	87	3/25	88	3/29	90	Continue programs.
Altman, Susan	3/9	94	3/10	93	3/15	98	Continue programs; try a contract.
Baron, Mary	3/15	82	3/21	80	3/10	85	Supplement vocab program with games.
Brice, Amy	3/9	89	3/20	81	3/23	86	Supplement vocab program with games.
Caldor, John	3/10	76	3/15	75	3/20	75	Try instructional packages.
Friedman, Joan	3/10	96	3/12	98	3/17	100	Continue programs; alternate with small groups; try a contract or two.

FIGURE 7–4 Record-keeping Form for Programmed Learning.

Sample Programs

Following are several samples of programs developed by teachers and used successfully at different levels with students whose learning styles matched the approach central to Programmed Learning Sequences.

This PLS on the Great Depression includes graphs, illustrations, Task Cards, a crossword puzzle, and a built-in Pic-A-Hole to reinforce the text for visual and tactual students. (Photographs courtesy Center for the Study of Learning and Teaching Styles, St. John's University, New York.)

The Great Depression:
Don't Let It Get You Down

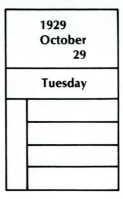

If you wish to listen to this Programmed Learning Sequence as you read, start the accompanying tape right after you read this section. Each time a question is read, turn the tape recorder off, write your answer with a grease pencil, and then turn the tape recorder on again to learn whether you were correct.

Each page in this program is called a frame. On one side of each frame, information is presented and a question is asked. Mark your answer on the frame itself with a grease pencil. Then turn the frame over to the back to see if your response was correct. If it was, move on to the next frame. If it was incorrect, study the frame to find out why. It is important to understand your mistake before you go ahead.

Here are some terms I will be using to describe that terrible time in our history. Perhaps you'll want to look at them before you read on. By the time you have finished reading my letter, you will know every one of them.

1. Depression: A severe decline in business activity, especially marked by high levels of unemployment.

2. Stock: Shares of ownership in a business which are sold to people to allow them to share some of the money earned by the company.

This Programmed Learning Sequence on "The Great Depression" was designed by Camille Sinatra, Manhasset Public Schools, Manhasset, New York.

3. <u>Stock market</u>: A place where people buy and sell stocks (which are shares in business companies).

4. <u>Dividend</u>: Money paid to a person who owns stock; the money is a share of the total amount the company earns.

5. <u>Stock market crash of 1929</u>: A sharp fall in the price of stocks in October 1929, which helped to bring about the Great Depression.

6. <u>Black Tuesday</u>: October 29, 1929, the day the stock market crashed.

7. <u>Banking panic</u>: An event that happened in February 1933, when people all over the United States withdrew their savings from banks.

8. <u>Soup kitchens</u>: Places where food was served to the needy during the Great Depression.

9. <u>Breadlines</u>: Lines of people waiting to be given food during the Great Depression.

10. <u>Lodging houses</u>: Places where the homeless could spend the night during the Great Depression.

11. <u>Prosperity</u>: A time of high production of goods and low unemployment.

12. <u>Recovery</u>: A time when the economy of a country is improving after a period of poor business activity and high unemployment.

Turn on the recorder if you wish!

Frame 1

Dear _____,

Reading about the Great Depression has really gotten me down in the dumps. Teachers are always saying that one important reason for studying history is that we must learn from our past mistakes to avoid making the same mistakes in the future. The years of the Great Depression are a time I wouldn't have wanted to live through for anything. If I thought such a thing might happen again, that would really put a damper on my spirits.

By the time you finish reading my letter, you will know all about this depressing period of our history, and you will be able to describe what it must have been like to live in the United States during the years we know as the Great Depression.

I understand that before 1929 there was a long period of prosperity (a time when many goods were being produced and most people were employed).

A time of high production of goods and low unemployment

is referrred to as _____.

Back of Frame 1

A time of high production of goods and low unemployment is referred to as <u>prosperity</u>.

Frame 2

This period of prosperity made people very ambitious and optimistic. Many people developed a get-rich-quick attitude and spent a lot of money buying stock, or shares, in companies that were doing well.

Shares of ownership in a business which are sold to people and which allow them to share some of the money

earned by the company are called _____.

Back of Frame 2

Shares of ownership in a business which are sold to people and which allow them to share some of the money earned by the company are called <u>stock</u>.

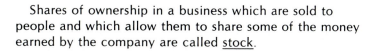

Frame 3

By 1929, so many people owned so much stock that the big companies listed on the New York Stock Exchange were paying out three times as much money in dividends as they had in 1920. The people who owned the shares of stock must have loved that!

In 1929, companies were paying three times as much

money in _____ to stock shareholders.

Back of Frame 3

In 1929, companies were paying three times as much money in <u>dividends</u> to stock shareholders as they had in 1920!

Frame 4

This boom in business could not go on forever, however. Suddenly, on October 24, 1929, everyone wanted to sell their stock and make a profit. People stopped buying stock altogether, and prices of stocks fell. This continued for five days. On October 29, 1929, a day known as Black Tuesday, came an even steeper decline and people began to panic. The greedy get-rich-quickers were losing all their money!

An even steeper drop in stock prices occurred on

_____, a day known as _____.

Back of Frame 4

An even steeper drop in stock prices occurred on October 29, 1929, a day known as Black Tuesday.

WALL ST. LAYS AN EGG

This is one of the most famous headlines from Variety, a newspaper for people in the entertainment industry.

Frame 5

The Great Stock Market Crash continued day after day until, by the middle of November, many major stocks were at rock bottom. Many people had lost thousands, even millions, of dollars!

The period during which stock prices plunged in 1929 is known as the Great Stock Market Crash. Draw an arrow on this graph showing the fall in stock prices.

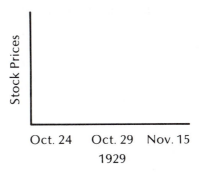

Oct. 24   Oct. 29   Nov. 15

1929

Back of Frame 5

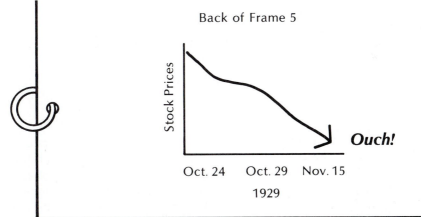

Ouch!

Oct. 24   Oct. 29   Nov. 15

1929

Frame 6

Review directions:
Use the words from the list on the bottom of this page to complete the following paragraph.

Before 1929 there was a period of high _____ and low _____, which made people very ambitious and optimistic. During this period of _____, many people spent a lot of money buying _____, or shares, in companies that were making a great deal of money. These companies were paying high _____ to the shareholders who owned stock, and everyone was very prosperous. On _____, a day known as _____, the _____ began and the period of prosperity came to a sudden end.

Black Tuesday	October 29, 1929
unemployment	production
prosperity	Great Stock Market Crash
dividends	stocks

Back of Frame 6

Before 1929 there was a period of high <u>production</u> and low <u>unemployment,</u> which made people very ambitious and optimistic. During this period of <u>prosperity</u>, many people spent a lot of money buying <u>stocks</u>, or shares, in companies that were making a great deal of money. These companies were paying high <u>dividends</u> to the shareholders who owned stock, and everyone was very prosperous. On <u>October 29, 1929</u>, a day known as <u>Black Tuesday</u>, the <u>Great Stock Market Crash</u> began and the period of prosperity came to a sudden end.

Frame 7

The 1920s period of prosperity was over. The country was in bad shape economically and about to enter a period known as the Great Depression. Although there had been many earlier periods of financial struggle in the United States, none had been as bad as this. Now the whole country was in deep trouble.

The stock market crash in 1929 was the first event of

what we call the _____.

Back of Frame 7

The stock market crash in 1929 was the first event of what we call the <u>Great Depression.</u>

Frame 8

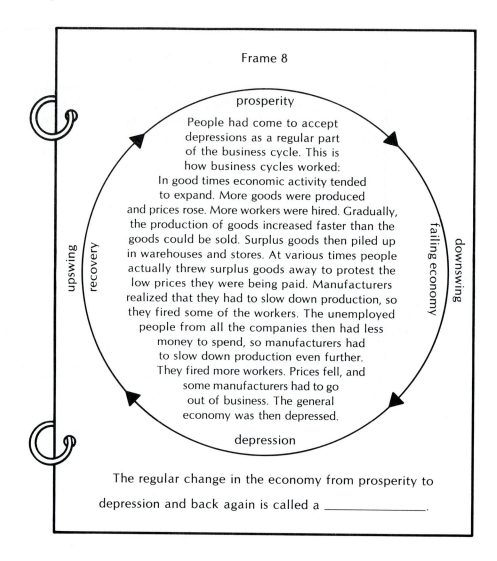

prosperity

People had come to accept depressions as a regular part of the business cycle. This is how business cycles worked: In good times economic activity tended to expand. More goods were produced and prices rose. More workers were hired. Gradually, the production of goods increased faster than the goods could be sold. Surplus goods then piled up in warehouses and stores. At various times people actually threw surplus goods away to protest the low prices they were being paid. Manufacturers realized that they had to slow down production, so they fired some of the workers. The unemployed people from all the companies then had less money to spend, so manufacturers had to slow down production even further. They fired more workers. Prices fell, and some manufacturers had to go out of business. The general economy was then depressed.

depression

upswing

recovery

failing economy

downswing

The regular change in the economy from prosperity to depression and back again is called a _____.

Back of Frame 8

The regular change in the economy from prosperity to depression and back again is called a <u>business cycle.</u>

Here farmers are dumping milk to protest the low prices of farm products.

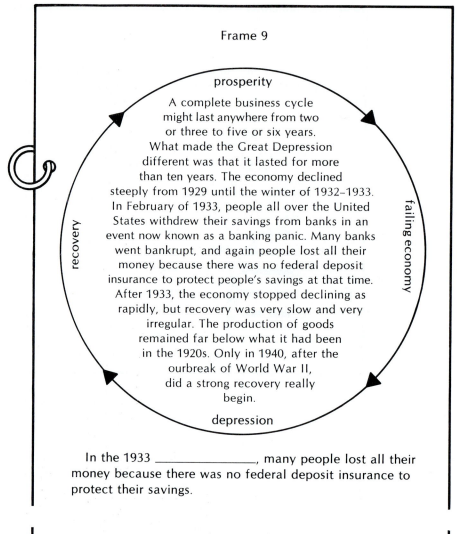

Frame 9

prosperity

recovery

failing economy

A complete business cycle might last anywhere from two or three to five or six years. What made the Great Depression different was that it lasted for more than ten years. The economy declined steeply from 1929 until the winter of 1932–1933. In February of 1933, people all over the United States withdrew their savings from banks in an event now known as a banking panic. Many banks went bankrupt, and again people lost all their money because there was no federal deposit insurance to protect people's savings at that time. After 1933, the economy stopped declining as rapidly, but recovery was very slow and very irregular. The production of goods remained far below what it had been in the 1920s. Only in 1940, after the ourbreak of World War II, did a strong recovery really begin.

depression

In the 1933 _____, many people lost all their money because there was no federal deposit insurance to protect their savings.

Back of Frame 9

In the 1933 <u>banking panic,</u> many people lost all their money because there was no federal deposit insurance to protect their savings.

Frame 10

Throughout the long period of the Depression, ten out of every one hundred people were unemployed. At the lowest point in early 1933, 25 out of every 100 people had no jobs. Less money was spent on food, clothing, furniture, automobiles, jewelry, recreation, and medical care. Many people lost their homes and took to the road looking for work. Families would camp wherever they could. Some people even erected squatters' shacks in Central Park in New York! I can just imagine how everyone's lifestyle must have changed!

During the worst period of the Great Depression,

_____ percent of the American people were unemployed.

Back of Frame 10

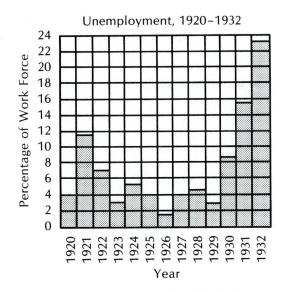

Unemployment, 1920–1932

Source: *Historical Statistics of the United States.*

During the worst period of the Great Depression,
<u>25</u> percent of the American people were unemployed.

Frame 11

From what I can tell, there must have been a great deal of human suffering and discouragement during the Great Depression. Shopkeepers who had worked hard for many years lost their businesses. Thousands of people lost all the money they had saved in bank accounts when the banks went out of business. Many people who had good jobs lost them. Students graduating from schools and colleges could not find work. People with good skills could not use them. But the weakest and poorest suffered most. Married women were fired because employers thought they did not need the work if their husbands were employed. In the Southwest, Mexican-born farm workers who were unable to find work were rounded up and shipped back to Mexico. Even some who had jobs were shipped home so that American citizens could take their places. Unemployment was also very high among blacks and other minority groups.

The term <u>depression</u> describes the mood of the people as well as the state of the _____ in the United States for ten years beginning in 1929.

Back of Frame 11

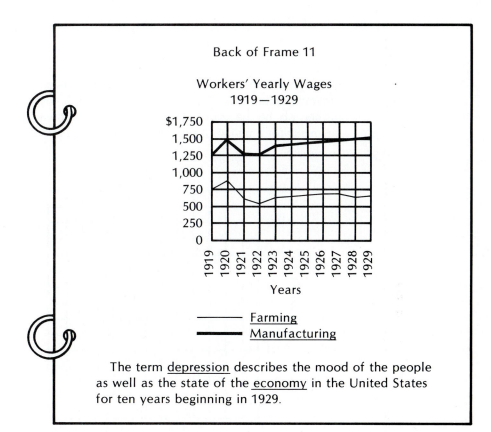

Workers' Yearly Wages
1919—1929

Years

—————— Farming
━━━━━━━ Manufacturing

The term <u>depression</u> describes the mood of the people as well as the state of the <u>economy</u> in the United States for ten years beginning in 1929.

Frame 12

Until the middle of the 1930s there was no system of umemployment insurance. If a person suddenly lost his/her job, he/she could not collect unemployment payments for a period of time until he/she found another job.

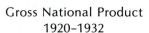

Gross National Product
1920–1932

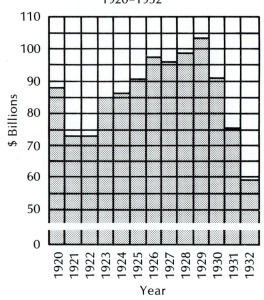

Source: *Historical Statistics of the United States.*

(The gross national product, or GNP, is the total dollar value of all goods and services produced by a country in one year. It is considered a good measure of overall economic health.)

A program that did not exist in the United States until the mid-1930s was _____ insurance.

Back of Frame 12

Fred Bell, a rich man
before the depression,
sold apples on a
San Francisco corner
in 1931...

A program that did not exist in the United States until
the mid-1930s was <u>unemployment</u> insurance.

Frame 13

There also was no national welfare assistance program to help the unemployed and their families. Welfare payments were not available to feed, clothe, and house children if their parents were out of work.

This child is standing in a soup line.

Another program that did not exist before the 1930s was

_____ assistance to help people who lose their jobs.

Back of Frame 13

Another program that did not exist before the 1930s was <u>welfare</u> assistance to help people who lose their jobs.

Frame 14

So what did people do if they desperately needed help?
Many victims of the Depression received help from
relatives and friends. Others stood on street corners trying
to sell apples or pencils. In fact, my great grandmother
told me that's what she always thinks of when she
remembers the Depression years. Some people began begging
on street corners, and others became tramps, wandering
around the country and stealing rides on railroad freight
cars. Unfortunately, other people became thieves, and still
others actually starved to death.

A young man
selling apples
from his little
cart in 1932.

During the Depression, some people became

_____ and _____.

Back of Frame 14

During the Depression some people became…any two of
the following:

beggars, thieves, tramps, street-corner salespeople,
squatters, ill and starved

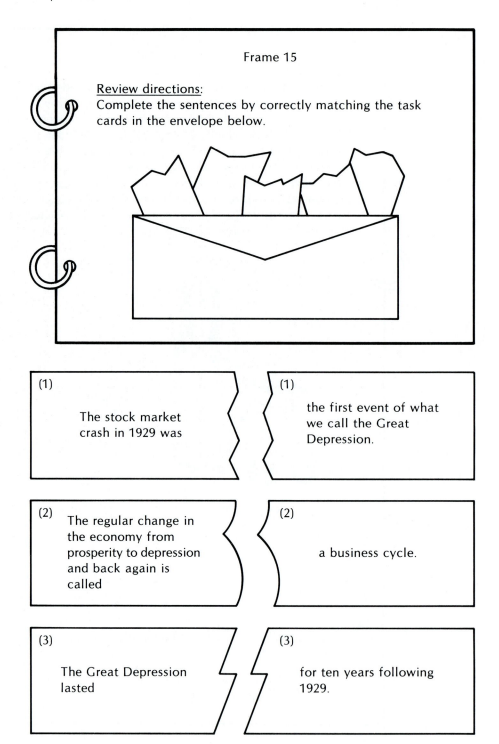

Frame 15

<u>Review directions:</u>
Complete the sentences by correctly matching the task cards in the envelope below.

(1)

The stock market crash in 1929 was

(1)

the first event of what we call the Great Depression.

(2) The regular change in the economy from prosperity to depression and back again is called

(2)

a business cycle.

(3)

The Great Depression lasted

(3)

for ten years following 1929.

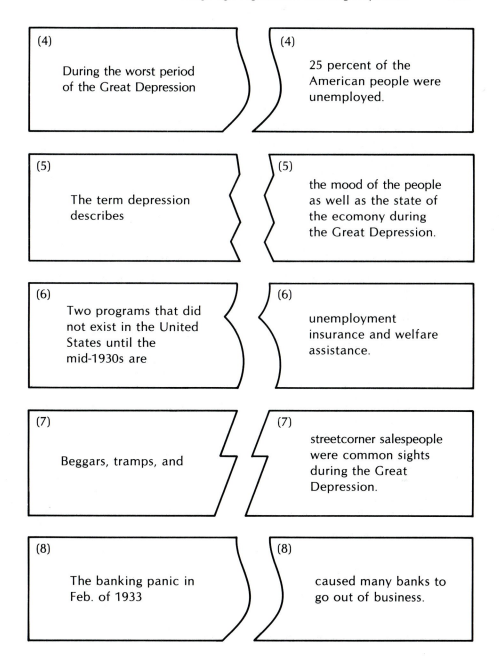

(4) During the worst period of the Great Depression

(4) 25 percent of the American people were unemployed.

(5) The term depression describes

(5) the mood of the people as well as the state of the ecomony during the Great Depression.

(6) Two programs that did not exist in the United States until the mid-1930s are

(6) unemployment insurance and welfare assistance.

(7) Beggars, tramps, and

(7) streetcorner salespeople were common sights during the Great Depression.

(8) The banking panic in Feb. of 1933

(8) caused many banks to go out of business.

Frame 16

Great efforts were made to help the jobless. Relatives tried to help the unemployed and their families, of course. State and city governments and private charities raised money to feed the poor and to provide them with a little cash for their other needs. Special "drives" were conducted to collect food and clothing for the unemployed and their families.

Some people and groups who tried to help the jobless were _____ and _____.

Back of Frame 16

Some people and groups who tried to help the jobless were...any two of the following:

city governments, state governments, relatives, private charities, those involved in community drives

Frame 17

There also were soup kitchens and breadlines where hungry people could get a free meal or free food.

A city breadline during the Great Depression.

Hungry people could get a free meal or free food at
_____ and _____.

Back of Frame 17

Hungry people could get a free meal or free food at <u>soup kitchens</u> and <u>breadlines.</u>

Frame 18

Lodging houses were opened by local communities, charitable groups, and private individuals so that the homeless might have a place to spend the night.

Homeless people could spend the night in

_____.

Back of Frame 18

Homeless people could spend the night in <u>lodging houses.</u>

Frame 19

More than any other person, President Herbert Hoover received most of the blame for failing to find solutions to the problems that plagued the nation during the Great Depression. It wasn't until the next administration and the beginning of World War II that the United States really began to recover from the economic disaster of the longest depression in history.

_____ was President during the Great Depression.

Back of Frame 19

<u>Herbert Hoover</u> was President during the Great Depression.

Frame 20

<u>Review directions</u>:
Now let's see if you understand this abysmal subject. Use the Pic-A-Hole below to review some of the important concepts about the Great Depression before you try my final quiz. Don't be glum if you miss some, chum. Just practice again before you turn the page.

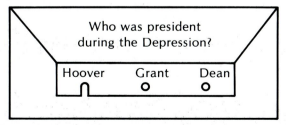

Who was president
during the Depression?

Hoover   Grant   Dean

Frame 21

Summary:
Personally, I think the American people were wrong to blame President Hoover for not being able to get them out of the fix their own greediness and lack of foresight had gotten them into. I'm really relieved that we have federal programs like unemployment insurance, welfare assistance, and federal deposit insurance now, but I would still hate to live through another Great Depression. Can you just imagine having to camp out in Central Park or in a tent next to your car?! How depressing...

   We'll be old enough to vote in a few years, and I don't know about you, but I'm going to keep a close eye on our future and try to elect people who can help the country avoid another serious depression.

Frame 22

Directions:

Use a continuity tester to match the items in Column A with the items in Column B. Every time the tester lights up, add another ten (10) points to your score.

Column A		Column B	
O	Black Tuesday, October 29, 1929	federal programs begun as a result of the Great Depression	O
O	stock market	the beginning of the Stock Market Crash	O
O	February 1933	a regular change in the economy from depression to recovery and properity.	O
O	breadlines, soup kitchens, and lodging houses	amounts of money paid to shareholders who own stock in a company	O
O	beggars, tramps, street-corner salespeople	President during the Great Depression	O
O	business cycle	what many people were forced to become during the Depression	O
O	unemployment insurance welfare assistance, and federal deposit insurance	a place where stocks are bought and sold	O
O	dividends	a severe decline in business accompanied by high unemployment	O
O	Herbert Hoover	the time of the banking panic when people lost all their savings as banks closed	O
O	depression	relief programs to help the hungry and homeless during the Depression	O

Sure hope you enjoyed my letter.
'Bye for now,
Your Friend

This heart-shaped PLS "Heart: Takes a Licking, But Keeps on Ticking," includes a tape for students who would like to hear the contents read to them and visual/tactual Task Cards (inside heart-shaped envelope) for review. (Photograph courtesy Center for the Study of Learning and Teaching Styles, St. John's University, New York.)

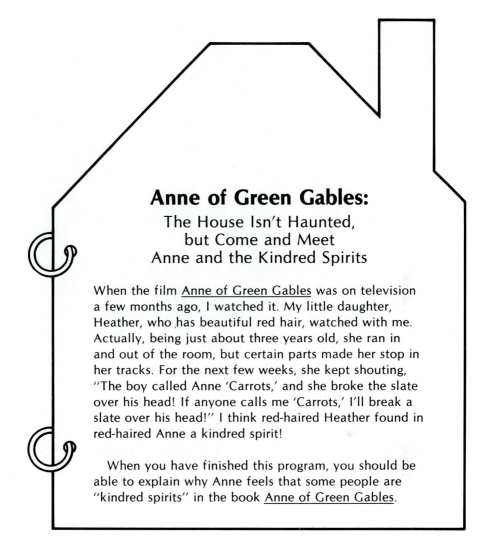

Anne of Green Gables:
The House Isn't Haunted,
but Come and Meet
Anne and the Kindred Spirits

When the film <u>Anne of Green Gables</u> was on television
a few months ago, I watched it. My little daughter,
Heather, who has beautiful red hair, watched with me.
Actually, being just about three years old, she ran in
and out of the room, but certain parts made her stop in
her tracks. For the next few weeks, she kept shouting,
"The boy called Anne 'Carrots,' and she broke the slate
over his head! If anyone calls me 'Carrots,' I'll break a
slate over his head!" I think red-haired Heather found in
red-haired Anne a kindred spirit!

When you have finished this program, you should be
able to explain why Anne feels that some people are
"kindred spirits" in the book <u>Anne of Green Gables</u>.

This Programmed Learning Sequence on *Anne of Green Gables* was designed by Vivian Valvano
Lynch, Associate Dean, St. Vincent's College, St. John's University, New York (1988).

This PLS on Anne of Green Gables was created in the shape of the house in which Anne lived and includes an accompanying tape to help nonachieving, underachieving, or insecure readers master the content. (Photograph courtesy Center for the Study of Learning and Teaching Styles, St. John's University, New York.)

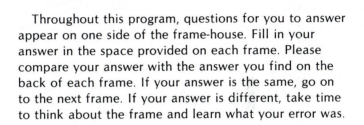

Throughout this program, questions for you to answer appear on one side of the frame-house. Fill in your answer in the space provided on each frame. Please compare your answer with the answer you find on the back of each frame. If your answer is the same, go on to the next frame. If your answer is different, take time to think about the frame and learn what your error was.

Vocabulary

These are new vocabulary words that you will use in the program.

<u>sympathetic</u>   Having the same feelings as another person; being understanding of another person because of sameness of feelings.

<u>confide</u>   To tell a secret.

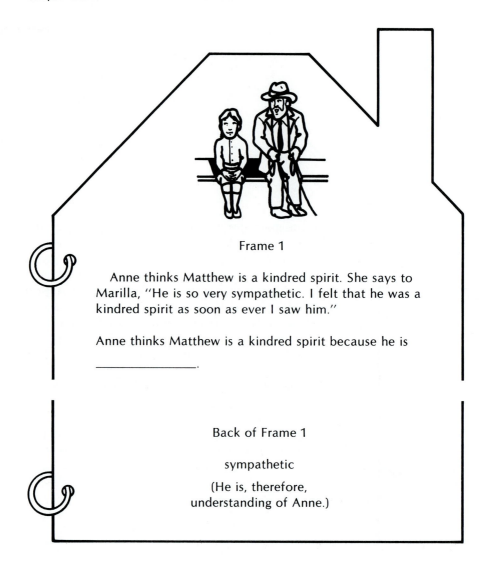

Frame 1

Anne thinks Matthew is a kindred spirit. She says to Marilla, "He is so very sympathetic. I felt that he was a kindred spirit as soon as ever I saw him."

Anne thinks Matthew is a kindred spirit because he is

_____.

Back of Frame 1

sympathetic

(He is, therefore,
understanding of Anne.)

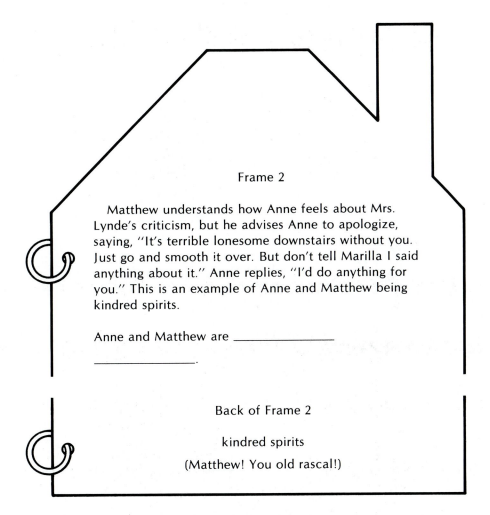

Frame 2

    Matthew understands how Anne feels about Mrs. Lynde's criticism, but he advises Anne to apologize, saying, "It's terrible lonesome downstairs without you. Just go and smooth it over. But don't tell Marilla I said anything about it." Anne replies, "I'd do anything for you." This is an example of Anne and Matthew being kindred spirits.

Anne and Matthew are _____

_____.

Back of Frame 2

kindred spirits

(Matthew! You old rascal!)

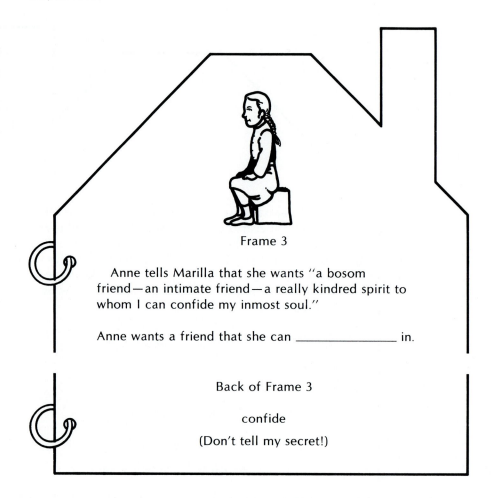

Frame 3

Anne tells Marilla that she wants "a bosom friend—an intimate friend—a really kindred spirit to whom I can confide my inmost soul."

Anne wants a friend that she can _____ in.

Back of Frame 3

confide

(Don't tell my secret!)

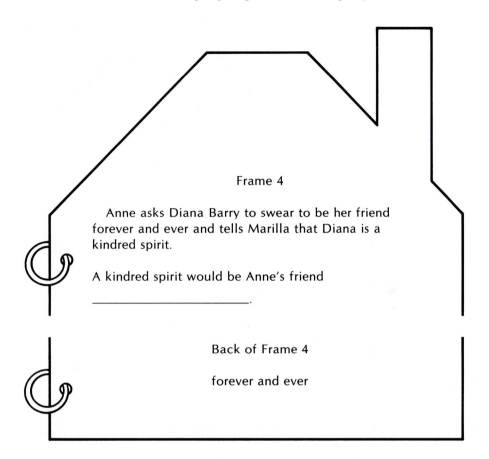

Frame 4

Anne asks Diana Barry to swear to be her friend forever and ever and tells Marilla that Diana is a kindred spirit.

A kindred spirit would be Anne's friend

_____.

Back of Frame 4

forever and ever

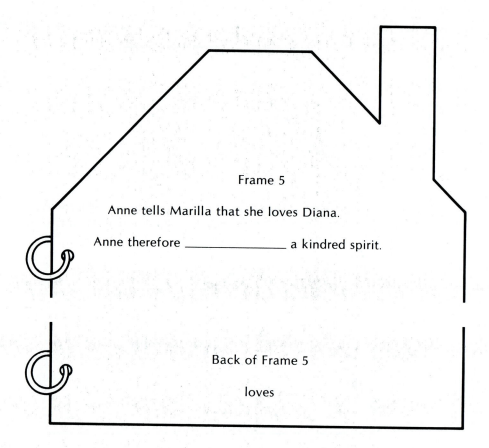

Frame 5

Anne tells Marilla that she loves Diana.

Anne therefore _____ a kindred spirit.

Back of Frame 5

loves

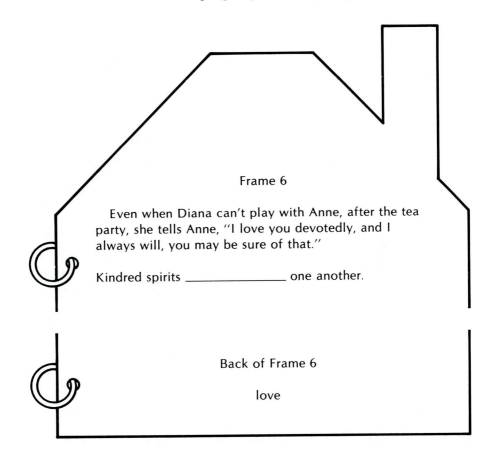

Frame 6

Even when Diana can't play with Anne, after the tea party, she tells Anne, "I love you devotedly, and I always will, you may be sure of that."

Kindred spirits _____ one another.

Back of Frame 6

love

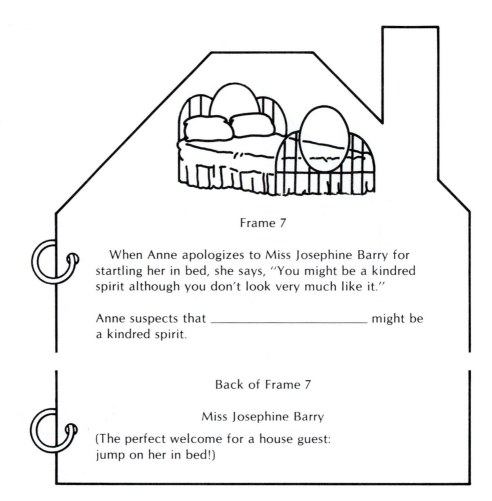

Frame 7

   When Anne apologizes to Miss Josephine Barry for startling her in bed, she says, "You might be a kindred spirit although you don't look very much like it."

Anne suspects that _____ might be a kindred spirit.

Back of Frame 7

Miss Josephine Barry

(The perfect welcome for a house guest: jump on her in bed!)

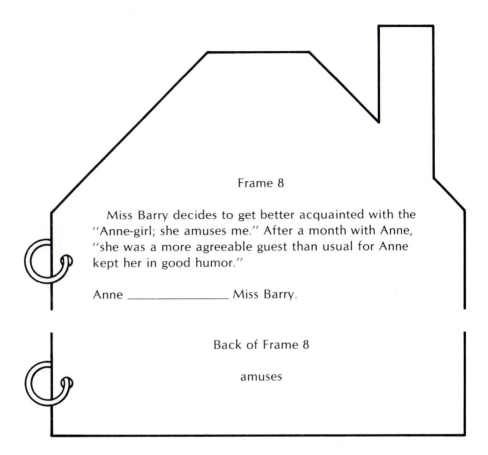

Frame 8

Miss Barry decides to get better acquainted with the "Anne-girl; she amuses me." After a month with Anne, "she was a more agreeable guest than usual for Anne kept her in good humor."

Anne _____ Miss Barry.

Back of Frame 8

amuses

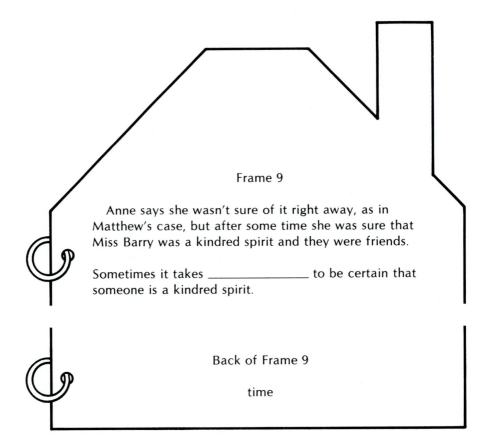

Frame 9

Anne says she wasn't sure of it right away, as in Matthew's case, but after some time she was sure that Miss Barry was a kindred spirit and they were friends.

Sometimes it takes _____ to be certain that someone is a kindred spirit.

Back of Frame 9

time

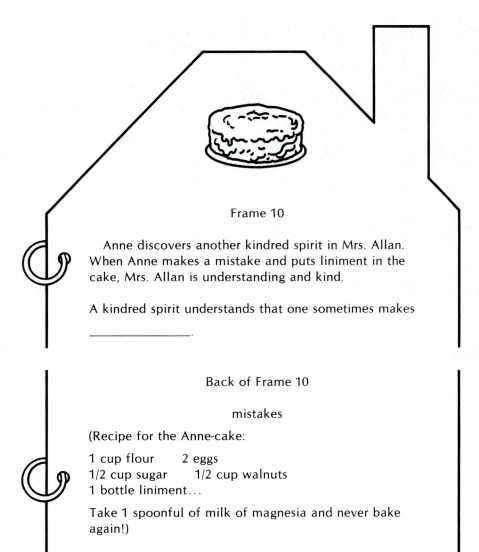

Frame 10

    Anne discovers another kindred spirit in Mrs. Allan.
When Anne makes a mistake and puts liniment in the
cake, Mrs. Allan is understanding and kind.

A kindred spirit understands that one sometimes makes

_____.

Back of Frame 10

mistakes

(Recipe for the Anne-cake:

1 cup flour   2 eggs
1/2 cup sugar   1/2 cup walnuts
1 bottle liniment...

Take 1 spoonful of milk of magnesia and never bake
again!)

Frame 11

Mini-Quiz

Complete this rhymed poem by filling in the right words. If you need help, look along the border. You'll find the answers there.

Anne Shirley is our heroine's name; Finding kindred spirits is her game.

Her bosom friend not a secret will carry; Of course, we mean _____.

A bachelor farmer, quiet and shy,

_____ likes Anne in a blink-of-an-eye.

A cake that's laced with  cannot Mrs. Allan's kindness dent.

Even Miss Josephine has to agree, "I like the Anne-girl; she _____ me."

Back of Frame 11

Quiz Answers

Diana Barry

Matthew

liniment

amuses

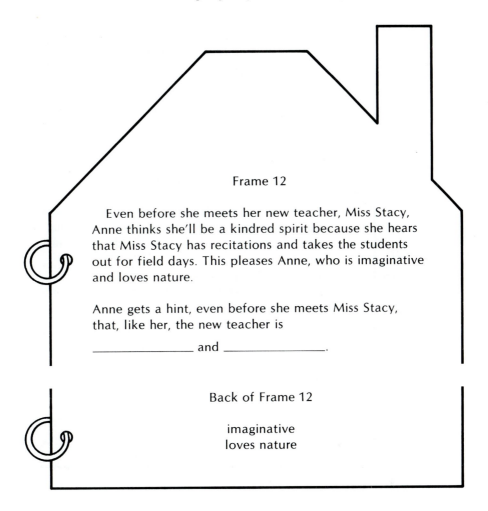

Frame 12

Even before she meets her new teacher, Miss Stacy, Anne thinks she'll be a kindred spirit because she hears that Miss Stacy has recitations and takes the students out for field days. This pleases Anne, who is imaginative and loves nature.

Anne gets a hint, even before she meets Miss Stacy, that, like her, the new teacher is

_____ and _____.

Back of Frame 12

imaginative
loves nature

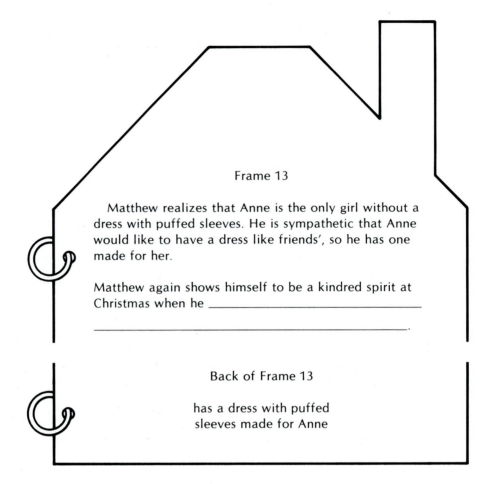

Frame 13

Matthew realizes that Anne is the only girl without a dress with puffed sleeves. He is sympathetic that Anne would like to have a dress like friends', so he has one made for her.

Matthew again shows himself to be a kindred spirit at Christmas when he _____

_____.

Back of Frame 13

has a dress with puffed
sleeves made for Anne

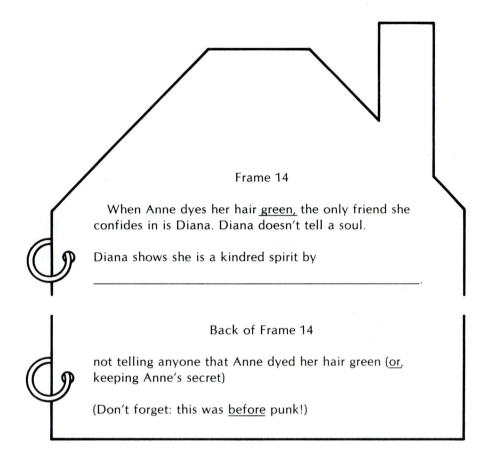

Frame 14

When Anne dyes her hair <u>green,</u> the only friend she confides in is Diana. Diana doesn't tell a soul.

Diana shows she is a kindred spirit by

_____.

Back of Frame 14

not telling anyone that Anne dyed her hair green (<u>or,</u> keeping Anne's secret)

(Don't forget: this was <u>before</u> punk!)

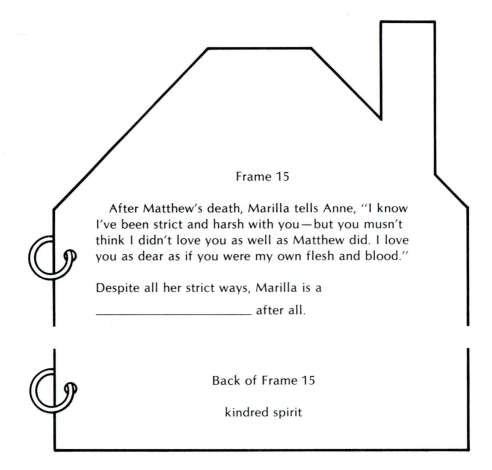

Frame 15

   After Matthew's death, Marilla tells Anne, "I know
I've been strict and harsh with you—but you musn't
think I didn't love you as well as Matthew did. I love
you as dear as if you were my own flesh and blood."

Despite all her strict ways, Marilla is a

_____ after all.

Back of Frame 15

kindred spirit

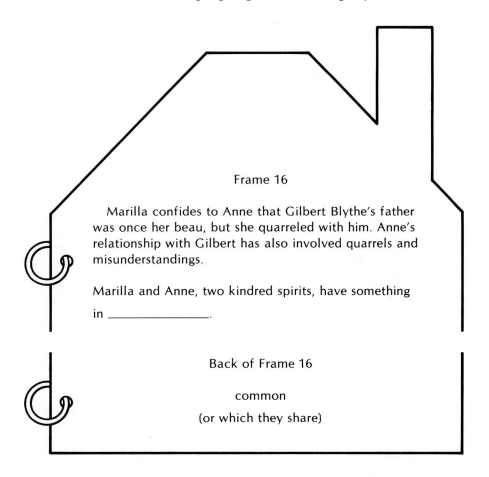

Frame 16

Marilla confides to Anne that Gilbert Blythe's father was once her beau, but she quarreled with him. Anne's relationship with Gilbert has also involved quarrels and misunderstandings.

Marilla and Anne, two kindred spirits, have something in _____.

Back of Frame 16

common
(or which they share)

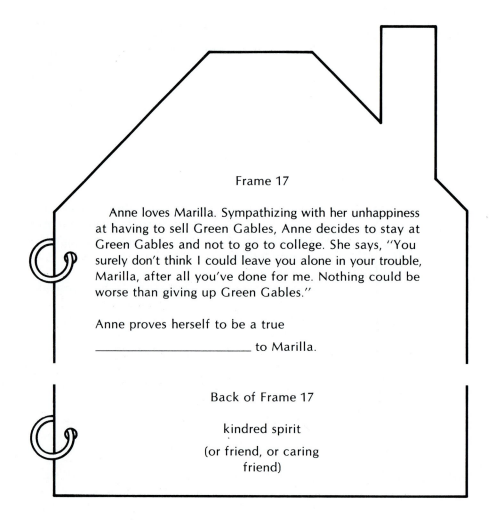

Frame 17

Anne loves Marilla. Sympathizing with her unhappiness at having to sell Green Gables, Anne decides to stay at Green Gables and not to go to college. She says, "You surely don't think I could leave you alone in your trouble, Marilla, after all you've done for me. Nothing could be worse than giving up Green Gables."

Anne proves herself to be a true

_____ to Marilla.

Back of Frame 17

kindred spirit
(or friend, or caring
friend)

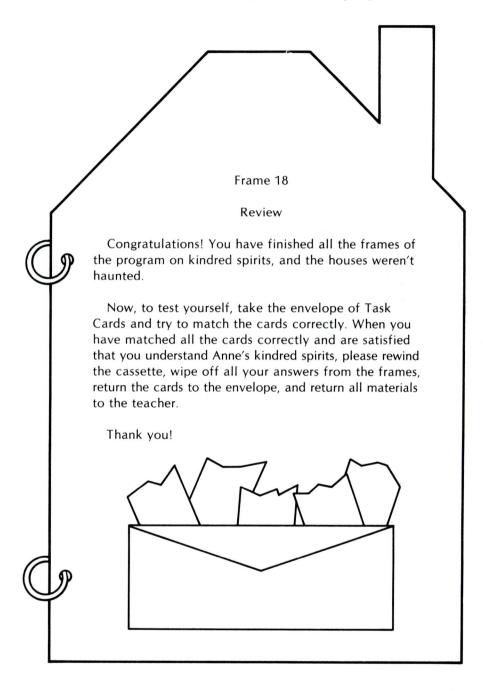

Frame 18

Review

Congratulations! You have finished all the frames of the program on kindred spirits, and the houses weren't haunted.

Now, to test yourself, take the envelope of Task Cards and try to match the cards correctly. When you have matched all the cards correctly and are satisfied that you understand Anne's kindred spirits, please rewind the cassette, wipe off all your answers from the frames, return the cards to the envelope, and return all materials to the teacher.

Thank you!

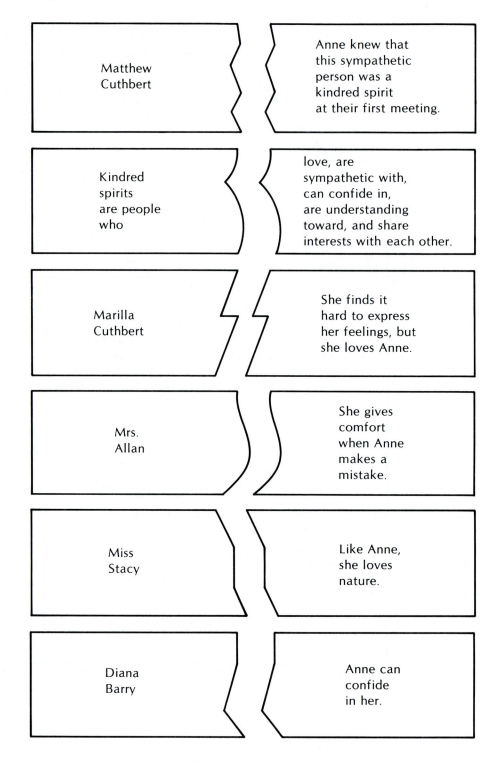

Matthew
Cuthbert

Anne knew that
this sympathetic
person was a
kindred spirit
at their first meeting.

Kindred
spirits
are people
who

love, are
sympathetic with,
can confide in,
are understanding
toward, and share
interests with each other.

Marilla
Cuthbert

She finds it
hard to express
her feelings, but
she loves Anne.

Mrs.
Allan

She gives
comfort
when Anne
makes a
mistake.

Miss
Stacy

Like Anne,
she loves
nature.

Diana
Barry

Anne can
confide
in her.

A Final Word about Programmed Learning Sequences

PLSs are the closest thing we know to a tape-recorded storybook, but they are based on the total school curriculum rather than only on literature. PLSs enable students to read text rapidly; they introduce material globally, and many adolescents are global rather than analytic. PLSs are structured but do not cause young people tension or pressure. They may be used in any environment or sociological pattern responsive to individuals' strengths. They stimulate interest; can be used without direct teaching; free the teacher to work with those who require immediate adult interactions; and can be made by parents, students, aides, and interested noneducators as well as by teachers.

PLSs are better than tape-recorded books because they (1) begin globally, thus appealing to global youngsters—the majority of our secondary population; (2) incorporate tactual devices into the frames, thus helping low auditory and low visual students reinforce through another sense; (3) are sequential, so they appeal to analytic youngsters, too; (4) reinforce every seven or eight frames to revitalize learning on an ongoing basis; and (5) are accompanied by a tape so that nonreading students or poor readers may learn content regardless of inadequate reading skills. They also (6) provide immediate feedback; (7) teach at each student's own pace; (8) question, answer, reinforce; and (9) often joke a bit—such a change from everyday instruction!

You may photocopy the PLSs in this chapter, duplicate them, and ask the students to experiment with them. You will need to read them onto a tape so that learners who use them can hear the contents being read—quietly and in relative privacy. We hope you will decide to make a PLS to teach a planned unit. If you do, check the following features to be certain you have created a PLS that can teach effectively.

The PLS should include:

1. An attractive cover in a shape related to the content
2. Both an analytic and a global title (with humor, if possible, or a clever play on words)
3. Clearly stated objectives
4. Specific directions for the students to follow (e.g., read, answer, check, wipe off, erase, put back, use the accompanying tape, handle carefully, etc.)
5. A global beginning
6. When possible, the story woven through the entire PLS
7. Interesting, upbeat phrases rather than academic directives
8. Step-by-step sequencing
9. Actual teaching with the identical concept or material repeated in different ways on several frames
10. Answers on the back of the frame, accompanied by humor, jokes, and illustrations
11. Illustrations related to the text, in color

12. Varied questioning types ("Circle"; "Write in . . . "; "Fill in the missing letters"; "Draw a line from the right side of the sheet to . . . ")
13. An accompanying tape
14. Answers provided in complete statements
15. No "Yes" or "No" answers
16. An interdisciplinary theme for global students
17. Appropriate review frames
18. Built-in tactual reviews
19. Neatness, attractiveness, legibility
20. Correct spelling and grammar
21. Original and creative touches
22. Themes or ideas related to students' interests, life-styles, or talents
23. A choice or two, at times
24. Laminated easy-to-handle frames
25. Frames that will turn in the correct position (not upside-down)

We know from experience that secondary students can create their own tactual materials—Flip Chutes, Electroboards, Pic-A-Holes, and Task Cards. If you give them the objectives, they will create simple, illustrated PLSs and *learn* the content as they create the resource. Allow two or three students to work together *if they wish to do so*. *Don't* think that they can't develop PLSs; you will be pleasantly surprised!

_8_

Designing Contract Activity Packages (CAPs) to Respond to Individual Learning Styles

Contract Activity Packages (CAPs) are one of the three basic methods of individualizing instruction. The other two, Programmed Learning Sequences (PLSs) and Multisensory Instructional Packages (MIPs), are described in Chapters 7 and 9. Sample CAPs, PLSs, and MIPs all have been designed to teach the same objectives. Thus, three diverse strategies are available to respond to three different basic learning style patterns and different ability and performance levels. Generally, CAPs are appropriate for average or above-average, gifted, and or nonconforming (LSI scores of below 40 on Responsibility) students. In addition to responding to specific learning style differences among learners, Contract Activity Packages are more effective than a large-group lecture or question-and-answer discussion for the following reasons:

Self-Pacing

When we stand before a group of students and explain what we are trying to teach, youngsters can absorb the content only as quickly as we are able to relate it. Given different resources through which to learn, many youngsters could achieve more rapidly than some of their classmates. Others, of course, find that the flow of our words is too rapid for them to understand fully. We teachers cover in each lesson what we believe the majority of students in that group are capable of assimilating, but we proceed with the full knowledge that some are capable of learning much more than they are being exposed to in a given time, whereas others are capable of learning only a fragment of what we are highlighting. We understand that the lecture method is effective for only a percentage of students, but for the most part we have not replaced it with better techniques.

If we teach too much too quickly, we are bound to lose the less able student. If we keep a pace that is slow enough so that the less able student may keep abreast, we unwittingly irritate or bore the brighter youngster. If we try to vary the pace to provide interest, both groups may miss important information during the presentation.

In contrast to a group lecture, Contract Activity Packages permit individual pacing so that students may learn as quickly or as slowly as they are able to master the material. In addition, youngsters are neither embarrassed because others grasp the content more quickly than they do, nor bored because they must wait for classmates to catch up with them before the class is introduced to the next knowledge or skill area. Each learner works independently but may, by choice, team up with classmates who can pace themselves similarly.

Varied Academic Levels

Whenever we address an entire class, instruction is, of necessity, geared to the academic level of the largest number of children present. We all know, however, that in every group some can absorb information in its simplest form, whereas others first become interested when the concepts become complex and challenging. Auditory students can hear something once and retain it, whereas others require extensive reinforcement before they are capable of either understanding or remembering. Those who learn easily in class are likely to be bored by the detailed repetition that certain classmates require; those who learn slowly may become frustrated by their inability to acquire the knowledge that their counterparts do with ease. In contrast to a group lecture, Contract Activity Packages can be designed so that students can function on their current academic level but master concepts or facts through resources that clarify the content because of their style responsiveness. This may be accomplished in four ways:

1. Resource Alternatives teach the required objectives at different reading levels.
2. Activity Alternatives require application of the content.
3. Reporting Alternatives cause review of the content with peer discussion and, if necessary, correction.
4. Small-group techniques provide another instructional strategy through peer learning.

Independence

When we speak to a large group, students are dependent on us for their intellectual growth and stimulation. Further, each youngster is required to learn the same thing at the same time to the same extent and in the same way. Since learners differ from one another in ability, achievement, interests, and learning styles, their dependence on us as a primary source seriously limits the academic progress of some. Finally, despite our skills and sensitivities as teachers, it is important to recognize that some students learn better through a multimedia approach, computer programs, simulations, projects, or tactual/kinesthetic resources than they do from an articulate, knowledgeable adult, and that the large-group lecture does not enable them to learn easily. Since nature has endowed each person with unique sensory strengths and limitations, many students are able to learn more and learn it better by beginning with visual, tactual, or kinesthetic resources rather than through an auditory approach—which is what a lecture or discussion is.

Through the use of Contract Activity Packages, youngsters become personally responsible for learning what is required. They are given specific objectives and a choice of media resources through which they may learn. Although they are told exactly what they must master, they are given no indication of which resources contain the necessary answers. Because of their exposure to a variety of materials in their search for the explicit information in their objectives, students obtain a great deal of ancillary knowledge. Often the required concepts are included in several resources, thus providing multisensory repetition.

Moreover, because students may select the resources they use (from a list of approved ones), the self-selection factor improves their motivation, reduces their nonconformity inclinations, and permits them to work in ways in which they feel most comfortable. Self-pacing permits them to learn as quickly as they can, but well enough to retain what they have studied. As they become accustomed to exercising freedom of choice and assuming responsibility, they become increasingly independent of their teacher and learn to use resources to their advantage. They begin to recognize that they can learn easily and well by themselves, and gradually they develop sufficient confidence to move into new studies and design their own resources. They eventually take pride in their ability to teach themselves, and ultimately they use the teacher as a guide and facilitator rather than as a fountain of knowledge from which to absorb information.

Teachers who believe that the greatest gifts they can give to their students are a love of learning and the tools to teach themselves easily will enjoy the effects of contracting. Those who teach for the self-gratification of having students serve as an admiring audience for their performances will find it more difficult to encourage independent learning and to adapt instructional strategies to their students' learning styles. Nevertheless, for optimal learning to occur, those teachers will need to identify the students who require an authority figure, those who learn by listening, those who are able to learn at the time of day when they are scheduled for classes, those who can remain seated passively for the length of each class or subject period, and those who are so motivated that they will learn merely because the teacher suggests or projects that it is important to do so.

Reduced Frustration and Anxiety

If education is important, as the compulsory education laws imply, then everyone should become educated. If everyone should be educated, everyone should be encouraged to learn as well and as quickly as is possible—for that person. Since the majority of youngsters are neither gifted nor extremely bright, imagine how discouraged they must feel every day of the week when they realize that they must use all their resources to live up to the teacher's expectations while a few of their classmates exert little effort and invariably appear to know all the answers.

Although some successfully hide their anxiety, many verbalize that they don't like school while others drop out even as they occupy their seats in the classroom. Despite the fact that both national and state commissions have recommended the development of alternative programs that respond to "the great diversity of students and needs . . . within the schools" (Rise Report, 1975), innovative or different approaches to learning often are suspect and are expected to continually produce higher academic achievement and more positive student attitudes than are evidenced in traditional educational settings.

Contract Activity Packages reduce student anxiety and frustration without requiring extensive changes in class organization. They can be used in a self-contained classroom at any level and with many students. Youngsters are permitted to learn in ways that they find most amenable—by themselves, with a peer or two, in a small group, with the teacher, through resources of their choice, at their seats, on the floor, and so on.

When students are permitted to learn through this method, it is important that rules be established to indicate clearly those behaviors that are acceptable and to insist that these regulations be adhered to firmly. It is also important that students be trusted to proceed seriously and to accomplish their objectives. Youngsters who do not work effectively on their CAPs should be cautioned and advised that they will not be permitted to continue learning in this way unless they achieve a certain minimum grade on each examination related to their studies. Research has demonstrated that, in many cases, teachers are unable to identify the special learning styles of youngsters. Instead, they teach all students in the ways the teachers feel most comfortable. When learning style strengths are complemented, however, student motivation and achievement increase significantly (see Appendix A). Moreover, independence is enhanced when students are allowed to take CAPs to the library, study areas, or their homes to pursue them at the right time of day, in quiet or with music, with food or not, and so forth.

Capitalizing on Individual Student Interests

All students must learn to read, to write, to express themselves well, and to compute. Beyond these *musts,* however, there is no curriculum that every student everywhere should, of necessity, master. There is no need for every youngster to know the annual rainfall in exotic places or to commit to memory foreign products, capital cities, rivers, and other such extraneous facts that make up the required curriculum for many classes. It is equally ludicrous for every student to be required to study algebra, a foreign language, industrial arts, music appreciation, or many of the subjects in a standard curriculum. We understand that the intent of extensive exposure to a variety of different studies is to expand the horizons and interests of students—but the opposite often occurs. When youngsters are forced to take specific subjects without choice, they often become recalcitrant and negative.

Perhaps schools might experiment with a series of cluster subjects, such as those that are found in most curricula, and offer their students a choice of any four out of seven, or five out of eight. It is true that some students might never be exposed to social studies, or literature, or the arts, but we suggest that most would learn in depth the areas that they do select to study. As Mager and McCann (1963) suggest, motivation increases with the amount of control we exercise over what, when, and how we learn.

If you believe it is necessary for all students to learn the conventional school curriculum, consider the topics that we seldom if ever discuss in school that often touch their lives directly—divorce, pollution, racism, sex roles, poverty, the energy crisis, inflation. A Contract Activity Package can be used to introduce these and other topics of interest to those for whom they will have value. CAPs, therefore, will free you to direct your major energies toward, first, students who need direct interaction with you and, second, subjects that require mastery by all—reading, language, computational skills, and interpersonal values. Basic knowledge in other areas can easily be added to interdisciplinary themes through the use of additional CAPs and other teaching strategies.

Learning Style Characteristics
Responsive to Contract Activity Packages

Contract Activity Packages are responsive to most learning style characteristics, for they may be used flexibly with some students and with a precise structure for others, as described in the following examples:

1. For students who need sound, an earplug may be used to isolate radio or recorded music for those who benefit from it. If discussion is important, an instructional area (such as a Learning Station or Interest Center) can be established in a section of the room and blocked off by perpendicular dividers to provide an inner sanctum for its occupants and to protect their classmates from being distracted by movement or talk. Rules for discussion need to be established so that no one outside the instructional area hears the words of anyone inside, but that is a management strategy that will be necessary whenever you begin to accommodate the classroom to individual learning styles.

Motivated, visual students may work alone and learn the information required by the Contract Activity Package's (CAPs) objectives through their choice of a variety of Resource Alternatives (books, transparencies, films, filmstrips, videotapes, television programs, tapes, lectures, games, interviews, trips, simulated experiences, or tactual manipulatives) which respond to their learning style strengths at an appropriate level of difficulty. (Photograph courtesy Center for the Study of Learning and Teaching Styles, St. John's University, New York.)

The youngster who requires silence can use another instructional area where no one may speak and where the adjacent dens or alcoves are used for essentially quiet activities.

2. When students are permitted to work on their CAPs anywhere in the classroom as long as they work quietly, do not interrupt others, and respect the rules that have been established, they will automatically adjust light, temperature, and design to their learning style characteristics.

3. The motivated, persistent, and responsible students should be given a series of objectives to complete, a list of the resources that they may use to obtain information, suggestions for how and where to get help should they experience difficulty, and an explanation of how they will be expected to demonstrate their achievement of the objectives. They then should be permitted to begin working and to continue—with occasional spot-checking—until their task has been completed. The unmotivated, the less persistent, and those who tend to be less responsible should be given only a few objectives, the listing of resources that may be used, and suggestions for obtaining assistance when they

Students may work on their CAPs either in a conventional seat and desk or in an informal design. (Photographs courtesy of Blake Middle School, Hopkins, Minnesota, and Brockport High School, Brockport, New York.)

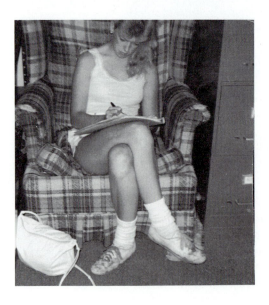

need it. These youngsters, however, require frequent supervision and constant encouragement and praise for their progress. You will need to circulate among them, ask questions, check on their understanding of what they are doing, and comment favorably when you observe their efforts. Were you to treat the motivated students in the same way, you would be interrupting their concentration and diverting them. But if you don't check on the unmotivated students when they have difficulty with an assignment, they will become frustrated, get involved in diversionary activities, or give up.

4. The CAP permits students to work either alone, with a friend or two, or as part of a team through the small-group activities that are included. Youngsters also may work directly with the teacher when difficult objectives require adult assistance.

5. The Resource Alternatives section of the CAP includes auditory, visual, and tactual or kinesthetic (T/K) resources (at different levels), thus permitting students to learn through their strongest perceptual strength and to reinforce what they've learned through the next strongest sense or senses. The CAP may be used anytime—during the early morning hours, after dinner—to match the individual learner's best time of day for concentrating and producing. Further, youngsters may snack on raw vegetables or other nutritious foods

A strong need to work in pairs can be accommodated for completion of either all or part of a Contract Activity Package merely by allowing students to study in ways responsive to their sociological preferences (60 or above on the Learning Style Inventory *Individual Printout). (Photographs courtesy of Franklin Township Middle and High Schools, Franklin Township, Indiana.)*

if they feel the need to, and they also may take short breaks for relaxation—as long as they return to their objectives and continue working on them until they have been completed. You are encouraged to experiment with CAPs for students who have the potential for mastering objectives either alone or with a classmate or two. However, when a youngster using a CAP does not perform well on the final assessment for that topic, immediately transfer him or her to another instructional approach, such as a PLS, an MIP, or T/K resources. CAPs are *best* for motivated, auditory, or visual learners; they also are responsive to nonconformists.

Basic Principles of Contract Activity Packages

A Contract Activity Package is an individualized educational plan that facilitates learning because it includes each of the following elements:

1. *Simply stated objectives that itemize exactly what the student is required to learn:* Do you recall studying for a test in college and trying to determine the important items on which you might be tested? Teaching at all levels is often conducted in an atmosphere of mystery; we introduce many concepts, facts, and skills and then require students to intuit those items that, in our opinion, are worthy of commitment to memory and retention. This approach, though common, is not logical. If specific knowledge is worthwhile, we ought to indicate that to our students and then encourage them to learn those things so well that they retain them. Knowing what is expected is central to individual motivation.

Instead of continuing the pedagogical game of "I'll teach many things, and you try to guess which I'll include on the test!," we recognize that all students cannot learn everything that we teach—because of their individual abilities, experiences, interests, and learning style differences. We then diagnose each student to identify whether he or she is capable of learning many

"Ancient Greece: It Burns a Torch for You" includes multiple instructional resources through which students with different learning styles may master the identical objectives through resources responsive to their individual strengths. They then apply the information they mastered through Activity Alternatives— original creative activities in which students demonstrate their new knowledge. They share their completed Activity Alternatives through Reporting Alternatives in which classmates use, and simultaneously check and/or correct, the original products. Small-group techniques are available for teamed interactions when students are peer-oriented. An assessment at the end permits students to determine how much they have learned and what still needs to be mastered. (Photographs courtesy Center for the Study of Learning and Teaching Styles, St. John's University, New York.)

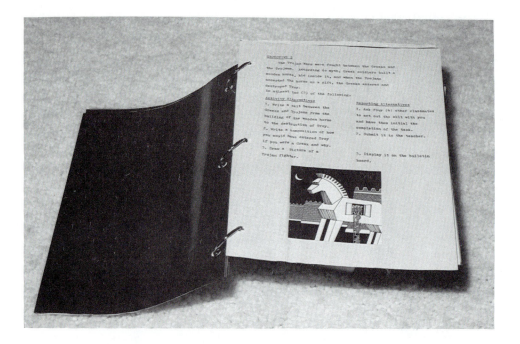

things sequentially (60 or above on Persistence) or just a few things in a series of short, multiple assignments (40 or below on Persistence), which can then be prescribed as a lesson, Contract Activity Package, Programmed Learning Sequence, or Multisensory Instructional Package. Motivated, persistent, responsible students may be given longer tasks to complete; their opposites should be given many, shorter tasks. Brighter students may be assigned a number of things to master; slower achievers should be given several shorter prescriptions.

When we tell youngsters what they are expected to achieve, we have given them their objectives. When we also explain the ways in which they may demonstrate that they have mastered their objectives, we are giving them a statement that is called a *behavioral objective*. More information about how to write objectives for students is provided in the next section of this chapter.

When students are given simple statements that itemize those objectives for which they are responsible, they need not be concerned about *everything* but can focus on just the tasks that they must master. This freedom from unnecessary anxiety reduces stress and permits them to proceed to and learn required objectives and aspects of specific interest to them.

    2. *Multisensory Alternative Resources that teach the information that the objectives indicate must be mastered:* Students are given a list of available resources that they may use to learn the information required by their objectives. The resources should be multisensory: visual materials such as books, films, filmstrips, study prints, computer programs, or transparencies; auditory materials such as Task Cards, Learning Circles, and games; and interesting kinesthetic materials such as body games or extremely large tactual devices. The resources are *suggested* sources of information, but the students are free either to use them or to identify other instructional materials through which they may learn. If students use resources that have not been listed in the teacher-designed Contract Activity Package, they must identify them by direct reference when demonstrating the knowledge they have gained. Because youngsters are free to select the materials through which they will learn, the choices are called *Resource Alternatives*. It is important, of course, to help students recognize their perceptual strengths so that they use Resource Alternatives that respond to their strongest sense to introduce information, and materials that respond to their next strongest senses to reinforce what they have learned.

Some authority-oriented, conforming students (60 or above on Authority Figure Present, Teacher Motivated, and Responsibility) learn best with interaction and direct feedback from their teacher. Thus, Robert Ballinger questions his French students concerning their findings with a Learning Circle designed to introduce new vocabulary and their completion of Activity Alternatives responsive to specific objectives. (Photographs courtesy Worthington High School, Worthington, Ohio.)

3. *A series of activities through which the information that has been mastered is used in a creative way:* When we first became involved in individualizing instruction in 1967, we used Learning Activity Packages (LAPs) that included behavioral objectives, special and assigned readings, resources through which to learn (which were called "activities"), and a posttest by which to assess the student's progress. We found that students were able to examine their objectives, use the resources, acquire the necessary information, and pass the test at the end of the LAP. Three months later, however, the average retention rate was approximately 58 percent.

When experimenting with alternatives to LAPs, we found that if we added two procedures to the existing system, we could increase students' ability to remember information that only had been learned by approximately 20 percent. The first was a series of activities in which students were required to use the information they had learned in a creative way. On the basis of Mager and McCann's studies completed in 1963, we gave students a choice from among approved alternatives of the activities they would complete. This section of the CAP is thus called *Activity Alternatives.* Activity Alternatives may be labeled A (auditory), V (visual), T (tactual), or K (kinesthetic). They provide multisensory options that match perceptual strength and learning style.

4. *A series of alternative ways in which creative instructional resources developed by one student may be shared with one or more—but no more than six to eight—classmates:* The second procedure that tends to increase retention for peer-oriented students is called *Reporting Alternatives.* We found that when students engage in a creative activity, they often want to share it with their peers. The sharing serves as either an introduction or a reinforcement of the material to the person who is being shown the activity, but it also provides the person who created it with reinforcement and a sense of accomplishment. This sharing—or reporting—increases retention of what has been learned and, in addition, serves as a self-fulfilling experience for some. Teaching others often promotes learning for the "student" teacher.

5. *At least three small-group techniques:* Individualization does not imply that children must work or learn in isolation. Rather, it suggests that each student's learning style be identified and that each learner be permitted to achieve in ways that complement his or her style. Since many students prefer to work in small groups or in a pair (Poirier, 1970), and since others evidence this preference when their requirements become difficult, at least three small-group techniques (of the teacher's choice) are added to each Contract Activity Package so that sections of the CAP that are difficult may be attacked (and conquered) by a few students working together. A Team Learning to teach each difficult objective should *always* be included among or in addition to the three small-group techniques.

Although the small-group requirements are not mandated for every youngster, they do serve as an aid for students who find it difficult to complete intricate tasks or to learn difficult concepts by themselves.

6. *A pretest, a self-test, and a posttest:* Each Contract Activity Package has a single test attached to it. This test may be used to assess the student's knowledge of the information required by the CAP's behavioral objectives before the CAP is assigned, so that students who have already mastered those concepts and skills need not be burdened with the same subject matter again. To avoid loss of motivation, the pretest should be eliminated in all cases where the teacher knows scores will be very low.

This pretest assessment also may be used as a self-assessment by the student to identify how much of the information required by the behavioral objectives he or she has already mastered and how much remains to be learned even after he or she has ostensibly completed the CAP. Self-assessment builds ownership of the contract and its objectives. Self-testing reduces stress and promotes self-confidence.

Finally, we may use the same assessment to test the student after resources have been used, the Activity Alternatives have been completed and shared with selected classmates, the three small-group techniques have been done, the self-test has been taken, and the behavioral objectives have been mastered. If you wish, you may develop three separate assessment devices, but since the test questions are directly related to the individual behavioral objectives, it is just as valuable to use the identical test for all three situations. This approach establishes a pattern of revealing what is expected, removes the mystery, and builds motivation. Should you become concerned about rote memorization of answers, you can change the order of the questions on the final CAP test. Your students' confidence and interest will be retained.

Step-by-Step Guide to Designing a Contract Activity Package

The first Contract Activity Package that you design takes time because you must adopt several new techniques with which you may be relatively unfamiliar. The second CAP is not difficult to write at all, and by the time you embark on your third, you'll be helping colleagues and administrators by explaining the process and the reasons for each stage. Most secondary students are capable of designing their own CAPs after they have worked successfully with three or four. Initially, you may want to provide the objectives and permit them to design the remaining parts. Eventually they will be able to create complete CAPs—whether alone or with a friend or two (see Chapter 10).

The design and creation of games, charts, stories, tapes, films, filmstrips, cartoons, Flip Chutes, Electroboards, Task Cards, Pic-A-Holes, Learning Circles, floor games, Programmed Learning Sequences, and other Activity Alternatives aid students in applying and remembering the difficult information they are required to learn. (Photographs courtesy of Center for the Study of Learning and Teaching Styles, St. John's University, New York.)

Step 1 Begin by identifying a topic, concept, or skill that you want to teach. Write the name of the topic, concept, or skill that you have decided to teach as a title at the top of a blank sheet of paper. There are two kinds of CAPs. The first, a curriculum CAP, covers a topic that you would like to teach to all or most of the students in your class. The second, an individual CAP, is designed for a topic in which only one or a few students might be interested. Because we are assuming that this is your first effort at CAP development, we suggest that you identify a topic that would be appropriate for most of your students. When you have completed this first CAP, you will have the skills to write as many as you wish—some for individuals, others for small groups, and the majority for use with an entire class at different times during the semester. The Center for the Study of Learning and Teaching Styles at St. John's Uni-

Sharing Activity Alternatives or reporting them to others further reinforces knowledge because the creators of the materials teach to classmates the information they used when making the original resource. The students with whom they share their projects examine, evaluate (in terms of correctness only), and also learn from the newly designed material. Moreover, the Activity Alternatives can be used as future Resource Alternatives the next time the same unit is taught. (Photographs courtesy Center for the Study of Learning and Teaching Styles, St. John's University, New York.)

versity provides excellent sample CAPs at almost cost to practitioners who prefer to follow perfected ones as a guide.

Curriculum contracts, once they are colored and laminated, will remain useful for years. Sharing copied CAPs and building a library of varied topics will provide an expanding resource for schools and districts. Gifted students, parents, aides, and education majors at local colleges can assist in the effort to stock a central "bank" of effective and valuable CAPs. All CAPs may be duplicated for multiple use by teachers in the appropriate subject classrooms.

Step 2 Develop a humorous or clever global subtitle.

Examples

"The Brain: or Getting Your Head Together"
"Life in the Universe: Give Me Some Space"
"Electricity: The Shocking Truth"
"Graphics: Get the Point?"
"DNA: The Double Helix Is Not a Roller Coaster Ride"

Step 3 List the things about this topic that you believe are so important that every student in your class should learn them. Then list the things about this topic that are important, but that slow achievers need not necessarily learn. Finally, consider the things about this topic that might appeal to special students—for example, the musician, the artist, the traveler, the carpenter, the cook, and so on. List these as special interest items.

Examine your developing list of objectives. Be certain that the most important ones to be learned are placed first. These should be followed by items that are also of consequence but that everyone need not necessarily master. Finally, add the items that you believe might be of interest to students with special talents or interests. Objectives concerning sports, dance, drama, music, or the culinary arts often increase interest when related to subject matter content.

All the most important items will become the required learning for your students. Many of the secondary list of important items will be required, but students should be given some choices among these items. Thus, the way in

At least three small-group techniques like Team Learning (to introduce difficult material), Circle of Knowledge (to reinforce it), Brainstorming (for problem solving), Role playing, and Simulations (for analyzing and reinforcing) are included in each Contract Activity Package. (Photographs courtesy of North Chicago High School, North Chicago, Illinois, Corsicana High School, Corsicana, Texas, and Robeson High School, Chicago, Illinois.)

which you assign the number of required objectives will help you personalize the CAP according to individual achievement and/or interest levels.

When the CAP is completed and ready for use, assign the first group of required objectives to all. Remember that motivation is increased by options— so if you can permit students some choice, even among the first objectives, you will observe nonconformists beginning to evidence interest in the assignment. For example, you might say that the class must master "any seven of the following nine objectives." Some teachers suggest: "Complete the first three and any additional five of your choice." Another alternative would be, "Do any three in the first group, numbers 1 to 3 in the second group, and any two in the third group." In short order, many gifted students will complete the most difficult questions, design two or three objectives of their own, or create an entire CAP!

Step 4 Translate the important items into behavioral objectives. When students are given a list of items that should be learned, these items are called *objectives,* and they become the students' short-term instructional goals. Be-

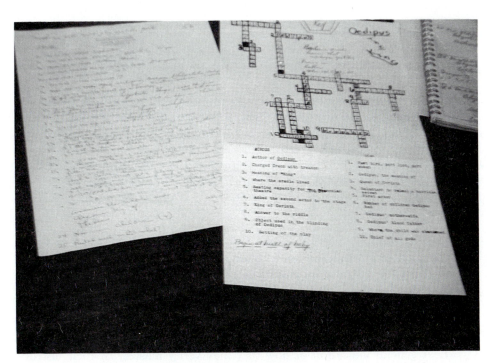

Crossword puzzles, scrambled definitions, and other challenging strategies may be added to review the content that needs to be learned. (Photograph courtesy Center for the Study of Learning and Teaching Styles, St. John's University, New York.)

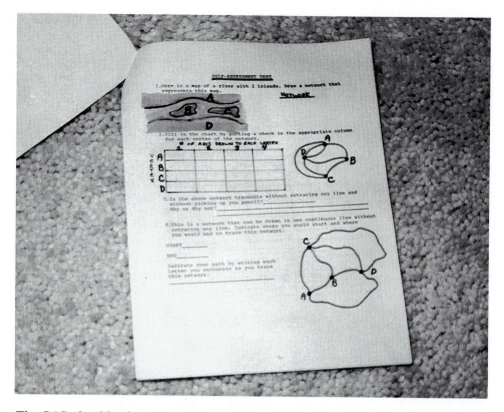

The CAP should culminate in a self-assessment test to show what has already been mastered and what remains to be studied again. The self-assessment also builds confidence in test-taking. The questions in the test relate directly to the CAP's objectives, but no answers are given. It is the student's responsibility to find the correct answers and determine how well he or she has progressed. It is permissible to study for the self-assessment alone, in a pair, or in a small group. (Photograph courtesy Center for the Study of Learning and Teaching Styles, St. John's University, New York.)

cause acquired information can be demonstrated in many ways, it is important that youngsters be given an idea of how they will be expected to demonstrate what they have mastered. Recognizing individual differences, we acknowledge that people are capable of evidencing knowledge through different skills and talents. We therefore give students:

1. A general indication of how they may verify mastery of their instructional objectives and
2. Specific alternatives to increase their motivation, diffuse their nonconformity inclinations, and capitalize on their strengths.

Many years ago, Mager (1962) suggested that a behavioral objective should include the following:

1. An identification and name of the overall behavioral act
2. The conditions under which the behavior was to occur
3. The criterion of acceptable performance

After years of working with objectives, we are convinced that when all three items are included, the objectives become too long and complicated for most students to comprehend; are not individualized, and therefore do not respond to learning style, interest, ability levels, or talents; and are not used as efficiently or as humanistically as is possible.

Therefore, we suggest that behavioral objectives—which list the behaviors that may be used to demonstrate mastery of specific learning goals—be written in the following generalized way, and that specific behaviors that may be used to demonstrate acquired knowledge or skills be *optional* through a series of Activity Alternatives. Further, the action prescribed at the beginning of the behavioral objectives should be direct and explicit—for example, list, divide, collect, identify, predict. See Figures 8-1 (subject applications) and 8-2 (general application for appropriate samples).

Example
Identify five major causes of World War II.

This objective clearly indicates what must be learned, but it does not restrict learners to explaining in a specific way. Because the causes of World War II can be described in many different ways, we give the students a choice of how they will show that they know the answer by listing a series of Activity Alternatives directly below the behavioral objective and permitting each individual to decide which of the activities he or she prefers.

Step 5 Design at least three or four Activity Alternatives for each behavioral objective (or for a group of related objectives) so that students may choose how they demonstrate that they have learned what the objectives require of them. In effect, the Activity Alternatives permit students to determine the conditions under which they will perform or demonstrate their mastery. See Figure 8-3 for samples of perceptually related Activity Alternatives that can be incorporated into a CAP.

Example
Behavioral Objective   List five (5) major causes of World War II:

1. With a group of your classmates, dramatize (role-play) at least five (5) major causes of World War II.
2. On a cassette, list at least five (5) major causes of World War II.

FIGURE 8–1 Sample Subject Applications

Arts and Crafts
assemble
blend
brush
build
carve
color
construct
crush
cut
dab
dot
draw
drill
finish
fit
fix
fold
form
frame
grind
hammer
handle
heat
illustrate
make
melt
mend
mix
mold
nail
paint
paste
pat
position
pour
press
process
roll
rub
sand
saw
sculpt
sew
shake
sharpen
sketch
smooth
stamp
stick
stir
trace

trim
varnish
wipe
wrap

Drama
act
clasp
correct
cross
direct
display
emit
enter
exit
express
leave
move
pantomime
pass
perform
proceed
respond
show
start
turn

Language
abbreviate
accent
alphabetize
argue
articulate
capitalize
edit
hyphenate
indent
outline
print
pronounce
punctuate
read
recite
speak
spell
state
summarize
syllabicate
translate
type
verbalize
write

Mathematics
add
bisect
calculate
check
compound
compute
count
derive
divide
estimate
extrapolate
extract
graph
group
integrate
interpolate
measure
multiply
number
plot
prove
reduce
solve
square
subtract
tabulate
tally
verify

Music
blow
bow
clap
compose
conduct
finger
harmonize
hum
mute
play
pluck
practice
sing
strum
tap
whistle

Physical Education
arch
bat

bend
carry
catch
chase
climb
coach
coordinate
critique
float
grip
hit
hop
jump
kick
knock
lift
march
perform
pitch
run
score
skate
ski
somersault
stand
stretch
strike
swim
swing
throw
toss

Science
calibrate
compound
connect
convert
decrease
demonstrate
dissect
graft
grow
increase
insert
lengthen
light
limit
manipulate
nurture
operate
plant
prepare

reduce
remove
replace
report
reset
set
specify
straighten
time
transfer
weight

Behavior
accept
agree
aid
allow
answer
buy
communicate
compliment
contribute
cooperate
disagree
discuss
excuse
forgive
greet
guide
help
inform
interact
invite
join
laugh
lend
meet
offer
participate
permit
praise
react
relate
serve
share
smile
supply
talk
thank
volunteer
vote

FIGURE 8-2 Sample General Applications

Simple Tasks
attend
choose
collect
complete
copy
count
define
describe
designate
detect
differentiate
discriminate
distinguish
distribute
duplicate
find
identify
imitate
indicate
isolate
label
list
mark
match
name
note
omit
order
place
point
provide
recall
repeat
select
state
tally
tell
underline

Study Skills
arrange
attempt
categorize
chart
cite

circle
classify
compile
consider
diagram
document
find
follow
formulate
gather
include
itemize
locate
map
organize
quote
record
relate
reproduce
return
search
signify
sort
suggest
support
underline
volunteer

Understanding
conclude
estimate
explain
fill in
justify
rephrase
represent
restate
transform
translate

Analysis Skills
analyze
appraise
combine
compare
conclude

contrast
criticize
deduce
defend
evaluate
explain
formulate
generate
induce
infer
paraphrase
plan
present
save
shorten
structure
substitute
switch

Knowledge
collect
complete
copy
count
define
duplicate
find
identify
imitate
list
label
mark
match
name
note
omit
order
place
point
recall
repeat
select
state
tally
tell
underline

Synthesis Skills
alter
change
design
develop
discover
expand
extend
generalize
modify
paraphrase
predict
propose
question
rearrange
recombine
reconstruct
regroup
rename
reorganize
reorder
rephrase
restate
restructure
retell
rewrite
signify
simplify
synthesize
systematize

Evaluation
argue
assess
judge
predict
validate

Application
construct
demonstrate
draw
illustrate
indicate
isolate
make
record

FIGURE 8-3   Alternative Activities Classified by Perceptual Responsiveness

Auditory
Develop an oral report.
Make a tape-recorded lesson.
Tape-record a court trial.
Tape a panel discussion.
Hear a debate.
Make a tape recording.
Write a song.
Tape-record an original poem.
Tape-record a musical performance.
Read a script aloud.
Write the dialogue for a play.
Tape-record an original radio program.
Design a verbal game on tape.
Develop a slide show with tape.
Develop a television program/show.
Create a travelogue lecture.
Tell different endings.
Share and ask about:
  • the most interesting
  • the best liked
  • the saddest
  • what might have been if. . . .
Tell the most humorous/exciting parts.
Using New Age type music, create . . .
Orally report on your research findings.
Create a choral group to . . .

Kinesthetic
Conduct a survey
Administer a questionnaire.
Participate in a court trial.
Conduct/participate in a panel discussion.
Conduct/participate in a debate.
Make up a game.
Design a machine.
Invent an alternative design.
Conduct a musical performance.
Dramatize a script.
Pantomime.
Put on a puppet show.
Conduct a campaign.
Create a dance to demonstrate . . .
Perform a television show.
Perform a videotape.
Make up a floor game/maze.
Make an enormous:
  • Electroboard
  • Flip Chute
  • set of Task Cards
  • Pic-A-Hole
Conduct a charade.
Create a sand table.
Role-play, simulate.
Conduct a research study.

Tactual/Visual Combination
Make a model.
Develop a learning kit.
Make a set of multipart Task Cards.
Make a Multisensory Instructional Package.
Make a puzzle.
Make an Electroboard.
Make a Pic-A-Hole.
Make a floor game.
Make a scrapbook.
Create a coloring book.
Develop a display.
Design a stage setting.
Make a collage.
Design an artistic creation representing . . .
Dress paper dolls as characters.
Recreate the environment in miniature.
Design a crossword puzzle.
Rewrite . . .
Write a job description
Write, illustrate directions for

Write:
  • a different ending
  • about the most humorous, most exciting,
    saddest . . .
Mark beautiful, descriptive passages
Design a new library card category for . . .
Write a letter to a person 100 years in either
  the past or the future.
Graphically suggest a better way of doing . . .
Develop a collection.
Sculpt . . .
Stitch . . .
Draw, illustrate, paint, finger-paint . . .
Design a cartoon.
Make a tapestry.
Create a three-dimensional map.
Make a tapestry.
Weave . . .
Review . . .
Graphically describe how to . . .

Using symbols only, create a . . .
List new and interesting:
- words, expressions
- information
- corroborative data

Visual (Pictorial)
Develop a(n):

diagram
map
graph
chart
photograph
original illustration
coloring book
display
poster
cartoon
collage
slide show
TV show
movie
filmstrip
game
design
book jacket design
costume design
flip book
mural
historical time line
illustrated report
transparency

Document original research.
Find original manuscripts and recreate . . .
Give a pictorial synopsis of . . .
Write a new interpretation of . . .

Visual (Words)
Develop a(n):

book of poems
poem
diary
words for a song
original story
book
tall tale
advertisement
written report
imaginary letter
newspaper article
recipe
magazine article
letter to editor
letter to legislator
book review
test/quiz on chart
game
biography
comparison report
editorial
collection of articles

   3. Write a story about at least five (5) different things that happened to cause World War II.
   4. Draw a map of Europe just before World War II. Use symbols, drawings, photographs, or artwork to portray five (5) causes of World War II.

Step 6 Create a Reporting Alternative for each of the Activity Alternatives that you have designed. As indicated before, the Activity Alternative gives students a choice of how they will apply the information they have learned so that it is reinforced. Once an activity has been completed, most students enjoy sharing their product with others. Sharing an Activity Achievement with classmates or friends provides additional reinforcement for the person who developed it. In addition, it serves as either an introduction of new material or a repetition of previously studied material for the students who serve as the listeners, viewers, players, or participants. Furthermore, the sharing may be another way of demonstrating acquired knowledge or skill.

Example

Behavioral Objective   State at least one (1) important date and event in the life of any eight (8) of the following people and explain how each person impacted on World War II.

1. Hitler
2. Mussolini
3. Franklin D. Roosevelt
4. Churchill
5. Chamberlain
6. Quisling

7. Hirohito
8. Patton
9. Montgomery
10. Eisenhower
11. Lenin
12. Stalin

If you can complete this for ten (10) of the above people, you have excellent potential for becoming a historian!

Activity Alternatives

1. Make a time line listing the dates and events in the lives of the eight (8) or ten (10) people that you choose. Through illustrations, show the role each played in World War II.

2. Draw and then dress paper dolls as they would have been dressed had they been the people listed above. Then talk for the dolls and describe at least one important date and event in their lives and how each person impacted on World War II.

3. Write a poem or produce a record that describes how each person impacted on World War II.

4. Write an original story, play, or radio or television script that describes a date and event in the life of each of the people about whom you

Reporting Alternatives

1. Mount the time line in our room and answer any questions your classmates may ask about it.

2. Give a two-minute talk to three or four people telling them about the characters you drew.

3. Mount your poem or record that tells at least one (1) important thing about these people.

4. Read the story or play, on a radio or television show. Rehearse the script with classmates and ask a few students to observe it and then com-

chose to learn. Explain the parts each played in World War II.

5. If you can think of an activity that you would prefer to the ones listed above, write it on a piece of paper and show it to your teacher for possible approval.

ment in writing. Add their comments to your CAP folder.

5. If your original activity is approved, develop a Reporting Alternative that complements (matches) it.

What follows is a list of Activity and Reporting Alternatives that may be used to develop options for all students. You will want to identify those activities that would be motivating for your students, adapt and rewrite them so that they are appropriate for the specific Contract Activity Package objectives that you are designing, and use them as part of the choices you permit. They may also be used as homework assignments to add interest to and provide application for required items. The application through development of an original creation using the student's perceptual strengths contributes substantially to retention of difficult information.

Examples

Activity Alternatives

1. Make a miniature stage setting with pipe-cleaner figures to describe the most important information you learned about your topic.

2. Make a poster "advertising" the most interesting information you have learned.

3. Describe costumes for people or characters you have learned about.

4. Prepare a travel lecture related to your topic.

Reporting Alternatives

1. Display the stage setting and figures and give a two-minute talk explaining what they represent and why you selected them.

2. Display the poster and give a two-minute talk explaining why you found the information interesting.

3. Describe to a group of classmates how you determined what the costumes should be, how you made them, and the people who would have worn them.

4. Give the lecture before a small group of classmates. You also may tape record it for others who are working on the same topic.

5. Draw a series of pictures on a long sheet of paper fastened to two rollers. Write a script for it.

6. Describe in writing or on tape an interesting person or character that you learned about.

7. Write or tell a different ending to one of the events you read about.

8. Pantomime some information you found very interesting.

9. Construct puppets and use them in a presentation that explains an interesting part of the information you learned. Have a friend photograph your presentation.

10. Make a map or chart representing information you have gathered.

11. Broadcast a book review of the topic, as if you were a critic. Tape record the review.

12. Make a clay, soap, or wooden model to illustrate a phase of the information you learned.

13. Construct a diorama to illustrate an important piece of information.

14. Dress paper dolls as people or characters in your topic.

15. Make a mural to illustrate the information you consider interesting.

16. Build a sand table setting to

5. Show your movie to one or more small groups of classmates.

6. Ask a few classmates to tell you what they think of the person you portrayed.

7. After sharing your thoughts with a classmate or two, ask them to think of other ways the event could have ended.

8. Let a few classmates try to guess what you are pantomiming.

9. Display the pictures and the puppets. Do the presentation.

10. Display the map or chart and answer questions about it.

11. Permit others to listen to your tape and tell you if they would like to read the book.

12. Display the model and answer questions about it.

13. Display the diorama and answer questions as an artist might.

14. Give a two-minute talk about the doll characters.

15. Display the mural and answer questions that arise.

16. Explain the setting to other

represent a part of your topic.

17. Rewrite an important piece of information, simplifying the vocabulary.

18. Make a time line, listing important dates and events in sequence.

19. Write a song including information you learned.

20. Make up a crossword puzzle.

21. Make up a game using information from your topic.

22. Direct and participate in a play or choral speaking about your topic.

23. Write a script for a radio or television program. Produce and participate in this program.

24. Develop commentaries for a silent movie, filmstrip, or slide show on your topic. Use your own photographs or slides, if possible.

25. With others, plan a debate or panel discussion on challenging aspects of your topic.

26. Write a news story, an editorial, a special column, or an advertisement for the school or class newspaper explaining your views concerning any one aspect of your topic.

27. Write an imaginary letter from one character to

students. Ask them to evaluate your effort in a few short sentences.

17. Develop a project about the information with two (2) classmates.

18. Display the time line and be prepared to answer questions.

19. Sing the song in person or on tape for a small group of students.

20. Let other students try to complete it. Check and return their answers to them.

21. Play the game with other members of your class.

22. Present the dramatic or choral creation to a small group of classmates.

23. Present the program for a group of classmates.

24. Present the program for a group of classmates.

25. Hold the debate and participate in it.

26. Mail your writing to the paper. Ask three students to write "letters to the editor" praising or chastising you as a reporter.

27. Display the letter.

another. Tell about something that might have happened had they both lived at the time and place of your topic.

28. Make up tall tales about characters in the topic.

29. Keep a make-believe diary about your memorable experiences as you lived through the period concerned with your topic.

30. Try to find the original manuscripts, old page proofs, first editions of books, book jackets, taped interviews with authors or other interesting persons in the community, autographs of authors, or any other documentation related to your topic. If the material cannot be brought to school, organize a small group trip to visit the place where you found the items.

31. Document some original research you've found on your topic using bibliographies, footnotes, and quotations.

32. Search the library card index and/or bring photographs and a description of new materials concerned with your topic to class.

33. Develop a computer software program for this objective.

28. Permit others to react to them.

29. Read a portion of your diary to some of your classmates. See whether they can identify the period concerned with the topic. And the diary to the Resource Alternatives available for other people who are studying the topic.

30. Take a group trip concerned with your topic. Either write or tape record something of interest that you learn.

31. Submit the research to your teacher.

32. Add the information to the Resource Alternatives for your topic.

33. Show two friends how to use the software.

34. Broadcast a program to another country giving your point of view about this topic.

34. Have four (4) students receive the broadcast and relate your conclusions.

Step 7 List all the resources you can locate that students may use to gain the information required by their behavioral objectives. Try to find multisensory resources if they are available. Categorize the materials separately—for example, books, transparencies, tapes, records, magazines, and games. If you have them, include Programmed Learning Sequences, Multisensory Instructional Packages, Pic-A-Holes, Flip Chutes, Electroboards, Task Cards, or Learning Circles. Use these broad divisions as titles; underline each title and, below it, list the names of the resources that are available. Students may use additional materials if they wish, but they should either show these materials to you or refer to them in their work. Because students may select which resources they will use, these materials are called Resource Alternatives. For examples, see the Resource Alternatives included in the sample CAPs in this chapter.

If available, include materials at different reading levels to bracket the range of abilities in the class using the CAPs. For example, a CAP on biological systems may present information at the seventh- through twelfth-grade levels for a heterogeneous ninth-grade class in health.

Step 8 Add at least three small-group techniques to the developing Contract Activity Package. Always include a Team Learning. Identify the most difficult objectives in your CAP. Develop a Team Learning to introduce those objectives that require in-depth knowledge, insight, or extensive explanation. Design a Circle of Knowledge to reinforce what you taught through Team Learning. Use any of the remaining strategies, such as Brainstorming, Group Analysis, or Case Study, to help peer-oriented youngsters gain information. Circles of Knowledge are simple to create; try a few. Team Learnings require more time but are well worth the effort, for they will enhance retention for many of your students and, simultaneously, free you to work directly with those who are authority-oriented and need your supervision and guidance. For examples, see the samples of small-group techniques included in Chapter 5 and in the CAPs in this chapter.

Step 9 Develop a test that is directly related to each of the behavioral objectives in your CAP. An assessment instrument or examination that is directly related to stated objectives is called a *criterion-referenced test.* Questions for such a test are formed by either restating the objective or phrasing it in a different way.

For example, if the behavioral objective was "List at least five (5) major causes of World War II," then the question on the examination should also be "List at least five (5) major causes of World War II."

You may, of course, be creative in the way you test your students. The test may include maps, puzzles, games, diagrams, drawings, and photos for those who learn best in those ways.

The test may be used at three different times: (1) as a pretest to assess whether the student knows a major portion of the topic and does not need to pursue all objectives in the CAP, (2) as a self-test to determine readiness for the final assessment, and (3) as the teacher's final evaluation of knowledge gained. Knowing what is expected improves attitudes toward learning and increases motivation. The order in which the questions are given on the pre-, self-, and posttests may be changed if the teacher suspects that individual students are memorizing answers without truly internalizing the knowledge. If that happens, those are the wrong students for a CAP!

Step 10 Design an illustrated cover for the Contract Activity Package. (See the sample CAPs that follow.)

Step 11 Develop an informational top sheet. On the page directly after the illustrated cover, provide information that you believe is important. Some items that may be included are as follows:

- The name of the Contract Activity Package
- The student's name
- The student's class
- The objectives that have been assigned to or selected by that student
- The date by which the CAP should be completed
- The dates by which selected parts of the CAP should be completed (for students in need of structure)
- A place for a pretest grade
- A place for a self-test grade
- A place for a final test grade
- The names of the classmates that may have worked on this CAP as a team
- Directions for working on or completing the CAP

Step 12 Reread each of the parts of the Contract Activity Package. Make certain that they are clearly stated, well organized, in correct order, and grammatically written. Check your spelling and punctuation.

Step 13 Add illustrations to the pages to make the CAP attractive and motivating.

Step 14 Duplicate the number of copies you will need.

Step 15 Design a record-keeping form so that you know which students are using and have used the Contract Activity Package and how much of it they have completed successfully (see Figure 8–4.)

NAME: _____   CONTRACT: _____
_____
_____

OBJECTIVES TO BE COMPARED _____

OBJECTIVES	DATE COMPLETED	ACTIVITIES COMPLETED	GROUP TECHNIQUES COMPLETED
1.			
2.			
3.			
4.			
5.			
6.			
7.			
8.			
9.			
10.			
11.			
12.			
13.			
14.			
15.			
16.			

FIGURE 8-4   This form provides an overview of a student's progress and is used with the contract system where students select their objectives from a list of enumerated options.

Step 16 Try a CAP with those students who can work well with any two or three small-group techniques. Be prepared to guide and assist the students through their first experiences with a CAP. Establish a system whereby they can obtain assistance if they need your help. Placing an ''I Need Assistance'' column on the chalkboard or on a chart and having youngsters sign up for help when they are stymied is usually effective. Direct them to place their names beneath the title and to return to their places until you are free to come to them. They should not interrupt you but, rather, should busy themselves on other objectives or tasks—or get help from a classmate—until you can get to them.

Suggestions for Perfecting a Contract Activity Package

Although it is not incorrect to state repeatedly: "You will be able to . . . ," it does become repetitious and often provokes humor. It is suggested, therefore, that at the top of the page you write:

Example

Behavioral Objectives

By the time you have finished this contract, you will be able to complete each of the following objectives:

 1. List at least five (5) major causes of World War II.
 2. State at least one important action taken by eight (8) important historical figures during the period just before and during World War II.

Any time that you use a number in the objectives, spell out the number; then, in parentheses, write the numeral. This technique is used to accentuate the number for youngsters who may overlook specific details.

Example

List at least three (3) tools that archeologists use in their work.

Use complete and grammatically correct sentences. Do not capitalize words that should not be capitalized. Contracts should be excellent examples of good usage, spelling, and grammar for students. If you wish to emphasize a word that may be new to the student's vocabulary, underline the word.

Use the phrase *at least* before any number of required responses to motivate selected students to achieve more than is required.

Example

List at least five (5) events leading up to World War II. Can you think of a sixth (6th)?

Be certain that the objective does not become an activity. The objectives state what the student should learn. The activity enables the youngster to demonstrate that he or she has learned it by using the information when making a creative, original product.

Example
Objective: Describe the events that directly led to the outbreak of World War II.

Activity Alternatives

1. Draw a mural showing the events that led directly to the outbreak of World War II.

or

2. Write a poem describing the events that directly led to the outbreak of World War II.

For each small-group technique, begin at the top of a new page. Name the technique and then number from one (1) through four (4) and place lines on which the students' names may be written. Add another line for the recorder's name.

Example
Team Learning

1. _____   3. _____

2. _____   4. _____

Recorder: _____

In the Reporting Alternatives, never ask a youngster to report to the entire class. Have an activity shared with one, two, or a few classmates, or with the teacher. It is difficult for a student to hold the entire class' attention; and if one student is given the opportunity, it should be offered to all. Instead, have the students report to a small group. If the activity is outstanding, ask the student to share it with a second small group. You may either assign students or ask for volunteers to listen to the report.

The title of each of the major parts of the CAP should be underlined— for example, Behavioral Objectives or Activity Alternatives.

Independent Contract

Individual CAPs also may be designed by gifted, bright, and/or creative students in the patterns described in this chapter. Those students could pursue a specific interest unrelated to the required curriculum. They need only think through and respond to the following curriculum questions.

1. What is a particular interest of mine that I would like to investigate?
2. What important things do I want to learn?
3. Which resource should I use?
4. How can I use what I need to learn in a creative, original way that I can eventually share with others?
5. If I rewrite the objectives (what I need to learn), how can I translate them into a self-assessment? See Chapter 10 for specifics concerning the development of student-designed CAPs.

Read the following Contract Activity Packages and perhaps try them with motivated or nonconforming students in your class. Then develop one based on your curriculum. Use the following guidelines for correcting a CAP so that you know you have a product with which your students are likely to succeed.

Guidelines for Correcting a CAP

1. Do you have both an analytic and a global title?
2. Are the objectives clearly stated, requiring absolutely no further explanation?
3. Do the objectives begin each page at the top?
4. Where multiple responses are required, do you say, "Describe *at least* ——————————. . ." so that motivated students may respond to more than the minimum number required?
5. When you use numbers, are they written *both* ways (in word and symbol form)?
6. Does each objective have related Activity and Reporting Alternatives?
7. Are the Activity Alternatives multisensory?
8. Does each Reporting Alternative ally itself *directly* with its Activity Alternative?
9. Do the Activity Alternatives require that the student *make* something creative?
10. Is only one Activity and Reporting Alternative required for each objective?
11. Does the CAP have a listing of multisensory Resource Alternatives?
12. Is there a Team Learning for each difficult objective?
13. Does the Team Learning *teach* something and then ask three different types of questions concerned with what was taught (factual, higher level cognitive, and creative)?
14. Does the CAP have one or more Circles of Knowledge?
15. Is there a *third* small-group technique, such as Case Study or Brainstorming?
16. Is the assessment directly related to the objectives?

17. Are there pictures, illustrations, or graphs directly related to the CAP content throughout the CAP?
18. Is the printing or typing well done and easy to read?
19. Are there any spelling or grammatical errors in the CAP?
20. Does each objective begin with a verb?
21. Does the CAP provide some choices for the student?
22. Is the CAP attractive and easy to use?
23. Is each of the objectives in the related PLS included in the CAP?

Suggest that students check each other's original CAP, complete the following form below, and submit it to you.

The CAP I have examined is: _____

created by _____

The following items need to be corrected: _____

_____

Name: _____

Date: _____

Sample Contract Activity Packages

Following are several samples of secondary school (grades 7–12) Contract Activity Packages developed by teachers and used successfully at different levels with students whose learning styles matched the approach of this method.

If this is your students' first experience with CAPs, assign only a few objectives to introduce them to the process. Give them a few opportunities to begin to feel secure with this method before deciding whether it is effective for each individual. If it stimulates and provokes their thinking and knowledge, continue using it. If you find that selected students do not respond well to it (even if they are permitted to work with just one or two classmates), set aside the CAP system for those youngsters and introduce either Programmed Learning Sequences or Multisensory Instructional Packages to them. The last of these methods is potent for students who require multisensory resources and structure, are self-oriented (rather than peer-oriented or teacher-oriented), and learn essentially through tactual or kinesthetic means.

The Contract Activity Package is most effective with youngsters who are motivated and either auditory or visual, or are nonconforming. You will note that it is an especially well organized system, although it does permit flexible learning arrangements and options for students.

Sample CAP: Social Studies
The Great Depression*
or
You Think *You've* Got Trouble?

Introduction and Objectives

The years of the Depression were difficult ones for the American people. Life was hard and people struggled to survive. It was not at all a pleasant period in our history. However, this contract is filled with many interesting activities to help you learn about the Great Depression.

First, take the pretest on the last page, and answer any questions you can. Check your answers with the teacher.

*This contract Activity Package was designed by Camile Sinatra, Reading Specialist, Manhasset Junior/Senior High School, Manhasset, New York.

The cover, title, and materials in a CAP should reflect the theme and illustrate what will be studied. Even at the high school level, it is wise to include a tape that reads the content of the CAP for students who do not comprehend well the things they read. (Photograph courtesy Center for the Study of Learning and Teaching Styles, St. John's University, New York.)

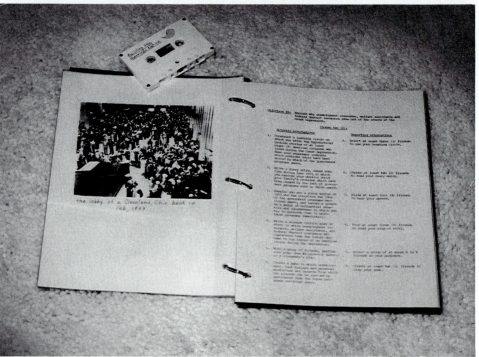

Everyone must complete all six (6) objectives and at least one (1) Activity and Reporting Alternative for each objective. You may work alone, with a classmate or two, or check in with me frequently.

Take the posttest when you finish.

Please keep track of your progress on the next page (see Figure 8–4). We will be using class time for the next three (3) weeks to complete these activities. You will also need to work on some of these activities as homework and/or during your study periods. All of the resources you will need are in the classroom, the home and career skills center, the technology lab., and the media center. Of course, you may also use your own books and materials and/or the public library if you wish.

By the time you have finished this CAP you will be able to complete each of the following requirements:

Objective #1 Describe the quality of life lived by many Americans who were affected by the Great Depression.
Choose two (2):

Activity Alternatives	Reporting Alternatives
1. Write a letter to a friend describing the hardships you and your family are facing as you live through the years of the Great Depression.	1. Choose at least four (4) friends to read your letter.

A city breadline

2. Create a mural that depicts the ways in which people made a living and tried to survive during the Great Depression.

3. Make a recording similar to an old-time radio newscast describing the hardships experienced by people during the Depression.

4. Make a You-Tell-It filmstrip or a roll paper movie showing life during the Great Depression, and write an accompanying script to describe the scenes.

5. List the ways in which unemployed people obtained food, clothing and shelter during the Great Depression and be ready to answer questions about the items on your list.

6. Create a set of Task Cards out of twelve (12) sentences which describe the quality of life lived by many Americans who were affected by the Depression.

2. Display your mural in the classroom or in the student activities center.

3. Choose three (3) friends to listen to your broadcast.

4. Share your filmstrip with at least five (5) friends.

5. Ask the teacher or a classmate to quiz you on your list.

6. Choose three (3) friends to reassemble your Task Cards.

Objective #2 Explain a business cycle. *Choose two (2):*

Activity Alternatives

1. Construct a board game that will lead two (2) to six (6) players through the various phases of a business cycle.

2. Pretend you are a financial analyst and prepare a recorded presentation describing the various phases of a business cycle.

Reporting Alternatives

1. Choose at least two (2) friends to play your game with you.

2. Select at least four (4) friends to listen to your recording.

3. Write a one-paragraph summary of a business cycle and illustrate it with a diagram of your own creation.

3. Share your summary and diagram with at least two (2) friends and be sure they understand how the summary and diagram match.

4. Create a crossword puzzle with at least twenty (20) words, including all of the important terms used in describing a business cycle.

4. Ask three (3) friends to do your puzzle for you.

5. Write a poem about a business cycle and include some lines describing how the cycle was different during the Great Depression.

5. Choose four (4) friends to read or listen to your poem.

6. Assemble an Electroboard which illustrates the various phases of a business cycle.

6. Select at least three (3) friends to use your Electroboard.

Objective #3   Tell what happened on these important dates: (a) October 29, 1929 and (b) February 1933.
   Choose two (2):

Activity Alternatives

1. Make an 8- to 10-frame comic strip on paper or You-Tell-It filmstrip which shows what happened on these two important dates.

Reporting Alternatives

1. Show your comic strip or filmstrip to at least four (4) friends.

2. Create and illustrate two (2) funny headlines for your local newspaper describing the events that happened on these important dates.

2. Post your headlines on the bulletin board.

3. Write a letter dated late February 1933, to the editor of a large newspaper. In the letter, describe your unhappiness with the events of that month, and also mention what happened to you on October 29, 1929.

3. Choose at least three (3) friends to read your letter.

4. Construct a two-sided diorama portraying each of the events that occurred on these important dates.

4. Exhibit your diorama in the classroom or in the student activities center.

5. With one other student, develop two (2) soap opera style mini-skits in which you each play characters involved in the events of 1929 and 1933.

5. Choose a small group of friends to be an audience for your performance.

6. Create a Learning Circle with at least eight (8) items which include these two important dates as well as terms that describe the repercussions of these events.

6. Ask at least four (4) friends to use your Learning Circle.

Objective #4   Describe the process of making an investment in the stock market.

Choose two (2):

Activity Alternatives

1. Write a song in which you complain about losing money on an investment during the stock market crash.

Reporting Alternatives

1. Choose at least three (3) friends to hear or read your song.

2. Make a graph showing the value of ten (10) shares of any stock you choose that is reported on the New York Stock Exchange from Tuesday through Thursday of this week.

2. Display your graph on the bulletin board.

3. Check the stock reports in the *New York Times* or your local newspaper for Tuesday through Thursday of this week, and calculate the amount of money you would have lost or gained on five different stocks if you had bought ten (10) shares of each on Monday.

3. Have at least three (3) friends check your figures.

4. As if you are the owner of a small business in the micro-community, draw up certificates to be used in selling shares of stock in your company.

4. Sell some stock to at least two (2) friends. (Remember, you will have to pay dividends!)

5. Pretend you are a stock broker working on Wall Street and write a letter to a client offering your reasons for suggesting that she or he buy a particular stock. (You may tie this Activity Alternative in with Activity #4 above.)

5. Choose at least (4) friends to read your letter.

6. Choosing the pasta letters that form at least ten terms connected with a stock investment, make a pot of soup.

6. Share it with a friend.

Objective #5   List the reasons the American people were unhappy with President Herbert Hoover.
   Choose two (2):

Activity Alternatives

1. Write a diary entry as though you were President Herbert Hoover worried about the growing discontent over the depression.

Reporting Alternatives

1. Choose at least three (3) friends to read your diary entry.

2. Make a poster depicting President Hoover worrying over the American people's reaction to the Great Depression.

2. Display your poster on the bulletin board.

3. Pretend you are President Hoover and record a speech in which you try to assure the American people that the problems they are facing during the Depression will soon be over.

3. Choose at least four (4) friends to listen to your speech.

4. Draw a political cartoon showing President Hoover troubled about events in America during the Great Depression.

5. Dress up as President Herbert Hoover and permit class members to interview you with questions about the country's economic problems during the Great Depression.

6. Make a Flip Chute with a set of flip cards that enumerate at least twelve (12) problems faced by President Hoover and the nation, and indicate whether the problems were social, economic, or political. (Make sure you have at least one of each kind of problem in your set.)

4. Publish your cartoon and distribute it to at least five (5) friends.

5. Choose at least three (3) friends to interview you.

6. Challenge at least three (3) friends to use your Flip Chute.

Objective #6   Explain why unemployment insurance, welfare assistance, and federal deposit insurance grew out of the events of the Great Depression. *Choose two (2):*

Activity Alternatives

1. Construct a Learning Circle on which you write the hypothetical problem stories of at least eight (8) American citizens who lived during the Great Depression. Have your responses indicate which problems could have been solved by which of the government programs above.

2. Write a diary entry, dated some time during late 1933, in which you express your worries about your family's

Reporting Alternatives

1. Select at least three (3) friends to use your Learning Circle.

2. Choose at least two (2) friends to read your diary entry.

problems, which have been caused by the lack of government programs such as those above.

3. Imagine you are a young genius in 1933 who has conceived the idea of the government programs mentioned above, and record a speech to a group of influential senators and congressmen in which you try to persuade them to begin those programs immediately.

3. Allow at least four (4) friends to hear your speech.

4. Write a science fiction play or story in which unemployment insurance, welfare assistance, and federal deposit insurance are characters from the future who come to the rescue of an American living during the Depression.

4. Find at least three (3) friends to read your play or story.

5. With a group of friends, perform your play (see #4 directly above) or a classmate's play.

5. Select a group of at least six (6) to eight (8) friends as your audience.

6. Create a game in which unemployment, bank failure, and personal misfortune are hazards from which the players can be rescued by assistance from the three programs mentioned above.

6. Choose at least two (2) friends to play your game.

**Crossword Puzzle:
The Great Depression**

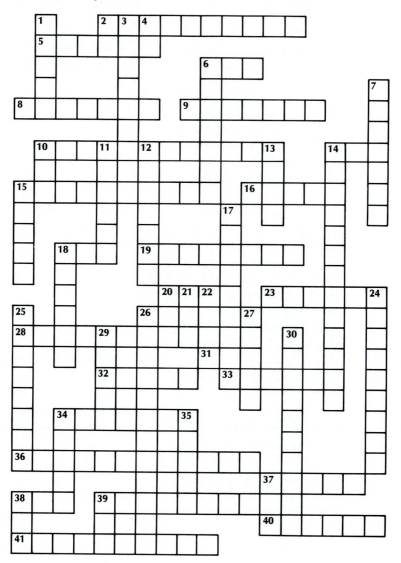

DOWN

1. portion of stock owned by an individual
2. abbreviation for television
3. government system of support for destitute families
4. suffix meaning a person
6. Black _____ (day of the week on which the stock market crashed)
7. feeling shared by many during the Great Depression
10. polite title of address for a gentleman
11. to fix
12. first name of President during the early part of the Depression
13. opposite of go
14. the regular change in the economy from prosperity to depression and back again
15. what happened in February 1933
17. payments collected by shareholders
18. same as #5 across
20. bashful, easily embarrassed
21. meat from a pig, goes with eggs
22. vicinity, environs
24. people who set up rustic campsites in parks or on other public land
25. days like the one on which the stock market crashed
26. places where people could get a hot meal during the Depression
27. share in a company
29. opposite of fancy
30. October 29, 1929, the date of the _____ market _____
34. places where squatters set up "Hoovervilles"
35. to tear into thin strips
37. more than one
38. opposite of happy
39. an insect that produces honey

ACROSS

2. percentage of people out of work during the worst part of the Depression
5. last name of President during early part of the Depression
6. number of years the Great Depression lasted
8. word used to describe the government of the entire country
9. During the Great Depression, people lost the money they had placed in bank accounts because of a lack of federal _____ insurance.
10. people who own stock in a company
14. comical word for hitting over the head; also, a style of jazz
15. a time of high production of goods and low unemployment
16. another word for tramps
18. feminine pronoun
19. period during which the economy is improving
20. fish prized for its roe
23. places where homeless people could find shelter during the Depression (lodging _____)
26. plural of #1 down
28. condition under which it is impossible for a person to earn money
31. fuss, bother, as in Shakespeare's "Much _____ about Nothing"
32. item sold by street corner salespeople during the Depression
33. place where one goes to receive an education
34. items sold by street corner peddlers
36. place where peddlers tried to sell their wares
37. opposite of late
38. signal sent when one is in trouble
39. place where people could go to receive free bread and other food items
40. homes in which squatters lived
41. name for the ten-year period 1929–1939

Q-A CARD GAME RULES

1. ———————————— 3. ————————————
2. ———————————— 4. ————————————

1. This game can be played by up to four people.
2. Shuffle the cards and deal until all cards have been distributed.
3. The player who has the card with the red star in the upper right-hand corner goes first. He or she reads the question on the card.
4. The player who has the card with the answer to the question reads the answer aloud. If all the players agree that the answer is correct, the same player then reads the question on the lower half of the card.
5. The player who has the answer to *that* question then reads it aloud, and the process continues as in number four (4) above. Each time a player reads an answer and question, that player may discard his card on a pile in the center of the table.
6. The game continues until one player has discarded all of his cards and is declared the winner.

Note: What makes this game tricky is that the player who reads the question may also be the player who has the answer in his hand!

Circle of Knowledge

1. ———————————— 3. ————————————
2. ———————————— 4. ————————————

Recorder ————————————————

List as many words having to do with this unit as you can. Take $2\frac{5}{8}$ minutes.

——————————————— ———————————————
——————————————— ———————————————
——————————————— ———————————————
——————————————— ———————————————
——————————————— ———————————————
——————————————— ———————————————
——————————————— ———————————————
——————————————— ———————————————

Team Learning for
Hoover Fights the Great Depression

1. _____   3. _____

2. _____   4. _____

Recorder _____

Directions: Read the following essay and work together on the questions that follow.

Herbert Hoover's work during the Great World War seemed good training for dealing with the Depression. He had helped the Belgians after the Germans invaded their country. He had run the American food program after 1917. As Secretary of Commerce during the 1920s he had won the confidence of most business leaders.

Hoover also understood economics better than most politicians. When he realized that the nation had entered a serious depression, he tried to stimulate recovery quickly. He urged Congress to lower taxes so that people would have more money to spend on goods and services. He called for more government spending on **public works,** such as road construction or building dams. These measures would increase the demand for goods and put jobless people back to work, he said.

Farmers in particular were hard hit by the Depression. The price of most farm products fell sharply. Hoover urged farmers to form cooperatives and to raise smaller crops until prices rose. He also favored holding down interest rates so business could borrow money more easily.

Above all, the President recognized that the American people had lost confidence in the economic system. This was part of their psychological depression. He tried to encourage them to have faith in the future. "Prosperity," he said, "is just around the corner."

But Hoover's strength as an organizer in wartime proved to be a weakness during the Depression. In both situations he insisted that voluntary cooperation would solve the nation's problems. In wartime his appeals to patriotism and self-sacrifice were effective. During the war people knew who the enemy was and what to do to protect themselves. In the Depression they could not identify any particular enemy. Therefore they did not have much confidence that they could protect themselves.

Hoover displayed still another weakness. He believed that the federal government should not increase its authority just because times were hard. If the United States took over powers that normally belonged to state and local governments, it would become a "super-state." Even when city after city proved unable to raise enough money to take care of the unemployed, Hoover opposed federal grants for relief purposes. Such aid would destroy the "real liberty" of the people, he said.

He supported federal assistance to banks and big industries. These loans were sound investments, he said. The money would be used to produce goods and earn profits. Then the loans could be repaid. Lending money to a farmer to buy pig feed or more seed or a tractor was also proper, according to Hoover's theory. But he opposed giving federal aid to farmers so that they could feed their children. That would be giving them something for nothing. Under the American system charity was the business of state and local governments and private organizations like the Red Cross and the Salvation Army.

As the Great Depression dragged on, Hoover became more and more unpopular. People began to think that he was hardhearted. He seemed not to care about the sufferings of the poor. His critics even claimed that he was responsible for the Depression.

Both charges were untrue. Hoover cared deeply about the suffering the Depression was causing. He sincerely believed that his policies were the proper ones. These policies had certainly not caused the Depression. After all, every industrial nation in the world then had high unemployment. The Great Depression affected all of Europe and most of the rest of the world.

The economies of nations that depended on agriculture were badly depressed. There was a depression in wheat-growing Australia and in beef-raising Argentina. The price of Brazilian coffee fell so low that farmers there burned the coffee beans in cookstoves. Coffee made a cheaper fuel than coal or kerosene.

Still, even if he was not responsible for the long depression, Hoover's rigid policies were not working. He was in charge of the government. Therefore people tended to blame him.

1. List two examples of public works. _____

_____

2. How did President Hoover try to stimulate the economy? _____

_____

3. Why did the American people believe that Herbert Hoover would be a good president? _____

_____

_____

4. What weaknesses did Hoover show in dealing with the Great Depression? _____

_____

_____

_____

5. What made the American people blame Hoover for the Great Depression? ─────────────────────────────────

───

───

───

6. Pretend that you are President Hoover. Prepare a speech to Congress outlining at least three things you want the government to do to help the nation recover from the Great Depression. (Please make your notes on a separate sheet of paper.)

7. Invent a fictitious planet that sends four of its citizens to study the earth during the Depression and to write a report listing three or more reasons for the Depression.

Solitaire—Challenge

1. ───────────────────── - ─────────────────────

2. ───────────────────── - ─────────────────────

3. ───────────────────── - ─────────────────────

4. ───────────────────── - ─────────────────────

5. Recorder ─────────── - ─────────────────────

Work together to create a set of at least twenty (20) flash cards about the major concepts and vocabulary involved in this unit. After you have played enough games of Solitaire individually, Challenge one another, and then each member of the team should Challenge one other student in the class to a game. Record your names above.

Reminders
Solitaire   An individual player places a set of flash cards on the table, term up and definition down. He or she then proceeds to pick up as many of the cards as possible by correctly identifying the meaning of the term as it is removed from the table.
    The more difficult version: The player proceeds with the same intent as above, but the cards are placed on the table, term down and definition up. This time the player must read the definition and recall the term correctly.

Challenge   Two players each attempt to gain the greater number of cards as they play the games described above, each player taking his or her turn.

Group Analysis

1. _____ 3. _____

2. _____ 4. _____

Recorder _____

Discuss these three (3) questions. Record some of your reactions.

1. Why is it important to understand the factors which brought about the Great Depression?

2. Consider the plight of the homeless in present-day America. Can you suggest any federal programs that might help to alleviate the problem?

3. Are there any other problems to which you feel our government is not responding adequately? What do you think the country should do?

Pre- and Posttest

Name _____

Date _____

Directions: Answer each of the following questions in a short paragraph.

1. Describe the quality of life lived by many Americans who were affected by the Great Depression.

2. Explain a business cycle.

3. Tell what happened on these important dates: (a) October 29, 1929 and (b) February 1933.

4. Describe the process of making an investment in the stock market.

5. List the reasons the American people were unhappy with President Herbert Hoover.

6. Explain why unemployment insurance, welfare assistance, and federal deposit insurance grew out of the events of the Great Depression.

Resources

Books
Brown, Richard C., and Herbert J. Bass. "The Great Depression and the New Deal." *One Flag, One Land.* Morristown, NJ: Silver Burdett, 1975, pp. 580–585.
Davidson, James West, and Mark H. Lytle. "From Prosperity to Despair." *The United States: A History of the Republic.* Englewood Cliffs, NJ: Prentice-Hall, 1986, pp. 546–553.
Garraty, John A. "The Great Depression and the New Deal." *American History.* New York: Harcourt Brace Jovanovich, 1982, pp. 737–742.
Reich, Jerome R., and Edward L. Biller. "The Great Depression." *Building the American Nation.* New York: Harcourt Brace Jovanovich, 1971, pp. 630–635.

You-Tell-It Filmstrip Supplies
You-Tell-It film with 48 story boards, calibrated layout guide, instruction manual, fifty feet of film, marking pens, and projector stage. Dev-Coa, Inc., Developmental Corporation of America, 83 Clover Avenue, Floral Park, NY 11001.

Game
"The Great Crash: Stock Market" with reading sheets, question sheets, and board game. From Games to Teach American History series, Opportunities for Learning, Inc., 20417 Nordhoff Street, Department F20, Chatsworth, CA 91311.

Magazine
"Back at Home" with a decade of pictures, including the roaring twenties, Hoover, and the stock market crash; news stories are written at a 3.5–4.5 reading level; 60–70 photographs. From Our Century Magazines series, Fearon Education, David S. Lake Publishers, 19 Davis Drive, Belmont, CA 94002.

Video Cassettes
"The Great Depression" including the bank panic, Wall Street on Black Tuesday, unemployment, Roosevelt's New Deal, the coming of World War II, and the return of prosperity. Two video cassettes, 32 minutes. Guidance Associates, Inc., Communications Park, Box 3000, Mount Kisco, NY 10549-0900.
"Witness to History: The Great Depression" including bank runs, unemployment, food lines, shantytown "Hoovervilles," Hoover, Roosevelt, and the Bonus Army. One cassette, 15 minutes. Guidance Associates. (See above.)

Filmstrips

"The Great Depression" with four filmstrips, cassettes, and simulations as well as spirit masters. Includes photographs, cartoons, commercial art, songs, and ballads. Opportunities for Learning, Inc. (Please see "Game" above.)

Additional Teacher-Made Materials

Learning Circle
Task Cards
Flip Chute
Pic-A-Hole
Electroboard
Hooverville Hopscotch or Do the Unemployment Shuffle (Floor Game)

Please see directions in the MIP script or listen to the tactual-kinesthetic learners' tape.

Q-A Card Game (please see CAP* activity #8).
Crossword Puzzle (please see CAP activity #7).
Team Learning on Herbert Hoover (please see CAP activity #10).
Solitaire and Challenge Card Games (please see CAP activity #11 and oral instructions on the MIP tape as well as in the script).
Tape recordings of reading from *Building the American Nation* and *American History*
Tape recording of the PLS
Tape recording of the script for the use of the MIP
Tapes for the visual learner, the auditory learner, and the tactual/kinesthetic learner

Sample Cap: Literature
Anne of Green Gables:
The House Isn't Haunted,
but Come and Meet
Anne and the Kindred Spirits*

*This Contract Activity Package on *Anne of Green Gables* was designed by Vivian Lynch, Associate Dean, St. Vincent's College, St. John's University, New York.

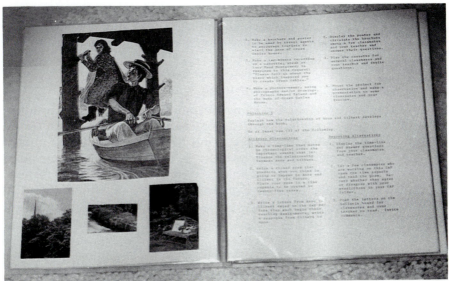

This CAP on Anne of Green Gables *includes numerous drawings, photographs, a tape, a puzzle, and a script (Photograph courtesy Center for the Study of Learning and Teaching Styles, St. John's University, New York.)*

You have read (and, I hope, enjoyed) *Anne of Green Gables.* I hope that you will know Anne and her home and her kindred spirits much better when you have completed this CAP.

Name ————————————————————————————————

Class ————————————————————————————————

Objectives Completed ——————————————————————————

Date Completed ————————————————————————————

Complete objectives 1, 2, and 6, and any other two (2).

Objective #1   In a novel, the people are called *characters.* How they look and how they act are called their *character traits.*

Describe the character traits of Anne. (Required)

Do at least one (1) of the following:

Activity Alternatives

1. Write a report that describes Anne's appearance, her ways of dealing with people, and her favorite pasttimes.

2. Make a collage of pictures clipped from magazines that remind you of Anne. Label the collage with at least four (4) words that describe Anne.

3. Make a two-minute recording on a cassette; speak as Anne in response to this question from readers: "What do you think are your best qualities and why?".

4. Pretend you are a stage actress and a writer. Play Anne in an original two-minute scene in which you describe your appearance and your feelings about your appearance. Play this scene in full costume and make-up.

Reporting Alternatives

1. Share your report with a small group of classmates and present it to your teacher.

2. Display the collage to several classmates and your teacher and explain it.

3. Play the cassette for classmates who are working on this CAP and ask for their reactions. Record reactions in your CAP folder.

4. Curtain up! Perform your scene for your audience: your classmates and teacher.

5. Make up a crossword puzzle that uses at least ten (10) words to describe Anne.

5. Make copies of the crossword puzzle for other students working on this CAP; let them try to solve it.

Objective #2   Explain the importance of "kindred spirits" in the book. (Required)

Do at least one (1) of the following.

Activity Alternatives

1. Make a chart which lists each of the people Anne considers "kindred spirits" along with a one-line reason why.

2. Write a composition which discusses in detail the relationship between Anne and one (1) of her "kindred spirits".

3. Pretend that you are Anne and it is Christmas. Write two (2) rhymed poems to two (2) "kindred spirits," telling them how you feel about them.

4. Draw a series of sketches showing the people Anne considers "kindred spirits." Bind them into a booklet and number the pages. On the last page, list the page numbers, the characters' names, and a one-line explanation of why they are in your booklet.

Reporting Alternatives

1. Mount the chart and explain it to a few classmates and your teacher.

2. Read your composition to several classmates and your teacher and answer their questions.

3. Display copies of the poems on a class bulletin board. Answer questions from classmates and your teacher.

4. Show your booklet to a few classmates who are working on this CAP and ask if they can recognize the "kindred spirits." Record results in your CAP folder.

Objective #3   Where a story takes place is called its *setting*. Much of this book takes place at the house and farm called Green Gables.

Explain why Anne's home, Green Gables, becomes important to her.

Do at least one (1) of the following.

Activity Alternatives

1. Make a large color painting or a model of Green Gables.

Reporting Alternatives

1. Display the painting or model to a few classmates and your teacher; point out at least three (3) things that made Green Gables special to Anne.

2. Pretend that you are a television reporter who has visited Green Gables, the home of the famous (although not rich!) Anne Shirley. Prepare a two-minute broadcast reporting on her lifestyle. Write your script; gather pictures to refer to; videotape your broadcast.

2. Play your broadcast for several classmates and your teacher. Invite reactions.

3. Pretend that you are Anne. Write a diary entry in which you discuss your feelings about Green Gables.

3. Leave your diary at the bulletin board for classmates and your teacher to read.

4. Construct a chart which displays the differences between Green Gables and the other places Anne has lived.

4. Display the chart and answer classmates' questions.

Objective #4   Explain how the success of this book has affected the real place which inspired its author.
   Do at least one (1) of the following.

Activity Alternatives

1. Write a report on the Anne of Green Gables House on Prince Edward Island.

Reporting Alternatives

1. Ask a few classmates to read the report and present it to your teacher.

2. Make a brochure and poster to be used by travel agents to encourage tourists to visit the Anne of Green Gables House.

2. Display the poster and circulate the brochure among a few classmates and your teacher and answer their questions.

3. Make a two-minute recording on a cassette; speak as Lucy Maud Montgomery in response to this request: "Please tell us about the place which inspired you to create Green Gables.

4. Make a picture-essay, using photographs and/or drawings, of Prince Edward Island and the Anne of Green Gables House.

3. Play the cassette for several classmates and your teacher and invite questions.

4. Mount the project for observation and make a presentation to some classmates and your teacher.

Objective #5 Explain how the relationship of Anne and Gilbert develops through the book.
Do at least one (1) of the following.

Activity Alternatives

1. Make a time line that notes in chronological order the important events that influence the relationship between Anne and Gilbert.

2. Write a rhymed poem that predicts what you think is going to happen to Anne and Gilbert in the future. Place your poem in a time capsule to be opened in twenty-five years.

3. Write a letter from Anne to Gilbert dated on the day before they each begin their teaching assignments; write a response from Gilbert to Anne.

4. Pretend that you are a cartoonist whose strip, "Carrots and Gil" is syndicated daily in national newspapers. Create at least three (3) episodes of the cartoon strip for publication.

Reporting Alternatives

1. Display the time line and answer questions from your classmates and teacher.

2. Let a few classmates who are working on this CAP open the time capsule and read the poem. Record whether they agree or disagree with your predictions in your CAP folder.

3. Post the letters on the bulletin board for classmates and your teacher to read. Invite comments.

4. Display the cartoon strip episodes and answer the questions of your classmates and teacher.

Objective #6   In literature, we look at ways that characters change because of experiences they have or problems they face.

Explain how Anne changes because of at least three (3) experiences or problems. (Required)

Do at least one (1) of the following.

Activity Alternatives

1. Make two (2) paintings or drawings of Anne, one as she looks as the book begins and one as she looks as the book ends. Make a poster, the same size as the paintings or drawings, on which you list experiences or problems that change Anne. Set up the poster as a connection between the two portraits.

2. Pretend that you are Marilla and you are keeping a personal journal. Write an entry on the day the book's action ends in which you discuss how you have seen Anne change.

3. Construct a one-dimensional diagram or a three-dimensional maze that illustrates Anne meeting experiences and problems.

Reporting Alternatives

1. Have your portraits and connecting poster mounted on an easel or bulletin board; explain them to a group of classmates and your teacher.

2. Ask a few classmates to read the journal entry and answer their questions; present it to your teacher.

3. Display the diagram or maze on a table and provide a guided "walk-through," with explanation, for a group of classmates and your teacher.

4. Make a two-minute recording on a cassette; speak as Anne at the end of the book in response to this question, and direct your answer to Miss Stacy: "What are some of the things you have learned over the past two years?".

4. Play the cassette for several classmates and your teacher. Answer their questions.

Resource Alternatives

Books
Commire, Anne, ed. *Yesterday's Authors of Books for Children.* Vol. 1. Detroit: Gold Research Company, Book Tower, 1977. Section entitled "Lucy Maud Montgomery" begins on p. 183.

Montgomery, L. M. *Anne of Green Gables.* Toronto: Farrar, Straus and Geroux, Inc., 1984.

Senick, Gerard J., ed. *Children's Literature Review.* Vol. 8. Detroit: Gold Research Co., Book Tower, 1986. Section entitled "Lucy Maud Montgomery" begins on p. 107 and includes a great deal of material on the author, the content of the book, and commentaries on the book.

Magazine Articles
"Where Books Are Born—Anne's Beloved Island." *Victoria,* Volume 2, Number 1, Spring 1988, pp. 74–81. This article includes material on Prince Edward Island, background material on the author, and information on the Anne of Green Gables house.

Video
Walt Disney Home Video Presents *Wonderworks: Anne of Green Gables.* Produced by Sullivan Films, 1987, The Walt Disney Company.

The next section of this CAP includes Group Activities, a Self-Assessment Test, and a Final Surprise.

Team Learning: *Anne of Green Gables*
Team Members:

1. _____   3. _____

2. _____   4. _____

Recorder _____

Read the following excerpts from *The Selected Journals of L. M. Montgomery* and complete the team assignment:

April 9, 1897— . . . I am still pegging away at my writing. The road of literature is at first a very slow one, but I have made a good deal of progress since this time last year and I mean to work patiently on until I win—as I believe I shall. . . .

August 23, 1901— . . . I have been industrious and respectable all summer. Have written stories and letters, read novels, histories and encyclopedias. . . .

August 16, 1907— . . . All my life it has been my aim to write a book—a "real live" book. Of late years I have been thinking of it seriously but somehow it seemed such a big task I hadn't the courage to begin it. Two years ago in the spring of 1905 I was looking over this notebook in search of some suitable idea for a short serial I wanted to write . . . and I found a faded entry written ten years before:—"Elderly couple apply to orphan asylum for a boy. By mistake a girl is sent to them." I thought this would do. . . . The result was *Anne of Green Gables*.

June 20, 1908—(upon receiving *Anne of Green Gables* from the publishers) . . . This book is mine, mine, mine . . . something which, but for me, would never have existed.

Team Assignment   Answer the following questions:

1. What was Lucy Maud Montgomery's lifelong ambition?

_____

2. Why did L. M. Montgomery hesitate before beginning to write a book?

_____

3. Did L. M. Montgomery believe that it was easy or hard to become a writer? Why?

_____

_____

_____

4. How did L. M. Montgomery feel when *Anne of Green Gables* was published? Why?

_____

_____

_____

5. Is L. M. Montgomery's notebook important? Why?

_____

_____

_____

6. Write a four- to six-line rhymed poem _by_ L. M. Montgomery the day she receives her book from the publisher, _or_ make an illustration of L. M. Montgomery the day she receives her book from the publisher.

_____

_____

_____

_____

_____

_____

Brainstorming: _Anne of Green Gables_
Group Members

1. _____   **3.** _____

2. _____   **4.** _____

　　　　　　Leader/Recorder _____

Brainstorm: Anne Shirley is as _____ as a _____.

Circle of Knowledge: Anne of Green Gables
Circle Members

1. _____   3. _____

2. _____   4. _____

Recorder _____

The Question: List as many words as you can to describe Anne Shirley.

_____   _____

_____   _____

_____   _____

_____   _____

_____   _____

_____   _____

_____   _____

_____   _____

Role Playing: Anne of Green Gables

Group Members   *Roles*

1. _____   _____

2. _____   _____

3. _____   _____

4. _____   _____

5. _____   _____

Choose an important episode in the book and dramatize it for the class. (Act it out with costumes and make-up and, if you wish, scenery.) Your "play" must be 5 to 10 minutes in length.

Here are some suggestions for topics; you may also see me for permission to do a different topic.

Anne's Arrival at Green Gables
Anne's Episode with Mrs. Lynde
Anne's First Days at School

The Tea Party with Diana
Anne Rescues Minnie May
The Allans Come to Dinner
Anne Plays the Lily Maid

Self-Assessment Test

1. Name three (3) character traits of Anne and give an example from the book to prove each.

    1. _____

    _____

    _____

    2. _____

    _____

    _____

    3. _____

    _____

    _____

2. Tell what Anne means by a "kindred spirit."

    _____

    _____

    _____

    _____

    _____

    _____

    _____

3. Name three (3) people who are kindred spirits to Anne and give an example that shows why.

    1. _____

    _____

    _____

2. _____

_____

_____

3. _____

_____

_____

4. Name three (3) experiences or problems that Anne must face and show how she changes because of each.

1. _____

_____

_____

2. _____

_____

_____

3. _____

_____

_____

Let's Celebrate!
(This is not a test.)

I found a book called *The Anne of Green Gables Cookbook* by Kate Macdonald (Toronto: Oxford University Press, 1985). It has recipes for all the dishes mentioned in Anne's book.

Let's celebrate the completion of everyone's work on *Anne of Green Gables* with a tea-party.

Please choose which dish you will prepare for our tea-party. You can look up the recipe in the cookbook. I will announce the date for the tea-party in time for you to prepare your recipe. Please check one line.

_____ Old-Fashioned Lemonade

_____ Diana Barry's Favorite Raspberry Cordial

_____ Afternoon Ruby Tea Biscuits

_____ Miss Ellen's Pound Cake

_____ Mrs. Irving's Delicious Shortbread

_____ Orange Angel Cake with Orange Glaze

_____ Chocolate Goblin's Food Cake with Chocolate Fudge Frosting

_____ I really don't like to bake, but I'll help set up for the tea-party!

When I know what everyone else is preparing, I will let you know what I will prepare. (You can sample my baking, too!)

Sample Cap: Basic Bookkeeping
or
Making Dollars & "Cents" of It*

Bookkeepers are the scorekeepers for business.

What is *business?* a formal definition is "all commercial activities designed to sell goods and services to customers at a profit." In other words, a group of people that receives, spends, borrows, saves, or lends money is a business. This could be from your paper route, to a drugstore, to a manufacturing plant to a professional practice like a Doctor's.

Business is a game with many players where bookkeepers keep the score. With this contract, you will learn how to keep score. In the business world, it is referred to as "keeping the books."

By the time you finish this contract, you will be able to do each of the following items:

1. Describe a transaction and its relationships.
2. Distinguish between debits and credits.
3. Explain the concept of double-entry bookkeeping.
4. Identify assets and their classifications.
5. Define *equity:* the different types and their classifications.
6. Illustrate the Accounting Equation.
7. Identify and describe a Balance Sheet.

*This Contract Activity Package was designed by Karen Robinson, graduate student, St. John's University.

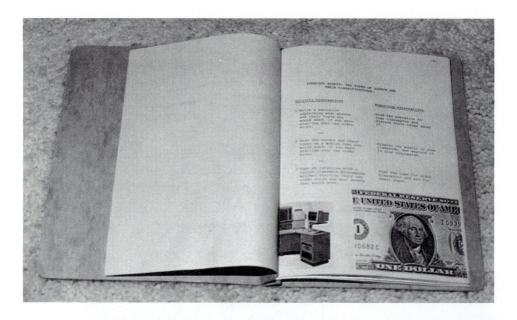

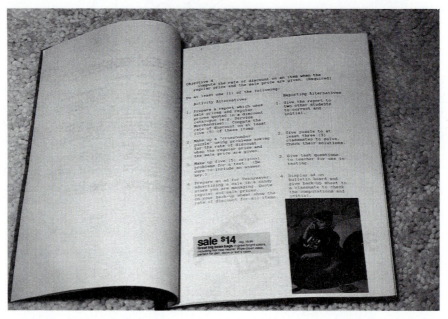

Technical language is made interesting to students through the use of Resource Alternatives of their choice and Activity Alternatives that permit them to apply the knowledge they are gaining through their personal perceptual strengths. (Photograph courtesy Center for the Study of Learning and Teaching Styles, St. John's University, New York.)

Describe a Transaction and Its Relationships

Activity Alternatives

1. Draw a diagram with stick figures showing how one transaction causes other transactions to occur.

or

2. Describe at least five (5) different types of of transactions and make a recording of your selections.

or

3. Tell a story about how transactions work if you were to purchase a CD player and some CDs.

Reporting Alternatives

1. Display the diagram so that 3 of your classmates can see how the transactions work.

2. Play the recording for 1 of your classmates and answer their questions.

3. Read the story to a classmate and discuss.

Distinguish Between Debits and Credits

Activity Alternatives

1. Draw a cartoon showing what a debit and credit would look like.

or

2. Make a tape explaining how you would teach the difference between debits and credits.

or

3. In a story, explain the debits and credits if you were to purchase a CD player and some CDs.

Reporting Alternatives

1. Mount the cartoon and display it.

2. Play the tape and teach 1 of your classmates how to debit and credit.

3. Read the story to 2 classmates and ask for their comments.

Explain the Concept of Double-Entry Bookkeeping

Activity Alternatives

1. Plan a radio talk show to discuss double-entry bookkeeping.

or

Reporting Alternatives

1. Put on the radio talk show and ask your classmates to participate.

2. Draw a sketch of double-entry bookkeeping.

2. Mount the sketch and display it for fellow classmates.

or

3. Illustrate how double-entry bookkeeping works if you were to purchase a CD player.

3. Explain the illustration to 2 classmates.

Identify Assets and Their Classifications

Activity Alternatives
1. Write a narrative explaining what assets and their types you would need, if you were starting your own video store.

Reporting Alternatives
1. Read the narrative to 2 class-mates and discuss their ideas about it.

or

2. Draw the assets and their types on a mobile that you would need, if you were starting your own video store.

2. Display the mobile in your classroom, and explain it to 2 classmates.

or

3. Tape an interview with a fellow classmate discussing starting his or her own video store and what assets he or she would need.

3. Play the tape for 2 other classmates and ask for their input.

Define Equity: The Different Types and Classifications

Activity Alternatives
1. In narrative form, detail the types of equity you would need if you started your own video store.

Reporting Alternatives
1. Read the narrative to 2 class-mates and discuss their ideas about it.

or

2. Draw the equities, types, and classifications on a mobile that you would need if you were starting your own video store.

or

3. Tape an interview with a fellow classmate discussing the equities she or he would need if he or she were starting a video store.

2. Display the mobile for your classmates and explain it to 3 of them.

3. Play the tape for 3 classmates and ask for their input.

Explain whether you would use a debit or a credit journal entry to show the following, choose at least six (6) items:

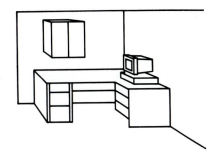

1. An increase to cash
2. A decrease in inventory
3. An increase in machinery
4. The spending of cash
5. Going into debt
6. Paying a bill that is due
7. An increase to your (the owner's) capital
8. An increase to accounts receivable
9. A decrease to notes payable

If you can complete all nine (9), you are on your way to becoming a bookkeeper!

Activity Alternatives

1. Draw T accounts displaying the items you have chosen on cardboard using your own money amounts.

or

2. Plan a quiz show in which contestants are called upon to answer the items chosen above.

or

Reporting Alternatives

1. Post the cardboard and explain each to 2 classmates.

2. Put on the quiz show with several classmates. Ask a small group of other classmates to watch the show.

3. Explain in a narrative why the accounts are debited or credited and what types of accounts they are.

3. Read the narrative to 2 classmates and answer their questions.

Illustrate the Accounting Equation

Illustrate the Accounting Equation by using the preceding information, giving the balancing entry to each of the items you have chosen.

If you can complete all nine (9), start looking for a bookkeeping job!

Activity Alternatives
1. Draw T accounts displaying the items you have chosen and key the balancing entry.

Reporting Alternatives
1. Make copies of your T accounts, hand out and discuss the entries with 2 classmates.

or

2. Plan a quiz show in which you are the host and ask your classmates to supply the balancing entry for those items chosen.

2. Put on the quiz show with several classmates and have a few classmates observe.

or

3. Explain in narrative form the balancing entry for the items chosen.

3. Read the narrative to 3 classmates and answer their questions.

Identify and Describe a Balance Sheet

Pretend you are the owner of a video store. What would your Balance Sheet look like?

Activity Alternatives
1. Diagram the Balance Sheet on poster board.

Reporting Alternatives
1. Display the Balance Sheet and explain it to 2 classmates.

or

2. Tape an interview with a fellow classmate explaining your Balance Sheet.

2. Play the tape for 3 classmates so they can comment on it.

or

3. Make a Learning Circle depicting the order of the items on the Balance Sheet and their classifications.

3. Play the Learning Circle with 2 classmates.

or

4. If you have access to a personal computer, print out your sample Balance Sheet.

4. Make copies of your printout and distribute to 3 classmates.

Identify each of the following, as an asset, a liability, or capital. Choose six (6):

1. Cash
2. Accounts payable
3. Michael Jackson, capital
4. Interest due to the bank
5. Supplies on hand
6. Land and building
7. Insurance paid in advance
8. Accounts receivable

Activity Alternatives
1. Draw each of those chosen in T accounts on cardboard and put dollars with them.

Reporting Alternatives
1. Display the T accounts and discuss with 4 classmates.

or

2. Make a Learning Circle of the ones you have chosen.

2. Play the Learning Circle with a few classmates.

or

3. Make Task Cards of the ones you have chosen.

3. Use the Task Cards with 2 classmates.

Define the words or phrases on the following list:
a. transaction
b. journal
c. chronological
d. debit
e. credit
f. assets
g. liabilities
h. inventory
i. accounts receivable
j. accounts payable

You're really special if you can also define at least two (2) of these words or phrases:
k. liquidity
l. balance sheet equation
m. initial capital
n. owner's equity

Activity Alternatives

1. Using the words you have chosen, write a few paragraphs about bookkeeping for your video store. Tape record what you have written.

or

2. Make a crossword puzzle using the items you have chosen.

or

3. Make a Learning Circle from the words you have chosen.

Reporting Alternatives

1. Play the tape for several classmates and ask them for their comments.

2. Mount the puzzle and play it with several classmates.

3. Show the Learning Circle to a few classmates. Ask them to use it.

Circle of Knowledge

Team Members

1. _____   4. _____

2. _____   5. _____

3. _____   6. _____

Recorder _____

In four and $\frac{1}{16}$ ($4\frac{1}{16}$) minutes, list as many assets, liabilities, and capital accounts you can and specify which type they are.

	Check appropriate column		
	Type of Account:		
Item	A	L	C
1.			

Team Learning

Team Members

1. _____   3. _____

2. _____   4. _____

Recorder _____

Read the following passage and then reach consensus with the other group members so that all the questions are answered. Where there is a lack of agreement, those who disagree with the majority may write their own answers.

Jon Bonjovi opened a video store known as Bonjovi's Video's on October 1, 1989. The store's transactions for October were entered directly in T accounts. The T accounts represent the store's current assets of cash, accounts and notes receivable, the store's inventory of video tapes, the prepaid insurance and office supplies; the capital assets of shelves, a VCR, and office equipment. The equity accounts consists of current liabilities of accounts payable, long-term liability of notes payable, and owner's equity.

On October 31, 1989, these accounts appeared as shown below.

Bonjovi's Video Ledger Accounts
as of October 31, 1989

Cash					Accounts Receivable			
Oct. 1	$20,000.00	Oct. 3	$5,000.00		Oct. 14	$3,000.00	Oct. 16	$800.00
16	800.00	6	1,000.00					
31	5,000.00	12	300.00					
		15	1,000.00					
		15	10,000.00					
		17	200.00					

Notes Receivable					Video Tapes			
Oct. 15	$10,000.00	Oct. 31	$5,000.00		Oct. 2	$10,000.00	Oct. 14	$3,000.00

Shelves				Jon Bonjovi Capital		
Oct. 1	$6,000.00				Oct. 1	$20,000.00

	VCR	
Oct. 3	$5,000.00	

	Office Supplies	
Oct. 4	$500.00	
7	200.00	

	Prepaid Insurance	
Oct. 6	$1,000.00	
12	300.00	

	Office Equipment	
Oct. 15	$4,000.00	

Accounts Payable			
Oct. 17	$200.00	Oct. 2	$10,000.00
		4	500.00
		7	200.00
		15	3,000.00

Notes Payable		
	Oct. 10	$6,000.00

Questions

1. How were the company's transactions entered?
2. Indicate the probable reason for the recorded debits and credits. Do this by describing the transactions that were recorded on the dates shown.
3. Determine the account balances as of October 31, 1989.
4. Prepare a Balance Sheet as of October 31, 1989.
5. Choose one (1) of these activities:

   A. List five (5) of your own transactions and post the additional debits and credits to the existing accounts; determine the account balances and prepare a Balance Sheet as of October 31, 1989.
      (If you can add another five (5) more transactions, you are really quite a bookkeeper!)

   or

   B. Change the dollar amounts on the existing T accounts; determine the account balances, and prepare a Balance Sheet as of October 31, 1989.

**Group Analysis
Case Study**

Team Members

1. _____   3. _____

2. _____   4. _____

       Recorder _____

The balance sheet below for B. Joel Service Company contains a number of errors in placement and headings.

B. Joel Service Company
Balance Sheet
For the Year ended December 31, 1989

Cash	$ 4,000.00	Accounts Payable	$ 20,000.00
Owner's Investment	84,000.00	Building	70,000.00
Equipment	16,000.00	Accounts Receivable	14,000.00
Total Assets	104,000.00	Total Liabilities	104,000.00

1. What are the errors presented in this Balance Sheet?
2. How would you correct the presented Balance Sheet?
3. Place the presented Balance Sheet in the correct form.
4. Add a few more of your accounts and add them to the corrected Balance sheet.

(Answer Sheet follows.)

ANSWER SHEET

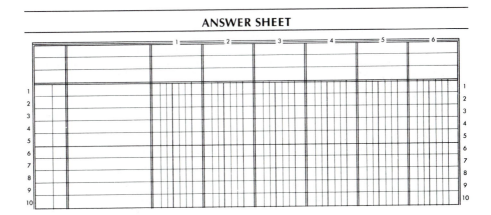

Resource Alternatives

Books

Cerepak, John R., and Donald H. Taylor. *Principles of Accounting.* Englewood Cliffs, NJ: Prentice-Hall, 1987.

Fields, Louis W. *Bookkeeping Made Simple.* New York: Doubleday, 1990.

Needes, Belverd E., Henry R. Anderson, and James C. Caldwell. *Principles of Accounting* (2nd ed.). Boston: Houghton Mifflin, 1984.

Other:

Programmed Learning Sequence
Electro Quiz Board
Flip Chute
Pic-A-Hole
Balance Sheet Body Game
Audio Tape
Script

Journals

Journal of Accountancy
C.F.O. The Magazine for Chief Financial Officers

Organizations

AICPA—American Institute of Certified Public Accountants, 1211 Avenue of the Americas, New York, New York. (212) 575-6200.

Student Name _____

Test

1. A _____ is any business deal that involves money.

2. The left side of an account is referred to as:

   a. the balance   c. a credit
   b. a debit   d. a footing

3. Bookkeeping is a single entry process. True or False

4. The basic tool for recording transactions is the _____.

5. A purchase of office equipment on credit requires a credit to:

   a. office equipment   c. accounts payable
   b. cash   d. equipment expense

6. The purchase of an asset for cash will:

   a. increase and decrease assets at the same time
   b. increase assets and increase liabilities
   c. increase assets and increase owner's equity
   d. increase assets and decrease liabilities

7. Payment for a two- (2) year insurance policy requires a debit to:

   a. prepaid insurance   c. cash
   b. insurance expense   d. accounts payable

8. Which of the following is a liability account?

   a. accounts receivable   c. rent expense
   b. withdrawals   d. accounts payable

9. The payment of a liability will:

   a. increase both assets and liabilities
   b. decrease both assets and liabilities
   c. decrease assets and increase liabilities
   d. increase assets and decrease liabilities

10. If a company has liabilities of $19,000.00 and owners' equity of $57,000.00, the assets of the company are:

    a. $38,000.00   c. $57,000.00
    b. $76,000.00   d. $19,000.00

11. Give an example of a business transaction that will result in (choose three (3)):

    a. an increase in one asset and a decrease in another asset.
    b. an increase in an asset and an increase in a liability.
    c. an increase in an asset and an increase in owner's equity.
    d. a decrease in an asset and a decrease in a liability.

12. Use the accounting equation to answer the questions below and show your calculations (choose two (2)):

    a. The assets of the White Snake Company are $480,000.00 and the owner's equity is $360,000.00. What is the amount of the liabilities?
    b. The liabilities of Stewart Enterprises equal one-third ($\frac{1}{3}$) of the total assets. The firm's owner's equity is $80,000.00. What is the amount of the liabilities?
    c. At the beginning of the year, Springsteen Company's assets were $180,000.00 and its owner's equity was $100,000.00. During the year, assets increased $60,000.00 and liabilities decreased $10,000.00. What was the owner's equity at the end of the year?

13. Supply the missing amount in the balance sheet data. Determine:

    a. A company's total liabilities when its total assets are $120,000.00 and its total owner's equity is $72,000.00.
    b. The equity of the owner when the business has total assets of $50,000.00 and total liabilities of $35,000.00.

c. A company's total assets when its total liabilities of $150,000.00 are equal to two-thirds ($\frac{2}{3}$) of its total owner's equity.

14. Using the following information, determine the company's total assets, total liabilities and owner's equity.

Accounts Payable	$12,000.00
Accounts Receivable	9,000.00
Michael Jordan, Capital	30,000.00
Building	40,000.00
Cash	8,000.00
Equipment	?
Land	6,000.00
Mortgage Payable	25,000.00

15. Using the form below, identify each transaction listed by letter and then indicate its effect on the company's total assets, total liabilities, and owner's equity. The effects of the first transaction are indicated as an example:

a. The owner invested cash to start the business.
b. Purchased office equipment for cash.
c. Purchased a vehicle on credit.
d. Borrowed money from a bank.
e. Paid in cash some of the amount owed on the company vehicle.
f. Lent money to another company on a promise that it would soon be paid back.
g. Received cash representing the entire amount lent previously.

	Total Assets	Total Liabilities	Owner's Equity
a.	Increase	No effect	Increase

16. From the following information, prepare a Balance Sheet for the Jackson Record Company as of August 31, 1989.

Accounts Payable	$ 3,400.00
Accounts Receivable	1,900.00
Building	46,000.00
M. Jackson, Capital	39,300.00
Cash	8,600.00
Land	7,500.00
Office Equipment	6,600.00
Mortgage Payable	19,000.00
Notes Payable	8,900.00

_9_

Designing Multisensory Instructional Packages to Respond to Individual Learning Styles

Multisensory Instructional Packages (MIPs) are especially appealing to students who find it difficult to sit quietly for long periods of time or who cannot listen to a teacher without frequently interrupting or losing attention. Using a package, these youngsters can concentrate for the amount of time that suits them, take breathers whenever they wish, and then continue with their work. Instructional packages are not as effective for students who need continual direct interaction with either adults or peers; but very often the same MIP on the identical objectives or topic may be suitable for several learners at the beginning of a semester, for others a few weeks later, for others at midterm, and so on. They also may be designed so that one or two of the multisensory activities may be bypassed if less concentration on the topic is necessary.

Instructional packages are a boon to teachers who want to individualize instruction through direct appeal to personal learning styles but who cannot stretch themselves thin enough for a class full of individuals with a variety of needs and problems. Because students work independently (or with a friend) and the materials are self-corrective, the packages can meet the needs of learners on several academic levels—youngsters with learning disabilities who require special attention; slow learners who need more time to grasp new material; average youngsters who prefer working on their own or for shorter or longer blocks of time; advanced students who are capable of progressing faster than their peers; and any interested student who wants to learn about a topic, concept, or skill at the moment that he or she desires, not when the teacher is able to get to the subject. The packages don't take up much classroom space and are particularly well suited to home study.

As an example of what is possible in a single classroom, six or seven highly visual students might be working on a PLS on vocabulary related to French food; three auditory students might be listening to a tape pronouncing the French food vocabulary; five highly kinesthetic students might be using a French vocabulary floor game to learn the words (*before* they hear the tape); four or five independent youngsters might be working on a CAP on the same lesson; three extremely tactual students would be *beginning* the lesson with an Electroboard, Flip Chute, or Pic-A-Hole; and students with no perceptual strengths would be using the MIP. After their first exposure through the strongest sense, students may exchange resources, but they need to *begin* correctly.

Learning Style Characteristics Responsive to Instructional Packages

Because of their multisensory activities, instructional packages are very motivating to slow learners, who usually require repetition and varied approaches through many senses before they are motivated to acquire and retain new knowledge and skills. The tape, written script, tactual, and kinesthetic materials may be used over and over again until the youngster masters the objectives of the package.

Each instructional package focuses on a single objective or concept to be taught. This isolated goal is well suited to the recalcitrant learner who often finds it difficult to concentrate on more than one thing at a time. Conversely, unless the material in the package is extremely challenging, it is unlikely to interest high achievers who quickly become bored by repetition.

Instructional packages are especially appropriate for those youngsters who require structure. The step-by-step procedures provide clear, sequenced directions that are repeated in a variety of ways until success is achieved.

Students who prefer working alone usually enjoy this multisensory method immensely. They can take the materials to an instructional area in the room, to the library, or even to their homes to work on intensively and without the distractions of the classroom and their peers.

Sound, in the form of your recorded voice, music, or other taped effects, can be provided or modulated through earphones or a cassette player.

All perceptual strengths are appealed to: by definition, instructional packages include visual, auditory, tactual, and kinesthetic activities. Even when a student has only a single perceptual strength, he or she is likely to learn and to complete objectives because everything that is taught is introduced and reinforced through the four major learning senses.

Teachers should be aware of those youngsters who prefer instructional packages but who lack responsibility. Encouragement and piecemeal success on portions of the package should be provided. Careful monitoring will aid those students in building responsibility. At times it may be necessary for the teacher or selected peers to work with those youngsters who respond well to instructional packages but who also require interaction with an authority figure or friends to stimulate learning.

Generally speaking, instructional packages are ideal for slower students who require structure and who can be sufficiently motivated by their multisensory activities to progress independently and successfully. MIPs may be signed out for home study. Instructions on the tapes guide students though each of all four multisensory activities, cautioning that the first one used should respond to each individual's perceptual strength—whichever modality is most to the right on the *Learning Style Inventory* (LSI) Individual Printout.

Learning Style Characteristics to Which Instructional Packages Can Be Accommodated

Instructional packages can be taken to wherever the light, temperature, and design of the physical environment are exactly as the student wishes them to be. Because instructional packages are portable and may be worked on alone, the choice of where to use these resources belongs to the student, who may select the amount of light, the degree of temperature, and the kind of design in which he or she feels most comfortable.

Motivation is often developed or stimulated through these packages because of (a) the choice that students have in their selection or in the topic that will be studied, (b) the way the packages accommodate to the environmental and physical elements of learning style, (c) the control that youngsters exercise over the amount and pace of learning in which they engage at a given time, and (d) the academic progress that is virtually assured by the package's multisensory repetition.

Three other important aspects of learning style—intake, time of day, and mobility—are accommodated by instructional packages. It is easy to take advantage of intake while working independently on an instructional package. Raw vegetables, nuts, raisins, or other nutritious foods can be available in a bowl wherever the youngster is working, provided that rules have been established beforehand for access, eating, discarding, and the care of the premises.

Packages may be used at any time of the day or night without interfering with others and without interrupting other scheduled activities. Therefore, students can select the most appropriate and effective time to complete a package.

Many growing adolescents cannot sit still or work in one place for a long time. Packages allow total mobility. A student may take the package with him, spread it out, walk away, come back, sprawl, kneel, or just sit. Since the activities themselves provide action and movement, mobility is well served by this method.

How Instructional Packages Facilitate Academic Achievement

Instructional packages are multisensory, self-contained teaching units that appeal to students who learn slowly or whose learning style characteristics respond to this method. All packages have certain basic elements in common:

This Multisensory Instructional Package (MIP) on "Let's Learn about Ancient Greece: It Burns a Torch for You" includes: a Programmed Learning Sequence to respond to students' needs for structure and visual and/or tactual materials; many manipulative resources such as an Electroboard, a Flip Chute, a Pic-A-Hole, Task Cards, and a Learning Circle; a kinesthetic Floor Game; a Contract Activity Package for youngsters who are motivated and who wish to reinforce through this technique after they have completed the items more responsive to their individual learning style strengths; and tapes to both direct the sequencing of instruction and to facilitate mastery by reading the text to students who need assistance with the printed content. (Photograph courtesy Center for the Study of Learning and Teaching Styles, St. John's University, New York.)

1. *Each package focuses on a single concept.*

Whether the package focuses on a novel such as *Anne of Green Gables*, a theme such as "War: Human Atrocity or Means of Protecting the Human Species?," or a single lesson, students know precisely what the focus is and can decide if it is appealing as a new topic or useful in reinforcing a previously learned skill. The cover and title always reveal what the package contains.

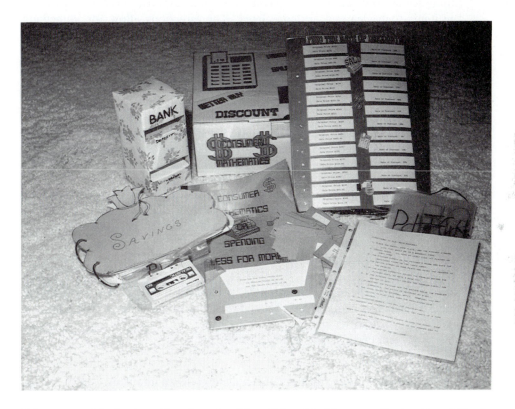

"Consumer Math: Spending Less for More" is a Multisensory Instructional Package designed for slowly achieving secondary students. The text is written on a sixth-grade reading level and emphasizes practical applications of purchasing and selling specific items based on many adolescents' interests—buying and trading in uniforms, sports equipment, tickets for baseball games, and so forth. Although it contains a Contract Activity Package for those who first complete the other enclosed instructional resources, it requires beginning the subject with the Flip Chute, Pic-A-Hole, Task Cards, Electroboard, or the kinesthetic Wall Game and then reviewing with the Programmed Learning Sequence. (Photograph courtesy Sr. Mary Buetner, graduate student, St. John's University, New York.)

2. *At least four senses are used to learn the contents.*

A typewritten script that is repeated by the taped voice of the teacher gives clear directions to students to construct, manipulate, piece together, write, draw, complete, play, and in several ways use their sense of touch and their entire bodies in kinesthetic activities related to the package's objectives.

3. *Feedback and evaluation are built in.*

Tests are included in the package, and students may respond by writing, taping, or showing results. Correct answers and responses may be checked as the items to be learned are completed. The directions allow for immediate feedback and self-evaluation. Mistakes can be corrected through repetition of the taped and printed directions and by comparing the students' answers with ones prepared for the games and activities.

4. *Learning is private and aimed at individual learning styles.*

Only the teacher and student know how well the youngster is doing. Self-image and success are enhanced as progress increases without peer competition for the slower students. The multisensory approach; colorful materials and packaging; working alone; motivating choices; selection of when, where, and how; and the ability to move about and to eat if necessary make the instructional package an effective teaching aid for many students.

Step-by-Step Guide to Designing an Instructional Package

Step 1   Identify the topic. For example, you may want your students to understand concepts or acquire skills related to scientific procedure, interpreting a novel, or synthesizing specific events in either history or current events, or how to solve a certain type of math problem.

Step 2   List the things you want the student to learn about the topic.

Step 3   Plan to tape record simple learning objectives for your students. Use such words as *explain, describe, list,* and *identify.* For example, if you were constructing a package on nouns, the taped objective might be: "By the time you finish this package, you will be able to explain what a noun is and to recognize one in a sentence." (For specific instructions, see the section of this chapter on "How to Tape Directions for Instructional Packages.")

Step 4   Pretend you are teaching your class the most important aspects of the selected topic. Write out exactly what you would say to them. Plan to tape-record this explanation.

Step 5   Develop a visual, a tactual, and a kinesthetic activity that emphasizes these aspects in different ways. Write the directions for each of the activities as they will be taped.

Step 6   Make up a short test that will reveal whether the student has learned the skills and concepts after using the package. This may be recorded as well as written.

Step 7   Use a colorful cardboard box with a design that reveals the topic and contents. Cover the entire box, including the typewritten topic and contents, with clear Contact paper, or laminate them to ensure longevity.

Examples of Appropriate Instructional Packages

Language Arts   Parts of speech, correct grammar, selected skills such as:

Recognizing and Using Adjectives

What Does an Adverb Do?

Interpreting and Creating Poetry

Writing in the Style of Tom Clancy

Writing a Creative Story

How to Write an Original Ending

How to Write a Business Letter

How to Develop Complete Sentences

When to Use the Possessive Form

Describing the Differences between Romanticism and Realism

Quotation Marks: Where Do They Go?

Social Studies   Map skills, geographical locations, community workers, common interests, such as:

East and West

Locating Capital Cities

Estimating Mileage

Congressional Powers

How Climate Affects Industrial Growth

What Is a Family?

A Different Kind of "Key"

A Visit to Paris

The Third World Nations

Customs of the Algonquins

Say "Hello!" in Many Languages

The Energy Crisis: How Does It Affect You?

How Do We Change "Man's Inhumanity to Man"?

The Canadian Pipeline

How Can We Erase Urban Blight?

How to Cope with Divorce in the Family

Mathematics   Telling time, counting, explaining money, sets, shapes, or signs:

Computing Your Future Income

The Things All Nations Share in Common: Economic Interdependence

One World: First Steps: Dividing Food Equitably among Humanity

Geometric Proofs

Precalculus Equations

Finding the Perimeter of Right Triangles

Solving Simple Alegbra Problems

Logarithms

Science   Explaining sources of power, food, growth, and health:

What Can a Magnet Do for You?

Making a Bulb Light

The Respiratory System

The Impact of Drugs on Your Mind

Static Electricity

Who Is Taller than Whom?

What Can Marijuana Do to You?

Geological Remnants in Our Area

Become an Inventor! Create a ———.

Would You Like to Make a Bell Ring?

The Greenhouse Effect

Are your Teeth Falling Out? They Will Unless . . .

You Can Have Beautiful Skin

Electromagnetic Control of the Universe

How to Tape Directions for Instructional Packages

The cassette tape is, perhaps, the most important part of a Multisensory Instructional Package. To be effective, the tape must provide simple, concise directions and explanations so that students can use the package without your assistance. The following suggestions can help you develop a good tape:

1. State the objectives clearly and simply.
2. Speak slowly and vary your speech pattern, tone, and inflection to add listening interest. Be dramatic, but not overly so.
3. Avoid picking up background noises or taping where electrical appliances can cause interference.
4. Use explicit directions for each action that the student must take. For example, request that the package's cover be placed on the table, that items be taken out carefully, that each envelope be returned to the box, and so on.
5. Pause after giving directions so that the listener has time to consider them and carry them out. Or, to allow longer periods of time, you could say, "Turn off the tape recorder while you are putting these materials away. But remember to turn the recorder back on when you are ready to continue."
6. Don't ask questions that require only "yes" or "no" responses. Avoid saying, "Are you ready to begin the next activity?" or "Did you know the answer to that riddle?" Instead say, "I hope you are ready for the next activity! Please take out the blue box with the cotton cloud on it." Or, "I hope you knew that the answer to that riddle was 'a clock.' A clock has 'hands' but never washes them!"
7. Be certain that the tape is completely self-instructional. Put yourself in the student's place and see if you can work alone without assistance or additional resources and without having to leave the area.
8. Repeat important directions or difficult passages in a slightly different way to reinforce in an interesting manner.
9. Use good grammar and appropriate vocabulary.
10. Be certain that the tape and the materials are self-corrective. If you ask questions, pause sufficiently and then provide answers.
11. Use supplementary sounds (music, bells, animal imitations, other people's voices). These add interest and help to sustain attention.
12. Use a good tape recorder and fresh batteries; place the microphone in a comfortable position for you; place a "Taping" sign on your door to avoid bells and other intrusions; take the telephone off the hook; leave enough footage at the beginning of the tape so that your introduction is recorded in its entirety; watch that the tape does not run out while you are still speaking; check the volume; and test as you are recording to be certain the pickup is clear.
13. Your students need only use two or three MIPs before they will be ready to create their own (see Chapter 10). Designing original MIPs, either individually, in pairs, or in small groups, will help students internalize the information they must master and will teach them to translate any difficult material they encounter in the future into instructional resources from which they will be able to learn anything.

Sample Multisensory Instructional Packages
Social Studies: The Great Depression*

Script

Hi! I hope you enjoy using this Multisensory Instructional Package on the Great Depression. It contains materials and activities for all kinds of learning styles. In this carton you will find a tape that says, word for word, exactly what you are reading here. Get it out now. Look for the tape with the yellow circle designed like a smiling face. I'll wait for you while you find it.

Hello, again. You may stop this tape whenever you need to take a break or to have more time to think something over. You may also replay any parts of the tape whenever you wish.

If you're ready, let's begin. By the time you complete this MIP, you should be able to:

1. Describe the quality of life lived by many Americans who were affected by the Great Depression.
2. Explain a business cycle.
3. Tell what happened on these two important dates: (a) October 29, 1929; and (b) February 1933.

*This Multisensory Instructional Package on "The Great Depression: Don't Let It Get You Down" was designed by Camille Sinatra, Reading Specialist, Manhasset Junior-Senior High School, Manhasset, NY.

"The Great Depression: Don't Let It Get You Down!" is replete with actual photographs and descriptions of what the United States was like during that period of economic deprivation. Note the component instructional strategies—a Contract Activity Package, a Programmed Learning Sequence, a variety of tactual materials, a kinesthetic Floor Game, a script, and accompanying tapes. (Photograph courtesy Center for the Study of Learning and Teaching Styles, St. John's University, New York.)

4. Describe the process of making an investment in the stock market.
5. List the reasons the American people were unhappy with President Herbert Hoover.
6. Explain why unemployment insurance, welfare assistance, and federal deposit insurance grew out of the events of the Great Depression.

All the materials you will need to achieve these objectives are in this carton. The materials are color-coordinated and marked with letters and colored circles or stars for easy identification. In the carton you will find:

1. The MIP script and tape you are using now
2. A PLS with accompanying tape (look for the smiling blue face)
3. A tape to accompany the two assigned readings from *American History* and *Building the American Nation*
4. Special tapes with advice for:
     a. the visual learner
     b. the auditory learner
     c. the tactual/kinesthetic learner
5. Two sets of cards for five different card games (instructions are in the CAP and also on this tape)
6. A Flip Chute
7. A Pic-A-Hole
8. A Learning Circle
9. An Electroboard
10. Task Cards
11. A Floor Game which is also a dance
12. An MIP package pre- and posttest (which is identical to the CAP test)

Directions for the use of all these things follow immediately. Specific directions and advice for the visual, auditory, and tactual kinesthetic learner can be found on separate clearly marked tapes. Remember to do the activities in the order of your perceptual strengths. Use the materials that are addressed to your greatest strength first. Then use the materials addressed to your second and third strengths, and so on. Do as many activities as you need to master the objectives—and enjoy yourself!

First, everyone must begin by taking the pretest, which is on the last page of this script. Answer whichever questions you can, and check with the teacher. Stop the recorder and do it now. (Pause)

Good. You're back. Here are the directions I promised you:

Electroboard Directions

1. Take the continuity tester and lay it out in front of you.
2. Put one end of the tester near the question, or left side of the board.
3. Put the other end of the tester near the right, or answer side of the board.
4. Read the word or phrase on the left side.
5. Place one end of the continuity tester on the silver circle next to that word or phrase.
6. Read the choice words and phrases on the right side.
7. When you find a match, put the other end of the continuity tester onto the silver circle next to it.
8. If you choose the correct match, the continuity tester will light up.
9. It it doesn't light, try again.

10. Continue until you have matched all the items on both sides (A and B) of the Electroboard. Try to remember the answers to each question. Write them into your notebook.

On side A of the Electroboard, the left column reads:

- Lodging houses
- Ten (10)
- October 29, 1929
- Apples and pencils
- Breadlines
- "Wall Street Lays an Egg"
- Herbert Hoover
- Stock
- Recovery
- Welfare

On side A of the Electroboard, the right column reads:

- A president during the Great Depression
- Date of the Great Stock Market Crash
- Queues on which people stood waiting for free bread and other food items during the Great Depression
- Shares of ownership in a business
- A stage in the business cycle during which the economy begins to improve
- Two items sold by street corner peddlers during the Great Depression
- Program in which the government assumes responsibility for the support of its citizens
- Length (in years) of the Great Depression
- Newspaper headline the day after the Great Stock Market Crash
- Places where homeless people could spend the night

On side B of the Electroboard, the left column reads:

- Soup kitchens
- Business cycle
- Unemployment insurance
- February 1933
- Twenty-five (25)
- Prosperity
- Boom

- Depression
- Black Tuesday
- Dividends

On side B of the Electroboard, the right column reads:

- Amounts of money paid to stockholders who own shares in a company
- A time of low production of goods and high unemployment
- Regular change in the economy from depression to recovery and prosperity and back again
- A time of high production of goods and low unemployment
- Payments made for a period of time to an unemployed worker
- Name we have given to the day the stock market crashed
- Places where free meals were provided during the Great Depression
- Date of the banking panic
- Percentage of unemployed people at the worst point in the Great Depression
- A period of abnormal economic prosperity usually followed by a severe depression

Pic-A-Hole Directions*

1. Take the golf tee that is attached to the Pic-A-Hole out of its pocket.
2. Read the question that is in the top window.
3. In the smaller, bottom window are three choices to answer the question. Only one of them is correct.
4. Take the golf tee. Put it into the hole under the correct answer.
5. Gently try to pull the card out of the pocket. If your answer is correct, the card will slide freely from the pocket. If you choose an incorrect answer, however, the card will not slide out.
6. Continue until you have answered all the questions.

These are the questions and answer choices on the cards in the Pic-A-Hole:

- During the Depression, many people lost the money they had deposited in bank accounts because there was no
  welfare   federal deposit insurance   stock

*See Chapter 6 for drawings of the actual Pic-A-Hole cards for this topic.

- A time of high production of goods and low unemployment is referred to as
  prosperity   a business cycle   depression
- An item commonly sold by streetcorner salespeople was
  apples   diamonds   watches
- A period during the business cycle when the economy is on the upswing from depression is called
  recovery   prosperity   economy
- Shantytown villages set up on public land by homeless people were called
  squatters   Hoovervilles   lodges
- The banking panic took place in
  October 1929   1940   February 1933
- The Great Depression affected almost all aspects of life in the United States and abroad, but especially the
  politics   social programs   economy
- During the worst period of the Great Depression _____% of the American people were unemployed.
  15   25   10
- _____ is the day in October 1929 when stock prices fell sharply and the Great Depression began.
  Black Monday   Black Tuesday   Blue Tuesday
- Monies paid to shareholders who own stock in a company are called
  shares   stock   dividends
- Shares of ownership in a business that are sold to people and allow them to share some of the money earned by the company are called
  shareholders   stock   dividends
- Street corner salespeople selling apples and pencils, beggars, and _____ were common sights during the Depression.
  tramps   millionaires   prosperity
- There was no such thing as _____ before the 1930s.
  depression   unemployment insurance   prosperity
- A program that did not exist before 1930 was
  prosperity   unemployment   welfare
- The Great Stock Market Crash occurred in
  1929   1933   1940
- The regular change in the economy is called
  recovery   depression   a business cycle
- The Great Depression lasted for _____ years.
  10   5   25
- Free meals were provided at
  drives   soup kitchens   banks
- Homeless people could spend the night in
  breadlines   parks   lodging houses
- The President, during the early part of the Great Depression, was
  Hoover   Roosevelt   Wilson

Flip Chute Directions*

1. Be certain all the cards in the envelopes on the sides of the container are facing you so that the missing corner is on the upper right side like this:

2. Read the word or phrase on the first card and try to think of a definition.
3. Insert the card face up into the top slot of the Flip Chute.
4. The card will come out the bottom slot with the definition showing. Is each what you thought it would be?
5. Work on the terms until you know all of them before the Flip Chute confirms your answer.

Here are the words or terms that appear on the Flip Chute cards. (Remember that your definition does not have to match the definition on the Flip Chute card word for word. What is important is the *meaning*.)

- Black Tuesday
- Unemployment insurance
- Depression
- February 1933
- Business cycle
- Dividends
- 25%
- Herbert Hoover
- Federal deposit insurance
- Breadlines
- Stocks
- Ten years
- Hoovervilles
- Welfare assistance
- Soup kitchens
- Street corner salespeople, tramps, beggars
- Prosperity
- Recovery
- October 29, 1929
- Lodging houses

Floor Game: Hooverville Hopscotch, or Learn to Do the Unemployment Shuffle

This floor game may be played by two to four people in one of two ways: either as an ordinary game of hopscotch, or as a dance. To begin:

*See Chapter 6 for drawings of the actual Flip Chute cards for this unit.

1. Find the bright red plastic floor game and spread it out onto a carpeted part of the floor.
2. Find the deck of cards that goes with the game. (Look for the green circle that matches the green circle on the game.)
3. Remove your shoes so that you can walk on the game squares.
4. *To play hopscotch:* Choose one person to read the questions on the cards. The remaining players must take turns answering the questions. As each player answers a question correctly, he or she may move from his or her position in the squatters' shack onto the consecutively numbered squares, one foot at a time. When the player reaches number eight (8), he or she must pivot on one foot and make his or her way back to the squatters' shack, one numbered square at a time. The players may take turns, completing the entire course individually before the next player begins, or the reader may choose to read the questions to alternate players so that two or three people are on the course at the same time.
5. *To learn the unemployment shuffle:* During this game, one player at a time must complete the entire course before another player begins. To play, follow the same directions as in #4 above, except that you must step into square 1 with your right foot, square 2 with your left foot, square 3 with your right foot and so on. You will see as you begin to do this that you must execute a number of spins and backward steps—the dance steps to the Unemployment Shuffle! Have fun!

The questions and answers on the Hooverville Hopscotch cards read:

- The Great Depression lasted for _____. ten years
- Places where homeless people could go to spend the night were called _____. lodging houses
- The President during the early part of the Great Depression was _____. Herbert Hoover
- October 29, 1929 is often called _____. Black Tuesday
- February 1933 is the date of the _____. banking panic
- October 29, 1929 is the date of the _____. Stock Market Crash
- Monies paid to shareholders who own stock in a company are called _____. dividends
- During the Depression, many people lost the money they had deposited in bank accounts because there was no _____. federal deposit insurance
- Shares of ownership in a company are called _____. stock
- People who lived in shacks in Hoovervilles were called _____. squatters
- During the Great Depression, ____% of the American people were unemployed. 25

- Two places where hungry people could receive food were _____ and _____.   soup kitchens and breadlines
- A time of high production and low unemployment is called _____.   prosperity
- Two items commonly sold on street corners during the Great Depression were _____ and _____.   pencils and apples
- When a person loses his or her job today, he or she can collect _____ until another job is found.   unemployment insurance
- The regular change in the economy is called a _____.   business cycle.

Game: Solitaire-Challenge

1. _____ − _____
2. _____ − _____
3. _____ − _____
4. _____ − _____
5. Recorder _____ - _____

Work together to create a set of at least twenty (20) flash cards about the major concepts and vocabulary involved in this unit. After you have played enough games of Solitaire individually, Challenge one another, and then each member of the team Challenge one other student in the class to a game. Record your names above.

Reminders:

Solitaire   An individual player places a set of flash cards on the table, term up and definition down. He or she then proceeds to pick up as many of the cards as possible by correctly identifying the meaning of the term as it is removed from the table.

The more difficult version: The player proceeds with the same intent as above, but the cards are placed on the table, term down and definition up. This time the player must read the definition and recall the term correctly.

Challenge: Two players each attempt to gain the greater number of cards as they play the games described above, each player taking his or her turn.

Special Note

If the Flip Chute from the MIP is not in use, you may use the cards that are in the envelopes on the container, or you may wish to use them just to help you create your own set. If you would like to hear the words and phrases read to you, please listen to the MIP tape for the Flip Chute.

Q-A Card Game Rules

1. _____   3. _____

2. _____   4. _____

1. This game can be played by up to four people.
2. Shuffle the cards and deal until all cards have been distributed.
3. The player who has the card with the red star in the upper right-hand corner goes first. He or she reads the question on the card.
4. The player who has the card with the answer to the question reads the answer aloud. If all the players agree that the answer is correct, the same player then reads the question on the lower half of the card.
5. The player who has the answer to *that* question then reads it aloud, and the process continues as in number four (4) above. Each time a player reads an answer and question, that player may discard his card on a pile in the center of the table.
6. The game continues until one player has discarded all of his cards and is declared the winner.

Note: What makes this game tricky is that the player who reads the question may also be the player who has the answer in his hand!

When the game is played in the correct sequence, the answers and questions on the Q-A cards read as follows:

Q—Who was President during the early part of the Great Depression?
A—Herbert Hoover

Q—For how many years did the Great Depression last?
A—ten years

Q—What do we call a period of high production and low unemployment?
A—prosperity

Q—During the worst part of the Great Depression, what percentage of the American people was unemployed?
A—25%

Q—What were places called where homeless people could spend the night?
A—lodging houses

Q—Shantytown villages erected on public land by the homeless were called _____.
A—Hoovervilles

Q—When did the Great Stock Market Crash occur?
A—October 29, 1929

Q—Where could hungry people go for a free meal during the Great Depression?
A—soup kitchens

Q—A business cycle is _____.

A—a regular change in the economy from prosperity to depression and back again.

Q—To protect citizens' deposits in bank accounts, a national program called _____ was begun as a result of the Depression.

A—federal deposit insurance

Q—During the Depression, an unemployed person could not receive _____ while he was temporarily out of work.

A—unemployment insurance

Q—A time of low production and high unemployment is referred to as a

A—depression

Q—Two items commonly sold by street corner salespeople during the Depression were

A—apples and pencils

Q—A period during the business cycle when the economy is on the upswing from depression is called

A—recovery

Q—The banking panic took place in

A—February 1933

Q—October 29, 1929 is often referred to as

A—Black Tuesday

Q—What do we call money paid to shareholders who own stock in a company?

A—dividends

Q—A program of financial assistance to the needy and their families that did not exist during the Depression is called

A—welfare support

Q—Places where people could receive bread and other food items were called

A—bread lines

Q—Certificates of ownership in a company that allow an investor to share in the profits of the company are called _____.

A—stock

Q—Who began the game with the card bearing a red star?

At this point, the person who asked the first question replies, and the game is over.

Learning Circle Directions

1. Take out the large yellow circle with the clothespins attached to it and remove all the clothespins.

2. Match each of the eight words or phrases on the circle with the word or phrase on each clothespin by clipping the clothespins in place on the circle.
3. When you have finished doing this, turn the circle over. On the back of the circle, you will see eight different designs in small colored circles.
4. If the designs match the designs on the clothespins, you will know that you have matched the items correctly.

Starting at the metal hanging ring and reading clockwise, the words and phrases on the learning circle read:

- President
- October 29, 1929
- ten years
- 25%
- Hoovervilles
- February 1933
- opposite of recovery
- bread lines

The words and phrases on the clothespins read:

- Herbert Hoover
- Black Tuesday
- Great Depression
- unemployed
- squatters' shacks
- banking panic
- failing economy
- free food

Task Card Directions*

1. Remove the Task Cards from the envelope marked with a plain red circle.
2. On each separate piece in the envelope is written half a statement about the Great Depression. The pieces fit together like jigsaw puzzles.
3. Your job is to match the halves and make the statements complete.
4. Continue until you have matched all of the pieces.

*See Chapter 6 for drawings of the actual Task Cards for this unit.

When you have finished, you will have the following statements:

- Depression is   /   a period of low production and high unemployment.
- Lodging houses were places where homeless people could   /   spend the night.
- During the worst part of the Great Depression   /   25% of the American people were unemployed.
- February 1933 was   /   the date of the banking panic.
- October 29, 1929 was   /   the date of the Great Stock Market Crash.
- The Great Depression lasted for   /   ten years.
- Herbert Hoover was   /   President during the Great Depression.
- Another term for the day of the Great Stock Market Crash is   /   Black Tuesday.
- Shantytown villages were called   /   Hoovervilles.
- Breadlines were places where hungry people could   /   receive free bread and other food items.

Now that you understand how each of the items in this package is to be used, find either the visual, the auditory or the tactual/kinesthetic tape for more specific advice related to your personal learning style.

Good luck and have fun!

Script for Tactual Students Using the Multisensory Instructional Package on the Great Depression

If you are a tactual learner, choose any of the tactual, tactual/visual, and/or tactual/kinesthetic activities in this Multisensory Instructional Package (MIP) to help you master this unit's objectives. Choose from among the Learning Circle, Task Cards, Flip Chute, Pic-A-Hole, or Electroboard. If you are tactual/kinesthetic—or if you might enjoy using a Floor Game—choose the Hooverville Hopscotch/Unemployment Shuffle.

Directions for how to use these resources are either on the back or on the bottom of each. If you prefer to hear them read to you, use the tape called "Directions for Using Tactual Resources."

If you are tactual and visual, and if you prefer a structured resource, you probably will learn easily from the Programmed Learning Sequence (PLS) in this MIP. It contains many tactual resources in miniature—a small Pic-A-Hole, Electroboard, and set of Task Cards. If you have not previously used a PLS to master a unit's objectives, do experiment. You may like it very much. The PLS is clearly marked with a smiling face—the same smiling face (in yellow) that matches the PLS's tape (in case you prefer hearing it as you read along).

People who like to move and can think while they are doing so (kinesthetic learners) usually enjoy learning through Floor Games. If you are kinesthetic, or tactual and kinesthetic, do try the Hooverville Hopscotch Floor

Game or the Unemployment Shuffle Floor Game. They are resources that entail a bit of dancing, but the better you become at answering the questions, the better you will be able to dance the Floor Game! What do you have to lose? Even if you are shy about dancing, look at these resources. You may decide to try them!

Tactual learners who enjoy working with others—rather than alone— sometimes enjoy the Card Games named *Q-A, Solitaire,* and *Challenge.* Directions for five different games are on the MIP tape. "Directions for Using Tactual Resources."

Start with whichever resources appeal to you, and use as many as it takes for you to be certain that you know all (most of) the answers required by this unit's objectives—but aim for *all!* After all, why not? When you believe that you have used enough resources to "cement the information in your brain" (remember the information required in the first Six Objectives listed at the beginning of the MIP tape), take the Posttest in the envelope labeled Posttest at the bottom of the MIP box. Compare your answers with a classmate's or check them with any of the resources in this package. If you need a little repetition to correct some, try a different resource for review or clarification.

When you have finished working with this MIP's resources, please *rewind* all the tapes you have used, return the materials to their original containers, and return the carton to where it belongs (the shelf, the closet, the instructional area).

I hope you enjoyed using this MIP! After all, it would be very sad to have you feel *depressed* about learning *this* topic—the Great Depression! Good luck on the exam! I hope you never forget this information, because economic depressions appear to be cyclical. If you remember, you will be prepared for, and thus able to cope with, any in the future! I wish you well!

Script for Auditory Students Using the Multisensory Instructional Package on the Great Depression

If you are an auditory learner, you may prefer to listen to my lecture on the Great Depression first—before using any of the other available resources. Please check with me or with our Class Calendar for the day and time that introductory lesson has been scheduled. On the other hand, you may prefer to hear one or more of the textbook's related chapters read on a tape. The tapes are in the MIP package and are clearly marked, "Book Chapters on Tape." One is from the text, *American History,* and the other is from *Building the American Nation.* They both may be of help, or you may prefer one more than the other. Let me know your reactions, please! If your preference is to read the chapter but to use the tape to read along with you, both chapters' tapes *and* the books are in our class library—both in the Reading Corner and in the "Textbook" collection.

If you are an auditory/tactual learner who also likes to learn visually, the

Programmed Learning Sequence (PLS) may appeal to you. That is the spiral-bound black book shaped like a calendar. The PLS is also in the MIP package. There is a tape to accompany it, with a smiling face that matches identically (in color and shape) the smiling face on the PLS itself. The PLS is highly structured and, thus, is easy to follow and learn from.

Start with an auditory resource but, after that initial exposure, you may use any or all of those included in this MIP carton. When you believe you have used enough resources to ensure that you have mastered the first Six Objectives listed at the beginning of the MIP tape, take the Posttest in the envelope labeled "Posttest" at the bottom of the MIP box. Compare your answers with a classmate's or check them against any of the resources in this MIP. If you need a little repetition to correct some, try a different resource than the one(s) you already used. A new or different resource may be more interesting for review or clarification than a repeat.

When you have finished working with this MIP's resources, please rewind all the tapes you used, return the materials to their original containers, and return the carton to where it belongs—on the shelf, in the closet, or in the Social Studies instructional section.

I hope you enjoyed using this MIP! After all, it would never do to have you learn about the Great Depression and feel anything but exuberant about the fact that you luckily avoided those hard-hit, economically depressed days. Feel *good* about that—at least!

Script for Visual Students Using the Multisensory Instructional Package on the Great Depression

If you are either a visual or a visual/auditory student, you may prefer to begin this unit by viewing one of the videocassettes or the filmstrip which are listed under "Resources" on the last two pages of the MIP script. The videocassette is in the classroom in the "Software" section (unless someone else is using it at the moment). If you cannot find it, an extra copy is in the school Media Center.

Another alternative would be for you to begin by reading the chapters in any of the four (4) books used in conjunction with this unit. Those, too, are listed under Resources on the last two pages of the MIP script. Two of the books, *American History* and *Building the American Nation,* have the chapters related to this unit on the Great Depression on tape. Those tapes are included in this MIP carton; the books *and* accompanying tapes are in our class library—both in the Reading Corner and in the "Textbook" collection.

If you are a visual learner who likes to work alone, you may be interested in using this MIP's Contract Activity Package (CAP). Please see me for a copy. There are *some* activities in the CAP (such as Team Learning, Circle of Knowledge, Case Studies, or Brainstorming) that you may care to engage in with one or more classmates or friends. The Reporting Alternatives *must* be shared with someone else. If this causes you a problem, please discuss it with me.

A Programmed Learning Sequence (PLS) is also available. It is an *excellent* resource for visual or tactual students who enjoy structure. Perhaps look at it and consider whether you would find that resource preferable to others. Although the PLS has an accompanying tape and several tactual resources, it is very readable and can be used without the tape if you wish.

Start with a visual resource but, after that initial exposure, you may use any or all of those included in this MIP carton. When you believe you have used enough resources to ensure that you have mastered the first Six Objectives listed at the beginning of the MIP tape, take the Posttest in the envelope labeled "Posttest" at the bottom of the MIP box. Compare your answers with a classmate's or check them against any of the resources in this MIP. If you need a little repetition to correct some, try a different resource than the one(s) you already used. A new or different resource may be more interesting for review or clarification than a repeat.

When you have finished working with this MIP's Resources, please rewind all the tapes you used, return the materials to their original containers, and return the carton to where it belongs—on the shelf, in the closet, or in the Social Studies instructional section.

I hope you enjoyed using this MIP! I would find it very depressing myself if you were to tell me that you did not enjoy learning this information this way after all the hard work it took to develop these many resources to help you learn about the Great Depression, in what I hoped would be an interesting way! In addition, there was absolutely no economic reimbursement for my effort, so the *least* you can do is elevate my spirits and tell me how much you appreciate my good work!

Incidentally, if, by any strange quirk of fate, you *did* enjoy learning this way, I would be pleased to give you the basic guidelines for creating an MIP. *Would you do that for our next unit?*

Pre- and Posttest

Name _____

Date _____

Directions: Answer each of the following questions in a short paragraph.

1. Describe the quality of life lived by many Americans who were affected by the Great Depression.

2. Explain a business cycle.

3. Tell what happened on these important dates: (a) October 29, 1929 and (b) February 1933.

4. Describe the process of making an investment in the stock market.

5. List the reasons the American people were unhappy with President Herbert Hoover.

6. Explain why unemployment insurance, welfare assistance, and federal deposit insurance grew out of the events of the Great Depression.

Resources

Books
Brown, Richard C., and Herbert J. Bass. "The Great Depression and the New Deal." *One Flag, One Land.* Morristown, NJ: Silver Burdett, 1975, pp. 580–585.
Davidson, James West, and Mark H. Lytle. "From Prosperity to Despair." *The United States: A History of the Republic.* Englewood Cliffs, NJ: Prentice-Hall, 1986, pp. 546–553.
Garraty, John A. "The Great Depression and the New Deal." *American History.* New York: Harcourt Brace Jovanovich, 1982, pp. 737–742.
Reich, Jerome R., and Edward L. Biller. "The Great Depression." *Building the American Nation.* New York: Harcourt Brace Jovanovich, 1971, pp. 630–635.

You-Tell-It Filmstrip Supplies
You-Tell-It film with 48 story boards, calibrated layout guide, instruction manual, fifty feet of film, marking pens, and projector stage. Dev-Coa, Inc., Developmental Corporation of America, 83 Clover Avenue, Floral Park, NY 11001.

Game
"The Great Crash: Stock Market" with reading sheets, question sheets, and board game. From Games to Teach American History series, Opportunities for Learning, Inc., 20417 Nordhoff Street, Dept. F20, Chatsworth, CA 91311.

Magazine
"Back at Home" with a decade of pictures, including the roaring twenties, Hoover, and the stock market crash; news stories are written at a 3.5–4.5 reading level; 60–70 photographs. From *Our Century Magazines* series, Fearon Education, David S. Lake Publishers, 19 Davis Drive, Belmont, CA 94002

Video Cassettes
"The Great Depression" including the bank panic, Wall Street on Black Tuesday, unemployment, Roosevelt's New Deal, the coming of World War II, and the return
of prosperity. Two video cassettes, 32 minutes. Guidance Associates, Inc., Communications Park, Box 3000, Mount Kisco, NY 10549–0900.
"Witness to History: The Great Depression" including bank runs, unemployment,
food lines, shantytown "Hoovervilles," Hoover, Roosevelt, and the Bonus
Army. One cassette, 15 minutes. Guidance Associates (see above).

Filmstrips
"The Great Depression" with four filmstrips, cassettes, and simulations as well as
spirit masters. Includes photographs, cartoons, commercial art, songs, and ballads. Opportunities for Learning, Inc. (please see "Game" above).

Additional Teacher-Made Resources

[Please *see* directions in the MIP script for using resources with which you
may be unfamiliar, or *listen to* the directions on the MIP tape.]

- Learning Circle (tactual/visual)
- Task Cards (tactual/visual)
- Flip Chute (tactual/visual)
- Pic-A-Hole (tactual/visual)
- Electroboard (tactual/visual)
- Hooverville Hopscotch Floor Game (kinesthetic/visual)
- Unemployment Shuffle Floor Game (kinesthetic/tactual)
- Q-A Card Game (see Contract Activity Package [CAP], Activity #8) (tac-
  tual/visual)
- Crossword Puzzle (see CAP, Activity #7)
- Team Learning on Herbert Hoover (see CAP, Activity #10)
- Solitaire Card Game (tactual/visual) (see CAP, Activity #11 and instruc-
  tions either on the MIP tape or in the MIP script)
- Challenge Card Game (tactual/visual) (see CAP, Activity #11 and instruc-
  tions on the MIP tape or in the MIP script)
- Tape recordings of the chapters related to The Great Depression in
  either *Building the American Nation* or in *American History*
- Tape recordings of the Programmed Learning Sequence (PLS)
- Tape recording of the MIP script
- Tape recordings for: (a) visual; (b) tactual; or (c) auditory learners. Kinesthetic learners, *stand or move* as you work with instructional resources
  that complement your secondary strength!;

Code: MIP = Multisensory Instructional Package; CAP = Contract Activity Package; PLS =
Programmed Learning Sequence.

Science: The Heart*

Hello! I'm happy that you chose this package on the heart to work with today. By the time you finish this package, you will understand the importance of the heart. This box contains many entertaining things for you to do to learn about the heart.

It is best for you to choose your first activity corresponding to your first strength, your second activity corresponding to your second strength, and your third activity corresponding to your third strength.

This Multisensory Instructional Package, "Heart: Takes A Licking But Keeps On Ticking," is a novel way of teaching science through students' very different learning style strengths. Every student completes the identical *objectives, but each does so by using instructional resources that are* complementary *to, rather than dissonant from, his or her learning style preferences. (Photograph courtesy Center for the Study of Learning and Teaching Styles, St. John's University, New York.)*

*This Multisensory Instructional Package, "The Heart: Takes a Licking, But Keeps On Ticking," was designed by Bernadette Kane, graduate student, St. John's University, Utopia Parkway, Jamaica, NY 11439.

If you do not remember your strengths, go to the bulletin board in the front of the room and check the LSI Class Chart[†] next to your name; you will see your first, second, and third strengths.

If you do not want to listen to the tapes, you do not have to listen. You are familiar with using the type of materials inside this box. If you have questions regarding particular material, refer to the tape describing that item.

The middle of this tape contains a reading of the Programmed Learning Sequence.

Tape Number Two (2) contains directions to the Flip Chute, Electroboard, Pic-A-Hole, and Floor Game, in that order. If you want to work with Task Cards, you can find them in the PLS, Frame 27.

This next portion of this tape contains a reading of the Programmed Learning Sequence (PLS).

Take out the PLS; it is a booklet designed in the shape of the heart. Open the PLS and read along with me. As we read the PLS, answer each question. If you need to think over a question, you can turn off the tape. Take your time and good luck. If you do not want to listen to this tape, turn it off and either choose the different activities most closely matched to your perceptual strength or read the PLS on your own.

Flip Chute

Take the question from the side pocket; read the question on the card. Think of an answer, then put the card with the question facing you into the top slot. Watch for the card to come out the bottom slot with an answer on it. Do this with each of the cards and you will see that it is an interesting tactual way to learn about the heart. When you finish all the questions, please put the cards back into the side pocket and put the Flip Chute back into the box.

Electroboard

Take out the red heart. In order to work this Electroboard, you need to use a continuity tester, which is available in the box. Put one end of the continuity tester onto the question being asked on the left-hand side of the heart. Put the other end of the circuit tester onto the answer you think is correct on the right hand side of the heart. The continuity tester will light up if you chose the correct answer. No light will show if your answer is incorrect, so try again! After you have worked with the Electroboard, please put it back into the box.

Pic-A-Hole

Take out the rectangular shaped material with the three (3) holes at the bottom. Read each card and choose an answer by placing the attached golf tee

---

[†]Class Charts are available through St. John's University's Center for the Study of Learning and Teaching Styles, New York. See Chapter 12.

into the hole. If you are correct, the card will come out; if you are incorrect, the card will remain in place. So, try again!

After you complete the Pic-A-Hole, please put it back into the box where you found it.

Floor Game

The Floor Game is designed for one (1) or two (2) players. If you are playing with two (2), flip a coin and heads will go first, tails second. Both players have a part to the heart.

Choose a card from the play card box. Read the question on the card (read out loud if you are playing with two (2) players.) Give your answer, then flip the card to check if you are correct. If you are right, move to the first box in your path. If you are wrong, your opponent then has a chance to answer the question. If your opponent gives the correct answer, then he can move to the first box in his path. After a question is answered, place the question into the answered question box.

For every correct answer you give, you advance a box toward the big heart. If you give an incorrect answer, then you move back a box. The first person who gets to the big heart is the winner. Please put the materials back into the box when the game has been completed.

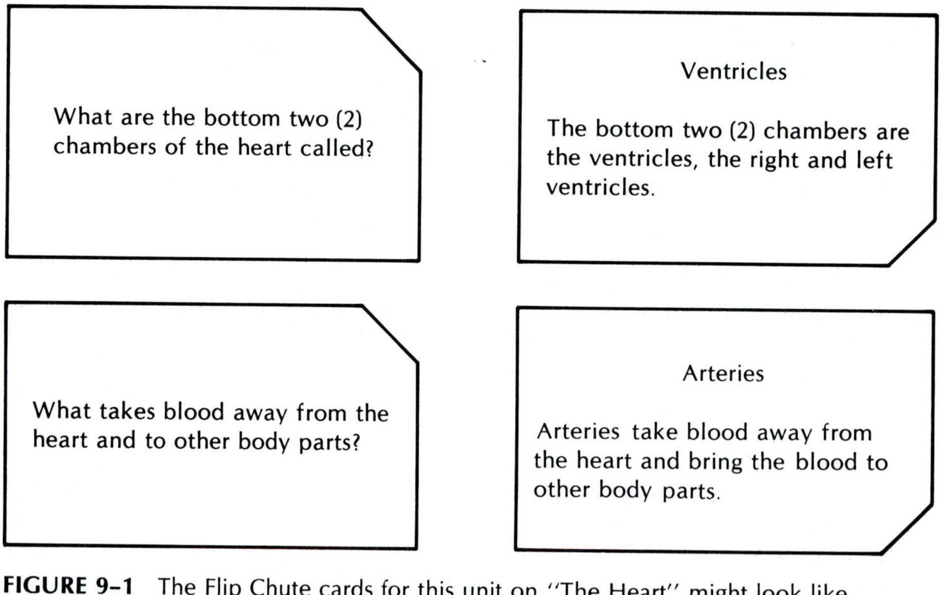

What are the bottom two (2) chambers of the heart called?

Ventricles

The bottom two (2) chambers are the ventricles, the right and left ventricles.

What takes blood away from the heart and to other body parts?

Arteries

Arteries take blood away from the heart and bring the blood to other body parts.

FIGURE 9–1   The Flip Chute cards for this unit on "The Heart" might look like these samples.

FIGURE 9-1 *Continued*

What are the top two (2) chambers of the heart called?	Atria (singular atrium) Right and left atrium are the top two (2) chambers of the heart.
What membrane encloses the heart?	Pericardium Pericardium is the membrane that the heart is enclosed in.
What muscular wall separates the heart into a right and left side?	Septum Septum is the muscular wall that separates the right and left side of the heart.
What prevents blood from flowing backwards?	Valves Valves prevent blood from flowing backwards.
What carries blood to the heart?	Veins Veins bring blood to the heart.

Continued

FIGURE 9-1 *Continued*

In which direction does the heart slant?

Downward

The heart slants downward.

How many chambers does the heart have?

Four (4)

The heart has four (4) chambers or compartments.

What type of organ is the heart?

Muscular

The heart is a muscular organ.

What is the largest artery in the body?

Aorta

The aorta is the largest artery in the body.

What are the largest veins in the body?

Superior and inferior vena cava

The superior and inferior vena cava are the largest veins.

Anne of Green Gables *is an MIP that makes literature come alive for students who require a variety of instructional materials but need to begin learning through resources most responsive to their unique learning style characteristics. (Photograph courtesy Center for the Study of Learning and Teaching Styles, St. John's University, New York.)*

"Basic Bookkeeping, or Making Dollars and Cents of It," designed by Karen Robinson, includes: both an analytic title and a global subtitle; a Programmed Learning Sequence for students who need structure and are either visual or tactual and motivated; a variety of tactual resources such as an Electroboard, a Pic-A-Hole, multipart Task Cards, and a Flip Chute; a kinesthetic Floor Game; a script that sequences the instructional resources based on each individual's primary and then secondary perceptual modality; a Contract Activity Package for those who wish to explore that method as a review after having first been exposed to the subject matter content through more responsive strategies; and a tape for each item to assist in mastery for students who either read below grade level or who enjoy being read to. (Photograph courtesy Center for the Study of Learning and Teaching Styles, St. John's University, New York.)

A Final Word on Multisensory Instructional Packages

Teachers often do not have the time or patience to teach and reteach each student who needs individualized attention. Instructional packages can do both and offer a variety of other benefits too. They develop listening skills, encourage independent work, and teach students to follow directions. They make students aware of their own growth and, gradually, build positive self-image and confidence. They provide a new teaching method when all else has failed.

Instructional packages may be used anywhere in the classroom, and thus respond to individual preferences for sound versus quiet, soft or bright light, temperature, and design. They permit students who wish to work by themselves to do so, while simultaneously allowing peer-oriented students to work cooperatively with one or two classmates. They minimize direct interaction between the learner and the teacher when a poor or negative relationship exists. However, when students are teacher-oriented, the teacher's voice on the tape or directions for usage provide a temporary substitute for direct personal proximity. They provide alternative activities for youngsters who enjoy variety and insure a specific pattern for those who feel secure with familiar strategies.

Instructional Packages are multisensory and, thus, respond to all perceptual modalities. Their activities can be sequenced so that each student learns *initially* through his or her strengths and then is *reinforced* through two different senses. They are private; no one except the learner and the teacher knows who is learning what and how. This resource permits students to move while learning, be directly involved in their own instruction, and proceed at a pace with which they can cope—and succeed.

This resource provides structure; youngsters who are extremely self-structured (LSI scores of 40 or below on structure) will not enjoy instructional packages as a routine, unless the content is challenging to them. Conforming students will find them interesting; nonconformists will enjoy the choices and variety of activities.

Gifted students can *make* instructional packages for use by others, thus capitalizing on their special creativity and talents. Parents can be involved by designing and developing packages too. Once completed, these resources can be used year after year by students who enjoy learning through multisensory materials. In effect, Multisensory Instructional Packages produce a more pleasant, nonconfrontational, constructive environment in which teachers who previously could not individualize instruction are able to do so. And, in addition to all these benefits, of course, instructional packages are fun!

10

Teaching Style: Expanding Your Strengths—Your Way!

Matching Learning and Teaching Styles

A growing body of research addresses the question of how matching learning and teaching styles affects cognitive outcomes. If instructional resources can be considered as having a *style* of their own, then several studies verified the increased academic achievement and improved attitudes toward learning evidenced when students' learning styles were matched with complementary methods or materials (Dunn, Bruno, Sklar, & Beaudry, 1990; Douglas, 1979; Gardiner, 1986; Ingham, 1989; Kroon, 1985; Trautman, 1979; White, 1980)—in the absence of any teacher's presence.

When addressing teachers' styles, however, depending on the instrument used to identify the instructor's style, different outcomes were realized. For example, Adams (1983), Cafferty (1980), and Mehdikhani (1980) all found a positive relationship between how each teacher taught and how well his or her students achieved. In each case, the closer the match between the teacher's teaching style and the student's learning style, the higher the student's grade-point average. However, each of those studies used single-dimension matches—for example, independent, self-paced; independent, teacher paced; lecture; or lecture/laboratory. With our concept of learning style, which includes 21 different variables, it is not easy to determine with which elements to match or mismatch teachers and students. In addition, when examining teachers on multidimensional variables, Gould (1987) reported that most teachers in her national sample had essentially similar teaching styles. Buell and Buell (1987) matched adult students with instructors whose perceptual strengths were similar to and different from theirs and, indeed, obtained both increased achievement and improved attitudes in the complementary treatments.

Studies of at-risk students in three different states (Gadwa & Griggs, 1985; Griggs & Dunn, 1988; Johnson, 1984; Thrasher, 1985) revealed that most underachievers strongly preferred collegial—rather than authoritative—teachers. (Photograph courtesy of John McNamara, Fremont, California.)

But how does one match students' perceptual strengths with those of their teachers when young children often are only tactual/kinesthetic (Crino, 1984; LeClair, 1986)? Apparently, the visual strengths develop among most youngsters by third or fourth grade *at the earliest,* and auditory memory does not begin to be strong for a majority of students much before sixth grade. Indeed, many male high school students are not auditory (Kroon, 1985). How do we match time-of-day preferences of children and their teachers when the majority of elementary school students are most alert in the late morning or early afternoon, whereas their teachers are either early-morning or night preferents?

Because there are so many elements of learning style that may influence individual students, it would seem that rather than try to match their styles with similar teaching styles, it is better to address practical ways of responding to students' diverse characteristics in a series of step-by-step procedures that gradually (1) increase the number of elements to which teachers respond; (2) demonstrate how to teach to each student's perceptual strength when we must lecture; (3) help teachers identify *their* current teaching styles so that they are aware of why certain students do or do not learn easily in their classes; (4)

A small group of underachievers, however, require an authoritative adult for direction and supervision. (Photo courtesy Madison Prep Junior High School, New York City.)

show teachers how to expand their current styles so that they become responsive to more students' styles; and ultimately, (5) teach those students who are capable of doing so to teach themselves new and difficult information by capitalizing on those methods that best respond to their individual strengths. Let's examine the steps in this process.

Which Elements of Learning Style Can Be Addressed by Redesigning the Classroom Environment?

Redesigning the conventional classroom should take no more than one period once each semester. Yet, consider the number of elements that are immediately addressed by that single effort. The varied sections will permit soft music for those who need sound, quiet for those who function best without it, bright or soft lighting, formal or informal seating arrangements, and the ability to move purposefully for those who need mobility. Students who are aware of their own style can wear more or less clothing to respond to their temperature preferences and, if the teacher is willing, can eat healthful vegetable snacks to

Allowing students to study in either formal or informal seating and/or in bright or dim illumination, as they feel most comfortable, addresses two important elements of learning style—classroom lighting and design. (Photograph courtesy Center for the Study of Learning and Teaching Styles, St. John's University, New York.)

resolve their intake needs. Thus, six elements of style can be dealt with merely by creating a few varied instructional areas, establishing rules and regulations for using them, and then permitting students to experiment with learning in ways that are both responsive to and dissonant from their styles so that each can find the right combination.

How Can Teachers Respond to the Emotional Elements?

Motivation will increase almost automatically as students' different styles are acknowledged, given credence, and responded to. It is particularly important to read *Two-of-a-Kind Learning Styles* (Pena, 1989) to middle school students and to encourage tenth- through twelfth-graders to read *Vive la Difference: A Guide to Learning for High School Students* so that they become secure in the realization that there is no good or bad style—that all styles are equally appropriate *as long as learning becomes easier and is retained longer.*

Awareness that students who appear to have "short attention spans" often process globally and need to work on multiple tasks simultaneously, in whichever sequence is most appealing to the individual, and with several short intervening breaks, permits teachers to allow them moments of needed "down-time" in which to relax between their periods of academic concentrations. (Photograph courtesy Madison Prep Junior High School, New York City.)

Students high in their need for "Authority Figure Present" (60 or above on the Learning Style Inventory*), require their teacher's frequent feedback—either assurances that they are "on track" or directions for how to improve. (Photograph courtesy Brockport High School, Brockport, New York.)*

Students who score low on Persistence on the LSI usually are global and process information differently than persistent analytics do. Most teachers expect such youngsters to stay on task and work diligently until each item is completed; they do not understand that global adolescents function better when permitted to work on several tasks simultaneously and begin anywhere in the sequence they wish—as long as they do complete their assignments. It also is easy to misunderstand the student who scores low on Responsibility. Such a youngster responds best to (1) knowing why the thing you want him or her to learn or do is important to *you;* (2) collegial rather than authoritative or directive, vocal tones; and (3) being given a choice of how he or she can demonstrate that the assignment *was* done. We encourage you to experiment with the following:

1. Every time you want to give your class an assignment, make it slightly longer than you ordinarily would. Thus, if you usually write 10 examples on the board, instead write 12; if you usually assign 20 vocabulary words, instead assign 22.

2. Divide the lengthened assignment into three parts by writing each part on one-third of the chalkboard. Tell the students that there are 12 examples on the board but that they are to complete "any 10 of the 12." (You only want 10, but the choice will be well received by those who need options.)

3. Tell the students that they may work on this assignment anywhere in the environment that they feel comfortable (on the floor, at the desk, in the rear or the front, in the bright or soft light, and so forth—as long as you can see them.

4. Too, tell the students that they may work on this assignment alone, if that is how they prefer; they also may work with a classmate. If they choose that alternative, establish rules for choosing a co-worker—for example, that they may pantomime their interest in working together but may not verbalize the request, or that classmates have a right to refuse to work with someone if they wish to function alone or with another whose style is more like their own. Also tell the youngsters that, if they wish, they may bring their chairs to a specific section of the room where you will be and that they may work with you. When students choose to work with you, know that they *need* to do that and be as nurturing as possible. You may leave the group that is working with you periodically to supervise the others, but you will see that, for the most part, the ones with you will gradually become increasingly independent and the ones working with classmates will tend to function collaboratively.

5. When certain students ask additional questions about the assignment, understand that they may need more structure or direction than others do and that they will not be able to function securely without it. When the same students pose questions frequently, offer them the option of sitting near you; that may help. When students do not do *exactly* what you directed, consider that they may be (1) low on Responsibility/Conformity and may need to do things their own way; (2) low on Auditory and unable to remember two or more directives when told in sequence; (3) unable, though willing, to follow external directives; (4) confused, not unwilling; and/or (5) under internal pressure and temporarily blocking. Place the directions on the chalk board or on a sheet of paper and allow the youngsters to read them and refer to them repeatedly. Also illustrate them or draw symbols to help the visual/global child comprehend procedures more easily.

How Can Teachers Respond to Sociological Elements?

It takes very little effort to permit students to complete all assignments, including homework, either alone, in a pair, or with an adult—provided that the youngster assumes the responsibility for learning everything that must be mastered and doing well on the test for each unit, theme, or lesson. Remember, however, that adult-oriented students may be unable to learn either alone *or* with a classmate and that the option of sitting near you and obtaining guidance, reinforcement, or assistance may be a necessary alternative. If you allow *these* choices, you are responding to four more elements—the need to learn alone, in a pair, as part of a team or group, and/or with an adult.

Students who need variety should be able to opt to do some things *their* way. If you provide alternatives as part of your assignments, that should help ease the boredom that some experience with routines and patterns. Students who do not choose to do things differently may very well prefer routines.

How Can Teachers Respond to Students' Varied Perceptual Strengths?

When trying to put together one of those multipart toys that their children begged for during the holidays, some parents begin by reading the accompanying directions and following from step 1 through to the last detail when the item is ready to be used. Such people tend to be analytic/visuals; they make sense out of printed words. Global visuals don't pay much attention to written or printed *words;* instead, they look at diagrams, pictures, and/or illustrations *first.*

Permitting students to complete assignments, including homework, *either alone, in a pair, with a small group, or with an adult, responds to their sociological learning styles. (Photographs courtesy: Robeson High School, Chicago, Illinois; Brockport Junior High School, Brockport, New York; and Corsicana High School, Corsicana, Texas, respectively.)*

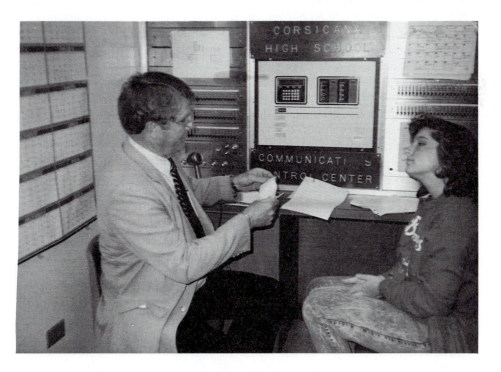

Some parents rarely look at directions. They take the parts out of the box, place them into a classification determined by size, shape, order, or color, and then sequentially analyze what to do first, pick things up as seem appropriate, and begin to experiment through a hands-on approach. Those are likely to be analytic/tactuals. Their counterparts, the global/tactuals, merely empty the box, let every piece fall where it may, and then proceed to pick up each interesting part, one by one—and sometimes several at a time—and push, pull, jab, alter, cajole, threaten, and eventually make each piece fit somewhere. When they are finished, leftover parts may still be lying on the floor or on the table, but the "mechanic" views them as not really necessary because the gadget works without them.

Not all parents fall neatly into one of these categories. Some reach for the directions, hand them to someone else, and say, "Read them to me." As the partner reads, the first person follows the verbal guidelines and puts the mechanism together. That is probably the easiest way for an analytic/auditory adult to accomplish the task. The global/auditory parent, however, will ask for the directions from the back forward, have the reader skip around, repeat, synthesize, and so forth.

All these adults will get the job done. *How* they do it depends on their *processing style* and *perceptual strengths*.

Understanding Perceptual Strengths

Auditory learners remember 75 percent of what they *hear* in a normal 40 or 50 minute lecture. Only 30 percent of the school-aged population appears to be auditory. It is the most difficult way for many people to remember new and demanding information. Visual learners remember 75 percent of what they *read* or *see*. Approximately 40 percent of the population is visual, but that number is divided into analytics and globals, with different percentages existing at different age levels.

Tactual learners remember what they *write* (if analytic) or *draw* or *doodle* (if global). Kinesthetic learners remember best the things they experience. Kinesthetics must be *actively involved* in going, doing, traveling, acting, and on-the-job training. Young children tend to be highly tactual and/or kinesthetic, but many people remain that way into adulthood. Some add visual and auditory strengths as they grow older; others do not.

Figure 10-1 provides information on 13 experimental studies wherein students were taught through matched and mismatched perceptual strengths. In each case, at the primary (Carbo, 1980; Urbschat, 1977), elementary (Hill, 1987; Jarsonbeck, 1984; Weinberg, 1983; Wheeler, 1980, 1983), secondary (Bauer, 1991; Kroon, 1985; Martini, 1986; Thorpe-Garrett, 1991) and adult (Buell & Buell, 1987; Ingham, 1989) levels, statistically higher test scores resulted when students were taught new and difficult information through their preferred, rather than their nonpreferred, modalities. Kroon (1985) obtained significantly higher (.01) test scores for students in matched rather than mismatched treatments, and an additional .05 significance when those same students were *reinforced* through their secondary or tertiary modality.

FIGURE 10–1 Experimental Research on Perceptual Learning Styles

Researcher and Date	Sample	Subject Examined	Perceptual Preference Examined	Significant Achievement
Bauer (1991)	Learning-disabled and emotionally handicapped junior high school underachievers	Mathematics	Auditory, visual, tactual	+
Buell & Buell (1987)	Adults	Continuing education	Auditory, visual, tactual	+
Carbo (1980)	Kindergartners	Vocabulary	Auditory, visual, "other" (tactual)	+
Hill (1987)	Elementary	Spelling	Auditory, visual, tactual	+
Ingham (1989)	Adults	Driver safety	Auditory/visual, tactual/visual	+
Jarsonbeck (1984)	4th-grade under-achievers	Mathematics	Auditory, visual, tactual	+
Kroon (1985)	9th-, and 10th-graders	Industrial arts	Auditory, visual, tactual, sequenced	+
Martini (1986)	7th-graders	Science	Auditory, visual, tactual	+
Thorpe-Garrett (1991)	9th-, 10th-, 11th-, 12-graders	Vocabulary	Auditory, visual, tactual	+
Urbschat (1977)	1st-graders	CVC Trigram Recall	Auditory, visual	+
Weinberg (1983)	3rd-grade under-achievers	Mathematics	Auditory, visual, tactual	+
Wheeler (1980)	Learning-disabled 2nd-graders	Reading	Auditory, visual, tactual, sequenced	+
Wheeler (1983)	Learning-disabled 2nd-graders	Reading	Auditory, visual, tactual	+

Source: Adapted by permission from "Survey of Research on Learning Styles" by R. Dunn, J. S. Beaudry, and A. Klavas, March, 1989, *Educational Leadership,* Vol. 46, No. 6, p. 52. Copyright © 1989 by the Association for Supervision and Curriculum Development.
Note: + represents significant positive findings.

Applications to Lecturing

Teaching students by lecture is likely to be effective only for auditory or auditory/tactual students who listen and then take good notes. However, note-taking requires that students understand the "most important things" the teacher is saying, and many students do not have that insight. Regardless, lecturing is a well-established, convenient method (for the teacher and for auditory students) and will undoubtedly continue in most classrooms. Thus, if a teacher is going to lecture, the following method for (1) *introducing* new and difficult material through each student's perceptual strength; (2) *reinforcing* through a secondary or tertiary strength; and (3) having the students then *use* the newly acquired knowledge in a *creative* way (to ensure application) is likely to increase the effectiveness of lecturing.

Step 1   Choose a topic or lesson where test scores will not be based on previously taught concepts or skills (Dunn, 1988). For example, begin a social studies or science unit, introduce a new artist or composer, or develop a new focus in current events. Any topic in your curriculum will do, as long as everything the students need to learn is included in the lecture. In other words, be certain that the test you later use to measure their knowledge gained through this lecture sequence includes only the information being taught in this lesson (or series of lessons) and is not dependent on prior knowledge.

Step 2   Be certain that you have at least two weeks' pretest and posttest scores on similarly difficult topics or lessons before you begin working with perceptual strengths. Keep the amount of time you spend on each lesson, the methods you normally use, and the youngsters' participation essentially similar throughout all the lessons—pre-experimental and experimental.

Step 3   Develop at least one set of Task Cards, one Flip Chute, one Pic-a-Hole, and one Electroboard to teach the important information (objectives of the lesson) you will introduce during the experimental period. For easy-to-follow guidelines for making those tactual resources, see Chapter 6. Also, develop a concise list of the objectives that should be mastered during the experimental lesson or unit and typed or printed material that actually teaches that information. The latter material may be taken from a textbook but should be brief and should respond directly to what the objectives indicate must be learned.

Step 4   Obtain one copy of the *Learning Style Inventory* (LSI) by Dunn, Dunn, and Price and Answer Sheets (the test itself) for each student in your class.[1] Different forms of the test are available for different grade levels, so specify how many Answer Sheets you need at each level. Also obtain a copy of either *Two-of-a-Kind* for grades 6–9 or *Vive la Difference: A Guide to Learning for High School Students* for grades 10–12.[2] Read the appropriate booklet to students who do not read well; others may read by themselves or in a pair or small group. Then discuss the contents so that students realize that (1) everyone has a learning style; (2) we are never too old to begin capitalizing on our style; (3) all styles are good—we all have strengths, albeit different ones; and (4) you are going to show them how to use their perceptual strengths to their best advantage.

Before administering the LSI, explain that students should answer its questions as if describing how they concentrate when they are trying to master difficult, new material. Administer the inventory and read the questions, even interpret them, for students who want/need assistance. Have the LSI Answer Sheets processed by Price Systems, Box 1818, Lawrence, KS 66046-0067.

Step 5   When the individual printouts have been processed, teach the students how to interpret them. A score of 60 or higher on auditory, visual, tactual, or kinesthetic means that that modality is strong; youngsters should be taught how to capitalize on those strengths. Conversely, students with a modality score below 40 should be cautioned to avoid beginning to learn difficult new material through that channel *initially,* although it can be used for reinforcement. Scores of 40 to 59 indicate that, if really interested in the material, the student can learn it through that modality; however, interest is a predetermining condition to concentration when scores are only in this middle range.

Step 6   Encourage the students to share, discuss, and compare their LSI data with each other and with their families and friends, and to explore similarities and differences. Then explain the need for each student to be introduced to difficult, new material through his or her strongest modality; to have the information reinforced in a secondary and tertiary modality; and then to use the information in a creative project or activity. Emphasize the need for all students to do assignments as directed by their sequenced perceptual strengths—strongest first, followed by a combined secondary and tertiary teamed modality, and then followed by making something creative that includes all the (correct) information they need to learn. If you would like to post large Wall Charts that provide for class information so that each student can merely look at the chart and follow his or her own perceptual sequence, those are available from the Center for the Study of Learning and Teaching Styles at St. John's University[3] (see Figure 10-2).

   Request the students' cooperation for a two-week period. Tell them that if they really study in accordance with the sequence you suggest, each should learn more, more easily, and remember it better than ever before.

Step 7   When students' auditory scores on the LSI are highest, they should hear the teacher's lecture or discussion first, before they read or take notes. Thus, auditory learners should listen in class, go home and read the succinct material the teacher developed to teach the objectives, and then simultaneously take notes and answer specific questions. The next day, such youngsters should make something creative with the information.

   For example, if the lesson were on idiomatic expressions, auditory students would listen to the explanation of idiomatic expressions in class. That night they would read a short description of idiomatic expressions and answer specific questions concerning the construct in writing. The next night, they would have a choice of completing any one of the following three activities:

FIGURE 10–2 Capitalizing on Students' Perceptual Strengths

Students' Perceptual Strength	Day One in School[a]	Day One at Home	Day Two in School	Day Two at Home	Day Three at School	Day Three at Home
Auditory			First exposure: Teacher's lecture. No notes need be taken.	Second exposure: Read. Write answers to the handout.[b]		Third exposure: Make a creative activity; make up a story or game from lesson content or ideas.
Visual		First exposure: Read text	Second exposure: Teacher's lecture. Write answers to the handout.			Third exposure: Make a creative activity.
Tactual	First exposure: Tactual materials geared to learning material; hands-on for short time period.	Second exposure: Read text or hear a tape of the reading material if available. Write answers to the handout.[b]	Third exposure: Teacher's lecture.			Fourth exposure: Make a creative activity.
Kines-thetic[c]		First exposure: Read text while walking	Second exposure: Teacher's lecture; may stand to take notes; write answers to the handout.[b]			Third exposure: Make a creative activity.

Source: Adapted from "Capitalizing on Students' Perceptual Strengths to Ensure Literacy While Engaging in Conventional Lecture/Discussion" by R. Dunn, 1988, *Reading Psychology: An International Quarterly,* vol. 9, No. 4, pp. 431–453. Copyright © 1988 by Hemisphere Publishing Corporation.

[a]On "Day One in School" after the first week, students should use and correct each other's completed creative activities, which will provide further reinforcement in a variety of interesting ways.

[b]Teacher prints what must be learned (objectives) onto a handout or a wall chart. The handout is the identical reading material for all students.

[c]Read text on next page for alternative kinesthetic sequences.

1. Write a rhyming poem that explains what idiomatic expressions are and how to recognize them in literature. Include at least ten (10) different idiomatic expressions in your poem.
2. Illustrate at least ten (10) idiomatic expressions and explain what they actually mean.
3. Make up a crossword puzzle with at least ten (10) idiomatic expressions and an explanation of what they mean.

When students' visual scores on the LSI are highest, they first should read the succinct material the teacher developed to teach what idiomatic expressions are. The next day, the visual student should listen to the teacher's lecture and, simultaneously, answer the questions that were included with the succinct material they read the previous night—but did not have to answer. The next night, the visual students should complete a creative activity chosen from among the teacher's listed alternatives.

When students' tactual scores on the LSI are highest, they first should be exposed to the new material through tactual materials such as multipart Task Cards, Flip Chutes, Pic-A-Holes, or Electroboards. After a short exposure to such materials (either alone, in pairs, or in a small group based on individuals' sociological preferences as revealed by their LSI printouts), tactual students should read the succinct material their teacher developed, take notes and answer questions, and then hear their teacher's lecture-explanation of idiomatic expressions. The next night, those youngsters should complete a creative activity chosen from among the teacher's listed alternatives.

When students' kinesthetic scores on the LSI are highest, they should stand and walk during the first exposure. Thus, students' whose highest scores are kinesthetic and auditory should be encouraged to stand and quietly move in place while they are listening to the teacher's introduction. However, a combined kinesthetic/auditory strength is not common. It is more likely that a kinesthetic student's next highest strength would be visual, in which case the introduction to the difficult new material should include reading at home while walking back and forth in a section of a room. The youngster then will be present on the next day to hear the teacher's presentation, during which he or she will take notes and answer the questions posed on the teacher-prepared succinct material. The following day, the creative activity should be completed. However, if the student's strongest modalities are combined kinesthetic/tactual, the first exposure should be by using the tactual materials while standing, then reading and answering the questions by writing, followed by the teacher's lecture and, subsequently, by completion of the creative activity.

Thus, every student will be present at the same time for the teacher's lecture, but each will have been introduced to the difficult new material through his or her perceptual strength, reinforced with a multisensory dual exposure, followed by application through the development of a creative resource.

Step 8 If students' early morning scores on the LSI are 60 or above, they should be advised to get up an hour earlier than usual and do their homework before they come to school. If their evening scores are 40 or below, they should do their homework in the evening. High-energy-level youngsters in the late morning or afternoon (scores of 60 or above on those LSI categories) should study or do their homework at those peak times. Explain to parents that their children's chronobiological levels are biologically imposed and that the youngsters should learn more, more easily if they concentrate on the material at the time of their best energy high.

Step 9 Encourage the students to follow this prescribed perceptual/time-of-day pattern for at least two weeks. Pre- and posttest them in each of the two weeks. Compare the students' grades on the tests you give in each of these two weeks, while they follow this suggested study/homework/lecture sequence, with the grades they achieved during the first two weeks' pre-experimental period's grades. Notice the differences (if any) in the amount of gain between the two sets of pretest and posttest scores. Share the achievement results with the students, their parents, and a colleague.

How Many Elements Can Be Responded to Easily?

We've just described how to respond to sound (#1), light (#2), design (#3), and mobility (#4) needs merely by redesigning a section or two or three of the conventional classroom. Sociological preferences can be handled just as easily by giving students options as to whom they are permitted to complete assignments with—alone (#5), with one classmate (#6), in a small cooperative group (#7), or with you nearby (#8). If you will remember to look at your classroom Wall Charts (see Chapter 11) and to be firm (but caring) with authority-oriented students and collegial with collegial or nonconforming students, you will be responding to the kind of adult each youngster needs (#9, #10). When you diversify the instruction and use various options, those who need variety will benefit (#11). Remember not to require that *everyone* try everything; those who feel secure with patterns and routines need time to get used to the innovation or new method *before* they are ready to experience it.

When you recognize that some students need to wear a sweater but others will be warm in the same environment at the same time, *and you permit each to dress appropriately,* you will have mastered temperature requirements for individuals (#12).

Options in assignments respond to nonconformists who score low on Responsibility. If you speak to such youngsters collegially and also explain why whatever you want them to do is important to *you,* you will make headway with this usually off-the-main-track group (#13). Dealing with structure also is not difficult (#14) if you are willing to provide more or fewer directions on the basis of individuals' requests. In fact, just being *aware* of these learning style differences will help you work better than previously with many young-sters.

The foregoing list includes 14 elements of style. Add to that the under-standing that nonpersistent children should be allowed to work on several items or tasks simultaneously and should be permitted a moment's breather when necessary, and we also will be addressing persistence (#15). If you can permit students to move from section to section of the room as they complete designated parts of their assignment, a combination of mobility, kinesthesia, design, responsibility, and sociological needs will be accommodated (#16).

If you permit youngsters to bring raw vegetables or fruit juice (within whatever restrictions *you* establish), intake can be addressed (#17). *You do not need to do everything;* whatever you try will yield positive results. Decide ex-actly what you will experiment with and what you choose *not* to try. Whatever you try, you should observe better student grades, behavior, *and* attitudes in your classroom within *six* weeks. If that does not happen, *stop!*

If you can get yourself sufficiently organized so that you can show your students how to read either before *or* after your classroom lecture or discus-sion and then how to reinforce with their own secondary or tertiary modalities, you will have made a big move forward and dealt efficiently with students' perceptual strengths (#18). For many, that is a certain way of improving test scores!

What Is Another Easy Way to Move into Learning Styles?

Using Team Learning to *introduce* new and difficult material and Circle of Knowledge to *reinforce* what you introduced through Team learning will (1) begin to organize instruction so that both structure and options are provided simultaneously; (2) permit low auditory or low visual students to learn through a multisensory approach; (3) show students who cannot learn alone how to achieve with classmates (or with you!); (4) provide opportunities for develop-ing higher level cognitive skills *and* creativity; (5) reduce tension in the environ-ment and permit youngsters to enjoy learning; (6) teach students how to work with objectives and begin to demonstrate that they *have* learned; and (7) help students internalize what they are learning and, therefore, remember it better (because of the application through creative projects).

How Difficult Is It to Teach Globally and Analytically?

If you are an analytic processor, you never concentrated on how to teach read-ing, math, or science globally, and you never took a required course in how to teach basic skills through the use of humor or drawings, so this is a brand new area for you. On the other hand, if you are a global processor, you rarely stay on task without deviating from a structured lesson plan. In fact, although you may be required to develop lesson plans, you rarely take them seriously.

To you, the thrill of teaching is to get the students' interests responding and to help them become creatively involved in the subject.

Both approaches are correct; it is important to teach children the entire required curriculum *and* it is important to teach it through their interests and frames of reference, and to help them relate it to their own lives. Thus, both analytic and global teachers can profit from understanding how to reach both types of student processors. However, having tested thousands of teachers during the past 20 years, we find that the majority seem to be fairly strong analytic processors, whereas the majority of secondary school students are strong global processors. Thus, this is one extremely important element of style, particularly for math teachers, who tend to be very analytic. For example, it is not uncommon for math teachers to say, "I don't care if your answer is correct. You must show me every step of the process." Globals cannot do that. They *intuit* the answers.

Thus, although this *is* a difficult element to confront, it is important. Read Chapter 4 and experiment with *planning* one lesson to include both styles. Then, two weeks later, plan for a second. As you become more and more adept at using the opposite style, you gradually will begin to incorporate it into major lessons. When you do, you will have mastered the nineteenth (19th) element!

What Can We Do with Time-of-Day?

Time-of-day energy levels are easier to respond to than initially seems feasible. For example, with a bit of organization, why wouldn't it be possible to experiment with some of these suggestions:

1. Teach a given subject at the same time of day for one semester and note which students are most alert and which are least alert at that time of day. Then change the time that subject is taught *drastically*—for example, from early morning to late afternoon or from just after lunch to first thing in the morning. Note changes in individuals' attitudes, achievement, attention spans, tensions, behaviors, and/or attendance. Only those students with strong preferences (LSI scores below 31 or above 69) will reveal dramatic differences; but for those youngsters, time of day is a critical factor. You should, however, observe differences among students with LSI scores between 31 and 40 and between 60 and 69—although of a less obvious nature.

2. Identify those students with LSI scores indicating strong preferences for a specific time period, particularly if that youngster has only one energy high during the day. Note each of those students' most important subject (required and core disciplines first). Tape-record your lessons in those important subjects at *your* best time of day, and instruct students to use the recordings at *their* highest energy level—even if that entails duplicating tapes and permitting youngsters to borrow them for home use.

3. Move school underachievers onto a schedule that allows *them* to learn their most important subjects at their best time of day. Dropouts (Gadwa & Griggs, 1982), truants (Lynch, 1981), and poor math achievers (Carruthers & Young, 1980) all reversed achievement *and* behavior when permitted to attend school during their energy-high, rather than energy-low periods. In fact, poor achievers almost consistently reveal late-morning, afternoon, and evening preferences, in contrast with early morning attendance and concentration (Dunn & Griggs, 1988).

4. Administer standardized achievement tests at the *best* time of day for students with strong preferences or strong opposite preferences on the LSI. Lemmon (1985) found that children in her elementary school achieved significantly better when taught at their highest energy level; Gadwa and Griggs (1985) revealed similar results at the high school level. Expect between 15 and 20 percent to reveal no time preference; they are the lucky ones who can perform well at any time of day *if* they are interested in what they are learning.

5. Assign "morning" students (LSI scores of 60 or above on the Evening–Morning continuum) to "morning" teachers (PEPS scores of 60 or above on the Evening–Morning continuum; see Appendix C) and "afternoon" students (LSI scores of 60 or above on Afternoon) to "afternoon" teachers (PEPS scores of 60 or above on Afternoon)—if the school has any of these adults. If there are more of one type than another, consider the extras as mismatches. Compare their performance with those of their matched classmates. Bear in mind that we are not controlling for IQ or achievement when experimenting in this way with time-of-day effects. If you take even one or two steps in this direction, you will have begun to respond to the 20th element of learning style. Now let's see if you are ready/willing to identify your own current *teaching* style so that you can recognize which students' styles are advantaged—or disadvantaged—by the strength of your own special brand of instruction.

Can You Identify Your Own Teaching Style Strengths?

If you are interested in appraising your teaching style, read the next few paragraphs that explain the various components of the construct. Then answer the questions honestly. You can self-score the instrument and have a fairly clear understanding of the students who are most, and least, complemented by the strengths of how you instruct. The next step will be to decide whether you are willing to try to expand at least one component of your style so that it becomes more responsive to other students' styles. Let's take one step at a time.

What *Is* Teaching Style?

There are many ways of teaching the same content; some people do it verbally, others do it visually, others experientially, and others tactually. All approaches are effective—but not for the same students. Just as with learning style, perceptual communication is only *one* part of teaching style. There are nine major components of style, including each of the following:

1. *Instructional planning* (Dunn & Dunn, 1977, pp. 75–87): Instructional planning encompasses the diagnosis, learning prescriptions, and evaluations completed for each student or group of students. Knowledge of each student's ability, learning style, interests, skill development, ability to retain information, concept formation, and so forth is essential to the diagnosis. The prescription includes the design and/or use of objectives, materials, techniques, and multisensory learning activities at various levels. Evaluation encompasses pretesting, student self-assessment, and teacher assessment based on the original objectives established for each student.

2. *Teaching methods:* Teaching methods usually refer to the instructor's behavior in the learning environment—the way he or she groups students for learning, designs and/or assigns resources, uses interaction techniques with students, and employs basic approaches to the teaching and learning of each student. Since the advent of individualization strategies, teaching methods also include the specific materials through which youngsters may achieve independently, such as Contract Activity Packages, Multisensory Instructional Packages, and Programmed Learning Sequences.

3.1 *Student groupings:* Student grouping is defined as the way a teacher assigns or permits learning to occur through small groups, pairs, individuals, large groups, varied groupings, or one-to-one tutoring. Because different youngsters respond to varied sociological interactions, a teacher should have at his or her fingertips a series of alternative grouping strategies that provide a wide range of interesting activities.

3.2 *Room design:* Room design reflects the ways in which the teacher divides, decorates, and designs instructional spaces or areas to match the characteristics of his or her students. The various types of furniture arrangements, alcoves, "offices," work areas, and the like, and how they make up the instructional environment, are included in this element.

3.3 *Teaching environment:* The teaching environment includes time schedules, the different types of instructional stations and centers, the optional learning activities that are available, and the provisions that are made for mobility, multilevel resources, and nutritional intake.

4. *Evaluation techniques:* Evaluation techniques encompass the methods the teacher uses to assess the progress of individual students. Testing, observations, performance assessments, and self-evaluation are part of the assessment of each student.

5. *Teaching characteristics:* Teaching characteristics are the values and standards a teacher holds and the operational approaches used to transmit those values and standards. The degree of flexibility, the importance of what is learned, and the amount of direction given to students are examples of teaching characteristics.

6. *Educational philosophy:* Educational philosophy refers to the attitudes a teacher holds toward key program descriptions, such as open education, a theme-centered curriculum, or a basic skills approach.

7. *Student preference:* Student preference describes the types of youngsters the teacher prefers to have as students. Characteristics of students are itemized—the gifted, the learning-impaired, the motivated, the nonachieving, and so on—to permit easy identification.

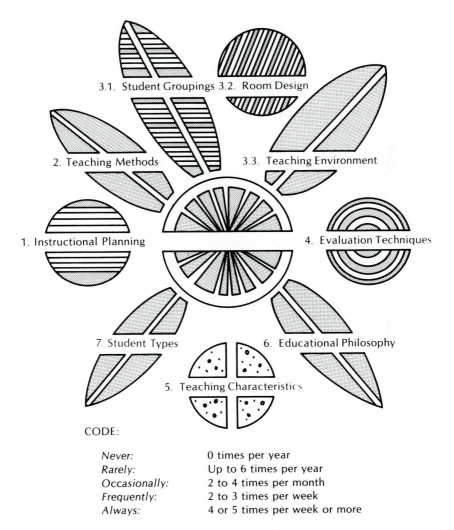

CODE:

Never:	0 times per year
Rarely:	Up to 6 times per year
Occasionally:	2 to 4 times per month
Frequently:	2 to 3 times per week
Always:	4 or 5 times per week or more

FIGURE 10–3 Teaching Style Elements and Scoring Code. This figure, illustrated by Dr. Edward J. Manetta, chairman, Department of Fine Arts, St. John's University, represents the nine elements of Teaching Style and a code to follow in the self-examination of how individuals communicate information to others. The number of times used from 0 times per year (''Never'') to four or five times per week or more (''Always'') aid in identifying teaching characteristics.

Teaching Style Inventory

FIGURE 10–4 The Teaching Style Inventory
This instrument results in a Teaching Style Profile.

Question I: *Instructional Planning*

Directions:

Circle the number that best describes how often you use each of the following planning techniques.

		Never	Rarely	Occasionally	Frequently	Always
a)	Diagnosis and prescription for each student..................	1	2	3	4	5
b)	Whole-class lessons	5	4	3	2	1
c)	Contracts, Programmed Learning Sequences, or Multisensory Instructional Packages	1	2	3	4	5
d)	Creative activities with student options	1	2	3	4	5
e)	Programmed materials or drill assignments..................	1	2	3	4	5
f)	Small-group assignments	1	2	3	4	5
g)	Task Cards or games	1	2	3	4	5
h)	Objectives, varied for individuals...........................	1	2	3	4	5
i)	Peer tutoring or Team Learning	1	2	3	4	5
j)	Role playing or Simulations................................	1	2	3	4	5
k)	Brainstorming or Circles of Knowledge	1	2	3	4	5
l)	Students design their own studies	1	2	3	4	5

Question II: *Teaching Methods*

Directions:

Circle the number that best describes how often you use each of the following teaching methods.

		Never	Rarely	Occasionally	Frequently	Always
a)	Lecture (whole class)	5	4	3	2	1
b)	Teacher demonstration	5	4	3	2	1
c)	Small groups (3–8)	1	2	3	4	5
d)	Media (films, tapes, etc.)	1	2	3	4	5
e)	Class discussion (question–answer)	5	4	3	2	1
f)	Individualized diagnosis and prescription for each student	1	2	3	4	5

Question III: Teaching Environment
Question 3.1: *Student Groupings*

Directions:

Circle the number that best describes how often you use each of the following types of groupings.

		Never	Rarely	Occasionally	Frequently	Always
a)	Several small groups (3–8 students)	1	2	3	4	5
b)	Pairs (2 students)..	1	2	3	4	5
c)	Independent study assignments (student works alone)	1	2	3	4	5
d)	One-to-one interactions with the teacher	1	2	3	4	5

		Never	Rarely	Occasionally	Frequently	Always
e)	Two or more of the above groupings at one time	1	2	3	4	5
f)	One large group (entire class).	5	4	3	2	1

Question 3.2: *Room Design*

Directions:

Circle the number that best describes how often you use each of the following classroom designs.

		Never	Rarely	Occasionally	Frequently	Always
a)	Rows of desks.	5	4	3	2	1
b)	Small groups of 3–8 students	1	2	3	4	5
c)	Learning Stations or Interest Centers	1	2	3	4	5
d)	A variety of areas	1	2	3	4	5
e)	Individual and small-group (2–4) alcoves, dens, "offices"	1	2	3	4	5
f)	Three or more of the above arrangements at the same time . . .	1	2	3	4	5

Question 3.3: *Teaching Environment*

Directions:

Circle the number that best describes your present instructional environment.

		Never	Rarely	Occasionally	Frequently	Always
a)	Varied instructional areas are provided in the classroom for different, simultaneous activities.	1	2	3	4	5
b)	Nutritional intake is available for all students as needed.	1	2	3	4	5
c)	Instructional areas are designed for different groups that need to talk and interact.	1	2	3	4	5
d)	Varied time schedules are in use for individuals	1	2	3	4	5
e)	Students are permitted to choose where they will sit and/or work.	1	2	3	4	5
f)	Many multisensory resources are available in the classroom for use by individuals and groups	1	2	3	4	5
g)	Alternative arrangements are made for mobile, active, or overly talkative students	1	2	3	4	5

Question IV: *Evaluation Techniques*

Directions:

Circle the number that best describes how often you use each of the following evaluation techniques.

		Never	Rarely	Occasionally	Frequently	Always
a)	Observation by moving from group to group and among individuals.	1	2	3	4	5
b)	Teacher-made tests.	1	2	3	4	5
c)	Student self-assessment tests	1	2	3	4	5
d)	Performance tests (demonstrations rather than written responses)	1	2	3	4	5
e)	Criterion-referenced achievement tests[a] based on student self-selected, individual objectives	1	2	3	4	5

Continued

FIGURE 10–4 *Continued*

	Never	Rarely	Occasionally	Frequently	Always
f) Criterion-referenced achievement tests[a] based on small-group objectives	1	2	3	4	5
g) Standardized achievement tests based on grade-level objectives	1	2	3	4	5
h) Criterion-referenced achievement tests[a] based on the individual student's potential	1	2	3	4	5

Question V: *Teaching Characteristics*[a]
  Directions:
  Circle the number that best describes you as a teacher.
  I tend to be:

	Not At All	Not Very	Somewhat	Very	Extremely
a) Concerned with *how* students learn (learning style)	1	2	3	4	5
b) Prescriptive (with student options)	1	2	3	4	5
c) Demanding—with high expectations based on *individual* ability	1	2	3	4	5
d) Evaluative of students as they work	1	2	3	4	5
e) Concerned with *how much* students learn (grade-level standards)	5	4	3	2	1
f) Concerned with what students learn (grade-level curriculum) . .	5	4	3	2	1
g) Lesson plan–oriented	5	4	3	2	1
h) Authoritative to reach group objectives	5	4	3	2	1

Question VI: *Educational Philosophy*
  Directions:
  Circle the number that best describes your attitude toward each of the following approaches and concepts.

	Strongly Disagree	Disagree	Undecided	Support	Strongly Support
a) Open education	1	2	3	4	5
b) Diagnostic-prescriptive teaching	1	2	3	4	5
c) Multiage groupings	1	2	3	4	5
d) Matched teaching and learning styles	1	2	3	4	5
e) Alternative education	1	2	3	4	5
f) Student-centered curriculum	1	2	3	4	5
g) Behavioral or performance objectives	1	2	3	4	5
h) Humanistic education	1	2	3	4	5
i) Independent study	1	2	3	4	5

[a]Criterion-Referenced Achievement Tests: The questions on these tests are based directly on the objectives assigned to or selected by the students.

		Strongly Disagree	Disagree	Undecided	Support	Strongly Support
j)	Individualized instruction	1	2	3	4	5
k)	Traditional education...................................	5	4	3	2	1
l)	Whole-group achievement	5	4	3	2	1
m)	Grade-level standards	5	4	3	2	1
n)	Teacher-dominated instruction..........................	5	4	3	2	1

[a]When teachers respond that they are "concerned with *how* students learn," the inference is that they permit options in the learning environment because of their awareness of individual differences. An observer should, thus, be able to see students working alone, with a peer or two, or with the teacher; sitting on chairs or on carpeting; using self-selected resources of a multisensory nature (if available); mobile (if necessary and without disturbing others), etc.

When a teacher indicates that he or she tends to be "prescriptive" but permits some student options, observers should be able to locate written objectives that include selected choices.

"Evaluative . . . as (students) work" suggests that observers will be able to see the teacher moving among the students while checking their progress and questioning them.

"Concerned with . . . grade-level curriculum" suggests that observers will see that objectives, lessons, and/or assignments tend to respond to a suggested or required grade-level curriculum.

"Authoritative to reach group objectives" suggests that observers will see the identical objectives, lessons, and/or assignments for every student in the same class.

SCORING KEY

All questions are weighted according to the relative importance of each item. Simply multiply the weight assigned to the technique by the number selected for the frequency.

Example:

1 a) Diagnosis and prescription for each student—3—Occasionally

Item	Weight		Frequency		Score
a	5	×	3	=	15

Complete each item and the total for each question. Then chart the totals on the Teaching Style Profile. This analysis and the predictor profile will aid you in matching students and teachers.

WEIGHT KEY

5. Highly individualized
4. Somewhat individualized
3. Transitional
2. Somewhat traditional
1. Traditional

Continued

FIGURE 10–4 *Continued*

1. Instructional Planning			
Item	Weight	× Frequency	= Score
a	5		
b	1		
c	5		
d	3		
e	4		
f	3		
g	3		
h	4		
i	3		
j	3		
k	3		
l	5	I: Total Score _____	

2. Teaching Methods			
Item	Weight	× Frequency	= Score
a	1		
b	2		
c	3		
d	3		
e	2		
f	5		
		II: Total Score _____	

3.1 Student Groupings			
Item	Weight	× Frequency	= Score
a	3		
b	3		
c	5		
d	2		
e	4		
f	1		
		III: Total Score _____	

3.2 Room Design			
Item	Weight	× Frequency	= Score
a	1		
b	3		
c	4		
d	5		
e	4		
f	5		
		IV: Total Score _____	

3.3 Teaching Environment			
Item	Weight	× Frequency	= Score
a	5		
b	4		
c	4		
d	5		
e	4		
f	4		
g	4		
		V: Total Score _____	

4. Evaluation Techniques			
Item	Weight	× Frequency	= Score
a	4		
b	2		
c	4		
d	4		
e	5		
f	4		
g	1		
h	4		
		VI: Total Score _____	

5. Teaching Characteristics			
Item	Weight	× Frequency	= Score
a	4		
b	5		
c	4		
d	3		
e	1		
f	1		
g	1		
h	1		
		VIII: Total Score _____	

6. Educational Philosophy			
Item	Weight	× Frequency	= Score
a	4		
b	5		
c	3		
d	5		
e	4		
f	3		
g	4		
h	3		
i	4		
j	5		
k	1		
l	1		
m	1		
n	1	VII: Total Score _____	

FIGURE 10–5   Teaching Style Profile

	Individ-ualized	Somewhat Individualized	Transi-tional	Somewhat Traditional	Tradi-tional
1. Instructional planning					
	210	168	126	84	42
2. Teaching methods					
	80	64	48	32	16
3.1 Student groupings					
	90	72	54	36	18
3.2 Room design					
	110	88	66	44	22
3.3 Teaching environment					
	150	120	90	60	30
4. Evaluation techniques					
	140	112	84	56	28
5. Teaching characteristics					
	100	80	60	40	20
6. Educational philosophy					
	220	176	132	88	44

Place the total score that you obtained for each of the previous categories on the line pertaining to the item by making a dot on the line closest to the appropriate numeral (see Figure 10–5). After you have placed a dot on each line indicating your total score for each category, link each dot in succession.

The following sample Teaching Style Profile should provide you with a graphic representation of teaching style. After linking the dots in succession and examining your own teaching style, draw a perpendicular line from top to bottom through your philosophy score, as shown in Figure 10–6. *Most teachers' philosophy is far more individualized than their methods—but that is why they recognize the need for at least some expansion of their style.*

How to Select Objectives and Reach Them

If your philosophy suggests that you believe in either individualized or somewhat individualized teaching, you may wish to consider expanding your current teaching style in one area; for example, you may decide to do a little

	Individualized	Somewhat Individualized	Transitional	Somewhat Traditional	Traditional
1. Instructional planning					
2. Teaching methods	210	168	126	84	
3.1 Student groupings	80	64	48	32	
3.2 Room design	90	72	54	36	
3.3 Teaching environment	110	88	66	44	
4. Evaluation techniques	150	120	90	60	
5. Teaching characteristics	140	112	84	56	
6. Educational philosophy	100	80	60	40	
	220	176	132	88	

FIGURE 10–6 Sample Teaching Style Profile

After completing your Teaching Style Profile, draw a perpendicular line from top to bottom through your philosophy score as shown in Figure 10–6—a typical profile.

redesigning of your classroom, as the teacher whose Teaching Style Profile is shown in Figure 10–7. She thought she could do a few things with the desk and seats that might allow for at least one section where some youngsters could work informally. She also thought she could tolerate youngsters sitting in either bright or soft lighting, so she arranged for that alternative. She decided to establish an Interest Center and a Learning Station (see Chapter 3) to permit some mobility for a few boys she always had thought of as hyperactive. The more she experimented, the more she realized that the youngsters were really "good kids" who had just been unable to conform to the formality of the seating and the restrictiveness of passive attention. As her teaching style changed rapidly in this one area, she found that she enjoyed teaching more than she had before.

	Individualized	Somewhat Individualized	Transitional	Somewhat Traditional	Traditional
1. Instructional planning					
2. Teaching methods	210	168	126	84	
3.1 Student groupings	80	64	48	32	
3.2 Room design	90	72	54	36	
3.3 Teaching environment	110	88	66	44	
4. Evaluation techniques	150	120	90	60	
5. Teaching characteristics	140	112	84	56	
6. Educational philosophy	100	80	60	40	
	220	176	132	88	

FIGURE 10-7   Sample Teaching Style Profile (Year One)

This teacher said "No" to rows of desks and gained 3 points; increased small-group work from occasionally to frequently and gained 3 points; established Learning Stations and Centers frequently instead of rarely and gained 8 points; created a variety of areas frequently as opposed to rarely and gained 10 points; designed alcoves, dens, "offices" frequently instead of never and gained 12 points; and established three or more of these arrangements frequently instead of rarely and gained 10 points—thus elevating her score from 43 to 89 to reach her objective. Her actual practice now is consistent with her philosophy (see Figure 10-8).

As this teacher gained success and confidence through redesigning her room to match learning style needs, she elected to improve her planning and methods the following year (see Figure 10-9).

FIGURE 10-8 How One Teacher Expanded Her Teaching Style through Increased Frequency of Selected Items in Room Design

	Last Year			Now		
	Weight	Frequency	Total	Weight	Frequency	Total
a) Rows of desks	1 ×	2	= 2	1 ×	5	= 5
b) Small groups	3 ×	3	= 9	3 ×	4	= 12
c) Learning Stations	4 ×	2	= 8	4 ×	4	= 16
d) Variety of areas	5 ×	2	= 10	5 ×	4	= 20
e) Alcoves, "offices"	4 ×	1	= 4	4 ×	4	= 16
f) Three or more of the above at the same time	5 ×	2	= 10	5 ×	4	= 20
	Total		43			89

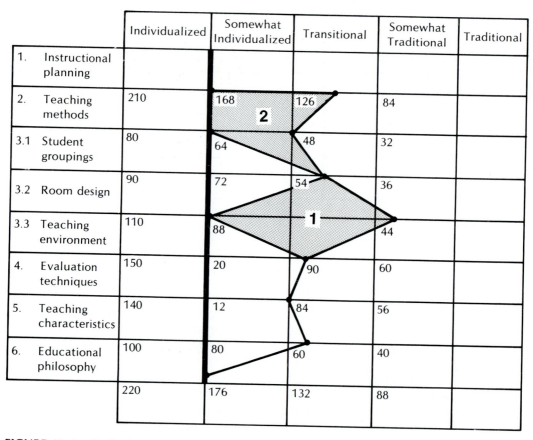

	Individualized	Somewhat Individualized	Transitional	Somewhat Traditional	Traditional
1. Instructional planning					
2. Teaching methods	210	168 **2**	126	84	
3.1 Student groupings	80	64	48	32	
3.2 Room design	90	72	54	36	
3.3 Teaching environment	110	88 **1**		44	
4. Evaluation techniques	150	20	90	60	
5. Teaching characteristics	140	12	84	56	
6. Educational philosophy	100	80	60	40	
	220	176	132	88	

FIGURE 10-9 Gradual Expansion of One Teacher's Teaching Style as She Began to Experiment with Increased Frequency of Items with Which She Felt Comfortable (Year Two)

Note: 1 = First year—room design.
2 = Second year—planning and methods.

422

Should you wish to consider expanding your teaching style in the same way, review the items under "Room Design" in the *Teaching Style Inventory*. Choose those items with which you feel fairly comfortable and decide to use them more frequently than you have heretofore. You will see your style expand to become increasingly responsive to students' multiple styles. If you *do* try this, retake that portion of the inventory in one month and note the difference in your score!

If you prefer to expand your teaching style in another area, choose one that interests you and, again, examine the section of the inventory related to that component. Choose the items with which you feel relatively comfortable and increase the frequency with which you do those things. Go slowly. You will enjoy the gradually developing appreciation of the difference your expanding style makes to your students.

As each area gradually expanded toward her philosophy, the teacher in the previous example discovered that several other areas (Student Groupings, Teaching Environment, and Teaching Methods) also began to move toward the left on her Teaching Style Profile. The *Teaching Style Inventory* offers an objective, self-determined approach to improved teaching and learning. If you would like to use this profile to focus on helping some youngsters you may not have been able to reach effectively in the past, experiment. If the process isn't working, obviously you will stop. But if you enjoy each change, you may find a very special delight in being able to use the right methods for the right students, instead of the same method for everyone.

The following questionnaire is related to student types with which you are most successful. It offers another dimension of matching teaching style to types of learners.

Question 7: Student Types

Directions:
Rate the degree of success you tend to have with each type of student.

CODE:

5. Almost always successful
4. Frequently successful
3. Occasionally successful
2. Rarely successful
1. Almost never successful

A. Learning Rate

———— Quickly achieving

———— Average achieving

———— Slowly achieving

———— Nonachieving

B. Motivation Scale

———— Motivated

———— Conforming

———— Persistent

———— Responsible

———— Apathetic

———— Unmotivated

———— Nonconforming

———— Not persistent

———— Not responsible

C. Emotional Stability

———— Emotionally stable

———— Active-mobile

———— Quiet-passive

———— Emotionally troubled

D. Learning Potential

———— Gifted

———— Creative

———— Far above-average I.Q.

———— Average I.Q.

———— Below-average I.Q.

———— Learning-impaired

E. Verbal Communication Ability

———— Articulate

———— Average verbal ability

———— Below-average verbal ability

———— Bilingual

———— Non-English-speaking

F. Independence Level

———— Peer-oriented

———— Adult-oriented

———— Independent

———— Authority-oriented

List all the types of students that received 5s under Question 7 for each of the categories A through F. You now know how to identify faculty teaching styles and the students with whom individuals believe they are successful.

TEACHER SUCCESS WITH STUDENT TYPES/PREDICTOR PROFILE

A: Learning rate ——————————————————————

B: Motivation scale ——————————————————————

C: Emotional stability ——————————————————————

D: Learning potential ——————————————————————

E : Verbal communications ability _____

F : Independence level _____

The next step is to identify individual youngsters' learning styles and then to match the right student with the right teacher—for him or her.

What Are the Next Steps?

Once you feel comfortable responding to at least some of the elements of learning style that are important to your students, you will want to share what you are doing with your students' parents. See Chapter 11 for resources that may assist you in this vein—for example, a booklet explaining the concept of learning styles specifically designed for parents, or a cartoon-like filmstrip and accompanying cassette explaining the concept. You may be able to solicit parental assistance in developing Contract Activity Packages (CAPs), Programmed Learning Sequences (PLSs), tactual/kinesthetic manipulatives (T/K), and/or Multisensory Instructional Packages (MIPs) for use with your students. You surely will want parents to see that their children do their homework according to their learning style strengths, so before you send home the Homework Disc prescriptions (see Chapter 11), explain to both the students *and* their parents how these should be used.

Next decide on which group of students you most wish to concentrate. Is it the gifted or nonconforming? Try a CAP. Is it the ones who need structure? Begin with a PLS. Are you most concerned with children who do not seem to remember much of what you discuss in class? Introduce them to the tactual materials in Chapter 6 and then have them reinforce what they were exposed to with a follow-up PLS. If your greatest concern is with the at-risk, underachievers, and potential dropouts, begin with MIPs.

Figure 10–10 illustrates graphically different departure points for moving into a learning styles instructional program. It is necessary to begin with identification of individuals' learning style strengths with the *Learning Style Inventory* and to share the results with students and their parents, but after that you may choose any path toward your objective of working with students through their strengths rather than through hit-or-miss approaches. Figure 10–11 presents an analytic diagram of steps and specific strategies on the path to responding to individual learning style characteristics.

What Are the Ultimate Steps?

Students will learn more, more easily, and retain it longer when they are taught through resources that complement their learning styles, but it is not always necessary to continually design new tactual resources, Programmed Learning Sequences, and Contract Activity Packages *for* them. After students have had at least three or four experiences *using* these methods, many of them will be

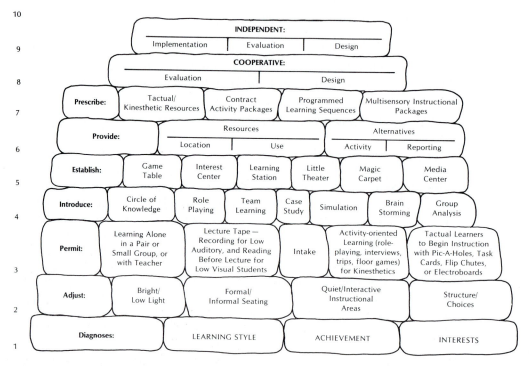

FIGURE 10–10 Stepping-Stones to Effective Instruction

able to begin designing their own, particularly when encouraged to work with peers. (On the other hand, remember that some learners prefer to work alone, so do not mandate that they work with others.) Teaching young people to translate their textbooks into resources that respond to how they, as individuals, learn, is the biggest step we can take toward helping them to become independent learners. Eventually they will be able to teach themselves anything by using their knowledge of style and translating printed matter into the method that best matches their strengths.

Teaching students to create their own materials is easy with some and difficult with others, but *often we anticipate problems where they never emerge* and vice versa. Thus, after youngsters have had experience using a specific method, assign the development of the appropriate resource either for homework or as a unit project.

Helping Students to Create Tactual Materials

Make a transparency of the directions for creating multipart Task Cards, Flip Chutes, Pic-A-Holes, or Electroboards and their pictorial representations. Project each transparency, one at a time, onto a blank classroom wall and—

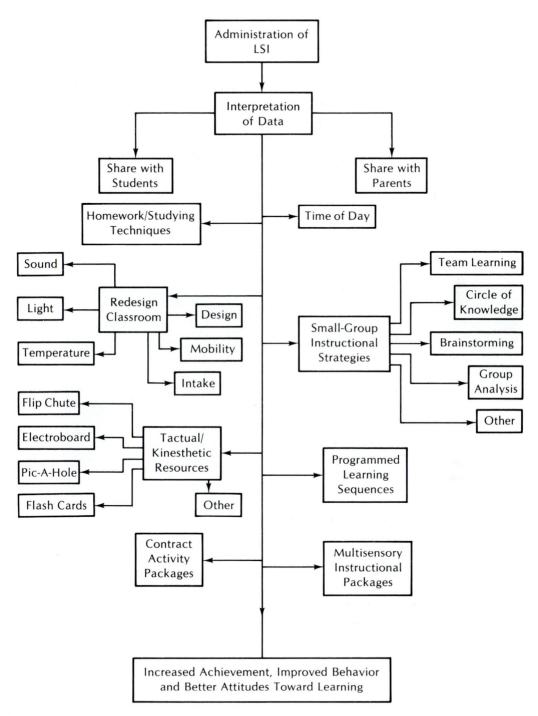

FIGURE 10-11 Learning Styles Process of Implementation with Dunn and Dunn Model designed by Dr. Angela Klavas.

keeping the overhead far away from the wall so that you project a very big image onto a large sheet of either oaktag or colored tagboard—trace the graphic and printed directions for each. Number the oaktag sections in sequence so that youngsters know with which to begin and when the manipulative has been completed. If you prefer to have these devices made at home, either photocopy the directions in Chapter 6, or have them copied from the large posters you will make for classroom display.

An alternative is to make it a class project to create one of the tactuals as part of a class or unit lesson. You will see that many tactual students will complete that assignment easily and with confidence; they also will help their auditory and visual classmates with an aplomb rarely evidenced by these children in school! After all, *that* (using their hands skillfully) is what they are best at!

After the manipulatives have been completed, have each student be re-

Tactual students learn more when they create *hands-on instructional resources than when they use teacher-made or commercial materials. Corsicana High School students have made and used a variety of tactual items, including Electroboards, Pic-A-Holes, Flip Chutes, and games. In this photo, several are using Task Cards to master a literature unit. Photograph courtesy Corsicana High School, Corsicana, Texas.)*

This high school student is industriously creating an Electroboard to demonstrate mastery of difficult academic information. (Photograph courtesy Cedar Crest High School, Lebanon, Pennsylvania.)

sponsible for having at least two classmates *use* their original manipulative and then either sign their name on a sheet of paper indicating that they checked the device and its information is totally correct *or* refuse to sign their names until the material has been corrected. Explain that they are not helping classmates by signing when information is *incorrect;* indeed, they are harming the offender by not showing where the errors are.

Recognize that, by using each other's materials, all students are having the difficult material required for that topic reinforced through varied instructional resources—which may be motivating.

Helping Students to Create Programmed Learning Sequences

Once students have used Programmed Learning Sequences (PLSs) three or four times, many will be able to create their own either together with a classmate or, perhaps, working with a parent. Tell them to follow these steps and to use one of the PLSs you have in the classroom as a guide.

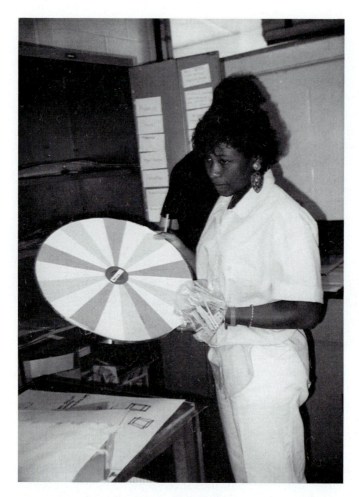

*Three different secondary school staffs have taught stu-
dents to learn and reinforce new and difficult academic
knowledge by creating and studying with their own
Learning Circles. (Photographs courtesy: Robeson High
School, Chicago, Illinois; Corsicana High School, Corsicana, Texas; and Sacred Heart Seminary, Hempstead,
New York, respectively.)*

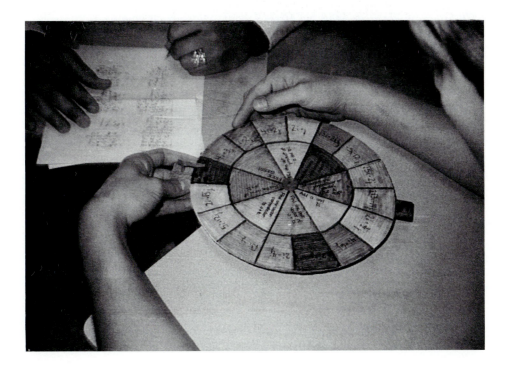

Once students have created a Pic-A-Hole, Flip Chute, and Electroboard, many begin to design original games and other three-dimensional instructional re-sources. (Photograph courtesy Midwest High School, Midwest, Wyoming.)

PLS Guidelines for Students

1. Assuming that you need to design a PLS to teach yourself difficult information in the curriculum, adopt the straight analytic title of the chapter in the book as your major title. Thus, if the title is "Graphing," that becomes the title of your developing PLS.

2. Make up a funny subtitle to appeal to global classmates. Use a play on words or an idea. Being corny is acceptable, but good grammar and decorum must be adhered to. Examples of funny subtitles might be:

- "Graphing: Get the Point?"
- "The Mind and the Brain: Or Getting Your Head Together!"
- "Vowel Sounds: The Long and Short of It"
- "Adjectives: Words that Defy Description"
- "Figurative Language: Say What You Mean and Mean What You Say"
- "Fractions: Dividing Problems into Parts We Can Handle"
- "Descriptive Research": Tell It Like It Is!"

This teacher, Mary Ellen Kasax-Saxler, taught her foreign language students to create their own tactual resources for learning French. (Photograph courtesy Blake Middle School, Hopkins, Minnesota.)

3. Think of a shape that represents the topic. If no shape is at all related, then use any shape that is different from an 8 × 10 rectangle.

4. Think of a way to get someone interested in this topic. How might it be helpful to know this information? Is there something practical that others can do with it? Is there a special reason that someone would find it interesting?

5. Develop a short story (one or two paragraphs) to show why this information might be important or interesting to someone studying this topic. For example, to learn about how to predict weather, you might write:

Timmy was soaked through and through. He had walked four miles to the gym because his mom was busy and, halfway there, it had begun to thunder and rain. He had been so engrossed thinking about basketball practice this morning, that he had not even glanced at the sky. Had he just looked skyward, he probably would have noticed the huge, black nimbus clouds that dominated the horizon. He might have remembered that nimbus clouds bring rain.

These students are translating information required by their unit objectives into visual/tactual charts and games as Activity Alternatives for their Contract Activity Packages. (Photograph courtesy Cedar Crest High School, Lebanon, Pennsylvania.)

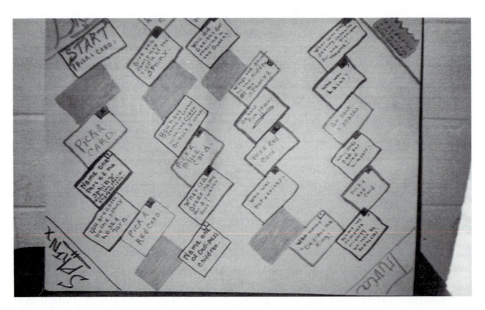

This is a game several students cooperatively designed to demonstrate mastery of their mathematics objectives. (Photograph courtesy Corsicana High School, Corsicana, Texas.)

434

6. Then write clearly what the PLS you are developing will teach. For example, ''This program will show you how to recognize different weather signs so that you probably will be prepared for rain when it happens—unlike poor Timmy!'' Decide what the PLS will teach by reading the questions at the end of the chapter. Those questions pertain to what the author believes are the most important things in this chapter. The most important things are what you must learn. Those are called your *objectives*. Thus, *objectives* are what must be learned in each chapter and in each PLS.

7. Clearly write the objectives for your developing PLS. For example:

By the time you complete this PLS, you should be able to do all the following things:

1. Name at least five (5) different cloud types and explain the kind of weather each cloud type predicts.
2. Explain each of the following words and phrases and use them correctly when writing a story about how to predict weather: (a) precipitation, (b) predicting, (c) atmosphere, (d) wind-chill factor, (e) high/low pressure area, and (f) weather alert.

8. Copy the objectives you wrote and keep them near you as you begin to read the book chapter, beginning with the first paragraph. Keep the first two objectives in mind and *read to find the answers* to those objectives. When you find them, neatly copy the sentence or paragraph that explains the information required by the objective and the answer onto a 5 × 7 index card in the shape that you decided to use for this PLS. After you either have printed or typed the information, add a question related directly to that information at the bottom of the index card (same side). Require that whoever uses this PLS after it has been completed provides an answer to that question. Clearly state how the question must be answered. For example:

Read the following question and circle the correct answer. (In that case, you might have given three choices of answers).

or

Read the following questions and then write your answer onto the dotted line.

or

Read the following questions and then look at the answers in the column on the left. Then find the answer to each question by drawing a line across to its correct answer in the right-hand column.

or

Fill in the missing letters and form the correct answer. You might do this: What is the name of the black cloud that predicts rain?

$$n \text{ \_\_ \_\_ } b \text{ \_\_ \_\_}$$

or

Open the small envelope attached to the back of this frame, carefully take the miniature Task Card pieces out, and put together the letters so that they form the answer.

9. Turn the index card over *as if you were turning a page in your textbook*. Neatly print the answer to the question on the reverse side of the index card.

10. After you print the answer on the back of the index card, draw a straight horizontal line halfway across the card and add either an illustration to further explain the answer (for example, a drawing of a nimbus cloud), a humorous or interesting comment about the answer, or additional information.

For example:

———————————————— Index card ————————————————

Answer: nimbus

————————————————

I hope you never have nimbus clouds in your life!—except when we need rain to make the crops and flowers grow!

11. Continue reading the textbook until you find every answer to each of the questions that were listed in the back of the chapter (your objectives). On each subsequent frame, write the important information to teach those answers. Continue to ask about the information on each frame and require answers to the questions *you* develop for each frame. Write the answers on the back of each frame and add illustrations throughout and additional statements on the rear. Think of, and add, humorous statements related to the information—but be polite and use good spelling and grammar.

12. Every seven or eight frames, *review* everything you taught to that point. You may design a miniature tactual resource to reteach the information. If you do, glue it onto a new frame whenever you want to reinforce what has already been presented. For example, make a Pic-A-Hole or an Electroboard to reteach what the frames included. Give directions for using the resource you design.

13. After all the questions have been answered—meaning that all the information for each objective has been printed or typed onto the index cards—begin a new frame with:

You have read all the information in this PLS to this point. See how much you remember. Answer all the following questions. If you are not *certain* that you know all the answers, either turn back to the frames that explain the information and reread them *or* use the tactual resources in your classroom and find the correct answers in the Flip Chute, the Electroboard, the multipart Task Cards, or the Pic-A-Hole related to this topic. You need to know all the answers, so be certain that you do.

14. On the next frame, write:

Please go back and wipe all your answers off this PLS so that the next person may use it. I hope you liked using it. It was a lot of work to make!

15. Go back through all the frames and be certain that you have illustrations related to the information wherever possible. Check the answers you printed on the back of the frames to be certain they are all there—and correct! Add funny comments if you can, but be certain they are in good taste.

16. Ask someone older than you to check your PLS for spelling and grammar. Make all necessary corrections. Then show it to your teacher. After he or she corrects it, make it perfect by doing whatever needs to be done (as your teacher suggests). Then laminate the PLS or cover it with clear contact paper to keep it in good shape. Before you laminate the back cover, neatly print or type your name, class, grade, and the date. Students who use your PLS to learn this information will always know that *you* were the author!

Helping Students to Create Contract Activity Packages (CAPs)

Before you begin to use CAPs with students, print colored oaktag lists of Activity Alternatives and Reporting Alternatives side by side and mount them in the classroom. Give the students choices of Activity Alternatives and matched Reporting Alternatives as a way of doing their homework. Applying new and difficult information in making something original and creative is one of the best ways to ensure retention. In addition, the use of these alternative activities will familiarize students with the concept and practice. When they need to design similar activities for CAPs later on, they will understand what to write.

CAPs are designed for motivated students who enjoy working independently and for nonconformists who need to work alone. Both groups will *want* to design additional CAPS once they have exhausted your supply. They also will be enticed into creating their own when they become interested in a topic for which you do not have a CAP available.

If you are willing to list the objectives for a unit, CAP students will find it relatively easy to decide on Activity Alternatives and Reporting Alternatives they would enjoy for each. Remind them to create activities that respond to diverse perceptual strengths—auditory, visual, tactual, and/or kinesthetic.

Playing detective in a library or Media Center to see how many Alternative Resources they are able to locate will interest most CAP enthusiasts. Remind them that using multimedia is appropriate (videotapes, filmstrips, records, "talking books," and so forth). They can list or illustrate all the resources they find and mount them on charts somewhere in the classroom so that others may benefit from their pioneering efforts.

A Circle of Knowledge is easy for most students to develop after they have been exposed to and participated in several. Even a Team Learning is not difficult to design once the students have been made aware of the specifically stated objectives. If you are willing to experiment, encourage students either to convert questions found at the end of the their textbook chapter into objectives for the next unit *or* to develop their own with a classmate or two or in a small group. The CAP student enjoys challenges, competes willingly, and sometimes designs more interesting objectives and/or activities than we adults devise.

Having worked with CAPs, motivated auditory or visual students and nonconformists will thrive as they develop them. After those have been submitted and corrected, ask the youngsters to make them attractive and to sign their name, class, grade, age, and the date on the rear cover. They will enjoy having their CAPs duplicated and distributed among other students who have become interested in using this instructional system.

Once students can be helped to become independent learners by learning how to translate new and difficult textbook materials into instructional resources responsive to their learning styles, there is no limit to their ability to eventually teach themselves information and skills that they become interested in learning or that become important to them. Figure 10–10 describes the process as a series of stepping-stones. Take whichever steps you feel most comfortable with in the beginning. As you begin to find your way, you may alter the path and go as far as you successfully can. We've suggested a road map; chart your own course!

Helping Students to Redesign Their Classroom on the Basis of Their Individual Learning Styles

When encouraged to experiment with redesigning their conventional classroom to respond to the learning styles of their classmates and themselves, students often suggest creative, attractive alternatives. We recommend that the strengths of each youngster in the class (as diagnosed by the *Learning Style Inventory*) be recorded on a large Wall Chart (see Chapter 11). Then discuss the differences that exist among members and why it is important that each learns through strengths. Finally, distribute copies of Figure 10–12 to individuals, pairs, or groups—depending on how individuals care to work—and ask them to create their own representations of a learning style classroom. The illustrated items can be cut out, shaded, pasted onto large colored pieces of oaktag, and then considered for adoption. Given this opportunity to engage in a bit of classroom interior decorating, many students develop both practical and artistic possibilities. Why not experiment with one or more of their suggestions? Because *they* revised the room, they will consider the privilege soberly and consciously appreciate your concern for their comfort. At the same time, they will take care not to take advantage of the privilege.

Whether or not you adopt one or more of the student-redesigned possibilities, mount and label them, giving their designers credit (in writing) for their interesting creations. Carolyn Brunner, director of the Erie 1 Board of Cooperative Educational Services' Instructional Development Center in Depew, New York, designed Figure 10–12, used it as described previously, and reported, ''mind-boggling'' successes as perceived by *both* the students and their teachers!

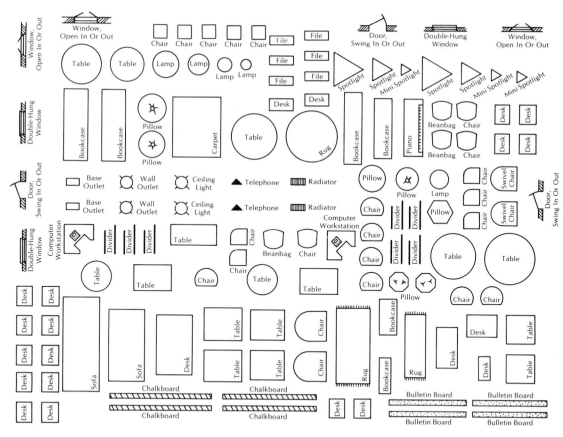

FIGURE 10–12 Items to Facilitate Student Redesigning of Conventional Classroom Space Based on Classmates' Learning Style Strengths
Source: Designed by Carolyn Brunner, director, Erie 1 BOCES, Depew, New York.

A Final Word on Teaching Style

Begin slowly. Use new strategies that make sense to you and with which *you* feel comfortable. Expand your teaching strengths gradually over a period of three to five years. As you expand your style to respond to more students' diverse styles, you will experience increasing success and your students will achieve better and enjoy learning more.

Notes

1. The *Learning Style Inventory* is available from Price Systems, Box 1818, Lawrence, KS 66046–0067.
2. *One-Of-A-Kind Learning Style* and *Vive la Difference: A Guide to Learning for High School Students* are obtainable from the Center for the Study of Learning and Teaching Styles, St. John's University, Utopia Parkway, Jamaica, NY 11439.
3. Perceptual Sequencing Wall Charts are available from the Center for the Study of Learning and Teaching Styles, St. John's University, Utopia Parkway, Jamaica, New York 11439.

_11_

Resources for Teachers and Trainers Getting Started with Learning Style

You believe in the learning style concept that students learn differently from one another. You believe that if they are taught with methods and resources that match their strengths rather than their weaknesses, academic achievement will increase and attitude toward school will improve. After investigating several learning style models, you have made the decision to adopt the Dunn and Dunn approach because it is a comprehensive model encompassing many different elements, its assessment instrument is the one used most in schools today, and it is easy to administer and interpret. Most important, it is backed with valid and reliable award-winning research conducted by more than 70 universities.

Whether you are a teacher beginning to implement learning style in your classroom, an administrator eager to get teachers interested in the concept, or a trainer helping teachers in the implementation process, you ask yourself, "What resources are available to get started?" Fortunately, the Center for the Study of Learning and Teaching Styles at St. John's University in New York City has many resources specifically designed to help people begin a learning styles instructional program.

This chapter was written by Dr. Angela Klavas, Assistant Director, Center for the Study of Learning and Teaching Styles, St. John's University, New York.

Background Information

Your first step is to become thoroughly acquainted with the Dunn and Dunn model by reading this book. To get an overview of the model and directions on how to assess for learning style and interpret a learning style profile, you may want to do one or more of the following:

- Read Chapters 1 and 2 carefully.
- Attend or sponsor a workshop on learning style with the Dunn and Dunn model.
- Attend a weekend or eight-day Leadership Certification Conference sponsored by the Center for the Study of Learning and Teaching Styles.
- Do an ERIC search for journal articles on learning style with the Dunn and Dunn approach (there is an excellent article on synthesis of research in *Educational Leadership,* Volume 46, Number 6, March 1989).
- Join the National Network on Learning Styles, a nonprofit organization sponsored by the National Association of Secondary School Principals and St. John's University. Members receive information about developments in the field of learning style and teaching style. Services include three newsletters annually providing summaries of the latest research, practical applications, and experimental programs; information about conferences, institutes, and inservice workshops for teachers and administrators; descriptions of publications and dissertations in the field; identification of resource personnel and exemplary school sites; an updated bibliography of publications and films; and responses to written or telephone requests for information.

Publications for Adults

The following are publications available from the Center for the Study of Learning and Teaching Styles that provide background information to teachers, administrators, and trainers interested in implementing learning styles.

- *Teaching Elementary Students through Their Individual Learning Styles* by Doctors Rita and Kenneth Dunn is a practical, hands-on guide to implementing learning styles.
- *Teaching Students to Read through Their Individual Learning Styles* by Dr. Marie Carbo and Doctors Rita and Kenneth Dunn provides a diagnostic-prescriptive approach for teaching children to read. It involves the identification of individual learning styles and the subsequent matching of complementary reading strategies, resources, and environments.

- *Learning Styles: Quiet Revolution in American Secondary Schools* by Dr. Rita Dunn and Dr. Shirley Griggs contains descriptions of the achievement and attitude gains of urban, suburban, and rural middle and high schools' learning style programs.
- *A Review of Articles and Books* is a compilation of articles and research studies and their implications for gifted, special education and regular instruction. Administrators and trainers can duplicate the journal articles for distribution to teachers. This publication also provides the documentation needed for writing proposals for grants, term papers, theses, and dissertations on learning styles and hemisphericity.
- *Unlocking the Giftedness in Every Child: A Guide for Parents* by Drs. Rita and Kenneth Dunn and Donald Treffinger describes how to capitalize on children's learning style strengths to develop talents and interests.

Administrators, teachers, and doctoral students interested in the research behind various learning style models will find the following resources informative and valuable.

- *The Curry Report* is a psychometric review of the major instructional preference, information-processing, and cognitive personality instruments that bear on individuals' learning styles.
- *The DeBello Report* compares learning style models and the psychometric analyses of their instruments. It contains an audiotape, script, extensive reference list, and diagram comparing eleven models, with variables, appropriate populations, validity of instrumentation, and the research behind each.
- *Annotated Bibliography* is an updated review of articles, books, dissertations, and research on learning style. This is an invaluable resource for anyone involved in writing term papers, theses, proposals for funding, or manuscripts.

Videotapes

Videotapes are excellent resources for training administrators, trainers, and teachers by providing an overview of the Dunn and Dunn model, the research, and the step-by-step strategies and techniques in its implementation process. Each of these tapes provides a complete inservice course for introducing faculty to beginning steps for teaching students through their individual learning styles.

- *Videotapes: Teaching Students through Their Individual Learning Styles* is a six-hour complete training program narrated by Dr. Rita Dunn. It introduces the Dunn and Dunn learning style model by explaining the environmental, emotional, sociological, physiological, and psychological elements of style. It describes how to identify individual strengths, redesign classrooms to respond to diverse styles, and teach students to do their homework through their learning style strengths.

- *Teaching At-Risk Students through Their Individual Learning Styles* is a complete training program narrated by Doctors Rita and Kenneth Dunn. It is a six-hour, hands-on, how-to description that provides the research and the methods for teaching at-risk students through their individual learning styles.
- *Personal Learning Power* is a musical rap video that explains learning style and prepares high school students for learning about their own unique strengths. This was created by Dr. Kenneth Dunn specifically for students in grades 5–12.
- *How to Conduct Research in Your Own Classroom* is a three-hour narration by Dr. Rita Dunn designed to help teachers monitor the effectiveness of their instruction.

The following videotape is an excellent resource for everyone interested in observing learning style techniques and strategies in a secondary school classroom. It can be used either as an introduction to the concept or as a culminating workshop activity.

- *Videotape: The Look of Learning Styles* presents learning style programs in four secondary schools located in different parts of the United States. It demonstrates how students' unique characteristics are matched with appropriate environments, resources, and methods in the classroom. This is also an excellent explanation of learning style resources for students.

Instrumentation

Before assessing the learning styles of students, teachers and administrators should have their own learning styles identified with the *Productivity Environmental Preference Survey* (PEPS). They will discover how they prefer to function, learn, concentrate, and perform in their own educational settings. Analyzing their personal style allows them to understand the process, thus making them better able to interpret the learning styles of students. More important, when they realize that they themselves have unique learning styles, they will better understand and accept the diversity in their students' styles. Administrators and trainers find that their staff development sessions become more effective after they administer and interpret the PEPS to the participants.

- *Productivity Environmental Preference Survey* (PEPS) by Dunn, Dunn, and Price is available in a specimen set, a computerized program, and a Scan-and-Score packet.

- The *Learning Style Inventory* (LSI) is the instrument used to identify learning style for students in grades 3 through 12. It is available in a specimen set, a computerized program, and a Scan-and-Score packet. Before the test is administered, students need to understand the concept of learning style and that, regardless of intelligence, age or gender, everyone has a unique learning style. Students should be informed that the LSI is not an IQ test or a reading test and that there are no "right" or "wrong" answers.

Publications for Students

The following are available to assist teachers in preparing students to take the LSI. They should be read by students before testing so that they can understand that the inventory is not an IQ test or a reading test, that there are no right or wrong answers, and that everyone has strengths—only different ones.

- *Two-of-a-Kind* by Rosy Pena is a storybook that explains learning style to junior high school students. In a high-interest story, GLOBAL Myrna and ANALYTIC Victor are close friends who respect their differences and study difficult material through their own unique learning styles.
- *Vive la Difference: A Guide to Learning for High School Students* by Connie Bauman was written specifically for secondary school students.

Doing Homework

Research indicates that improved academic achievement occurs when students do their homework through their individual learning style. Available at the Center for the Study of Learning and Teaching Styles are resources relating to homework and learning style for teachers, parents, and students.

- *Learning How to Learn* is a programmed Learning Sequence (PLS) on how to learn, study, and do homework through one's own perceptual strengths. In 36 frames, it explains how to learn more easily and remember better by introducing new information or skills through each person's strongest modality and then reinforcing through others. This PLS can be duplicated.
- *How to Do Homework through Learning Style* is a colorful and animated filmstrip with cassette tape that shows students how to do their homework. This resource also can be shown to individual parents or PTA groups so that they can provide the proper home environment to study and do homework.
- *Perceptual Strength Homework Charts* are two inexpensive posterboard charts that are an aid to both teachers and students. The *Learning Style*

Instructional Chart lists the correct sequence of instruction for the tactual, visual, auditory, or kinesthetic student and for teacher-directed lessons. The *Learning Style Class Chart* cites the six-step perceptual sequence of instruction for student, teacher-directed, and whole-group lectures. Using the primary perceptual strength from the LSI, the student is given his or her own personal sequence of self-instruction for homework assignments.

- *Homework Disk* is a software package that provides students (individually) with individual prescriptions for doing homework and studying in ways that complement their personal learning styles. Because they work through their strengths, students find doing homework more enjoyable and productive. This computer disk (available in IBM and Apple) works only with LSI data.

Teacher Inservice Packages

The four Teacher Inservice Packages (TIPs) available at the Center for the Study of Learning and Teaching Styles are designed to provide staff development through teachers' learning style preferences.

- The *Teacher Inservice Package (TIP) on Contract Activity Packages (CAPs)* demonstrates alternative methods of instructing gifted students in ways that many research studies suggest high-IQ, creative youngsters enjoy achieving. The TIP includes: (1) a series of colored slides instructing teachers explicity on how to design Contract Activity Packages on the junior high, middle, and high school levels, with a cassette tape that explains the slides; (2) a Programmed Learning Sequence on how to develop and use CAPs to accommodate selected learning style characteristics; and (3) three reproducible CAPs.
- The *Teacher Inservice Packages (TIP) on Programmed Learning Sequences (PLSs)* is designed for teaching motivated, persistent, visual students who need structure and like to work alone or in pairs. Environmental preferences, time of day, and intake also can be accommodated. The package includes a Programmed Learning Sequence on the design and use of a PLS, a cassette tape, overhead transparencies, and a script.
- The *Teacher Inservice Package (TIP) on Alternatives to Lecture* is designed to show teachers better ways to teach than talking and discussing. Four small-group instructional strategies (Team Learning, Circle of Knowledge, Brainstorming, and Group Analysis) are taught through three activities accommodating teachers' learning style preferences. The activities include: (1) scripts, worksheets, and samples; (2) transparencies and an audiotape; and (3) a Programmed Learning Sequence (PLS) that can be reproduced.
- The *Teacher Inservice Package (TIP) on Conducting Staff Development Workshops* contains tips and materials for conducting inservice with the

Dunn and Dunn model with suggested resources, techniques, and strategies. The package includes transparencies, a research list, an audiotape on overview, and other material to assist teachers in implementing the Dunn and Dunn model.

Instructional Resources for Students

Stimulating resources for students include *Contract Activity Packages* (CAPs) on the intermediate, and secondary levels. These CAPs are self-contained units of study for motivated, persistent students. They include (1) clearly stated Behavioral Objectives; (2) suggested multisensory Resources through which students may learn the information required in the objectives; (3) Activity Alternatives offering creative ways for students to apply the information acquired through the Resources; (4) Reporting Alternatives or ways in which the Activity Alternatives are shared; (5) at least three small-group techniques such as Circle of Knowledge, Team Learning, and Brainstorming; and (6) pre- and posttests. Contract Activity Packages are an excellent resource for gifted students. They are reproducible.

The Mind and the Brain—or Getting Your Head Together is available in both a Contract Activity Package (CAP) for the motivated and a Programmed Learning Sequence (PLS) for those who need structure. It teaches (1) parts and functions of the brain and (2) careers related to the brain and mind.

Additional resources specifically designed to teach students through their individual learning styles include the following:

- *Comics in the Classroom: A Learning Style Approach* by Pat McCoubrey is a 175-page kit that uses comics as a practical and enjoyable resource for teaching basic skills to underachievers. It spans all grade levels and covers a range of subject areas that include language arts, mathematics, creative arts, dramatic arts, social studies, and others. It also introduces and explains the concept of individual learning style, which greatly enhances its value as a unique and comprehensive resource. It contains 150 suggested activities and a teacher's manual.
- *Thinking Network (TN) Software Kit* for reading and writing is an Apple microcomputer software program (grades 7–9) on theme writing for improving thinking, reading, and writing skills. TN combines computer technology with high-interest, grade-appropriate reading selections through a variety of hands-on, global reading activities not available in other software programs.

Resources for Parents

To implement learning style fully, it is important to inform parents of their childrens' styles. The following resources are designed specifically for parents to help them understand the concept of learning style.

- *Learning Style—an Explanation for Parents* contains a filmstrip and audiotape explaining the concept of learning style. If followed by a discussion of learning style, it is an excellent resource to use at parent–teacher conferences.
- *Learning Styles: A Guide for Parents* explains learning style as it relates to parents and provides a written account of how they can accommodate their children's learning style at home.
- *Amazing Grades* includes a videotape and series of booklets designed to show parents how to help their children identify and capitalize on their learning style strengths so that their school achievement is improved.

Resource for Counselors

The Center for the Study of Learning and Teaching Styles also has an excellent resource specifically designed for school counselors. *Counseling Students through Their Individual Learning Styles* by Dr. Shirley Griggs is a monograph that enables counselors (K–12) to diagnose learning styles, use compatible interventions, and consult with teachers about accommodating diverse styles in the classroom. This book should be read *before* troubled and difficult-to-teach students are assigned to alternative programs, psychologists, or county agencies. Though written specifically for counselors, it also should be read by teachers and parents.

Where to Obtain Resources for Getting Started

If you are interested in obtaining any of the resources listed, please write to the Center for the Study of Learning and Teaching Styles, St. John's University, Utopia Parkway, New York, NY 11439, for a free resource brochure.

A Final Word on Implementing the Dunn and Dunn Learning Style Model

Extensive and often prize-winning research has shown that improving instruction relies on teaching each student through his or her learning style strengths. Each chapter in this book has suggested strategies for gradually changing conventional teaching into instructional approaches and resources that better match *individuals'* unique characteristics.

Dr. Angela Klavas, Assistant Director, Center for the Study of Learning and Teaching Styles, St. John's University, visited elementary schools that had implemented the Dunn and Dunn Learning Styles Model in geographical locations throughout the United States. Her report (Klavas, 1991) describes those factors that both helped and hindered the development of their successful learning styles programs. Hindering factors revolved around Central Office mandates and intrusions, supervisors with a different agenda, and, in some cases, lack of financial resources for staff development. Helpful factors revolved around the understanding and insight that both staff and students developed once they became familiar with the research and theory concerned with this model and the statistically higher achievement and attitude scores that resulted from implementation.

Figure 11–1 is a graph Dr. Klavas designed to represent the four stages of implementation of the Dunn and Dunn model. Although many of the schools had been involved in learning styles instruction for five or more years, few had moved into in-depth evaluation as indicated in the fourth stage. All had completed stages 1 and 2 to varying degrees; many had moved into stage

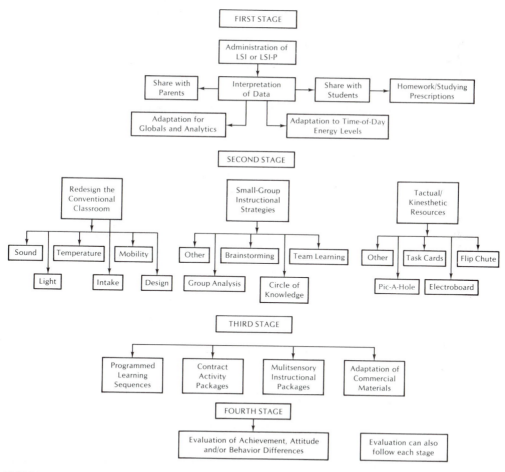

FIGURE 11–1 Learning Style Process of Implementation with Dunn and Dunn Model
Designed by Angela Klavas, Ed.D.

3. *All had obtained increased test achievement.* Of those that had tested for attitudinal improvement, all had obtained significantly higher attitude test scores based on how the students felt about learning in this type of program. *All* reported improved behavior and fewer incidences (if any) of the need for referrals because of discipline problems.

Thus, follow the Klavas design as closely as possible (see Figure 11–1). Begin with the administration of the appropriate instrument to identify each student's learning style; see Appendix B for a listing of learning style instruments and the grade levels for which each is recommended. Share the students' learning style strengths with them and their parents. Interpret the results in terms of how you will alter the classroom, resources, and/or instruction to respond better to students' identified strengths. Use the St. John's University Homework Disc to give each student and parent a prescription for how the youngster should study and do assignments based on individual learning style strengths. Be certain to explain that (1) in each family, parents and their siblings often have styles that are dramatically different from each other and (2) all styles are equally valuable. Do what you can to teach globals globally and analytics analytically (see Chapter 4), and remind students to do their most demanding cognitive work at the time of day that best matches their energy highs.

Next consider with which elements in Stage 2 you feel most comfortable. If redesigning the room does not appear overwhelming, choose those aspects that make sense to you and begin improving the instructional environment. If you are willing to experiment with introducing new and difficult material through Team Learning and then reinforcing through Circle of Knowledge, begin with those. If you are concerned about underachievers or bored students, begin with tactual/kinesthetic (T/K) instructional resources—the Flip Chute, Pic-A-Hole, Task Cards, Electroboards, Learning Circles, and so forth. Permit intake (water, juice, vegetables) if you are so inclined. You do *not* need to adopt all facets of learning styles instruction; do what you can!

The third stage entails translating your objectives—what you want the students to master—into appropriate methods—CAPs, PLSs, or MIPs. You also can adapt commercial materials to reflect similar approaches. At each stage, determine the effectiveness of the approach you are implementing with each child. Thus, compare individuals' grades during a three-week interval immediately *before* and *after* you begin each phase of the learning styles approach. Youngsters should perform better with learning styles methods and resources than they did previously. Share your comparison of the students' before-and-after test scores with them. Discuss how to change instruction to better appeal to each. The final stage should be teaching students to develop their own materials (T/K, CAP, PLS, MIP) by translating their textbook into resources that benefit them most.

Move into learning styles instruction slowly; take only one step at a time into those stages you believe you can manage. Do not undertake too much, but *do* keep trying new things. You will be amazed at how well certain methods "work" for certain youngsters and not for others. With each new stage you move into, your students will (1) achieve better, (2) like school more, and (3) behave better than before. In addition, they will develop a healthy appreciation of their own—and others'—styles, and will feel better about themselves, their classmates, and their teachers than they have for a long, long time! And they will owe it all to you.

REFERENCES AND RESEARCH BASED ON THE DUNN AND DUNN LEARNING STYLES MODEL

Adams, J. F. (1983). The effects of the satisfaction of learning style preferences on achievement, attention and attitudes of Palm Beach junior college students. Doctoral dissertation, Florida Atlantic University, 1983. *Dissertation Abstracts International, 83,* 15060.

Andrews, R. H. (1990, July–September). The development of a learning styles program in a low socioeconomic, underachieving North Carolina elementary school. *Journal of Reading, Writing, and Learning Disabilities International, 6*(3), 307–313. New York: Hemisphere.

Annotated Bibliography. (1992). New York: St. John's University's Center for the Study of Learning and Teaching Styles, Utopia Parkway, Jamaica, NY 11439.

Avise, M. J. (1982). The relationship between learning styles and grades of Dexfield junior and senior high school students in Redfield, Iowa. Doctoral dissertation, Drake University, 1982. *Dissertation Abstracts International, 43,* 09A, 2953.

Bass, B. M. (1965). *Organization psychology.* Boston: Allyn and Bacon, M p. 13.

Bauer, E. (1991). The relationships between and among learning styles perceptual preferences, instructional strategies, mathematics achievement, and attitude toward mathematics of learning disabled and emotionally handicapped students in a suburban junior high school. Doctoral dissertation, St. John's University, New York.

Beaty, S. A. (1986). The effect of inservice training on the ability of teachers to observe learning styles of students. Doctoral dissertation, Oregon State University, 1986. *Dissertation Abstracts International, 47,* 1998A.

Biggers, J. L. (1980). Body rhythms, the school day, and academic achievement. *Journal of Experimental Education, 49*(1), 45–47.

Bonham, L. A. (1987). Theoretical and practical differences and similarities among selected cognitive and learning styles of adults: An analysis of the literature, Volumes I and II. Doctoral dissertation, University of Georgia, 1987. *Dissertation Abstracts International, 48,* 2530A.

Braio, A. (1988). *Mission from no-style.* New York: Center for the Study of Learning and Teaching Styles, St. John's University.

Branton, P. (1966). The comfort of easy chairs. *FIRA Technical Report 22.* Hertfordshire, England: Furniture Industry Research Association.

Brennan, P. K. (1984). An analysis of the relationships among hemispheric preference and analytic/global cognitive style, two elements of learning style, method of instruction, gender, and mathematics achievement of tenth-grade geometry students. Doctoral dissertation, St. John's University, 1984. *Dissertation Abstracts International, 45,* 3271A.

Brunner, C. E., & Majewski, W. S. (1990, October). Mildly handicapped students can succeed with learning styles. *Educational Leadership, 48,* 21–23. Alexandria, VA: Association for Supervision and Curriculum Development.

Bruno, A. P., & Jessie, K. (1983). *Hands-on activities for children's writing.* Englewood Cliffs, NJ: Prentice Hall.

Bruno, J. (1988). An experimental investigation of the relationships between and among hemispheric processing, learning style preferences, instructional strategies, academic achievement, and attitudes of developmental mathematics students in an urban technical college. Doctoral dissertation, St. John's University, 1988. *Dissertation Abstracts International, 48*(5), 1066A.

Buell, B. G., & Buell, N. A. (1987). Perceptual modality preference as a variable in the effectiveness of continuing education for professionals. Doctoral dissertation, University of Southern California, 1987. *Dissertation Abstracts International, 48,* 283A.

Cafferty, E. (1980). An analysis of student performance based upon the degree of match between the educational cognitive style of the teachers and the educational cognitive style of the students. Doctoral dissertation, University of Nebraska, 1980. *Dissertation Abstracts International, 41,* 07A, M p. 2908.

Calvano, E. J. (1985). The influence of student learning styles on the mathematics achievement of middle school students. Doctoral dissertation, East Texas State University, 1985. *Dissertation Abstracts International, 46,* 10A.

Carbo, M. (1980). An analysis of the relationship between the modality preferences of kindergartners and selected reading treatments as they affect the learning of a basic sight-word vocabulary. Doctoral dissertation, St. John's University, 1980. *Dissertation Abstracts International, 41,* 1389A. (Recipient of the Association for Supervision and Curriculum Development National Award for Best Doctoral Research, 1980.)

Carbo, M., Dunn, R., & Dunn, K. (1986). Teaching students to read through their individual learning styles. Englewood Cliffs, NJ: Prentice Hall.

Carns, A. W., & Carns, M. R. (1991, May). Teaching study skills, cognitive strategies, and metacognitive skills through self-diagnosed learning styles. *The School Counselor, 38,* 341–346.

Carruthers, S. A., & Young, A. L. (1979). Do time preferences affect achievement or discipline? *Learning Styles Network Newsletter, 1*(2), 1. New York: St. John's University and the National Association of Secondary School Principals.

Center for the Study of Learning and Teaching Styles, St. John's University, Utopia Parkway, Jamaica, NY 11439.

Cholakis, M. M. (1986). An experimental investigation of the relationships between and among sociological preferences, vocabulary instruction and achievement, and the attitudes of New York, urban, seventh, and eighth grade underachievers. Doctoral dissertation, St. John's University, 1986. *Dissertation Abstracts International, 47,* 4046A.

Clairborne, A. (1988) Loose cannons and red herring: A book of lost metaphors. New York: Norton.

Clark-Thayer, S. (1987). The relationship of the knowledge of students' perceived learning style preferences and study habits and attitudes to achievement of college freshmen in a small urban university. Doctoral dissertation, Boston University, 1987. *Dissertation Abstracts International, 48,* 872A.

Clark-Thayer, S. (1988). Designing study-skills programs based on individual learning styles. *Learning Styles Network Newsletter, 9*(3), 1. New York: St. John's University and the National Association of Secondary School Principals.

Clay, J. E. (1984). A correlational analysis of the learning characteristics of highly achieving and poorly achieving freshmen at A & M University as revealed through performance on standardized tests. Normal: Alabama A & M University.

Cody, C. (1983). Learning styles, including hemispheric dominance: A comparative study of average, gifted, and highly gifted students in grades five through twelve. Doctoral dissertation, Temple University, 1983. *Dissertation Abstracts International, 44,* 1631A.

Cohen, L. (1986). Birth order and learning styles: An examination of the relationships between birth order and middle school students' preferred learning style profiles. Doctoral dissertation, University of Minnesota's Graduate Department of Educational Psychology, 1986. *Dissertation Abstracts International, 47,* 2084A.

Coleman, S. J. (1988). An investigation of the relationships among physical and emotional learning style preferences and perceptual modality strengths of gifted first-grade students. Doctoral dissertation, Virginia Polytechnic Institute and State University, 1988. *Dissertation Abstracts International, 50*(04), 873A.

Cook, L. (1989). Relationships among learning style awareness, academic achievement, and locus of control among community college students. Doctoral dissertation, University of Florida. *Dissertation Abstracts International, 49*(03), 217A.

Cooper T. J. D. (1991). An investigation of the learning styles of students at two contemporary alternative high schools in the District ofColumbia. Doctoral dissertation, The George Washington University, School of Education and Human Development, 1991.

Copenhaver, R. W. (1979). The consistency of student learning styles as students move from English to mathematics. Doctoral dissertation, Indiana University, 1979. *Dissertation Abstracts International, 80,* 0610.

Cramp, D. C. (1991). A study of the effects on student achievement of fourth- and fifth- grade students' instructional times being matched and mismatched with their particular time preference. Doctoral dissertation, University of Missouri.

Crino, E. M. (1984). An analysis of the preferred learning styles of kindergarten children and the relationship of these preferred learning styles to curriculum planning for kindergarten children. Doctoral dissertation, State University of New York at Buffalo, 1984. *Dissertation Abstracts International, 45,* 1282A.

Cross, J. A., Jr. (1982). Internal locus of control governs talented students (9–12). *Learning Styles Network Newsletters, 3*(3), 3. St. John's University and the National Association of Secondary School Principals.

Curry, L. (1987). *Integrating concepts of cognitive learning style: A review with attention to psychometric standards.* Ontario, Canada: Canadian College of Health Service Executives.

Davis, M. A. (1985). An investigation of the relationship of personality types and learning style preferences of high school students (Myers-Briggs Type Indicator). Doctoral dissertation, George Peabody College for Teachers of Vanderbilt University, 1985. *Dissertation Abstracts International, 46,* 1606A.

Dean, W. L. (1982). A comparison of the learning styles of educable mentally retarded students and learning disabled students. Doctoral dissertation, University of Mississippi, 1982. *Dissertation Abstracts International, 43,* 1923A.

DeBello, T. (1985). A critical analysis of the achievement and attitude effects of administrative assignments to social studies writing instruction based on identified, eighth grade students' learning style preferences for learning alone, with peers, or with teachers. Doctoral dissertation, St. John's University, 1985. *Dissertation Abstracts International, 47,* 68A.

DeBello, T. (1990). Comparison of eleven major learning style models: Variables, appropriate populations, validity of instrumentation, and the research behind them. *Journal of Reading, Writing, and Learning Disabilities International, 6*(3), 315–322. New York: Hemisphere.

DeGregoris, C. N. (1986). Reading comprehension and the interaction of individual sound preferences and varied auditory distractions. Doctoral dissertation, Hofstra University, 1986. *Dissertation Abstracts International, 47,* 3380A.

Delbrey, A. (1987, August). The relationship between the *Learning Style Inventory* and the *Gregorc Style Delineator.* Doctoral dissertation, The University of Alabama, 1987. *Dissertation Abstracts International, 49*(2).

DellaValle, J. (1984). An experimental investigation of the word recognition scores of seventh grade students to provide supervisory and administrative guidelines for the organization of effective instructional environments. Doctoral dissertation, St. John's University, 1984. *Dissertation Abstracts International, 45,* 359A. Recipient of the Phi Delta Kappa National Award for Outstanding Doctoral Research, 1984; National Association of Secondary School Principals' Middle School Research Finalist Citation, 1984; and Association for Supervision and Curriculum Development Citation for National Research (Supervision), 1984.

DellaValle, J. (1990, July–September). The development of a learning styles program in an affluent, suburban New York elementary school. New York: Hemisphere Publishing Corporation, 6(3), 315–322.

Douglas, C. B. (1979). Making biology easier to understand. *The Biology Teacher, 4*(50), 277–299.

Dunn, K. (1985, January). Small-group techniques for the middle school. *Early Years, 15*(5), 41–43. Darien, Connecticut: Allen Raymond, Inc.

Dunn, K., & Dunn, R. (1987). Dispelling outmoded beliefs about student learning. *Educational Leadership, 44,*(6), 55–62.

Dunn, K., & Frazier, E. R. (1990). Teaching styles. Reston, VA: National Association of Secondary School Principals.

Dunn, R. (1984, December). How should students do their homework? Research vs. Opinion. *Early Years, 15*(8), 43–45. Darien, Connecticut: Allen Raymond, Inc.

Dunn, R. (1985). A research-based plan for doing homework. *The Education Digest, 9,* 40–42.

Dunn, R. (1987, Spring). Research on instructional environments: Implications for student achievement and attitudes. *Professional School Psychology, 2*(1), 43–52.

Dunn, R. (1988). Commentary: Teaching students through their perceptual strengths or preferences. *Journal of Reading, 31*(4), 304–309.

Dunn, R. (1989). Capitalizing on students' perceptual strengths to ensure literacy while engaged in conventional lecture/discussion. *Reading Psychology: An International Quarterly, 9,* 431–453. New York: Hemisphere Publishing Corporation.

Dunn, R. (1989a, May–June). Can schools overcome the impact of societal ills on students' achievement? The research indicates—yes! *The Principal, 34*(5), 1–15. New York: Board of Jewish Education of Greater New York.

Dunn, R. (1989b, Summer). Do students from different cultures have different learning styles? *International Education, 16*(50), 3–7. New Wilmington, PA: Association for the Advancement of International Education.

Dunn, R. (1989). Individualizing instruction for mainstreamed gifted children. In R. R. Milgram (Ed.), *Teaching Gifted and Talented Learners in Regular Classrooms.* Springfield, IL: Charles C Thomas, Chapter 3, pp. 63–111.

Dunn R. (1989). Recent research on learning and seven applications to teaching young children to read. *The Oregon Elementary Principal, 50*(2), 29–32.

Dunn, R. (1989, February). A small private school in Minnesota. *Teaching K–8, 18*(5), 54–57. Norwalk, CT: Early Years, Inc.

Dunn, R. (1989c, Fall). Teaching gifted students through their learning style strengths.

International Education, 16(51), 6–8. New Wilmington, PA: Association for the Advancement of International Education.

Dunn, R. (1990a, January). Bias over substance: A critical analysis of Kavale and Forness's report on modality-based instruction. *Exceptional Children, 56*(4), 354–356. Reston, VA: Council for Exceptional Children.

Dunn, R. (1990b, October). Rita Dunn answers questions on learning styles. *Educational Leadership, 48*(15), 15–19. Alexandria, VA: Association for Supervision and Curriculum Development.

Dunn, R. (1990c, Winter). Teaching underachievers through their learning style strengths. *International Education, 16*(52), 5–7. New Wilmington, PA: Association for the Advancement of International Education.

Dunn, R. (1990d, Summer). Teaching young children to *read:* Matching methods of learning style perceptual processing strengths, Part One. *International Education, 17*(54), 2–3. New Wilmington, PA: Association for the Advancement of International Education.

Dunn, R. (1990e, Fall). Teaching young children to read: Matching methods to learning styles perceptual processing strengths, Part Two. *International Education; 17*(55), 5–7. New Wilmington, PA: Association for the Advancement of International Education.

Dunn, R. (1990f, July–September). Understanding the Dunn and Dunn learning styles model and the need for individual diagnosis and prescription. *Journal of Reading, Writing, and Learning Disabilities International, 6*(3), 223–247. New York: Hemisphere.

Dunn, R. (1991, Winter). Are you willing to experiment with a tactual/visual/auditory global approach to reading? Part 3, *International Education,18*(56), 6–8. New Wilmington, PA: Association for the Advancement of International Education.

Dunn, R., Beaudry, J. A., & Klavas, A. (1989). Survey of research on learning styles. *Educational Leadership, 46*(6), 50–58.

Dunn, R., & Bruno, A. (1985). What does the research on learning styles have to do with Mario? *The Clearing House, 59*(1), 9–11.

Dunn, R., Bruno, J., Sklar, R., & Beaudry, J. (1990, May–June). Effects of matching and mismatching minority development college students' hemispheric preferences on mathematics test scores. *Journal of Educational Research, 83*(5), 283–288. Washington, DC: Heldref.

Dunn, R., Cavanaugh, D., Eberle, B., & Zenhausern, R. (1982). Hemispheric preference: The newest element of learning style. *The American Biology Teacher, 44*(5), 291–294.

Dunn, R., DeBello, T., Brennan, P., Krimsky, J., & Murrain, P. (1981, February). *Educational Leadership, 38*(5), 372–375. Alexandria, VA: Association for Supervision and Curriculum Development.

Dunn, R., Deckinger, L., Withers, P., & Katzenstein, H. (1990). Should College Students Be Taught How to Do Homework? *Illinois Research and Development Journal, 26*(2), 96–113.

Dunn, R., DellaValle, J., Dunn, K., Geisert, G., Sinatra, R., & Zenhausern, R. (1986). The effects of matching and mismatching students' mobility preferences on recognition and memory tasks. *Journal of Educational Research, 79*(5), 267–272.

Dunn, R., & Dunn, K. (1972). *Practical approaches to individualizing instructional programs: Contracts and other effective teaching strategies.* Nyack, NY: Parker Publishing Company, Division of Prentice Hall.

Dunn, R., & Dunn, K. (1975). *Educator's self-teaching guide to individualizing instructional programs.* Nyack, NY: Parker Publishing Company, Division of Prentice Hall.

Dunn, R., & Dunn, K. (1977). *Administrator's guide to new programs for faculty management and evaluation.* New York: Parker Publishing Company, Subsidiary of Prentice Hall.

Dunn, R., & Dunn, K. (1978). *Teaching students through their individual learning styles: A practical approach.* Englewood Cliffs, NJ: Prentice Hall.

Dunn, R., & Dunn, K. (1988). Presenting forwards backwards. *Teaching K–8, 19*(2), 71–73. Norwalk, CT: Early Years, Inc.

Dunn, R., Dunn, K., & Freeley, M. E. (1984). Practical applications of the research: Responding to students' learning styles—step one. *Illinois State Research and Development Journal, 21*(1), 1–21.

Dunn, R., Dunn, K., & Price, G. E. (1975, 1977, 1978, 1979, 1985, 1987, 1989). *Learning Style Inventory.* Obtainable from Price Systems, Box 1818, Lawrence, KS 66044. $12.00.

Dunn, R., Dunn, K., & Price, G. E. (1979, 1980, 1990). *Productivity Environmental Preference Survey.* Obtainable from Price Systems, Box 1818, Lawrence, KS 66044. $12.00.

Dunn, R., Dunn, K., & Price, G. E. (1977). Diagnosing learning styles: A prescription for avoiding malpractice suits against school systems. *Phi Delta Kappan, 58*(5), 418–420.

Dunn, R., Dunn, K., Primavera, L., Sinatra, R., & Virostko, J. (1987). A timely solution: A review of research on the effects of chronobiology on children's achievement and behavior. *The Clearing House, 61*(1), 5–8.

Dunn, R., Gemake, J., Jalali, F., & Zenhausern, R. (1989). Cross-cultural differences in learning styles. *Journal of the Missouri Association for Supervision and Curriculum Development Journal, 1*(2), 9–15.

Dunn, R., Gemake, J., Jalali, F., Zenhausern, R., Quinn, P., & Spiridakis, J. (1990, April). Cross-cultural differences in the learning styles of fourth-, fifth-, and sixth-grade students of Afro, Chinese, Greek, and Mexican heritage. *Journal of Multicultural Counseling and Development, 18*(2), 68–93. Alexandria, VA: American Association for Multicultural Counseling and Development.

Dunn, R., Giannitti, M. C., Murray, J. B., Geisert, G., Rossi, I., & Quinn, P. (1990). Grouping students for instruction: Effects of individual vs. group learning style on achievement and attitudes. *Journal of Social Psychology, 130*(4), 485–494. Washington, DC: Heldref Publications.

Dunn, R., & Griggs, S. A. (1988). *Learning styles: Quiet revolution in American secondary schools.* Reston, VA; National Association of Secondary School Principals.

Dunn, R., & Griggs, S. A. (1989, January). Learning styles: Key to improving schools and student achievement. *Curriculum Report.* Reston, VA: National Association of Secondary School Principals, 4 pp.

Dunn, R., & Griggs, S. A. (1989, October). The learning styles of multicultural groups and counseling implications. *Journal of Multicultural Counseling and Development, 7*(4), 146–155. Alexandria, VA: American Association for Multicultural Counseling and Development.

Dunn, R., & Griggs, S. A. (1989a, September). Learning styles: Quiet revolution in American secondary schools. *The Clearing House, 63*(1), 40–42. Washington, DC: Heldref.

Dunn, R., & Griggs, S. A. (1989b, April). A matter of style. *Momentum, 20*(2),W66–70. Washington, DC: National Catholic Education Association.

Dunn, R., & Griggs, S. A. (1989c, January), A quiet revolution in Hempstead. *Teaching K–8, 19*(4), 55–57. Norwalk, CT: Early Years, Inc.

Dunn, R., & Griggs, S. A. (1989d, Winter). A quiet revolution: Learning styles and their application to secondary schools. *Holistic Education, 2*(4), 14–19. Greenfield, MA: Holistic Education Review, Association of Secondary School Principals.

Dunn, R., & Griggs, S. A. (1989e, February). A small private school in Minnesota. *Teaching K–8. 19*(5), 54–57. Norwalk, CR: Early Years, Inc.

Dunn, R., & Griggs, S. A. (1990). A comparative analysis of the learning styles of multicultural subgroups. *Journal of Reading, Writing, and Learning Disabilities International, 6*(3). New York: Hemisphere.

Dunn, R., & Griggs, S. A. (1990). Research on the learning style characteristics of selected racial and ethnic groups. *Journal of Reading, Writing, and Learning Disabilities, 6*(3), 261–280. Washington, DC: Hemisphere.

Dunn, R., Krimsky, J., Murray, J., & Quinn, P. (1985). Light up their lives: A review of research on the effects of lighting on children's achievement. *The Reading Teacher, 38*(9), 863–869.

Dunn, R, Pizzo, J., Sinatra, R., & Barretto, R. A. (1983, Winter). Can it be too quiet to learn? *Focus: Teaching English Language Arts, 9*(2), 92.

Dunn, R., & Price, G. E. (1980). The learning style characteristics of gifted children. *Gifted Child Quarterly, 24*(1), 33–36.

Dunn, R., & Price, G. E. (in press). Comparison of the learning styles of fourth-, fifth-, and sixth-grade male and female Mexican-American students in southern Texas and same-grade students in the general population of the United States. *The Journal of Multicultural Counseling and Development.*

Dunn, R., Price, G. E., Dunn, K., & Griggs, S. A. (1981). Studies in students' learning styles. *Roeper Review, 4*(2), 38–40.

Dunn, R., and Smith, J. B. (1990). Chapter Four: Learning styles and library media programs, In J. B. Smith (Ed.), *School Library Media Annual.* Englewood, CO: Libraries Unlimited, Inc., pp. 32–49.

Dunn, R., White, R. M., & Zenhausern, R. (1982). An investigation of responsible versus less responsible students. *Illinois School Research and Development, 19*(1), 19–24.

Fadley, J. L., & Hosler, V. N. (1979). *Understanding the alpha child at home and at school.* Springfield, IL: Charles C Thomas.

Fitt, S. (1975). The individual and his environment. In T. G. David & B. D. Wright (Eds.), *Learning environments.* Chicago: University of Chicago Press.

Fleming, V. J. (1989, August). Vocational classrooms with style. *Vocational Education Journal, 10*(1), 36–39. Alexandria, VA: American Vocational Association.

Freeley, M. E. (1984). An experimental investigation of the relationships among teachers' individual time preferences, inservice workshop schedules, and instructional techniques and the subsequent implementation of learning style strategies in participants' classrooms. Doctoral dissertation, St. John's University, 1984. *Dissertation Abstracts International, 46,* 403A.

Gadwa, K., & Griggs, S. A. (1985). The school dropout: Implications for counselors. The School Counselor, *33,* 9–17.

Gardiner, B. (1983). Stepping into a learning styles program. *Roeper Review, 6*(2),W90–92.

Gardiner, B. (1986). An experimental analysis of selected teaching strategies implemented at specific times of the school day and their effects on the social studies achievement test scores and attitudes of fourth grade, low achieving students in an urban school setting. Doctoral dissertation, St. John's University, 1986. *Dissertation Abstracts International, 47,* 3307A.

Garger, S. (1990, October). Is there a link between learning style and neurophysiology? *Educational Leadership, 48*(2), 63–65. Alexandria, VA: Association for Supervision and Curriculum Development.

Garrett, S. L. (1991). The effects of perceptual preference and motivation on vocabulary and attitude scores among high school students. Doctoral dissertation, University of LaVerne.

Geisert, G., Dunn, R. (1991a, March). Computers and learning style. *Principal, 70*(4), 47–49. Reston, VA: National Association of Elementary School Principals.

Geisert, G., & Dunn, R. (1991b, March). Effective use of computers: Assignments based on individual learning style. *The Clearing House, 64*(4), 219–224. Washington, DC: Heldref Publications.

Geisert, G., Dunn, R., & Sinatra, R. (1990). Reading, learning styles, and computers. *Journal of Reading, Writing, and Learning Disabilities, 6*(3), 297–306. Washington, DC: Hemisphere.

Giannitti, M. C. (1988). An experimental investigation of the relationships among the learning style sociological preferences of middle-school students (grades 6, 7, 8), their attitudes and achievement in social studies, and selected instructional strategies. Doctoral dissertation, St. John's University, 1988. *Dissertation Abstracts International, 49,* 2911A.

Gotkin, L. (1963, December–1964, January). Individual differences, boredom, and styles of programming. *Programmed Instruction.*

Gould, B. J. (1987). An investigation of the relationships between supervisors' and supervisees' sociological productivity styles on teacher evaluations and interpersonal attraction ratings. Doctoral dissertation, St. John's University, 1987. *Dissertation Abstracts International, 48,* 18A.

Griggs, S. A. (1989, November). Students' sociological grouping preferences of learning styles. *The Clearing House, 63*(3) 135–139. Washington, DC: Heldref Publications.

Griggs, S. A. (1990). Counseling students toward effective study skills using their learning style strengths. *Journal of Reading, Writing, and Learning Disabilities: International,6*(3) 223–247. New York: Hemisphere.

Griggs, S. A., & Dunn, R. (1988, September–October). High school dropouts: Do they learn differently from those students who remain in school? *The Principal, 34*(1), 1–8. New York: Board of Jewish Education of Greater New York.

Griggs, S. A., & Price G. E. (1980). Learning styles of the gifted versus average junior high school students. *Phi Delta Kappan, 62,* 604.

Griggs, S. A., & Price, G. E. (1982). A comparison between the learning styles of gifted versus average junior high school students. *Creative and Gifted Child Quarterly, 7,* 39–42.

Griggs, S. A., Price, G. E., Kopel, S., & Swaine, W. (1984). The effects of group counseling with sixth-grade students using approaches that are compatible versus incompatible with selected learning style elements. *California Personnel and Guidance Journal, 5*(1), 28–35.

Guianta, S. F. (1984). Administrative considerations concerning learning style, its relationship to teaching style, and the influence of instructor/student congruence on high schoolers' achievement and educators' perceived stress. Doctoral dissertation, St. John's University, 1984. *Dissertation Abstracts International, 45,* 32A.

Guzzo, R. S. (1987). Dificuldades de apprenddizagem: Modalidade de atencao e analise de tarefas em materisla didaticos. Doctoral dissertation, University of Sao Paulo, Institute of Pyschology, Brazil, 1987.

Hankins, N. E. (1973). *Psychology for contemporary education.* Columbus, OH: Charles E. Merrill, Chapter 7.

Hanna, S. J. (1989). An investigation of the effects on achievement test scores of individual time preferences and time of training in a corporate setting. Doctoral dissertation, St. John's University, 1989.

Harp, T. Y., & Orsak, L. (1990, July–September). One administrator's challenge: Implementing a learning style program at the secondary level. *Journal of Reading, Writing, and Learning Disabilities International, 6*(3), 335–342. New York: Hemisphere.

Hart, L. A. (1983). *Human brain and human learning.* New York: Longman.

Harty, P. M. (1982). *Learning styles: A matter of difference in the foreign language classroom.* Unpublished master's dissertation, Wright State University.

Hawk, T. D. (1983). A comparison of teachers' preference for specific inservice activity approaches and their measured learning styles. Doctoral dissertation, Kansas State University, 1983. *Dissertation Abstracts International, 44,* 12-A, 3557.

Hill, G. D. (1987). An experimental investigation into the interaction between modality preference and instructional mode in the learning of spelling words by upper-elementary learning disabled students. Doctoral dissertation, North Texas State University, 1987. *Dissertation Abstracts International, 48,* 2536A.

Hodges, H. (1985). An analysis of the relationships among preferences for a formal/informal design, one element of learning style, academic achievement, and attitudes of seventh and eighth grade students in remedial mathematics classes in a New York City junior high school. Doctoral dissertation, St. John's University, 1985. *Dissertation Abstracts International, 45,* 2791A. Recipient of the Phi Delta Kappa National Finalist Award for Outstanding Doctoral Research, 1986.

Homans, G. (1950). *The human group.* New York: Harcourt Brace. *Homework Disc.* (1990). New York: Center for the Study of Learning and Teaching Styles, St. John's University.

Ingham, J. (1989). An experimental investigation of the relationships among learning style perceptual preference, instructional strategies, training achievement, and attitudes of corporate employees. Doctoral dissertation, St. John's University, 1989. *Dissertation Abstracts International, 51,* 02A.

Ingham, J. (1991). Matching instruction with employee perceptual preference significantly increases training effectiveness. *Human Resource Development Quarterly, 2*(1), 53–64. CA: Jossey-Bass.

Ignelzi-Ferraro, D. M. (1989). Identification of the preferred conditions for learning among three groups of mildly handicapped high school students using the *Learning Style Inventory.* Doctoral dissertation, University of Pittsburgh, 1989. *Dissertation Abstracts International, 51*(3), 796A.

Interpreting Adults' Productivity Style. (1991). New York: Center for the Study of Learning and Teaching Styles, St. John's University.

Jacobs, R. L. (1987). An investigation of the learning style differences among Afro-American and Euro-American high, average, and low achievers. Doctoral dissertation, Peabody University, 1987. *Dissertation Abstracts International.*

Jalali, F. (1988). A cross cultural comparative analysis of the learning styles and field dependence/independence characteristics of selected fourth-, fifth-, and sixth-grade students of Afro, Chinese, Greek and Mexican heritage. Doctoral dissertation, St. John's University, 1988. *Dissertation Abstracts International.*

Jarsonbeck, S. (1984). The effects of a right-brain mathematics curriculum on low achieving, fourth grade students. Doctoral dissertation, University of South Florida, 1984. *Dissertation Abstracts International, 45,* 2791A.

Johnson, C. D. (1984). Identifying potential school dropouts. Doctoral dissertation, United States International University. *Dissertation Abstracts International, 45,* 2397A.

Johnson, D. W., & Johnson, R. T. (1975). *Learning together and alone: Cooperation, competition, and individualization.* Englewood Cliffs, NJ: Prentice Hall.

Kahre, C. J. (1985). Relationships between learning styles of student teachers, cooperating teachers, and final evaluations. Doctoral dissertation, Arizona State University, 1984. *Dissertation Abstracts International, 45,* 2492A.

Kaley, S. B. (1977). Field dependence/independence and learning styles in sixth graders. Doctoral dissertation, Hofstra University, 1977. *Dissertation Abstracts International, 38,* 1301A.

Keefe, J. W. (1982). Assessing student learning styles: An overview of learning style and cognitive style inquiry. *Student Learning Styles and Brain Behavior.* Reston: Virginia National: Association of Secondary School Principals.

Kelly, A. P. (1989). Elementary principals' change-facilitating behavior as perceived by self and staff when implementing learning styles instructional programs. Doctoral dissertation, St. John's University, 1989.

Kirby, P. (1979). *Cognitive style, learning style and transfer skill acquisition.* Columbus: National Center for Research in Vocational Education, The Ohio State University.

Klavas, A. (1991). Implementation of the Dunn and Dunn learning styles model in United States' elementary schools: Principals' and teachers' perceptions of factors that facilitated or impeded the process. Doctoral dissertation, St. John's University, New York.

Knapp, B. (1991). An investigation of the impact on learning styles factors upon college students' retention and achievement. Doctoral dissertation, St. John's University.

Koester, L. S., & Farley, F. H. (1977). *Arousal and hyperactivity in open and traditional education.* Paper presented at the Annual Convention of the American Psychological Association, San Francisco. ERIC Document Reproduction Service No. ED 155 543.

Kreitner, K. R. (1981). Modality strengths and learning styles of musically talented high school students. Master's dissertation, The Ohio State University.

Kress, G. C., Jr. (1966). *The effects of pacing on programmed learning under several administrative conditions.* Pittsburgh: American Institute for Research.

Krimsky, J. (1982). A comparative analysis of the effects of matching and mismatching fourth grade students with their learning style preference for the environment element of light and their subsequent reading speed and accuracy scores. Doctoral dissertation, St. John's University, 1982. *Dissertation Abstracts International, 43,* 66A. Recipient of the Association for Supervision and Curriculum Development First Alternate National Recognition for Best Doctoral Research (Curriculum), 1982.

Kroon, D. (1985). An experimental investigation of the effects on academic achievement and the resultant administrative implications of instruction congruent and incongruent with secondary, industrial arts students' learning style perceptual preference. Doctoral dissertation, St. John's University, 1985. *Dissertation Abstracts International, 46,* 3247A.

Kulp, J. J. (1982). A description of the processes used in developing and implementing a teacher training program based on the Dunns' concept of learning style. Doctoral dissertation, Temple University, 1982. *Dissertation Abstracts International, 42,* 5021A.

Lam-Phoon, S. (1986). A comparative study of the learning styles of southeast Asian and American Caucasian college students of two Seventh-Day Adventist campuses. Doctoral dissertation, Andrews University, 1986.

Lan Yong, F. (1989). Ethnic, gender, and grade differences in the learning style preferences of gifted minority students. Doctoral dissertation, Southern Illinois University at Carbondale, 1989.

Learning Styles Network Newsletter. (1980–1991). New York: St. John's University and the National Association of Secondary School Principals.

LeClair, T. J. (1986). The preferred perceptual modality of kindergarten aged children. Master's thesis, California State University, 1986. *Master's Abstracts, 24,* 324.

Lemmon, P. (1985). A school where learning styles make a difference. *Principal, 64*(4), 26–29.

Lengal, O. (1983). Analysis of the preferred learning styles of former adolescent psychiatric patients. Doctoral dissertation, Kansas State University, 1983. *Dissertation Abstracts International, 44,* 2344A.

Levy, J. (1979, September). Human cognition and lateralization of cerebral functions. *Trends in neurosciences,* 220–224.

Levy, J. (1982, Autumn). What do brain scientists know about education? *Learning Styles Network Newsletter, 3*(3), 4.

Li, T. C. (1989). The learning styles of the Filipino graduate students of the Evangelical seminaries in metro Manila. Doctoral dissertation, Asia Graduate School of Theology, Phillipines, 1989.

Lorge, I., Fox, D., Davitz, J., & Brenner, M. (1958). A survey of studies contrasting the quality of group performance and individual performance, 1920–1957. *Psychological Bulletin, 55,* 337–372.

Lux, K. (1987). Special needs students: A qualitative study of their learning styles. Doctoral dissertation, Michigan State University, 1987. *Dissertation Abstracts International, 49,*(3), 421A.

Lynch, P. K. (1981). An analysis of the relationships among academic achievement, attendance, and the learning style time preferences of eleventh and twelfth grade students identified as initial or chronic truants in a suburban New York school district. Doctoral dissertation, St. John's University, 1981. *Dissertation Abstracts International, 42,* 1880A. Recipient of the Association for Supervision and Curriculum Development, First Alternate National Recognition for Best Doctoral Research (Supervision), 1981.

MacMurren, H. (1985). A comparative study of the effects of matching and mismatching sixth-grade students with their learning style preferences for the physical element of intake and their subsequent reading speed and accuracy scores and attitudes. Doctoral dissertation, St. John's University, 1985. *Dissertation Abstracts International, 46,* 3247A.

Madison, M. B. (1984). A study of learning style preferences of specific learning disability students. Doctoral dissertation, University of Southern Mississippi, 1984. *Dissertation Abstracts International, 46,* 3320A.

Mager, R. F. (1962). *Preparing instructional objectives.* Palo Alto, CA: Fearon,W pp. 1–2, 53.

Mager, R. F., & McCann, J. (1963). *Learner-controlled instruction.* Palo Alto, CA: Varian.

Marcus, L. (1977). How teachers view learning styles. *NASSP Bulletin, 61,* (408), 112–114.

Mariash, L. J. (1983). *Identification of characteristics of learning styles existent among students attending school in selected northeastern Manitoba communities.* Unpublished master's dissertation, University of Manitoba, Winnipeg.

Martini, M. (1986). *An analysis of the relationships between and among computer-assisted instruction, learning style perceptual preferences, attitudes, and the science achievement of seventh grade students in a suburban New York school district.* Doctoral dissertation, St. John's University, 1986. *Dissertation Abstracts International, 47,* 87A. Recipient of the American Association of School Administrators (AASA) First Prize, National Research, 1986.

McEwen, P. (1985). *Learning styles, intelligence, and creativity among elementary school students.* Unpublished master's dissertation, Center for Studies on Creativity, State University of New York at Buffalo.

McFarland, M. (1989). An analysis of the relationship between learning style perceptual preferences and attitudes toward computer assisted instruction. Doctoral dissertation, Portland State University. *Dissertation Abstracts International, 50*(10), 3143A.

Mehdikani, N. (1980). The relative effects of teacher teaching style, teacher learning style, and student learning style upon academic achievement. Doctoral dissertation, Catholic University of America, 1980. *Dissertation Abstracts International.*

Mein, J. R. (1986). Cognitive and learning style characteristics of high school gifted students. Doctoral dissertation, University of Florida, 1986. *Dissertation Abstracts International, 48,* 04, 880A.

Melone, R. A. (1987). The relationship between the level of cognitive development and learning styles of the emerging adolescent. Doctoral dissertation, State University of New York at Buffalo, 1987. *Dissertation Abstracts International, 38,* 607A.

Mickler, M. L., & Zippert, C. P. (1987). Teaching strategies based on learning styles of adult students. *Community/Junior College Quarterly, 11,* 33–37.

Miles, B. (1987). An investigation of the relationships among the learning style sociological preferences of fifth and sixth grade students, selected interactive classroom patterns and achievement in career awareness and career decision-making concepts. Doctoral dissertation, St. John's University, 1987. *Dissertation Abstracts International, 48,* 2527A. Recipient of the Phi Delta Kappan Eastern Regional Research Finalist, 1988.

Miller, L. M. (1985). *Mobility as an element of learning style: The effect its inclusion or exclusion has on student performance in the standardized testing environment.* Unpublished master's dissertation, University of North Florida.

Miller, M., & Zippert, C. (1987). Teaching strategies based on learning styles of adult students. *Community/Junior College Quarterly, 11,* 33–37.

Monheit, S. L. (1987). An analysis of learning based upon the relationship between the learning style preferences of parents and their children. Doctoral dissertation, The Fielding Institute, 1987. *Dissertation Abstracts International, 50*(02), 395A.

Morgan, H. L. (1981). Learning styles: The relation between need for structure and preferred mode of instruction for gifted elementary students. Doctoral dissertation, University of Pittsburgh, 1981. *Dissertation Abstracts International, 43,* 2223A.

Morris, V. J. P. (1983). The design and implementation of a teaching strategy for language arts at Chipley High School that brings about predictable learning outcomes. Doctoral dissertation, Florida State University, 1983. *Dissertation Abstracts International, 44,* 3231A.

Moss, V. B. (1981). The stability of first-graders' learning styles and the relationship between selected variables and learning style. Doctoral dissertation, Mississippi State University, 1981. *Dissertation Abstracts International, 43*(3), 665A.

Murrain, P. G. (1983). Administrative determinations concerning facilities utilization and instructional grouping: An analysis of the relationships between selected thermal environments and preferences for temperature, an element of learning style, as they affect word recognition scores of secondary students. Doctoral dissertation, St. John's University, 1983. *Dissertation Abstracts international, 44,* 1749A.

Murray, C. A. (1980). The comparison of learning styles between low and high reading achievement subjects in the seventh and eighth grades in a public middle school. Doctoral dissertation, United States International University, 1980. *Dissertation Abstracts International, 41,* 1005.

Napolitano, R. A. (1986). An experimental investigation of the relationships among achievement, attitude scores, and traditionally, marginally, and underprepared college students enrolled in an introductory psychology course when they are matched and mismatched with their learning style preferences for the element of structure. Doctoral dissertation, St. John's University, 1986. *Dissertation Abstracts International, 47,* 435A.

Nganwa-Baguma, M. J. (1986). *Learning styles: The effects of matching and mismatching pupils' design preferences on reading comprehension tests.* Bachelor's dissertation, University of Transkei, South Africa.

Orsak, L. (1990, October). Learning styles versus the Rip Van Winkle syndrome. *Educational Leadership, 48*(2), 19–20. Alexandria, VA: Association for Supervision and Curriculum Development.

Ostoyee, C. H. (1988). The effects of teaching style on student writing about field trips with concrete experiences. Doctoral dissertation, Teachers College, Columbia University, 1988. *Dissertation Abstracts International, 49,* 2916A.

Paskewitz, B. U. (1985). A study of the relationship between learning styles and attitudes toward computer programming of middle school gifted students. Doctoral dissertation, University of Pittsburgh, 1985. *Dissertation Abstracts International, 47,* 03, 697A.

Pederson, J. K. (1984). The classification and comparison of learning disabled students and gifted students. Doctoral dissertation, Texas Tech University, 1984.

Pena, R. (1989). Two-of-a-kind learning styles. New York: St. John's University. Obtainable from Center for the Study of Learning and Teaching Styles, Utopia Parkway, Jamaica, NY 11439.

Perrin, J. (1984). An experimental investigation of the relationships among the learning style sociological selected instructional strategies, attitudes, and achievement in problem solving and rote memorization. Doctoral dissertation, St. John's University, 1984. *Dissertation Abstracts International, 46,* 342A. Recipient of the American Association of School Administrators (AASA) National Research Finalist Award, 1984.

Perrin, J. (1990, October). The learning styles project for potential dropouts. *Educational Leadership, 48*(2), 23–24. Alexandria, VA: Association for Supervision and Curriculum Development.

Pizzo, J. (1981). An investigation of the relationships between selected acoustic environments and sound, an element of learning style, as they affect sixth grade students' reading achievement and attitudes. Doctoral dissertation, St. John's University, 1981. *Dissertation Abstracts International, 42,* 2475A. Recipient of the Association for Supervision and Curriculum Development First Alternate National Recognition for Best Doctoral Research (Curriculum), 1981.

Pizzo, J. (1982). Breaking the sound barrier: Classroom noise and learning style. *Orbit, 64, 13*(4), 21–22.P. Ontario: Ontario Institute for Studies in Education.

Pizzo, J., Dunn, R., & Dunn, K. (1990, July–September). A sound approach to reading: Responding to students' learning styles. *Journal of Reading, Writing, and Learning Disabilities, 6*(3), 249–260. New York: Hemisphere.

Poirier, G. A. (1970). *Students as partners in team learning.* Berkeley, CA: Center of Team Learning, Chapter 2.

Ponder, D. (1990). An analysis of the changes and gender differences in preferences of learning styles at adolescence and the relationship of the learning styles of adolescents and their parents when matched and mismatched according to gender. Doctoral dissertation, East Texas State University, 1990. *Dissertation Abstracts International, 64*(4), 1170A.

Price, G. E. (1980). Which learning style elements are stable and which tend to change over time? *Learning Styles Network Newsletter, 1*(3), 1.

Price, G. E., Dunn, K., Dunn, R., & Griggs, S. A. (1981). Studies in students' learning styles. *Roeper Review, 4*(2), 223–226.

Rahal, B. F. (1986). The effects of matching and mismatching the diagnosed learning styles of intermediate level students with their structure preferences in the learning environment. Doctoral dissertation, West Virginia University. *Dissertation Abstracts International, 47*(6), 2010A.

Ramirez, A. I. (1982). Modality and field dependence/independence: Learning components and their relationship to mathematics achievement in the elementary school. Doctoral dissertation, Florida State University, 1982. *Dissertation Abstracts International, 43,* 666.

Rea, D. C. (1980). Effects on achievement of placing students in different learning environments based upon identified learning styles. Doctoral dissertation, University of Missouri, 1989.

Reid, J. M. (1987, March). The learning style preferences of ESL students. *TESOL Quarterly, 21,* 87–105. Available to members only. TESP, 1118 22nd Street, N.W., Georgetown University, Suite 205, Washington, DC 20037.

Restak, R. (1979). *The brain: The last frontier.* New York: Doubleday.

Ricca, J. (1983). Curricular implications of learning style differences between gifted and non-gifted students. Doctoral dissertation, State University of New York at Buffalo, 1983. *Dissertation Abstracts International, 44,* 1324-A.

The Rise Report: Report on the California commission for reform of intermediate and secondary education. (1975). Sacramento: California State Department of Education.

Roberts, O. A. (1984). Investigation of the relationship between learning style and temperament of senior high students in the Bahamas and Jamaica. Graduate dissertation, Andrews University, 1984.

Roderick, M., & Anderson, R. C. (1968). Programmed instruction in psychology versus textbook style summary of the same lesson. *Journal of Educational Psychology, 59,* 383–387.

Sage, C. O. (1984). The Dunn and Dunn learning style model: An analysis of its theoretical, practical, and research foundations. Doctoral dissertation, University of Denver, 1984. *Dissertation Abstracts International, 45*(12), 3537A.

Shands, R., & Brunner, C., (1989, Fall). Providing success through a powerful combination: Mastery learning and learning styles. *Perceptions, 25,*(1), 6–10. New York: New York State Educators of the Emotionally Disturbed.

Shea, T. C. (1983). An investigation of the relationships among preferences for the learning style element of design, selected instructional environments, and reading achievement with ninth grade students to improve administrative determinations concerning effective educational facilities. Doctoral dissertation, St. John's University, 1983. *Dissertation Abstracts International, 44,* 2004A. Recipient of the National Association of Secondary School Principals' Middle School Research Finalist Citation, 1984.

Siebenman, J. B. (1984). An investigation of the relationship between learning style and cognitive style in non-traditional college reading students. Doctoral dissertation, Arizona State University, 1984. *Dissertation Abstracts International, 45,* 1705A.

Sims, J. E. (1988). Learning styles: A comparative analysis of the learning styles of Black-American, Mexican-American, and White-American third and fourth grade students in traditional public schools. Doctoral dissertation, University of Santa Barbara, 1988. *Dissertation Abstracts International, 47,* 02, 650A.

Sinatra, C. (1990, July-September). Five diverse secondary schools where learning style instruction works. (1990, July-September). *Journal of Reading, Writing, and*

Learning Disabilities International. New York: Hemisphere Publishing Corporation, *6*(3), 323–334.

Sinatra, R., Hirshoren, A., & Primavera, L. H. (1987). Learning style, behavior ratings and achievement interactions for adjudicated adolescents. *Educational and Psychological Research, 7*(1), 21–32.

Sinatra, R., Primavera, L., & Waked, W. J. (1986). Learning style and intelligence of reading disabled students. *Perceptual and Motor Skills, 62,*(1), 243–252.

Slavin, R. E. (1983). *Cooperative learning.* New York: Longman.

Slavin, R. E. (1988). Synthesis of research on cooperative learning. *Educational Leadership, 38*(8), 655–660. Alexandria, Virginia: Association for Supervision and Curriculum Development.

Smith, S. (1987). An experimental investigation of the relationship between and among achievement, preferred time of instruction, and critical-thinking abilities of tenth- and eleventh-grade students in mathematics. Doctoral dissertation, St. John's University, 1987. *Dissertation Abstracts International, 47,* 1405A.

Smith, T. D. (1988). An assessment of the self-perceived teaching style of three ethnic groups of public school teachers in Texas. Doctoral dissertation, East Texas University, 1988. *Dissertation Abstracts International, 49* A-08, 2062A.

Snider, K. P. (1985). A study of learning preferences among educable mentally impaired, emotionally impaired, learning disabled, and general education students in seventh, eighth, and ninth grades as measured by response to the *Learning Styles Inventory.* Doctoral dissertation, Michigan State University, 1985. *Dissertation Abstracts International, 46,* (05), SECA, 1251.

Solberg, S. J. (1987). An analysis of the Learning Style Inventory, the Productivity Environmental Preference Survey, and the Iowa Test of Basic Skills. Doctoral dissertation, Northern Arizona University, 1987. *Dissertation Abstracts International, 48,* 2530A.

Spires, R. D. (1983). The effect of teacher inservice about learning styles on students' mathematics and reading achievement. Doctoral dissertation, Bowling Green State University, 1983. *Dissertation Abstracts International, 44,* 1325A.

Steinauer, M. H. (1981). Interpersonal relationships as reflected in learning style preferences: A study of eleventh grade students and their English teachers in a vocational school. Doctoral dissertation, Southern Illinois University, 1981. *Dissertation Abstracts International, 43,* 305A.

Stiles, R. (1985). Learning style preferences for design and their relationship to standardized test results. Doctoral dissertation, University of Tennessee, 1985. *Dissertation Abstracts International, 46,* 2551A.

Stokes, B. M. (1989). An analysis of the relationship between learning style, achievement, race, and gender. Doctoral dissertation, The University of Akron, 1989. *Dissertation Abstracts International, 49,* 757A.

Svreck, L. J. (1990). Perceived parental influence, accommodated learning style preferences, and students' attitudes toward learning as they relate to reading and mathematics achievement. Doctoral dissertation, St. John's University, 1990.

Sykes, S., Jones, B., & Phillips, J. (1990, October). Partners in learning styles at a private school. *Educational Leadership, 48*(2), 24–26. Alexandria, VA: Association for Supervision and Curriculum Development.

Tanenbaum, R. (1982). An investigation of the relationships between selected instructional techniques and identified field dependent and field independent cognitive styles as evidenced among high school students enrolled in studies of nutrition. Doctoral dissertation, St. John's University, 1982. *Dissertation Abstracts International, 43,* 68A.

Tappenden, V. J. (1983). Analysis of the learning styles of vocational education and nonvocational education students in eleventh and twelfth grades from rural, urban, and suburban locations in Ohio. Doctoral dissertation, Kent State University, 1983. *Dissertation Abstracts International, 44,* 1326A.

Thies, A. P. (1979). A brain behavior analysis of learning style. In *Student learning styles: Diagnosing and prescribing programs.* Reston, VA: National Association of Secondary School Principals, M pp. 5–61.

Thrasher, R. (1984). *A study of the learning style preferences of at-risk sixth and ninth graders.* Pompano Beach: Florida Association of Alternative School Educators.

Tingley-Michaelis, C. (1983). Make room for movement. *Early Years, 13*(6), 26–29.

Trautman, P. (1979). An investigation of the relationship between selected instructional techniques and identified cognitive style. Doctoral dissertation, St. John's University, 1979. *Dissertation Abstracts International, 40,* 1428A.

Urbschat, K. S. (1977). A study of preferred learning modes and their relationship to the amount of recall of CVC trigrams. Doctoral dissertation, Wayne State University, 1977. *Dissertation Abstracts International, 38,* 2536–5A.

Vazquez, A. W. (1985). Description of learning styles of high risk adult students taking courses in urban community colleges in Puerto Rico. Doctoral dissertation, Union for Experimenting Colleges and Universities, San Juan, Puerto Rico, 1985. *Dissertation Abstracts International, 47,* 1157A.

Vignia, R. A. (1983). An investigation of learning styles of gifted and non-gifted high school students. Doctoral dissertation, University of Houston, 1983. *Dissertation Abstracts International, 44,* 3653A.

Virostko, J. (1983). An analysis of the relationships among academic achievement in mathematics and reading, assigned instructional schedules, and the learning style time preferences of third, fourth, fifth, and sixth grade students. Doctoral dissertation, St. John's University, 1983. *Dissertation Abstracts International, 44,* 1683A. Recipient of the Kappa Delta Pi International Award for Best Doctoral Research, 1983.

Weinberg, F. (1983). An experimental investigation of the interaction between sensory modality preference and mode of presentation in the instruction of arithmetic concepts to third grade underachievers. Doctoral dissertation, St. John's University, 1983. *Dissertation Abstracts International, 44,* 1740A.

Wheeler, R. (1980). An alternative to failure: Teaching reading according to students' perceptual strengths. *Kappa Delta Pi Record, 17*(2), 59–63.

Wheeler, R. (1983). An investigation of the degree of academic achievement evidenced when second grade, learning disabled students' perceptual preferences are matched and mismatched with complementary sensory approaches to beginning reading instruction. Doctoral dissertation, St. John's University, 1983. *Dissertation Abstracts International, 4,* 2039A.

White, R. (1980). An investigation of the relationship between selected instructional methods and selected elements of emotional learning style upon student achievement in seventh grade social studies. Doctoral dissertation, St. John's University, 1980. *Dissertation Abstracts International, 42,* 995A. Recipient of the Kappa Delta Gamma International Award for Best Doctoral Research Prospectus, 1980.

Wild, J. B. (1979). *A study of the learning styles of learning disabled students and non-learning disabled students at the junior high school level.* Unpublished Master's dissertation, University of Kansas, Lawrence.

Williams, G. L. (1984). The effectiveness of computer assisted instruction and its relationship to selected learning style elements. Doctoral dissertation, North Texas State University, 1984. *Dissertation Abstracts International, 45,* 1986A.

Wingo, L. H. (1980). Relationships among locus of motivation, sensory modality and grouping preferences of learning style to basic skills test performance in reading and mathematics. Doctoral dissertation, Memphis State University, 1980. *Dissertation Abstracts International, 41,* 2923.

Wittenberg, S. K. (1984). A comparison of diagnosed and preferred learning styles of young adults in need of remediation. Doctoral dissertation, University of Toledo, 1984. *Dissertation Abstracts International, 45,* 3539A.

Wittig, C. (1985). *Learning style preferences among students high or low on divergent thinking and feeling variables.* Unpublished Master's dissertation, Center for Studies on Creativity, State University College of Buffalo at New York, 1985.

Wolfe, G. (1983). Learning styles and the teaching of reading. Doctoral dissertation, Akron University, 1983. *Dissertation Abstracts International, 45,* 3422A.

Yeap, L. L. (1987). Learning styles of Singapore secondary students. Doctoral dissertation, University of Pittsburgh, 1987. *Dissertation Abstracts International, 48,* 936A.

Young, B. M. P. (1985). Effective conditions for learning: An analysis of learning environments and learning styles in ability-grouped classes. Doctoral dissertation, University of Massachusetts, 1985. *Dissertation Abstracts International, 46,* 708A.

Zak, F. (1989). Learning style discrimination between vocational and nonvocational students. Doctoral dissertation. University of Massachusetts. *Dissertation Abstracts International, 50,* 12A, 3843A.

Zenhausern, R. (1980). Hemispheric dominance. *Learning Styles Network Newsletter 1*(2), 3. New York: St. John's University and the National Association of Secondary School Principals.

Zikmund, A. B. (1988). The effect of grade level, gender, and learning style on responses to conservation type rhythmic and melodic patterns. Doctoral dissertation, The University of Nebraska, 1988. *Dissertation Abstracts International, 50* (1), 95A.

─── APPENDIX A───────

Instruments for Identifying Learning or Teaching Styles

- *Adults' Learning Styles: Productivity Environmental Preference Survey* (PEPS). Specimen Set, Tests, and Processing. Price Systems, Box 1818, Lawrence, KS 66044–1818.
- *Students' Learning Styles (Grades 3–12): Learning Style Inventory* (LSI). Specimen Set, Tests, and Processing. Price Systems, Box 1818, Lawrence, KS 66044–1818.
- *Students' Learning Styles (Grades K–2): Learning Style Inventory: Primary Version* (LSI:P). Center for the Study of Learning and Teaching Styles, St. John's University, Utopia Parkway, Jamaica, NY 11439.
- *Teachers' Teaching Styles: Teaching Style Inventory* (TSI) (Chapter 10).

INDEX